Lecture Notes in Computer Science 12089

More information about this series at http://www.springer.com/series/7409

Elisabeth Métais · Farid Meziane ·
Helmut Horacek · Philipp Cimiano (Eds.)

Natural Language Processing and Information Systems

25th International Conference on Applications
of Natural Language to Information Systems, NLDB 2020
Saarbrücken, Germany, June 24–26, 2020
Proceedings

 Springer

Editors
Elisabeth Métais
Laboratoire Cédric
Conservatoire National des Arts et Métiers
Paris, France

Helmut Horacek
Language Technology
German Research Center for Artificial
Intelligence
Saarbrücken, Germany

Farid Meziane
School of Science, Engineering
and Environment
University of Salford
Salford, UK

Philipp Cimiano
Semantic Computing Group
Bielefeld University
Bielefeld, Germany

ISSN 0302-9743   ISSN 1611-3349 (electronic)
Lecture Notes in Computer Science
ISBN 978-3-030-51309-2   ISBN 978-3-030-51310-8   (eBook)
https://doi.org/10.1007/978-3-030-51310-8

LNCS Sublibrary: SL3 – Information Systems and Applications, incl. Internet/Web, and HCI

This Springer imprint is published by the registered company Springer Nature Switzerland AG
The registered company address is: Gewerbestrasse 11, 6330 Cham, Switzerland

Preface

This volume contains the papers presented at NLDB 2020, the 25th International Conference on Applications of Natural Language to Information Systems held June 24–26, 2020, as a video conference at the German Research Center for Artificial Intelligence in Saarbrücken, Germany. We received 68 submissions for the conference. Each paper was assigned to three reviewers, taking into account preferences expressed by the Program Committee members as much as possible. After the review deadline, Program Committee members were asked to complete missing reviews. In addition, Organization Committee members and the Program Committee chair acted as meta-reviewers – they wrote additional reviews for borderline cases and for the papers which received reviews with considerably conflicting assessments. At the end, each paper received at least three reviews. On the basis of these reviews, the Organization Committee members and the Program Committee chair decided to accept papers with an average score around *weak acceptance* as full papers, papers with a slightly lower score as short papers. In borderline cases, credit was given to experimentally-oriented papers with novel and ambitious concepts.

The final acceptance rate counting the number of full papers according to NLDB tradition was 22% (15 out of 68), similarly competitive in comparison to the previous years. In addition, 10 submissions were accepted as short papers, and no posters, since NLDB 2020 had to be a video conference. Full papers were allowed a maximum of 12 and short papers a maximum of 8 pages. Originally, two more short papers were accepted, but the authors preferred to retract their submissions for personal reasons.

Following the trends of previous years, there is more diversification in the topics and specific issues addressed in comparison to a decade ago. Several papers address some languages for which not too rich resources are available – Arabic and Russian. Some currently hot topics are dealt with intensively, including sentiment analysis and chatbots, and successful tools are reused and adapted such as the transformer BERT. Finally, going beyond language proper is examined by several contributions, including visual data, affect, emotions, and personality.

In addition to the reviewed papers, there were three invited talks at NLDB 2020:

– Claire Gardent, LORIA Nancy, France
– Ehud Reiter, University of Aberdeen and Arria, UK
– Josef van Genabith, DFKI Saarbrücken, Germany

The accepted contributions (long and short papers) covered a wide range of topics, which we classified in six topic areas, each covering a section in this volume:

– Semantic Analysis
– Question Answering and Answer Generation
– Classification
– Sentiment Analysis

- Personality, Affect, and Emotion
- Retrieval, Conversational Agents, and Multimodal Analysis

Semantic Analysis

Two long and two short papers were categorized in this section. The first one incorporates psycholinguistic evidence into subword properties for training vector representations. The next two papers address named-entity recognition, both in non-standard domains. The first one works in the cybersecurity domain in Russian, showing superiority of the BERT model. The second one addresses biomedical data using a deep neural network (NN) architecture. The final paper in this section features explanations about semantic parsing, in the context of a natural language programming task.

Question Answering and Answer Generation

Three long and two short papers were categorized in this section. The first paper obtains performance increase through query expansion and coreference resolution measures. The next two papers extend question answering by dialog patterns, the first one automates building chatbots including clarification dialogs, the second one organizes answering procedural questions by incrementally following hierarchically organized knowledge. The last two papers address limitations of knowledge; the first one deals with large data in open domains, the second one obtains control over limitations caused by missing knowledge.

Classification

One long and three short papers were categorized in this section. There are two technology-based and two application-oriented contributions. One of the technology-based contributions applies an iterative procedure, exemplified for classifying short texts, the other one introduces systematic selection techniques to increase stability in Latent Dirichlet Allocation. The application-oriented contributions aim at identifying reports about defects and associated requests for improvements within dedicated reviews and court decisions in the area of housing law, respectively.

Sentiment Analysis

Two long and one short paper were categorized in this section. Each approach features a specific, non-standard perspective. The first approach features the role of positional information attributed to a word contributing to an aspect of interest. The second one studies the role of attention and demonstrates its relevance for assessing analytical texts. The last one emphasizes the exploitation of sentiment to drive strategies for curriculum learning.

Personality, Affect, and Emotion

Four long and one short paper were categorized in this section. The first two papers in this category address the role of personality for quite diverse purposes, one for the discrimination of honest versus deceptive authors, the other one to model language behavior of literary figures. The next two papers analyze emotions, one in the context of movies, the other one by analyzing low-level linguistic properties in social media blogs. The last one attempts to infer doubts about a specific disease from analyzing social media dialogs.

Retrieval, Conversational Agents, and Multimodal Analysis

Three long and one short paper were categorized in this section. The first two address extended mechanisms for answer choice taking into account the dialog context and semantic similarity between a new question and already processed ones, respectively. The next paper features anchoring entities based on textual and visual data, and the final paper describes a compound practical system with occasional human intervention.

The conference organizers are indebted to the reviewers for their engagement in a vigorous submission evaluation process. We would also like to thank, for the organization help, some members of the DFKI GmbH.

June 2020

Philipp Cimiano
Helmut Horacek
Elisabeth Métais
Farid Meziane

Organization

Conference Organization

Elisabeth Métais	Conservatoire des Arts et Métiers, France
Farid Meziane	University of Salford, UK
Helmut Horacek	German Research Center for AI, Germany

Program Chair

Philipp Cimiano	Bielefeld University, Germany

Program Committee

Jacky Akoka	CNAM & TEM, France
Hidir Aras	FIZ Karlsruhe, Germany
Faten Atigui	Conservatoire des Arts et Métiers, France
Pierpaolo Basile	University of Bari, Italy
Nicolas Béchet	IRISA, France
Gloria Bordogna	IREA, CNR, Italy
Sandra Bringay	LIRMM, France
Christian Chiarcos	University Frankfurt am Main, Germany
Raja Chiky	ISEP, France
Isabelle Comyn-Wattiau	CNAM, France
Flavius Frasincar	Erasmus University Rotterdam, The Netherlands
André Freitas	The University of Manchester, UK
Ahmed Guessoum	University of Science and Technology Houari Boumediene, Algeria
Yaakov Hacohen-Kerner	Jerusalem College of Technology, Israel
Siegfried Handschuh	University of Passau, Germany
Michael Herweg	IBM, Germany
Helmut Horacek	German Research Center for AI, Germany
Dino Ienco	IRSTEA, France
Ashwin Ittoo	HEC, University of Liège, Belgium
Paul Johannesson	Stockholm University, Sweden
Epaminondas Kapetanios	University of Westminster, UK
Zoubida Kedad	UVSQ, France
Eric Kergosien	GERiiCO, University of Lille, France
Christian Kop	University of Klagenfurt, Austria
Valia Kordoni	Humboldt University Berlin, Germany
Elena Kornyshova	Conservatoire des Arts et Métiers, France
Els Lefever	Ghent University, Belgium
Jochen Leidner	Thomson Reuters, USA

Deryle W. Lonsdale	Brigham Young University, USA
Cédric Lopez	Emvista, France
John P. Mccrae	National University of Ireland, Ireland
Elisabeth Métais	Conservatoire des Arts et Métiers, France
Farid Meziane	University of Salford, UK
Luisa Mich	University of Trento, Italy
Balakrishna Mithun	Limba Corp., USA
Rafael Muñoz	Universidad de Alicante, Spain
Le Minh Nguyen	Japan Advanced Institute of Science and Technology, Japan
Davide Picca	Université de Lausanne, Switzerland
Mathieu Roche	Cirad, TETIS, France
Paolo Rosso	Technical University of Valencia, Spain
Mohamad Saraee	University of Salford, UK
Imran Sarwar	The Islamia University of Bahawalpur, Pakistan
Bahar Sateli	Concordia University, Canada
Khaled Shaalan	The British University in Dubai, UAE
Max Silberztein	Université de Franche-Comté, France
Veda Storey	Georgia State University, USA
Vijay Sugumaran	Oakland University Rochester, USA
Maguelonne Teisseire	Irstea, TETIS, France
Dan Tufis	RACAI, Romania
Luis Alfonso Ureña	Universidad de Jaén, Spain
Sunil Vadera	University of Salford, UK
Wlodek Zadrozny	UNCC, USA
Fabio Massimo Zanzotto	University of Rome Tor Vergata, Italy

Webmaster

Christian Willms	German Research Center for AI, Germany

Additional Reviewers

Bernhard Bermeitinger
Matthias Cetto
Miguel Ángel García Cumbreras
Deborah Ferreira
Anastasia Giachanou
Frank Grimm
Philipp Heinisch
Andrea Iovine
Rémy Kessler
Arturo Montejo-Ráez
Christina Niklaus

Alejandro Piad
Juliano Efson Sales
Fernando Martinez Santiago
Gretel Liz De La Peña Sarracén
Lucia Sicilian
Hendrik Ter Horst
Mokanarangan Thayaparan
Pilar López Úbeda
Marco Valentino
Christian Witte

Contents

Retrieval, Conversational Agents and Multimodal Analysis

Semantic Analysis

Enhancing Subword Embeddings
with Open N-grams

Csaba Veres$^{(\boxtimes)}$ ⓘ and Paul Kapustin

University of Bergen, Bergen, Norway
{csaba.veres,pavlo.kapustin}@uib.no

Abstract. Using subword n-grams for training word embeddings makes it possible to subsequently compute vectors for rare and misspelled words. However, we argue that the subword vector qualities can be degraded for words which have a high orthographic neighbourhood; a property of words that has been extensively studied in the Psycholinguistic literature. Empirical findings about lexical neighbourhood effects constrain models of human word encoding, which must also be consistent with what we know about neurophysiological mechanisms in the visual word recognition system. We suggest that the constraints learned from humans provide novel insights to subword encoding schemes. This paper shows that vectors trained with subword properties informed by psycholinguistic evidence are superior to those trained with ad hoc n-grams. It is argued that physiological mechanisms for reading are key factors in the observed distribution of written word forms, and should therefore inform our choice of word encoding.

1 Introduction

There is currently a great deal of research activity around solutions using continuous representations of words. The most popular methods for learning word vectors, or *embeddings*, produce a single vector for each word form in the training set, for example GloVe [18], word2vec [15], and SVD [12]. These methods do not attempt to exploit syntactic or morphological regularities behind the word forms, as the unit of analysis is the single word.

These methods could be regarded as modern day experiments inspired by Zellig Harris' hypotheses about the distributional structure of language. Harris proposed that word meanings give rise to observable distributional patterns in language, such that two semantically unrelated words A and C would be less likely to be found in common linguistic contexts as two semantically related words A and B [10]. Modern machine learning techniques have made it computationally possible to *embed* very high dimensional distributional patterns in a much lower dimensional vector space, in which the distances between any given vectors are related to the similarities of context in which the corresponding words are found in the training set. Semantic relatedness is therefore correlated with the calculated distance (e.g. cosine distance) between vectors.

© Springer Nature Switzerland AG 2020
E. Métais et al. (Eds.): NLDB 2020, LNCS 12089, pp. 3–15, 2020.
https://doi.org/10.1007/978-3-030-51310-8_1

Since the unit of analysis in such machine learning models is the word, it is generally the case that rare words, and words formed by novel morphological combinations, are not represented in the training set with sufficient frequency to obtain a vector embedding. In response, Bojanowski et al. [2] trained vectors by decomposing words into subword components. Their embeddings had the advantage that low frequency and out-of-vocabulary words could be assigned a vector representation from the sum of their subword units. The training model is a modification of the skipgram model [15], in introducing a scoring function over the sum of the component n-grams (including the word itself). A word is therefore represented as the sum of the vector representation of the word and its constituent n-grams. Conversely, the vector representation of individual n-grams is shared between all words containing the particular n-gram, and therefore rare words can acquire reliable representations by taking advantage of the shared representations.

While the reported evaluations of the embedding vectors look promising, our experience in using them in an application has been mixed. Using the standard implementation[1] *fastText* and our own vectors trained with the latest Wikipedia dumps[2], we observed some examples where the related words would not be particularly useful for some tasks, for example query expansion. Consider the fairly common word *dictionary*, which has the following nearest vectors: *dictionaries, dictionarys, dictionarian, dictionarie, dictions, dictionarial, dictioneer, dictioner, dictionaric, dictionay*. These are highly overlapping morphological variations and not particularly useful in applications where more heterogeneous semantically related concepts are required for information retrieval. In contrast, word2vec[3] provided the following results for this example: *dictionaries, lexicon, oed, merriam, encyclopedia, bibliographical, lexicography, britannica, websters, encyclopaedia, glossary*. In general we had the intuition that fastText was more likely to include overlapping orthographic clusters in the results set, which motivated the experiments reported in this paper. We wanted to understand why, and under what circumstances the *fastText* results might suffer, and developed the hypothesis that psycholinguistic factors were involved. The approach is similar in spirit to emerging efforts which explore modern machine learning results from a psycholinguistic perspective. For example, Mandera et al. [14] use *semantic priming* results from psycholinguisic experiments instead of semantic similarity judgements to evaluate word vectors, and report new insights in the quality of embeddings.

The subword embedding approach presupposes that orthography to semantics mappings can be established for words as well as for the summation of the subword fragments. Thus, the vector obtained for out-of-vocabulary items acquires its position in semantic 'co-occurance' space as a function of the

---

[1] https://github.com/facebookresearch/fastText.

[2] We also used publicly available pretrained vectors, e.g. wiki-en.bin https://s3-us-west-1.amazonaws.com/fasttext-vectors/wiki.en.zip but found these even less satisfactory.

[3] https://github.com/dav/word2vec.

semantic space vectors in the constituent n-grams. Consider the following example adapted from [2], where the word *where* contains the following set of *tri*-grams. Note that the word is actually represented by n-grams where n is greater than or equal to 3 and less than or equal to 6, but for the sake of brevity we only list the trigrams:

<wh, whe, her, ere, re>

where the symbols ' < ' and ' > ' denote word boundaries.

Each of these trigrams are shared by many other words with very different meanings, for example:

< *wh* appears in *which, whence, whale, white, whack, whack − a − mole, wharf, whatever, ..*
whe appears in *anywhere, arrowhead, wheel, wheat, ...*
her appears in *whether, cherish, butcher, sheriff, thermometer, ...*

It seems clear that vectors generated from short n-grams will be at a point in semantic space that is not necessarily close to the semantics of any of the words which contain them, because they are contained in many words. The longer the n-gram, the fewer the containing words. It might seem odd that the inclusion of short n-grams in training would do any good at all, because they appear to introduce semantic noise. In fact, a systematic evaluation of n-gram length shows that embeddings that include bi- and tri- grams always show a slight degradation in performance when compared to those with only longer n-grams [2].

An additional consideration about the number of words sharing subword elements originates in psycholinguistic evidence about the mental representation of words. An important variable in human word recognition studies is the *orthographic neighbourhood*, commonly measured with Coltheart's N [3], where the orthographic neighbourhood of a word is determined by counting the number of other words of the same length, sharing all but one letter, and maintaining letter position. The measure of orthographic neighbourhood is correlated with the number of words related to the target word, which overlap significantly with the *set of* subword components. Every n-gram in a word is shared by a variety of semantically unrelated words, but the set of the constituent n-grams is unique to a particular word. Or, to put it in the opposite way, each word contributes its context to the training of its unique set of n-grams. When this set is re-assembled, the summed vector will be consistent with the vector just for the word itself. But this will be maximally effective when the combined set of constituent n-grams does not overlap significantly with another set of n-grams corresponding to a different word with a different meaning.

For example, the word *safety* has the *tri*-grams

<sa, saf, afe, fet, ety, ty>

and there are no other six-letter words which have a significant overlap with this set. On the other hand the word *singer* has the *tri*-grams

<si, sin, ing, nge, ger, er>

which overlap significantly with many semantically unrelated words such as *sinner, finger, linger*

<si, sin, inn, nne, ner, er>, <fi, fin, ing, nge, ger, er>, <li, lin, ing, nge, ger, er>

The result of this overlap is that if we present a rare word which overlaps significantly with these *n*-grams, its vector representation will be degraded to the extent that the set of overlapping *n*-grams is shared by semantically unrelated words. For example the semantically unrelated word *zinger* (a striking or amusing remark) will have similar sets of *n*-grams:

<zi, zin, ing, nge, ger, er>

which has a 67% overlap with *finger* and *linger*. The assembled vector for "zinger" would therefore be somewhere between "finger" and "linger".

The set of overlapping words in these examples is just what we have called the orthographic neighbourhood. In the previous example, this means that the trigrams for the high-N six-letter words have a 50%–67% overlap with N other words in its lexical neighbourhood, whereas for the low-N it is none, except for morphological variants of the word itself[4]. The higher the N, the more likely it is that a significant subset of *n*-grams will be shared by semantically unrelated words.

This paper explores the hypothesis that orthographic neighbourhood structure of English has some influence on the way subword *n*-grams are incorporated into word embeddings. We first describe some relevant findings involving orthographic neighbourhoods that have come to light as a result of psycholinguistic theories. We then show empirically how these properties can influence the quality of word embeddings, and propose alternative encoding schemes inspired by psycholinguistics and neuroscience, which solve some of the problems. Our main contribution is to show that a consideration of words as more than letter strings in some disembodied vocabulary, is beneficial. Words are the result of psycholinguistic processes. Based on this argument we develop a putatively better encoding scheme which takes into consideration the interdependency between word structure and human psychological and neural processing systems.

2   Orthographic Neighbourhood Density

Coltheart's N is the simplest measure of orthographic neighbourhood density, where two words are neighbours if they have the same length and differ in just one letter position. There have been many refinements, including the counting of words formed by letter transposition or repetition, and the use of Levenshtein distance. Nevertheless, many of the fundamental results hold for neighbourhoods with the Colthert's N measure, which we use in this paper [1,3,7,22].

The neighbourhood density of words is correlated with their length. [1] counted the number of neighbours for four, five, and six letter words in the

---

[4] In this example, *safe* has overlapping *n*-grams with *safety*.

CELEX linguistic database. In total these amounted to 8956 words, and she found a systematic difference; four-letter words had on average 7.2 neighbours, five-letter words had 2.4, and six-letter words, 1.1 neighbour. Not surprisingly, longer words tend to have fewer neighbours. Experiments which specifically manipulate neighbourhood density tend to use shorter words, typically four-letter words.

Orthographic neighbourhood N has an effect on how quickly people can respond to stimuli in a lexical decision task (LDT). In LDT, subjects are presented with a random sequence of words and nonwords, and asked to classify them as quickly as possible. Coltheart et al. [3] found that high-N nonwords (nonwords with many word neighbours) were classified more slowly than nonwords with few word neighbours. That is, people would be slower to respond that *dinger* was not a word than that *rafety* was not. This result is consistent with our view that nonword letter sequences that are similar to many words will be subject to more interference from existing word representations.

The effect of N on the word stimuli in LDT is less clear, but the preponderance of evidence suggests that words with high neighbourhoods are classified faster than words with low neighbourhoods. Thus, while having lots of neighbours hinders nonword classification, it helps word classification. Large lexical neighbourhood also helps in the naming task, where subjects are required to pronounce words presented to them. Andrews [1] reviewed eight studies and found that they all showed facilitatory effects. On the face of it, these findings appear to contradict the hypothesis that high neighbourhood words should have lower quality representations. However, one problem with interpreting the psycholinguistics evidence is that the results might not bear directly on the quality of the representations but, rather, on the decision process employed by the subjects in the experiment. That is, if a stimulus can generate lots of potential word vectors then a decision process might be more ready to accept it as a word - which is helpful if in fact it is a word, but unhelpful if it is not. The reaction time would then be influenced by the number of vectors rather than their quality.

However, a more intriguing possibility is that the human word recognition system constructs representations in such a way that high-N words are not disadvantaged by their overlapping lexical neighbours. If it is true that machine learning techniques can suffer in high-N environments but humans do not, then it would be advantageous to learn from the human system. We therefore decided to find more concrete evidence about the effects of neighbourhood density on the quality of trained embeddings.

2.1 Experiment 1: Effects of Orthographic Neighbourhood on Word Embeddings

Perhaps it goes without saying that there are currently no tests of word embeddings which take orthographic neighbourhood density into consideration. As a first step we decided to do a post-hoc analysis on popular data sets which are used for evaluating embeddings: SimLex-99 [11], WS353 [5], and the Stanford

Rare Word (RW) Similarity Dataset [13]. We counted the neighbourhood density of every unique word in each data set, as reported in Table 1. The average densities were surprisingly high; for example Forster and Shen [6] limit their high neighbourhood condition to $N \geq 4$, and other experimenters typically consider 4–5 as being high-N. Table 1 also shows the distribution of words of various lengths in the dataset, as well as the weighted mean length. WS353 has a slightly higher distribution of longer words and a correspondingly lower neighbourhood than SimLex, but most interestingly the RW set showed quite a different distribution with many more long words and a corresponding decrease in the N. We take this to be a completely uncontrolled and accidental feature of the datasets.

The differences in neighbourhoods suggest an alternative explanation for results obtained by [2], who found that English word embeddings from word2vec performed slightly better than fastText in the WS353 test set, but fastText performed better with RW. Their explanation was that the words in WS353 are common words for which good word2vec vectors can be obtained without exploiting subword information. The words in the RW dataset, on the other hand, are helped by subword information because their whole-word vectors are poor. Our analysis of neighbourhoods suggests a quite different explanation. By our hypothesis, fastText embeddings perform best in low-N words environments, which is only the case for the RW data set.

Encouraged by this evidence, we devised a more direct plausibility test for our hypothesis, further inspired by the observation that many of the high-N words we entered into the fastText nearest neighbour[5] query tool returned results where many of the words were morphologically related. They seemed to retain a core morphological stem. For example the high-N query word *tone* has the following semantic neighbours: *tones, overtone, staccato, toned, overtones, dissonantly, accentuation, accentuations, intonation, intonations*. One possible explanation for the morphological overlap is that a critical n-gram such as *ton* becomes central to the representation because it has to be intact to capture the semantic meaning. That is, *tone* has 20 orthographic neighbours, **one: bone done gone lone none cone hone pone sone zone t*ne: tine tune tyne to*e: toke tole tome tope tore tote ton*: tons* and disrupting the morpheme *ton* gives a completely different word. Interestingly, this phenomenon seems to extend to morphemes that are not part of the original query word. For example *bone* has fastText semantic neighbours: *bones, tooth, cartilage, marrow, teeth, osteo, arthroplastie, osteoarthritic, osteochondral, osteolysis* and word2vec neighbours: *bones, cartilage, tooth, skull, marrow, tissue, femur, fractures, teeth, spine*. Again, fastText appears to have latched on to an orthographic cluster which has stable semantic context, whereas word2vec has a much more varied answer set. We wanted to quantify this observation, and the test we proposed was to count the number of unique word stems returned for a nearest neighbour query. That is, by using a common stemming algorithm, we were able to eliminate results which shared

---

[5] It is unfortunate that words with similar embeddings are sometimes called 'neighbour', e.g. on http://fasttext.cc. To avoid confusion we will refer to these as 'semantic neighbours' from now on.

Table 1. Percentage of words of length l in three common data sets, the mean length of words in the data set and their observed Coltheart's N

Word Length	SimLex-99	WS353	RW
1	0	0.2	0
2	2	0.2	0.1
3	8	5.5	1.45
4	18	13	4.8
5	20	14.7	6.2
6	19	20	6.7
7	13.7	11.9	11.7
8	7	10	14.1
9	6.2	9	14.8
10	3.4	6	12.7
11	1.7	4.6	11
12	0.5	2	7.5
13	0.01	0.9	4.4
14	0.01	0.4	2.7
15			0.88
16			0.5
17		0.27	
18			0.03
19			0.03
Mean length	5.8	6.63	8.78
N	4.83	3.45	1.47

a common stem. There are several commonly used stemming algorithms [17], and none of them necessarily eliminate all the orthographically derived forms we would like, but after some experimentation we used the popular Snowball stemmer from NLTK.

We trained a word2vec and a fastText model on the latest WikiPedia data dump as of March 2018[6] (enwiki 20180320). All word2vec and fastText models were trained on the same dump to ensure consistency. The build of word2vec was obtained from https://github.com/dav/word2vec and fastText from https://github.com/facebookresearch/fastText.git.

A set of 9 low-N and 9 high-N, 4-letter words were assembled, keeping word length constant. These were submitted to word2vec and fastText to compute the top 10 nearest semantic neighbours. Each word was stemmed with the Snowball stemmer in the NLTK toolbox[7]. Finally the number of unique stems was subtracted from the total number of semantic neighbours for the two

---

[6] https://dumps.wikimedia.org/.
[7] http://www.nltk.org/howto/stem.html.

conditions. Table 2 shows the number of words that share some unique stem. fastText performed about as well as word2vec on low-N words, but seemed to suffer on the high-N words, corroborating our intuition that fastText vectors were sub optimal with high-N words.

Table 2. Number of words sharing a common stem

	Low-N	High-N
word2vec	14	15
fastText	12	20

3   Models of Word Encoding

Experiment 1 gave some reason to believe that the simple n-gram model of sub-word representation might be limiting the quality of the vectors obtained with fastText, because of the presence of high-N words. Since orthographic neighbourhoods effects are predominantly psycholinguistic, we reasoned that drawing on existing knowledge about human word encoding schemes, might help us to improve orthographic word representations. Our hypothesis is that the surface form of writing systems evolved in light of the properties of the human orthographic encoding mechanism, and an understanding of the properties of the human encoding system could help us implement coding schemes which are better suited to process those surface forms. The Latin alphabet provides discrete components which are combined to form words of various lengths. Interestingly, even though short words tend to have higher neighbourhood densities, there is an inverse relation between word length and frequency of use in English function words [16]. That is, the most frequently used words tend to be short with potentially high orthographic neighbourhoods, which could lead to errors if the perceptual system was not adapted to avoid the errors. Psycholinguistic results about neighbourhood density effects form a key source of evidence for models of visual word recognition.

There is general consensus in the literature that abstract letter identities, independent of type font and case, are involved in the initial stages of printed word recognition [7]. Beyond that, there are differing proposals for how the letter detectors combine to enable printed word recognition. It is clear, for example, that letter position must somehow be computed because readers have no trouble distinguishing between, say, *bale* and *able*. On the other hand humans seem to be unperturbed by letter transposition, deletion, or insertion, such that the intended meanings of *tmie*, *grdn*, and *garxden* are generally recognised [9].

One of the most well supported proposals for an orthographic encoding schema is the *open bigram* (or more generally open n-gram) model of spatial encoding. In the open bigram model, letter encoding includes distant bigram pairs in words, not just spatially contiguous ones. For example, the word *clam* could be coded by the set {*cl, ca, cm, la, lm, am*}. Here the character gap between the letters is not constrained.

Whitney [21] proposed an interesting version of the open bigram approach in the SERIOL model, which incorporates facts about the role of neural activation in information representation. The model postulates a *letter level* encoding stage in which the relative position of each letter in the word string is encoded by the temporal neural firing patterns. That is, the subsequent *bigram level* recognises ordered pairs of letters, converting the temporal sequence into a spatial one. Bigram nodes recognize ordered pairs of letters and fire only if, for example, input A is followed by input B but not if only A were received, or if B were received prior to A. The neuronal firing occurs if letter nodes transmit their information within an oscillatory cycle, so non contiguous letter pairs can also activate letter bigrams, but the strength of firing is diminished with the distance between characters.

The bigram encoding model has similarities with the model of subword encoding in fastText. There are also important differences, in that Whitney's model uses only bigrams as well as non-contiguous bigrams. We decided to try if the introduction of non-contiguous/open n-grams, in analogy with the human perceptual system, could improve the performance of fastText embeddings.

3.1   Experiment 2: Non-contiguous n-grams

In this experiment we tested the addition of open n-grams to subword features, to see if they improved fastText vector representations. We experimented many different encoding schemes, and found that including both open, and regular contiguous n-grams gave inferior results to just using open n-grams[8]. In other words, contiguous n-grams always degraded performance. The best results were obtained by 300 dimensional vectors trained with n-grams where $3 \leq n \leq 6$. We call the trained models with only open n-grams *fasterText*, because every word has fewer n-gram components, and the model is slightly faster to train[9].

To illustrate the reduction in the number of components compared to contiguous n-grams, consider just the *tri*-grams for the word *safety* from our previous example, showing a 66% reduction in just the number of *tri*-grams:

      contiguous trigrams: <sa   saf   afe   fet   ety   ty>
      open trigrams: <a e   s f t   a e y   f t>

The performance of the fasterText vectors is shown in Table 3 for the previously described tests in Table 1, as well as the SemEval2012 task 2, and the Google analogy task. The former of these adds some fine grained semantic relations, and the latter some syntactic as well as semantic analogies. The results

---

[8] This is an interesting result since it departs from theories of human representation. We return to this point in the discussion.

[9] For example time to train the two best performing models on an Intel(R) Xeon(R) CPU E5-2650 v3 @ 2.30 GHz, 40 cores, 62 GB RAM, fastText real time = 376 m 36.311 s, fasterText real time = 361 m 35.879 s.

Table 3. Correlation between human judgement and word vector similarity scores on SimLex999 (semantic similarity, **not** relatedness), WS353 (semantic similarity and relatedness combined), SemEval2012 task 2 (various complex semantic relations), Google (semnatic and syntactic analogy task), and RareWord dataset (semantic similarity). Non-contiguous n-grams in fasterText shown against word2vec and fastText. Five different hyperparamters in fasterText are shown, where the number in parentheses is the degree of n. o+c also includes closed bigrams.

	SimLex	WS353	SemEval	Google	RW
word2vec	.33	.64	**.18**	**.71**	.41
fastText	.33	.69	.17	.69	.44
fasterText(2o+c)	.33	.66	.17	.68	.38
fasterText(2)	.33	.67	.17	.69	.39
fasterText(2–3)	.33	.68	**.18**	.7	.4
fasterText(2–6)	.33	.69	**.18**	.69	.42
fasterText(3–6)	**.34**	**.70**	**.18**	**.71**	**.45**

show Spearman's rank correlation coefficient between vector cosine distance and human judgement. fasterText embeddings achieve the best result (or equal best) on all of the five tests. This in spite of the fewer total n-gram components. The table also shows that performance tended to increase as longer n-grams were included, and degraded if bigrams were also present. However, the important point again is that the open bigram trained embeddings outperformed or equalled the state-of-the-art algorithms on every test.

Table 4. Results from *jiant* target tasks.

	mnli (accuracy)	kerte (accuracy)	sts-b (spearman r)	wnli (accuracy)
fastText (pretrained)	0.408	0.552	0.218	0.563
fastText	0.408	0.552	0.244	0.563
fasterText	**0.440**	**0.578**	**0.248**	0.563

3.2   Downstream Tasks

We compared the embeddings on several downstream tasks using the *jiant*[10] toolkit to evaluate on several GLUE[11] benchmarks [20].

The network configuration, including pretrain tasks, was taken from the *jiant* tutorial. The core model is a shared BiLSTM and no effort was made to optimize the model, since we were looking for a comparison between the embeddings

---

[10] https://jiant.info/.
[11] https://gluebenchmark.com/.

rather than state-of-the-art performance. The test tasks were the Multi-Genre Natural Language Inference (MultiNLI) for textual entailment, the Recognizing Textual Entailment (RTE), the Semantic Textual Similarity Benchmark (sts-b) and the Winograd Natural Language Inference (WNLI or also known as The Winograd Schema Challenge), from the GLUE test set. These tasks are all putatively semantic, indicating semantic encoding in the word vectors [20]. Table 4 shows the results of the comparison between pretrained fastText vectors obtained through the *jiant* web site, the fastText vectors trained on our corpus and the fasterText vectors trained on the same corpus. There is a slight improvement with fasterText in these downstream tasks, suggesting that these embeddings encode more precise semantic information.

In a separate line of work, HaCohen-kerner et al. [8] used Skip Char Ngrams and other character level features in stance classification of tweets. Their goal was to maximise the available features for the short texts available in individual tweets, and to reduce the effect of noisy data due to misspellings. They generated a large number of skip character features, skipping the range between 2–6 characters depending on the word, and found that their skip character ngrams outperformed previous benchmarks. While this work did not use word embeddings directly, it nevertheless shows that non contiguous n-grams provide unique information about word meanings.[12]

4 Summary, Conclusions, and Future Work

The use of subword information for training word embeddings benefits rare words, and languages where words are spontaneously derived by compounding. It was argued that subword encoding is also intrinsic to human word recognition, and the experiments showed that by including aspects of the known human encoding scheme in machine learning, the results can be improved across the board.

One curious aspect of the results was that regular, closed n-grams tended to reduce the quality of the embedding vectors. This is unusual because all psychological models we are aware of include regular n-grams. One possible explanation is that our model misrepresented the role of closed n-grams because it used only a simple model of open n-grams. In our implementation we put equal weight on each n-gram, irrespective of its serial position in the word. In addition, we only used a gap of one character between letters. This corresponds most closely with a *discrete open bigram* model, where non contiguous bigrams within a specified inter-letter distance receive an activation of 1, all other bigrams 0. Other approaches allow larger gaps and weighting functions, which result in different contributions of the subword units. For example the unit *cm* is activated in the word *clam* if two intervening letters are permitted, but not by the word *claim*. On the other hand the *continuous open bigram* model assigns a continuous and decreasing activation to bigrams that are separated by more letters. Thus

---

[12] We would like to thank an anonymous reviewer for bringing our attention to this work.

cm would receive some activation from both words, but more from *clam*. An obvious next step is to implement a version of the continuous model. This could be achieved by repeating bigrams by a factor that is proportional to the distance between them. That is, spatially closer n-grams would get more training cycles in any given word. By doing this we might be able to re introduce shorter n-grams which would improve out of vocabulary performance as well as retain its other good characteristics.

Hannagan et al. [9] argue that orthographic encoding can be mathematically modelled as a string kernel, and different encoding schemes are simply different parameters of the kernel. String kernels are a general approach originally designed for protein function prediction, and are consistent with a general, biologically plausible model of sequence comparison that is tolerant of global displacement and local changes. Our main contribution is to show that subword embeddings based on biologically plausible string kernels produce better results than embeddings based on ad hoc letter combinations. The claims should therefore apply also to other languages and writing scripts, as well as to other methods for generating embedding vectors, for example BERT [4] and ELMo [19]. Observed word forms evolve in conjunction with the capabilities and properties of the human visual system. Encoding schemes used in artificial neural networks could benefit from learning about the properties of real neural networks and the environments in which they operate.

References

1. Andrews, S.: The effect of orthographic similarity on lexical retrieval: resolving neighborhood conflicts. Psychon. Bull. Rev. **4**(4), 439–461 (1997). https://doi.org/10.3758/bf03214334
2. Bojanowski, P., Grave, E., Joulin, A., Mikolov, T.: Enriching word vectors with subword information. arXiv:1607.04606 (2016)
3. Coltheart, M., Davelaar, E., Jonasson, J.T., fir Besner, D.: Access to the internal lexicon. Attent. Perform. **VI**, 535–555 (1977)
4. Devlin, J., Chang, M.W., Lee, K., Toutanova, K.: BERT: pre-training of deep bidirectional transformers for language understanding. arXiv:1810.04805 (2018)
5. Finkelstein, L., et al.: Placing search in context: the concept revisited. In: Proceedings of the 10th International Conference on World Wide Web, WWW 2001, pp. 406–414. ACM, New York (2001). https://doi.org/10.1145/371920.372094
6. Forster, K.I., Shen, D.: No enemies in the neighborhood: absence of inhibitory neighborhood effects in lexical decision and semantic categorization. J. Exp. Psychol. Learn. Mem. Cogn. **22**(3), 696 (1996). https://doi.org/10.1037/0278-7393.22.3.696
7. Grainger, J., van Heuven, W.: Modeling letter position coding in printed word perception. In: Bonin, P. (ed.) The Mental Lexicon (2004)
8. HaCohen-kerner, Y., Ido, Z., Ya'akobov, R.: Stance classification of tweets using skip char ngrams. In: Altun, Y., et al. (eds.) Machine Learning and Knowledge Discovery in Databases, vol. 10536, pp. 266–278. Springer, Cham (2017). https://doi.org/10.1007/978-3-319-71273-4_22

9. Hannagan, T., Grainger, J.: Protein analysis meets visual word recognition: a case for string kernels in the brain. Cogn. Sci. **36**, 575–606 (2012). https://doi.org/10.1111/j.1551-6709.2012.01236.x

10. Harris, Z.S.: Distributional structure. WORD **10**(2–3), 146–162 (1954). https://doi.org/10.1080/00437956.1954.11659520

11. Hill, F., Reichart, R., Korhonen, A.: Simlex-999: evaluating semantic models with (genuine) similarity estimation. arXiv:1408.3456 (2014)

12. Levy, O., Goldberg, Y., Dagan, I.: Improving distributional similarity with lessons learned from word embeddings. Trans. Assoc. Comput. Linguist. **3**, 211–225 (2015). https://scholar.google.com/scholar?cluster=6441605521554204538

13. Luong, M.T., Socher, R., Manning, C.D.: Better word representations with recursive neural networks for morphology. In: CoNLL, Sofia, Bulgaria (2013)

14. Mandera, P., Keuleers, E., Brysbaert, M.: Explaining human performance in psycholinguistic tasks with models of semantic similarity based on prediction and counting: a review and empirical validation. J. Mem. Lang. **92**, 57–78 (2017). https://doi.org/10.1016/j.jml.2016.04.001

15. Mikolov, T., Chen, K., Corrado, G., Dean, J.: Efficient estimation of word representations in vector space. arXiv preprint arXiv:1301.3781 (2013)

16. Miller, G., Newman, E., Friedman, E.: Length-frequency statistics for written English. Inf. Control **1**, 370–389 (1958). https://doi.org/10.1016/s0019-9958(58)90229-8

17. Moral, C., de Antonio, A., Imbert, R., Ramírez, J.: A survey of stemming algorithms in information retrieval. Inf. Res. Int. Electr. J. **19**(1) (2014). Paper 605

18. Pennington, J., Socher, R., Manning, C.D.: Glove: global vectors for word representation. In: Empirical Methods in Natural Language Processing (EMNLP), pp. 1532–1543 (2014). http://www.aclweb.org/anthology/D14-1162

19. Peters, M.E., et al.: Deep contextualized word representations. arXiv:1802.05365 (2018)

20. Wang, A., Singh, A., Michael, J., Hill, F., Levy, O., Bowman, S.R.: GLUE: a multitask benchmark and analysis platform for natural language understanding. In: The Proceedings of ICLR (2019)

21. Whitney, C.: How the brain encodes the order of letters in a printed word: the seriol model and selective literature review. Psychon. Bull. Rev. **8**(2), 221–243 (2001). https://doi.org/10.3758/BF03196158

22. Yarkoni, T., Balota, D., Yap, M.: Moving beyond Coltheart's N: a new measure of orthographic similarity. Psychon. Bull. Rev. **15**, 971–979 (2008)

Using BERT and Augmentation in Named Entity Recognition for Cybersecurity Domain

Mikhail Tikhomirov[(✉)], N. Loukachevitch, Anastasiia Sirotina, and Boris Dobrov

Lomonosov Moscow State University, Moscow, Russia
tikhomirov.mm@gmail.com, louk_nat@mail.ru, overnastuhed@yandex.ru,
dobrov_bv@mail.ru

Abstract. The paper presents the results of applying the BERT representation model in the named entity recognition task for the cybersecurity domain in Russian. Several variants of the model were investigated. The best results were obtained using the BERT model, trained on the target collection of information security texts. We also explored a new form of data augmentation for the task of named entity recognition.

Keywords: Cybersecurity · Named Entity Recognition · Pretraining · Augmentation

1 Introduction

Automatic named entity recognition (NER) is one of the basic tasks in natural language processing. The majority of well-known NER datasets consist of news documents with three types of named entities labeled: persons, organizations, and locations [1,2]. For these types of named entities, the state-of-the-art NER methods usually give impressive results. However, in specific domains, the performance of NER systems can be much lower due to necessity to introduce new types of entities, to establish the principles of their labeling, and to annotate them consistently.

In this paper we discuss the NER task in the cybersecurity domain [3]. Several additional types of named entities for this domain were annotated if compared to general datasets such as software programs, devices, technologies, hackers, and malicious programs (vulnerabilities). The most important entities for this domain are names of malicious software and hackers. However, the annotated dataset contains a modest number of entities of these types. This could be explained by the fact that usually names of viruses and hackers are not known at the time of an attack and are revealed later.

The research was supported by RSF (project No. 20-11-20166). Computational experiments were carried out using the equipment of the shared research facilities of HPC computing resources at Lomonosov Moscow State University.

E. Métais et al. (Eds.): NLDB 2020, LNCS 12089, pp. 16–24, 2020.
https://doi.org/10.1007/978-3-030-51310-8_2

To improve NER performance in such conditions, we suggest using BERT transformers [4] as well as an automatic dataset augmentation method, by which we mean extending a training dataset with sentences containing automatically labeled named entities. In this paper we study how quality of a NER system changes depending on variants of the BERT model used. We experimented with the following models: a multilingual model, a model fine-tuned on Russian data, and a model fine-tuned on cybersecurity texts. We also introduce a new method of dataset augmentation for NER tasks and study the parameters of the method.

2   Related Work

The information extraction task in cybersecurity domain has been discussed in several works. However, most works consider information extraction only from structured or semi-structured English texts [5]. The training corpus presented in [7] does contain unstructured blog posts, but those comprise less than 10% of the corpus. The proposed NER systems are based on such methods as principle of Maximum Entropy [5], Conditional Random Fields (CRF) [6,7]. Gasmi et al. [8] explored two different NER approaches: the CRF-model and neural network based model LSTM-CRF.

Currently, the state-of-the-art models for named entity recognition utilize various contextualized vector representations such as BERT [4], unlike static vector representations, such as word2vec [9]. BERT is pretrained on a large amount of unlabeled data on the language modeling task, and then it can be fine-tuned for a specific task. The paper [13] describes an approach to further training of the multilingual BERT model on the Russian-language data. The new model, called RuBERT, showed an improvement in quality in three NLP tasks in Russian, including named entity recognition [16].

In 2019, the NER shared task for Slavic languages was organized [14]. Most participants and the winner used BERT as the main model. The data had a significant imbalance among the types of entities. For example, the "product" entity was annotated only for 8% of all entities in the Russian data. The results of extracting this type of entities were significantly lower than for other entities.

As far as methods of data augmentation for natural language processing are concerned, they are mainly discussed for such tasks as machine translation and automatic text classification. The simplest augmentation method is to replace source words with their synonyms from manual thesauri or with similar words according to a distributional model trained on a large text collection [17]. In [18] the replacement words were selected among the most probable words according to a language model. The authors of [19] used four simple augmentation techniques for the classification tasks: replacing words with their synonyms, occasional word insertion, occasional word deletion and occasional word order changing. This method was applied to five datasets, showing average improvement of 0.8% for F-score. All four operations contributed to the obtained improvement.

In this paper we discuss a specialized method of data augmentation for named entity recognition. We obtain additional annotated data by inserting named entities in appropriate sentences and contexts.

3   Data

We use a renewed version of Sec_col[1] corpus [3] as a training dataset for the NER task. The final corpus contains 861 unstructured texts (more than 400 K tokens), which are articles, posts, and comments extracted from several sources on cybersecurity. The set of corpus labels (14K labeled entities) includes four general types: PER (persons excluding hackers), ORG (organizations excluding hacker groups), LOC, and EVENT; and five domain-specific types such as PROGRAM (computer programs excluding malware), DEVICE (for various electronic devices), TECH (for technologies having proper names), VIRUS (for malware and vulnerabilities), and HACKER (for single hackers and hacker groups). The annotation principles are described in detail in [3]. The authors of [3] compared different models of NER including CRF and several variants of neural networks on this corpus.

One of the labels, HACKER, is severely underrepresented in the dataset (60 occurrences). The VIRUS label was annotated 400 times, which is lower than for other tags.

4   BERT Models Used in Cybersecurity NER

We explore the use of the BERT model [4] for the NER task in the information-security domain. This model receives a sequence of tokens obtained by tokenization using the WordPiece technique [10] and generates a sequence of contextualized vector representations. BERT training is divided into two stages: pretraining and fine-tuning [12]. At the pretraining stage, the model is trained on the masked language modeling task. At the fine-tuning stage, the task-specific layers are built over BERT; the BERT layers are initialized with the pretrained weights, and further training for the corresponding task takes place.

For Russian, researchers from DeepPavlov [16] trained the model RuBERT on Russian Wikipedia and a news corpus [13]. To do this, they:

- took pre-trained weights from multilingual-bert-base,
- constructed a new vocabulary of tokens of a similar size, better suited for processing Russian texts, thereby reducing the average length of tokenized sequences by 1.6 times, which is critical for the model performance,
- initialized vector representations of new tokens using vectors from multilingual-bert-base in a special way,
- trained the resulting model with a new vocabulary on the Russian Wikipedia and the news corpus.

As part of this study, we evaluated BERT in the NER task in the field of information security with the following pretrained weights: 1) multilingual-bert-base model (BERT), 2) model trained on Russian general data RuBERT, 3) RuCy-BERT, which was obtained by additional training RuBERT on information-security texts. Training RuCyBERT was similar to training RuBERT, but

---

[1] https://github.com/LAIR-RCC/InfSecurityRussianNLP.

without creating a new vocabulary. To do this, the pretraining procedure was launched on 500K cybersecurity texts with the initialization of all weights from RuBERT. The training lasted 500k steps with batch size 6.

All three models have the same architecture: transformer-encoder [15] with 12 transformer blocks, 12 self-attention heads and H = 768 hidden size. The models are fine-tuned for 6 epochs, with B = 16 batch size, with learning rate 5e−5 and T = 128 maximum sequence length. When forming input for the model, only the first token of a word gets a real word label, the remaining tokens get a special label X. At the prediction step, the predicted label of the first token is chosen for the whole word.

5   Augmentation of Training Data

The important classes of named entities in the cybersecurity domain are names of viruses and hackers (including hacker groups). The Sec_col collection, however, includes a quite small number of hackers' names. Many texts related to cybersecurity include only unnamed descriptors (such as *hacker, hacker group, hacker community*).

The core idea of the NER augmentation is as follows: in most contexts where an entity descriptor is mentioned, some other variants of mentions are possible. For Russian, such variants can be: 1) a descriptor followed by a name or 2) just the name alone. The first above-indicated variant of entity mentioning is language-specific, depends on language-specific grammar rules. Consequently, we could augment the collection by adding names after descriptors or by replacing descriptors with names. The following sentences show the examples of the substitution operation for malware.

- **Initial sentence:** Almost 30% are seriously concerned about this issue, another 25% believe that the danger of **spyware** is exaggerated, and more than 15% do not consider this type of threat to be a problem at all.
- **Augmented sentence:** Almost 30% are seriously concerned about this issue, another 25% believe that the danger of **Remcos** is exaggerated, and more than 15% do not consider this type of threat to be a problem at all.

The suggested augmentation includes two subtypes: inner and outer. The inner augmentation involves sentences that contain relevant descriptors within the existing training data. If a sentence meets augmentation restrictions, then the descriptor is replaced with a name or a name is added after the descriptor with equal probability. In both cases, we require that the descriptor must not be followed by a labeled named entity and it must not be preceded by words that agree with the descriptor in gender, number or case, such as adjectives, participles, ordinal numbers, and others.

For the outer augmentation, we look for sentences with relevant descriptors in a collection of unannotated cybersecurity texts. There also must not be any evident named entities (words starting with a capital letter) in a window of certain width around the descriptor. As for this purpose an unannotated collection is used, we do not know the classes of potential named entities, thus we have to exclude sentences with such entities. Besides, we also require the absence of adjectives before the descriptor. The selected sentences also undergo the procedure of inserting a name after a descriptor or replacing the descriptor with a name with equal probability.

The augmentation has been implemented for two types of named entities: malicious software (VIRUS label) and hackers (HACKER label). 24 virus descriptors and 6 hacker descriptors were used. By means of inner augmentation, 262 additional annotated sentences for viruses and 165 annotated sentences for hackers were created. The outer augmentation can be of an unlimited size.

Inserted named entities are obtained in the following way. We took a large cybersecurity text collection and used it to extract names and sequences of names that follow target descriptors. We created the frequency list of extracted names and chose those names for which frequency was higher than a certain threshold (5). Then we excluded the names that appeared in the annotated training collection and belonged to classes that are different from the target class. The rest of the names were randomly used for insertion into the augmented sentences.

6   Experiments

We compare several variants of the BERT model on the NER task for information security domain. In addition, the results of using augmentation of the labeled data are investigated.

The CRF method was chosen as a baseline model, since in previous experiments with the Sec_col collection, this method showed better results than several variants of neural networks that are usually used for the NER task (BiLSTM with character embeddings) [3]. The CRF model utilizes the following features: token embeddings, lemma, part of speech, vocabularies of names and descriptors, word clusters based on their distributional representation, all these features in window 2 from the current token, tag of the previous word [3].

Table 1 shows the classification results for four models for all labels used, as well as the averaged macro and micro F-measures. It can be seen that the use of the multilingual-bert-base (BERT in the table) gives better results than the CRF model for all types of named entities. The use of the pretrained models on the Russian data (RuBERT) and information security texts (RuCyBERT) gives a significant improvement over previous models.

Since models based on neural networks due to random initialization can give slightly different results from run to run, the results in the tables for all BERT models are given as averaging of four runs. The last row of Table 1 indicates (F-macro std) the standard deviation of the results from the mean. It can be seen that the better the model fits the data, the better the results are, and the standard deviation decreases.

For CRF, all types of the augmentation improved the results of extracting target entities. The best augmentation was inner augmentation, which achieved 43.58 HACKER_VIRUS F-measure, which means an increase in the average

Table 1. Results of basic models

	CRF	BERT	RuBERT	RuCyBERT
DEVICE	31.78	34.04	43.13	**46.77**
EVENT	42.70	60.38	64.49	**67.86**
HACKER	26.58	42.69	52.43	**61.03**
LOC	82.30	90.00	**91.28**	90.01
ORG	68.15	76.10	**78.95**	78.58
PER	67.10	80.99	84.32	**84.56**
PROGRAM	62.15	63.15	64.77	**66.57**
TECH	60.65	67.08	67.60	**69.24**
VIRUS	40.90	40.21	46.92	**54.72**
F-micro	63.95	69.37	71.61	**72.74**
F-macro	53.59	61.63	65.99	**68.82**
F-macro std	–	1.52	0.93	**0.86**

quality of the target named entities by 10% points (almost a third). Macro F1 measure for all types of entities (57.39) was also improved significantly.

Table 2 shows the use of the proposed data augmentation approach to extract two types of named entities HÀCKER and VIRUS with inner and outer augmentations. For the outer augmentation, options for adding 100, 200, 400, 600 augmented sentences for each entity types (HÀCKER and VIRUS) were considered. However, the outer augmentation of 600 sentences gave a stable decrease in the results for all models, and therefore these results are not given in the tables. The "mean F1" column shows the averaging of the values of the F1 measure over all types of entities. The best achieved results are in bold. The results improving the basic results (without augmentation) are underlined.

It can be seen that the multilingual BERT model demonstrates a very high standard deviation on the two types of entities under analysis. Any variant of augmentation reduces the standard deviation, which, however, remains quite high (column F1 std). Two models of outer augmentation increase the quality of extraction of target entities while significantly reducing the standard deviation compared to the original model.

For the RuBERT model, the results are significantly higher than for the previous model, the standard deviation is lower. The augmentation in all cases reduces the standard deviation of F measures for target and all types of entities. The results on the target entities increased with outer augmentation of 200 sentences for both entities. Also, for some reason, the outer augmentation only with viruses positively influenced the extraction of both of them (100 and 200 sentences). The study of this phenomenon is planned to continue.

For RuCyBERT model, the basic performance is much higher, and there is no improvement from the augmentation. The augmentation on average reduces the standard deviation of F-measure, which leads to the fact that the performance of models with augmentation and the basic model is comparable.

It can be also seen that in almost all experiments the proposed augmentation significantly increases recall, but decreases precision.

Table 2. Models with augmentation

		HACKER_VIRUS				Macro	
		P	R	F1	F1 std	F1	F1 std
BERT	Base (no augmentation)	**46.43**	38.14	41.45	7.23	61.63	1.52
	Inner	36.81	45.44	39.92	3.53	61.26	0.86
	Outer 100	39.13	44.96	41.04	**2.18**	62.02	**0.55**
	Outer 200	39.32	48.24	**42.51**	4.33	**62.21**	0.74
	Outer 400	40.23	45.97	**42.53**	4.59	62.12	1.08
RuBERT	Base (no augmentation)	53.65	47.38	49.67	4.65	65.99	0.93
	Inner	45.01	**55.74**	48.87	3.48	65.92	0.68
	Outer 100	47.46	53.29	49.38	3.1	65.88	0.79
	Outer 200	47.83	55.34	50.71	2.96	66.24	**0.59**
	Outer 400	45.57	53.45	48.46	**2.36**	65.77	0.67
	Outer viruses 100	**57.14**	51.67	**53.79**	3.05	**66.85**	0.64
RuCyBERT	Base (no augmentation)	**61.33**	55.89	57.87	3.75	68.82	0.86
	Inner	52.51	**62.57**	56.03	2.54	68.61	0.53
	Outer 100	50.78	59.69	53.79	2.36	67.78	**0.43**
	Outer 200	52.82	59.61	54.82	3.94	68.06	0.74
	Outer 400	52.42	61.31	55.64	**2.16**	67.93	0.71

7 Conclusion

In this paper we present the results of applying BERT to named entity recognition for cybersecurity Russian texts. We compare three BERT models: multilingual, Russian (RuBERT), and cybersecurity model trained on specialized text collection (RuCyBERT). The highest macro F-score is shown by the domain-specific RuCyBERT model.

For each model, we have also presented a new form of augmentation of labeled data for the NER task, that is adding names after or instead of a descriptor of a certain type. The adding procedure is language-specific. In our case it is based on the Russian grammar. In practically all cases, the augmentation increases recall, but decreases precision of NER. A significant improvement from the augmentation was revealed for relatively weak CRF and multilingual BERT models. For the fine-tuned models, the quality has barely grown. Nevertheless, if in some cases it is impossible to fine-tune BERT on a specialized collection, the presented augmentation for named entities could be of great use while extracting named entities of non-standard types. The described Sec_col collection and the trained RuCyBERT model can be obtained from the repository[2].

References

1. Sang, E., Meulder, F.: Introduction to the CoNLL-2003 shared task: language-independent named entity recognition. In: Proceedings of the 7th conference on Natural language learning at HLT-NAACL 2003, vol. 4, pp. 142–147 (2003)
2. Mozharova, V.A., Loukachevitch, N.V.: Combining knowledge and CRF-based approach to named entity recognition in Russian. In: Ignatov, D.I., et al. (eds.) AIST 2016. CCIS, vol. 661, pp. 185–195. Springer, Cham (2017). https://doi.org/10.1007/978-3-319-52920-2_18
3. Sirotina, A., Loukachevitch, N.: Named entity recognition in information security domain for Russian. In: Proceedings of RANLP-2019, pp. 1115–1122 (2019)
4. Devlin, J., et al. Bert: Pre-training of deep bidirectional transformers for language understanding. arXiv preprint arXiv:1810.04805 (2018)
5. Bridges, R., Jones, C., Iannacone, M., Testa, K., Goodall, J.: Automatic labeling for entity extraction in cyber security. arXiv preprint arXiv:1308.4941 (2013)
6. Lafferty, J., McCallum, A., Pereira, F.: Conditional random fields: probabilistic: models for segmenting and labeling sequence data. In: International Conference on Machine Learning ICML-2001 (2001)
7. Joshi, A., Lal, R., Finin, T., Joshi, A.: Extracting cybersecurity related linked data from text. In: 2013 IEEE Seventh International Conference on Semantic Computing, pp. 252–259. IEEE (2013). https://doi.org/10.1109/ICSC.2013.50
8. Gasmi, H., Bouras, A., Laval, J.: LSTM recurrent neural networks for cybersecurity named entity recognition. In: ICSEA-2018, vol. 11 (2018)
9. Mikolov, T., et al.: Efficient estimation of word representations in vector space. arXiv preprint arXiv:1301.3781 (2013)
10. Wu, Y., et al.: Google's neural machine translation system: bridging the gap between human and machine translation. arXiv preprint arXiv:1609.08144 (2016)
11. Bahdanau, D., Cho, K., Bengio, Y.: Neural machine translation by jointly learning to align and translate. arXiv preprint arXiv:1409.0473 (2014)
12. Howard, J., Ruder, S.: Universal language model fine-tuning for text classification. arXiv preprint arXiv:1801.06146 (2018)
13. Kuratov, Y., Arkhipov, M.: Adaptation of deep bidirectional multilingual transformers for Russian language. arXiv preprint arXiv:1905.07213 (2019)
14. Piskorski, J., Laskova, L., Marcinczuk M., Pivovarova, L., Priban P., et al.: The second cross-lingual challenge on recognition, normalization, classification, and linking of named entities across slavic languages. In: 7th Workshop on Balto-Slavic Natural Language Processing BSNLP-2019, pp. 63–74 (2019)
15. Vaswani, A., et al.: Attention is all you need. In: Advances in Neural Information Processing Systems, pp. 5998–6008 (2017)
16. DeepPavlov documentation. http://docs.deeppavlov.ai/en/master/. Accessed 25 Dec 2019

---

[2] https://github.com/LAIR-RCC/InfSecurityRussianNLP.

17. Yang Wang, W., Yang, D.: That's so annoying!!!: a lexical and frame-semantic embedding based data augmentation approach to automatic categorization of annoying behaviors using #petpeeve tweets. In: 2015 Conference on Empirical Methods in Natural Language Processing, pp. 2557–2563 (2015)
18. Kobayashi, S.: Contextual augmentation: data augmentation by words with paradigmatic relations. In: 2018 Conference of the North American Chapter of the Association for Computational Linguistics, NAACL-2018, pp. 452–457 (2018)
19. Wei, J.W., Zou, K.: EDA: easy data augmentation techniques for boosting performance on text classification tasks. In: Conference on Empirical Methods in Natural Language Processing, EMNLP 2019, pp. 6381–6387 (2019)

Improving Named Entity Recognition for Biomedical and Patent Data Using Bi-LSTM Deep Neural Network Models

Farag Saad$^{(\boxtimes)}$, Hidir Aras, and René Hackl-Sommer

FIZ Karlsruhe – Leibniz Institute for Information Infrastructure,
Karlsruhe, Germany
{`farag.saad,hidir.aras,rene.hackl-sommer`}@fiz-karlsruhe.de

Abstract. The daily exponential increase of biomedical information in scientific literature and patents is a main obstacle to foster advances in biomedical research. A fundamental step hereby is to find key information (named entities) inside these publications applying Biomedical Named Entities Recognition (BNER). However, BNER is a complex task compared to traditional NER as biomedical named entities often have irregular expressions, employ complex entity structures, and don't consider well-defined entity boundaries, etc. In this paper, we propose a deep neural network (NN) architecture, namely the bidirectional Long-Short Term Memory (Bi-LSTM) based model for BNER. We present a detailed neural network architecture showing the different NN layers, their interconnections and transformations. Based on existing gold standard datasets, we evaluated and compared several models for identifying biomedical named entities such as chemicals, diseases, drugs, species and genes/proteins. Our deep NN based Bi-LSTM model using word and character level embeddings outperforms CRF and Bi-LSTM using only word level embeddings significantly.

Keywords: Biomedical · NER · Deep neural network · Bi-LSTM · CRF · Patent

1 Introduction

We have witnessed a massive growth of information in the biomedical domain in the last few decades due to the abundant research on various diseases, drug development, and gene/protein identification etc. However, a large percentage of the information related to the biomedical domain is available as unstructured document publications such as scientific articles, patents etc. In order to effectively exploit such unstructured resources, research in biomedical named entity recognition (BNER) is one of the most promising techniques for automating the utilization of biomedical data. Furthermore, BNER is considered an initial step for many downstream tasks, such as relation extraction, question answering, knowledge base completion, etc. [2].

© Springer Nature Switzerland AG 2020
E. Métais et al. (Eds.): NLDB 2020, LNCS 12089, pp. 25–36, 2020.
https://doi.org/10.1007/978-3-030-51310-8_3

Identifying biomedical entities is not a trivial task due to many factors such as complex entity structures, fuzzy entity boundaries, abundant use of synonyms, hyphens, digits, characters, and ambiguous abbreviations, etc. Despite significant efforts for building benchmark datasets to develop BNER, these datasets are still far from being optimal in quality and in size to speed up the development of BNER tools. For patents, the problem is even more complex as it is not easy to process the patent text due to peculiarities such as usage of generic terms, paraphrasing, and vague expressions, which makes it harder to narrow down the scope of the invention. This causes important contextual information to be lost, which has a negative effect on the performance of BNER tools [18]. A patent is a very important resource to consider as new chemical or biomedical entities are often shown in patent documents before they are even mentioned in the chemical or biomedical literature making patents a valuable, but often not a fully discovered resource. Furthermore, it is estimated that a significant portion of all technical knowledge is exclusively published in patents. For example, two-thirds of technical information related to the medical domain did not appear in non-patent literature [15].

On the basis of the encouraging results we have achieved in our ongoing work for using deep neural network models for the BNER task [17], in this paper, we show our improved deep learning approach that we evaluated on large biomedical datasets for the following biomedical entity types: chemical, disease, drug, gene/protein, and species. Moreover, we show the specific details of the developed neural network architecture and how the various neural network layers are designed to transform an input to a desired output – enabling the neural network to reduce the error/loss and optimize the learning task.

In the following, we firstly review the related work in Sect. 2, followed by a presentation of the proposed approach in Sect. 3. In Sect. 4 an empirical evaluation is presented and discussed. A conclusion is given in Sect. 5.

2   Related Work

In the literature, NER approaches are generally classified into hybrid (rule-based and statistical), supervised (feature-based) and unsupervised learning approaches [21]. In the biomedical domain, for example with regard to the hybrid approach, a two-fold method for Biomedical NER was proposed in which dictionary-based NER was combined with corpus-based disambiguation [1]. Due to the fact that a biomedical named entity can exist in different written forms, e.g., "SRC1", "SRC 1", and "SRC-1", performing the exact match of the biomedical named entity in a given text with the dictionary terms can result in very low coverage. Therefore, different forms of the same named entity were normalized and transformed into a unified representation. However, words from a common vocabulary may be mistakenly recognized as biomedical named entities. In order to tackle this issue a corpus-based disambiguation approach to filter out mistakenly recognized biomedical named entities was applied. The disambiguation process was accomplished based on a machine-learning classifier trained on an annotated corpus.

Tanabe and Wilbur used a combination of a statistical and a knowledge-based approach to extract gene and protein named entities from biomedical text [20]. First, a Brill POS tagger[1] was applied to extract candidates. These were then filtered based on manually curated rules, e.g., morphological clues, to improve the extraction accuracy. Furthermore, a Bayesian classifier was applied to rank the documents by similarity according to documents with known genes and proteins in advance. Hanisch et al. proposed *ProMiner*, which used a pre-processed synonym dictionary to extract gene and protein named entities from biomedical text [10]. ProMiner is composed of three parts, gene and protein named entity dictionary generation, gene/protein occurrence detection, and filtering of matched entities. Rule-based approaches are expensive and time consuming as rules need to be modified each time the data changes. Furthermore, rule-based approaches are usually domain dependent and cannot be smoothly adapted to a new domain.

In recent years, with the availability of the annotated biomedical corpora, several supervised approaches have been developed. For example, *GENIA*[2] and *BioCreative*[3] corpora were intensively used in supervising learning approaches such as Support Vector Machines (SVMs) [22], Conditional Random Fields [19] etc. In [22] Yang and Li proposed a SVM-based system, named *BioPPISVMExtractor*, to identify protein-protein interactions in biomedical text. Features that were set, such as word feature, protein names distance feature, link-path feature etc. were used for SVM classification. Based on these rich features, the SVM classifier was trained to identify which protein pairs have a biological relationship among them. In [19], Settles used the CRF (Conditional Random Field Approach) approach to recognize genes and proteins named entities with a variety of rich features set such as orthographic and semantic features obtained from a lexicon, etc. Based on the fact that a contextual feature is very important for the performance of the CRF approach, Settles models the local context feature by considering neighboring words, one word before and one word after the word in focus, besides other features for improving the sequence labeling task.

The clustering approach is considered as a standard unsupervised approach for biomedical NER. The assumption behind this unsupervised approach is that the named entities in the biomedical text can be clustered based on their contextual similarity. For example, in [23] Zhang and Elhadad proposed an unsupervised approach to extract named entities from biomedical text. The classification approach does not rely on any handcrafted rules, heuristics, or use of annotated data. It depends on corpus statistics and shallow syntactic knowledge, e.g., noun phrase extraction. Han et al. proposed a novel clustering based active learning method for the biomedical NER task [9]. They compared different variations of the proposed approach and discovered the optimal design of the active learning method. This optimal design employs the use of the vector representation

---

[1] https://www.npmjs.com/package/brill-pos-tagger.
[2] http://www.geniaproject.org/.
[3] https://biocreative.bioinformatics.udel.edu/.

of named entities, and the selection of documents that are representative and informative.

In the past few years, Deep Learning approaches for the NER task (mainly LSTM = Long Short-Term Memory) became dominant as they outperformed the state-of-the-art approaches significantly [5]. In contrast to feature-based approaches, where features are designed and prepared through human effort, deep learning is able to automatically discover hidden features from unlabelled data[4]. The first application for NER using a neural network (NN) was proposed in [3]. In this work, the authors used feature vectors generated from all words in an unlabelled corpora. A separate feature (orthographic) is included based on the assumption that a capital letter at the beginning of a word is a strong indication that the word is a named entity. The proposed controlled features were later replaced with word embeddings [4]. Word embeddings, which are a representation of word meanings in n-dimensional space, were learned from unlabelled data. A major strength of these approaches is that they allow the design of training algorithms that avoid task-specific engineering and instead rely on large, unlabelled data to discover internal word representations that are useful for the NER task.

The prowess of such approaches has since been observed many times. In the BioCreative V CEMP[5] and GPRO[6] tasks, the best algorithm combined deep learning and CRF [14]. Finally, in a study covering 33 datasets, an approach combining deep learning and CRF outperformed not only a plain CRF-based approach, but also entity-specific NER methods (e.g., a dictionary) in recall and F1-score [8]. In recent work, the original BERT (Bidirectional Encoder Representations from Transformers) model [6] was applied for the BNER task, e.g., to train models with biomedical text (BioBERT) [13]. Based on the achieved experimental results, BioBERT, e.g., slightly outperformed the BNER state-of-the-art approaches with 0.62% F-measure improvement and gained a significant improvement (12.24% MRR -Mean Reciprocal Rank-) for the biomedical QA task. The advantage of using the BERT model over other models is that it takes into account polysemous words. For example, Word2Vec produces only one embeddings vector for the polysemous word "apple", while the BERT model produces different embeddings: one embedding for the fruit and another one for the smart phone brand, etc.

3   Bidirectional Long-Short Term Memory (Bi-LSTM)

LSTM is a special case of Recurrent Neural Network (RNN) which is capable of remembering information of larger contexts. RNN is the most used approach for sequence labelling tasks due to its ability to consider a richer context compared to the standard Feed Forward Neural Network (FFNN). The main fundamental

---

[4] Readers interested in a more introductory text on the topic may wish to refer to [7].
[5] Chemical Entity Mention in Patents.
[6] Gene and Protein Related Object.

difference between the architecture of a RNN and a FFNN is that the information flow in the RNN is cyclic while the information flow in the FFNN only moves in one direction (feed and then forward). Each node in a RNN is making the prediction based on the current input into the RNN node and the past output of the same node. This mechanism makes RNN ideal for learning time-sensitive information as it doesn't neglect previous input. However, RNN suffers from the vanishing gradient problem which hinders handling wider contexts [11]. The reason therefore is that when fine-tuning the weights during the back propagation, the weight values update of the early layers will be strongly dependent on the weight values of the later layers. When the weight values of the later layers are very small (closer to zero), the weight values of the early layer will vanish very quickly, making it impossible for the RNN to learn the task effectively.

In LSTM instead of having a node with a single activation function as it is the case in RNN, the LSTM nodes can act as a memory cell which is able to store different types of information using a gate mechanism. Gates in LSTM regulate the flow of information, e.g., forget gates do not allow irrelevant information to pass through. There are two types of LSTM, unidirectional LSTM, which can handle information from the past, and bidirectional LSTM (Bi-LSTM), which can handle information from the past and from the future. One LSTM performs a forward operation so it can handle the information from the past and the second LSTM performs the backward operation so it can handle the information from the future and hence consider a wider context which can help with the predicting task. For more detailed information about the conceptual idea of the LSTM approach we refer the reader to the work proposed in [12].

The architecture of the Bi-LSTM deep neural network model is illustrated in Fig. 1. The input to the model is the *"mutant superoxide dismutase-1 gene"* sequence. The word embeddings is learned using unlabelled datasets, e.g., for chemical, drug, disease, gene, protein, etc. We used the Bi-LSTM to encode character-level information of a given word into its character-level representation (embeddings). If we consider the *"mutant"* token as an example, its characters *"M U T A N T"* will be used as input into the Bi-LSTM model and hence its character-based representation is generated. A combination of the character-based embeddings and the corresponding word embeddings which were generated using an unlabelled dataset will be the input to the Bi-LSTM layer. The result of this step is a richer contextual representation (vector representation) for the input sequence, which will be the input to the CRF model layer for the best label sequence tagging generation. The tagging layer (the CRF model) uses a probabilistic sequence-labelling model for sequence tagging. The CRF model takes as input a token sequence and assigns the most related label to each token based on the training dataset (see Sect. 4.1). As it is possible that a named entity spans over multiple tokens, and in order to tackle this issue, we used the *IOB* format scheme to define the entity boundaries. The training dataset represents the corresponding IOB-tags where IOB refers to *Inside, Outside* and *Beginning* and it is widely used as an encoding scheme for the NER task. Words tagged with *"O"* are outside of named entity, whereas words tagged with *"I"* lie inside

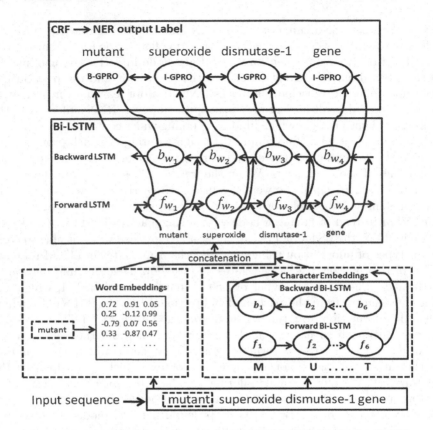

Fig. 1. The overall architecture of the Bi-LSTM-CRF Model for BNER.

of a named entity. *"B"* refers to words that represent the beginning of a named entity. To tag each token in the given sequence, the CRF model builds a set of inference rules based on the training corpus and the refined context obtained by the Bi-LSTM model. For the algorithm implementation we used the default value settings, e.g., embeddings dimensions of value 300, dropout of value 0.5, epochs of value 25, batch size of value 20. lstm size of value 100 etc.

4   Evaluation

In this section we present our empirical study of biomedical NER applied on various biomedical datasets obtained from biomedical literature and patents. Next, we briefly describe the datasets we used for training, word embedding generation, and evaluation of the proposed algorithm variants.

4.1   Dataset

We evaluated and trained several models on six different datasets employing five entity types: chemical, gene/protein, disease, drug, and species. Four datasets (chemical/drug, gene, disease and species) were acquired from biomedical litera-ture while two datasets (chemical and gene/protein) were acquired from patents belonging to various patent offices (cf. Table 1). All datasets were manually annotated by domain experts. The BC4CHEMD, BC2GM, CEMP and GPRO datasets were obtained from BioCreative[7], the NCBI-disease dataset from the National Center for Biotechnology Information[8], while the Linnaeus dataset was obtained from the Linnaeus website[9].

Table 1. The number of training and test instances for each dataset.

Dataset	Type	Training instances	Test instances
BC4CHEMD	The BioCreative IV chemical and drug	30682	26364
BC2GM	The BioCreative II gene	12574	5038
NCBI-disease	Diseases	4560	4797
Linnaeus	Species	11935	7142
CEMP chemical patent	Chemical	43307	19274
Chemdner GPRO patent	Gene/protein	10249	5652

Word embeddings are usually represented by lower-dimensional vectors of mostly up to 300 words in length, e.g., the vector of the word disease is very close to the vector's representation of, chronic, disorder, treatment, drugs etc. These relationships between vectors are not explicitly enforced by humans dur-ing training instead they are learnt by the training algorithm in an unsupervised manner based on large unlabelled datasets. The unlabelled datasets which we used to generate the word embeddings model are obtained from PubMedCentral (PMC)[10] full-text articles, English Wikipedia[11] full-text articles, and a combi-nation of them. We downloaded this data and performed basic cleansing steps such as removing unnecessary tags, references, authors sections etc. We then built the word embeddings models using the GloVe algorithm [16] based on a vector size of 300 and a contextual window size of 15.

Character embeddings can be used to improve the semantic representation of some words. Using word embeddings, we obtained the vector representations of most of the words included in the unlabelled dataset. However, in some cases word embeddings are not enough and won't capture all words such as out-of-vocabulary (OOV) words, different written forms of the same entity, misspelled words, etc. To identify such words, character embeddings are used to generate vector representations of words by considering their character-level structure, e.g., "alpha-lipoic-acid" and "α-lipoic-acid" will be considered as the same even though they not orthographically similar.

---

[7] https://biocreative.bioinformatics.udel.edu/resources/.
[8] https://www.ncbi.nlm.nih.gov/CBBresearch/Dogan/DISEASE/.
[9] http://linnaeus.sourceforge.net/.
[10] ftp://ftp.ncbi.nlm.nih.gov/pub/pmc/oa_bulk/ (until 12/2019).
[11] https://dumps.wikimedia.org/enwiki/latest/ (until 12/2019).

4.2 Experiments

We conducted five experiments as the baseline using the CRF approach. We then compared the results of the CRF approach with two variants of the Bi-LSTM model based on word- and character-level representations. We compared all methods in terms of precision, recall, and F1 score over the six test datasets. For the biomedical literature: Chemical and Drug (BC4CHEMD) with 26,364 test instances, Genes (BC2GM) with 5038 test instances, Disease (NCBI-Disease) with 4797 test instances and Species (Linnaeus) with 7142 test instances (See Table 1). For patent test datasets: Chemical (CEMP) with 19,274 test instances and Gene/Protein (GPRO) with 5652. The evaluation for the deep learning approach variants Bi-LSTM and CHARS-Bi-LSTM was performed based on the embedding vectors described in Sect. 4.1.

Table 2 shows the evaluation results of comparing both the Bi-LSTM and CHARS-Bi-LSTM models. The first embeddings model is learned based on the unlabelled dataset of PMC while the second embeddings model is learned using a combination of PMC and Wikipedia. The second word embeddings model was used to evaluate whether the combined embeddings model will have a significant impact on the Bi-LSTM model's performance. As shown in Table 2, for the BC4CHEMD test dataset (Chemical & Drug), the CHARS-Bi-LSTM model trained on the PMC unlabelled dataset achieved a significantly higher precision, recall, and F-measure with 0.90, 0.93, and 0.91, respectively, compared to the results of the CRF model (e.g., recall was improved by 15%) and compared to the Bi-LSTM model (e.g., recall was improved by 8%). However, the CHARS-Bi-LSTM model using word embedding trained on a combination of PMC and Wikipedia achieved a minor precision improvement by 1%, and has a drop of recall by 2% while the F-measure remains the same. The same applies for the BC2GM dataset where the CHARS-Bi-LSTM model using word embeddings trained on PubMed achieved a significant improvement over CRF (e.g., recall by 16%) and over Bi-LSTM (e.g., recall by 6%).

Using a word embedding trained on PMC and Wikipedia leads to a minor decrease in recall and F-measure by 1%. For the other test datasets (disease and species), the CHARS-Bi-LSTM trained on a combination of PMC and Wikipedia achieved a better improvement over the CHARS Bi-LSTM model using word embeddings trained only on a PMC dataset. For the disease dataset, precision improved by 10% while for species remains the same and F-measure improved by 4% while for species improved by 5%. Recall decreased by 1% while for species improved by 8%. The improvement can be interpreted as that Wikipedia is a significant resource for diseases and species, providing a richer data resource for the word embeddings learning task. For chemical and gene/protein patent test datasets, adding the Wikipedia data had almost no impact on the Bi-LSTM performance. This is due to the nature of the patent text since newly invented entities usually do not show up immediately in other resources, e.g., Wikipedia. To improve the BNER for biomedical data in patent resources, we built a new word embedding model trained in patent text to evaluate whether the developed patent model can raise the Bi-LSTM model's performance. We collected 1.5

million titles and abstracts obtained from EPO[12], USFULL[13] and PCTFULL[14] patent databases. We then kept only documents that belong to the life science domain by filtering over the International Patent Classification (IPC) code. Next, we combined the patents with PMC and applied the GloVe algorithm on the combined unlabelled dataset to build the word embedding model.

Table 2. Precision, Recall and F-measure of CRF and Bi-LSTM variants using various Word and Character level embeddings

Method	Word embeddings	Metrics	Test datasets					
			D1	D2	D3	D4	D5	D6
CRF	-	Precision	0.89	0.80	0.89	0.95	0.92	0.82
		Recall	0.78	0.72	0.76	0.49	0.87	0.74
		F-measure	0.83	0.76	0.81	0.62	0.90	0.79
Bi-LSTM-CRF	PubMed	Precision	0.87	0.78	0.87	**0.98**	0.92	0.81
		Recall	0.85	0.78	0.77	0.76	0.89	0.82
		F-measure	0.86	0.78	0.82	0.85	0.90	0.81
Bi-LSTM-CRF	PubMed + Wikipedia	Precision	0.85	0.79	0.97	**0.98**	0.92	0.80
		Recall	0.86	0.78	0.84	0.84	0.90	0.82
		F-measure	0.86	0.78	0.90	0.91	0.91	0.81
CHARS-Bi-LSTM-CRF	PubMed	Precision	0.90	**0.83**	0.88	**0.98**	0.93	0.82
		Recall	**0.93**	**0.84**	0.85	0.82	0.94	0.88
		F-measure	**0.91**	**0.84**	0.87	0.89	0.93	0.85
CHARS-Bi-LSTM-CRF	PubMed + Wikipedia	Precision	**0.91**	**0.83**	**0.98**	**0.98**	**0.94**	**0.84**
		Recall	0.91	0.83	**0.86**	**0.90**	0.95	0.87
		F-measure	0.90	0.83	**0.92**	**0.94**	**0.94**	0.85
CHARS-Bi-LSTM-CRF	PubMed + Patent	Precision	–	–	–	–	0.91	0.83
		Recall	–	–	–	–	**0.97**	**0.90**
		F-measure	–	–	–	–	**0.94**	**0.86**

Remarks: D1 refers to the BC4CHEMD, D2 refers to the BC2GM, D3 refers to the NCBI-Disease, D4 refers to the Linnaeus, D5 refers to the CEMP and D6 refers to the GPRO datasets

Using this combined word embeddings model applied on the patent chemical and gene/protein test datasets leads to a minor improvement of the CHARS-Bi-LSTM model (average recall improvement of 2%, see Table 2). This is an indication that patent data word embeddings models could slightly help to recognize more entities. For future evaluation, we will further increase the size and the focus of the patent data to include more chemical genes/proteins so a significant assessment can be performed.

Overall, the CHARS-Bi-LSTM model trained using character and word level embeddings achieved superior performance compared to the CRF and Bi-LSTM using only word embeddings. This indicates that character-level embeddings can be useful in handling out-of-vocabulary words, misspelled words, different forms of the same entity, etc., and hence the character-level representation is

---

[12] https://publication.epo.org/raw-data/product-list.
[13] http://patft.uspto.gov/.
[14] https://stn.products.fiz-karlsruhe.de/sites/default/files/STN/summary-sheets/ PCTFULL.pdf.

significantly able to infer a representation of unseen words in the training data and increase the Bi-LSTM model performance.

4.3   Application

In the following patent use case, we illustrate how BNER can be used for improving patent retrieval for discovering relevant inventions, technologies, and detailed information from text. As an example, a key term search for finding bio-technologies related to *biosensor devices* in medicine could be initiated using the key term "biosensor device". As biosensors are devices which have a broad range of applications such as in medicine, environmental research, agriculture, etc. a more-fine grained (entity-based) retrieval is required for finding more precise results. In our example, we can utilize biomedical annotations in order to narrow down our search to focus the domain of interest like biosensor device usage in medicine, e.g., DNA hybridization detection, glucose measurement, antibody detection, etc. In a different example, in case of the *"biosensor device"* query, the patent retrieval system will respond by suggesting specific biomedical terms, e.g., *"miRNA"*, which are related to the usage of biosensor devices in the biomedical domain. As a result, specific patents related to "miRNA" and biosensors can be retrieved more efficiently, e.g., "Method for preparing self-energized miRNA biosensor", "Biological probe and detection method for detecting miRNA and application", etc.

5   Conclusion

We have presented a deep neural network architecture based on Bi-LSTM and a setting for the efficient recognition of different classes of biomedical named entities. To achieve that goal, we have built and utilized several pre-trained embeddings models based on word and character level embeddings. Our experiments show that combining heterogeneous pre-trained word embedding models allows us to achieve better results in recognizing various types of biomedical named entities. For example, a small pre-trained patent word embeddings model combined with the PMC model has shown an improvement in the patent BNER task. Overall, the CHARS-Bi-LSTM model, trained using character and word level embeddings, achieved superior performance compared to the traditional CRF and Bi-LSTM approach using only word embeddings. This indicates that character-level embeddings seem to be very useful in handling out-of-vocabulary words, misspelled words, different forms of the same entity, etc.

References

1. Basaldella, M., Furrer, L., Tasso, C., Rinaldi, F.: Entity recognition in the biomedical domain using a hybrid approach. J. Biomed. Semant. **8**, 51 (2017)
2. Cokol, M., Iossifov, I., Weinreb, C., Rzhetsky, A.: Emergent behavior of growing knowledge about molecular interactions. Nat. Biotechnol. **23**(10), 1243–1247 (2005)

3. Collobert, R., Weston, J.: A unified architecture for natural language processing: deep neural networks with multitask learning, pp. 160–167 (2008)
4. Collobert, R., Weston, J., Bottou, L., Karlen, M., Kavukcuoglu, K., Kuksa, P.P.: Natural language processing (almost) from scratch. Computing Research Repository - CORR abs/1103.0398 (2011)
5. Dang, T.H., Le, H.Q., Nguyen, T.M., Vu, S.T.: D3NER: biomedical named entity recognition using CRF-BiLSTM improved with fine-tuned embeddings of various linguistic information. Bioinformatics **34**(20), 3539–3546 (2018)
6. Devlin, J., Chang, M.W., Lee, K., Toutanova, K.: BERT: pre-training of deep bidirectional transformers for language understanding. In: Proceedings of the 2019 Conference of the North American Chapter of the ACL: Human Language Technologies, Volume 1 (Long and Short Papers), pp. 4171–4186 (2019)
7. Goodfellow, I., Bengio, Y., Courville, A.: Deep Learning. MIT Press, Cambridge (2016)
8. Habibi, M., Weber, L., Neves, M., Wiegandt, D.L., Leser, U.: Deep learning with word embeddings improves biomedical named entity recognition. Bioinformatics **33**(14), i37–i48 (2017)
9. Han, X., Kwoh, C.K., Kim, J.: Clustering based active learning for biomedical named entity recognition. In: 2016 International Joint Conference on Neural Networks (IJCNN), pp. 1253–1260 (2016)
10. Hanisch, D., Fundel-Clemens, K., Mevissen, H.T., Zimmer, R., Fluck, J.: Prominer: rule-based protein and gene entity recognition. BMC Bioinform. **6**, S14 (2005)
11. Hochreiter, S.: The vanishing gradient problem during learning recurrent neural nets and problem solutions. Int. J. Uncertainty Fuzziness Knowl.-Based Syst. **6**, 107–116 (1998)
12. Hochreiter, S., Schmidhuber, J.: Long short-term memory. Neural Comput. **9**(8), 1735–1780 (1997)
13. Lee, J., et al.: BioBERT: a pre-trained biomedical language representation model for biomedical text mining. Bioinformatics **36**, 1234–1240 (2019)
14. Luo, L., et al.: A neural network approach to chemical and gene/protein entity recognition in patents. J. Cheminform. **10**(1), 1–10 (2018). https://doi.org/10.1186/s13321-018-0318-3
15. Mucke, H.: Relating patenting and peer-review publications: an extended perspective on the vascular health and risk management literature. Vasc. Health Risk Manag. **7**, 265–272 (2011)
16. Pennington, J., Socher, R., Manning, C.: Glove: global vectors for word representation. In: Proceedings of the 2014 Conference on Empirical Methods in Natural Language Processing (EMNLP), pp. 1532–1543 (2014)
17. Saad, F.: Named entity recognition for biomedical patent text using Bi-LSTM variants. In: The 21st International Conference on Information Integration and Web-based Applications & Services (iiWAS 2019) (2019, to appear)
18. Saad, F., Nürnberger, A.: Overview of prior-art cross-lingual information retrieval approaches. World Patent Inf. **34**, 304–314 (2012)
19. Settles, B.: Biomedical named entity recognition using conditional random fields and rich feature sets. In: Proceedings of the International Joint Workshop on Natural Language Processing in Biomedicine and Its Applications, JNLPBA 2004, pp. 104–107 (2004)
20. Tanabe, L., Wilbur, W.J.: Tagging gene and protein names in biomedical text. Bioinformatics **18**(8), 1124–1132 (2002)

21. Yadav, V., Bethard, S.: A survey on recent advances in named entity recognition from deep learning models. In: Proceedings of the 27th International Conference on Computational Linguistics, pp. 2145–2158, August 2018
22. Yang, Z., Lin, H., Li, Y.: BioPPISVMExtractor: a protein-protein interaction extractor for biomedical literature using SVM and rich feature sets. J. Biomed. Inform. **43**, 88–96 (2009)
23. Zhang, S., Elhadad, N.: Unsupervised biomedical named entity recognition: experiments with clinical and biological texts. J. Biomed. Inform. **46**(6), 1088–1098 (2013)

A User-centred Analysis of Explanations for a Multi-component Semantic Parser

Juliano Efson Sales[1,2]([envelope]), André Freitas[3], and Siegfried Handschuh[2]

[1] Department of Computer Science and Mathematics,
University of Passau, Passau, Germany
[2] Institute of Computer Science, University of St. Gallen, St. Gallen, Switzerland
{juliano.sales,siegfried.handschuh}@unisg.ch
[3] School of Computer Science, The University of Manchester, Manchester, UK
andre.freitas@manchester.ac.uk

Abstract. This paper shows the preliminary results of an initial effort to analyse whether explanations associated with a semantic parser help users to generalise the system's mechanisms regardless of their technical background. With the support of a user-centred experiment with 66 participants, we evaluated the user's mental model by associating the linguistic features from a set of explanations to the system's behaviour.

Keywords: Explainable AI · User-centred analysis · Semantic parsing

1 Introduction

Archetypal natural language understanding (NLU) systems, such as question answering, natural language interfaces and semantic parsers, typically require the complex coordination of multiple natural language processing components, where each component can explore a large spectrum of resources and learning methods [3]. Offering end-user explanations for intelligent systems has becoming a strong requirement either to comply with legal requirements [5] or to increase the user confidence [11]. However, while delivering a human-interpretable explanation for a single component is challenging, the problem is aggravated in the context of multi-component systems [3,11].

Although the literature shows explanation models evaluated from an user-centred perspective, none of them targeted an NLU system [9,13,19,21]. As natural language gives vast possibilities of expression, explanations of NLU systems can allow the users to adapt their writing styles to favour the system comprehension according to the underline model.

This work analyses different types of explanations instantiated in a multi-component semantic parsing system for an end-user natural language programming task to analyse to what extent users, irrespective of their technical background, are able to improve their mental models by associating the linguistic features from the explanations to the system's behaviour.

E. Métais et al. (Eds.): NLDB 2020, LNCS 12089, pp. 37–44, 2020.
https://doi.org/10.1007/978-3-030-51310-8_4

2   Related Work

Lipton [11] defined a comprehensive taxonomy of explanations in the context of AI, highlighting various criteria of classification such as motivation (*trust, causality, transferability, informativeness* and *fairness & ethics*) and property (*transparency* and *post-hoc interpretability*).

Trust is by far the most common motivation presented in the literature, like Pazzani [13], and Biran & Cotton [2] whose results showed users demonstrate higher confidence when using a system they understand how it works. *Fairness & ethics* is also a strong driver as the well-known European General Data Protection Regulation [5] guarantees both rights *"for meaningful information about the logic involved"* and *"to non-discrimination"* to prevent bias and unfair behaviour.

Diversely, *post-hoc* explanations make use of interpretations to deliver meaningful information about the AI model. Instead of showing how the model works, it presents evidences of its rationale by making use of *(i)* textual descriptions [18], *(ii)* visualisations able to highlight image parts from which the decision was made [17], *(iii)* 2D-representation of high-dimensional spaces [12], or *(iv)* explanation by similarity [4].

3   Semantic Parsing of Natural Language Commands

The Problem The problem of *semantic parsing of natural language commands* consists of mapping a natural language command to a formal representation, called *function signature*, from a knowledge base (KB) of APIs.

We formalise the target problem as follows. Let F be a KB composed of a set of k function signatures $(f_1, f_2, \ldots, f_k)$. Let $f_i = (n_i, l_i, P_i)$ be an element of F, where n_i is the *function's name*, l_i is the *function's provider*, and P_i is the set of *function's parameters*. Let f_i' be a call of f_i, which also holds values for their parameters, totally or partially. Let c_j be a natural language command which semantically represents a target function call f_j'. The parser aims at building a ranking model which, given a set of function signatures F and a natural language command c, returns a list B of ordered function calls, satisfying the command intent.

The Semantic Parser Our end-user study is focused on an explanation model for a multi-component semantic parser proposed by Sales et al. [14], which is composed of a chain of components. Given the space restriction, the semantic parser is briefly summarised in this section.

The first component performs a semantic role labelling (SRL) classification of the command tokens, segmenting and identifying the *(i)* function descriptor and *(ii)* the set of *command objects*. The *function descriptor* is the minimal subset of tokens present in the command that allows identifying the target function signature in the function KB. A *command object* represents a potential descriptor or value of a parameter. It is implemented based on an explicit grammar defined by dependency relations and POS-tags.

The second component is the *Type Inferencer* which plays the role of a named entity recogniser. The *Inferencer*'s implementation combines heuristics with a gazetteer.

Based on the function descriptor and the list of command objects, the model generates potential function calls by combining the set of command object and the list of function signatures. For each function call, the *Relevance Classifier* generates a classification as (i) wrong frame (score 0); (ii) right frame with wrong parameters (score 1); (iii) right frame with partial right parameters (score 2); (iv) right frame with right parameters (score 3). The classification phase is implemented as a Random Forest model [6], which take as input the *semantic relatedness scores* and *densities* (described below) to identify jointly the most relevant function signature and the best configuration of parameters values.

Originally, the proposed semantic parser [14] defined an extra component responsible for reducing the search space. As the explanation model is evaluated in a setting with a restricted data set, we simplified the architecture by removing this component. Thus, the inference process can be described by Eq. 1, which defines the ranking score of a given function call for a natural language command, where $\delta(x)$ is a type inferencer that, given an expression in natural language x, it return its semantic type. For example, $\delta(\text{"}dollar\text{"}) = \text{CURRENCY}$ and $\delta(\text{"john@domain.com"}) = \text{EMAIL}$; $\boldsymbol{x}$ is a vector representation of x in a word embedding model; $\cos(\boldsymbol{x}, \boldsymbol{y})$ is a semantic similarity function, which score how similar the vectors $\boldsymbol{x}$ and $\boldsymbol{y}$ are in the space. We use the cosine similarity for this purpose; $\bigodot_{i=1,j=1}^{n,k} (x_{ij})$ is a combinatorial optimiser that finds a maximum weight matching j to i. We use the Hungarian algorithm [8] for this purpose; and $den(p_i)$ is the set of the densities of the function parameters, which represents the inverse term-frequency in the function signatures vocabulary set.

$$cos(\boldsymbol{n}, \boldsymbol{d}) + \max_{j=1}^{k}(\cos(l, o_j)) + \sum \bigodot_{i=1,j=1}^{n,k} (cos(\boldsymbol{p_i}, \boldsymbol{\delta(o_j)})) + 1000 * \tau \quad (1)$$

The equation defines the sum of (i) the semantic relatedness of the function descriptor from the command and the function name, (ii) the maximum semantic relatedness of the command objects and the function provider, (iii) the combinatorial optimisation of the command objects' types and the function's parameters, and (iv) the function signature class τ multiplied by a large weight.

4   Explanation of a Multi-component Semantic Parser

As heterogenity is an intrinsic characteristic of a multi-component AI system, demanding different explanation methods to different parts of the application, we organised the explanation in a hierarchical fashion motivating the construction of a model that is suitable for users with different levels of knowledge in machine

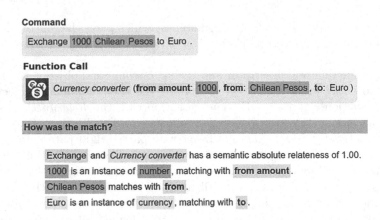

Fig. 1. Explanations of the *Semantic Role Labeler* and the *Type Inferencer*.

learning and linguistics. The explanation model, then, explores a hierarchical representation in an increasing degree of technical depth. In this context, it presents transparency-oriented explanations in the higher levels, going gradually to explanation that demand technical knowledge, and to the *post-hoc* ones.

The model presents seven explanations grouped by three layers focused on the components' behaviour and their input features. As expected in a heterogeneous architecture, each component operates under a different method and have different types of inputs.

SRL Rules and Syntactic Tree Layers. The first level describes the *Semantic Role Labeler* and the *Type Inferencer*. The explanations show the rules activated *(i)* to identify the command objects, *(ii)* to generated multi-word objects, and *(iii)* to identify the semantic types, highlighting the tokens and features involved in the process as shown in Fig. 1. The second level depicts the features on which the rules operate, namely the syntactic tree and the part of speech (POS) of each token. Figure 2 shows a natural language command and both the set of POS-tags and the dependency tree associated with its tokens. These layers aim at showing the connection between the linguistic features and main concepts of the parsing system, whose interpretability is dependent on the understanding of the role of linguistic features in the classification.

Word Embedding Layer. The matching process relies on the semantic relatedness scores, which represent the degree of semantic similarity the function descriptor and command objects have in relation to the function signature [16]. The semantic relatedness is calculated from a word embedding model, which represent terms as vectors in a high-dimensional space. The explanation provides a cluster-based visualisation using t-SNE [12], where it plots the semantic elements that plays a role in the matching process from both the command and the function signature as shown in Fig. 3. The cosine between the points represents the degree of semantic relatedness in a typical *post-hoc* explanation fashion.

The Ranking and Classification Layer. The lower level is devoted to the most technical explanations which shows the mathematical expression that defines the final ranking score of the function signature along with the features used in both the expression itself and in the function relevance classifier. To simplify the model to non-technical users, we reduced Eq. 1 to $\sum_{i=0}^{n}(z_i) + 1000 * \tau$, where all elements in the expression is represented by z, the vector of all features. Additionally, this level also presents the trained random forest classifier, showing the relevance of each feature in the final classification using the visualisation proposed by Welling et al. [20], called *Random Floor*.

5 Evaluation

We asked the participants to simulate the use of a semantic parser, in which the user inputs the natural language commands, and the system suggests a list of function calls as depicted in Fig. 4. We showed twelve pre-configured natural language commands and their corresponding list of 3 to 5 potential function calls as a result of the execution of the parser. The pre-configured commands as well as the function signatures came from the data set defined in the Task 11 of the SemEval 2017 [15], which presents a broader set of functions and describes commands closer to the daily routine of end users.

Mental Models. A mental model is a cognitive representation of the external world to support the human reasoning process [7]. In our task, the "external world" is represented by the semantic parsing system, and we evaluate the user's mental model by assessing whether the presented explanations help the user to generalise the system's mechanisms. So, we designed a set of questions to measure whether the user realised the correct influence of linguistic features in the overall performance of the parser in both SRL and classification phases. Given a contextual command, the participants were asked to judge affirmative sentences in a Likert 7-point scale [10]. We evaluated three aspects of the SRL: *(i)* the role of proper nouns, *(ii)* the importance of the correct spelling and use of grammar and *(iii)* the verb mood (indicative *vs.* imperative).

Proper nouns are generally written in capitalised letter in English. As proper nouns define a command object, we want to identify to what extend users identify the impact of this feature in the system's performance. After given a contextual command, we asked the participants to judge the veracity of sentences like *"Writing 'Swiss Francs' with capital letter increases the system comprehension"*.

Incomplete sentences might introduce errors in the POS-tagger and grammar tree parser, which on the other hand leads to wrong interpretation about the objects. In this task, we present grammatically incomplete commands (keyword-search style) to support users in the identification of the importance of grammatically correct sentences instead of keywords, such as traditional information retrieval systems. we asked the participants to judge the veracity of sentences

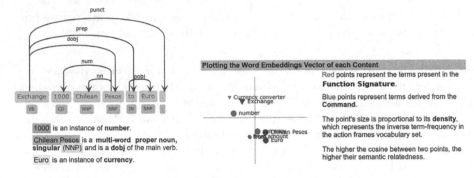

Fig. 2. Grammar tree.

Fig. 3. Plot of the elements from the command and function signature in which the cosine between the points represents the semantic relatedness.

Fig. 4. A natural language command and a list of potential function signatures representing its intent.

like *"Writing a set of keywords for the command has the same result as grammatically correct sentences"*.

Regarding verb moods, we presented to the participants commands written as questions and in the indicative form. After given a contextual command, we asked the participants to judge the veracity of sentences like *"Starting by 'I would like' increases the system comprehension"*.

Participants. We recruited 66 adult participants from the authors' professional networks whose unique requirement was to be fluent in English. The set of participants is composed of 26 females and 40 males, whose age vary from 20 to 49. They reported their level of knowledge in *machine learning* (ML) and *English grammar* (EG) according to the same scale suggested by Azaria et al. [1], to which we attributed a score from 1 to 6 respectively *none*; *very little*; *some background from high school*; *some background from university*; *significant knowledge, but mostly from other sources*; *bachelor with a major or minor in the related topic*.

The participants were divided randomly into the *control group* composed of 34 participants, which have access to the system without the explanation, and the *treatment group*, composed of 32 participants, with access to the explanation. The random division longed for balancing the number of participants with and without ML knowledge in each group.

We introduced the experiment to the participants by exposing its main goals and the expected procedures in the task. We highlighted that the idea behind the parser is to allow a user to find suitable functions and their parameters from her/his commands expressed in natural language, regardless of her/his technical knowledge. We asked them to select the correct function call for each pre-configured command, while examining the tool to infer how it works. For the users that participated in the treatment group, we encouraged them to see the explanations, which shows how the system maps commands to the function calls.

Table 1. The results regarding the mental model assessment.

Metrics	Treatment group	Control group	
Average	1.13	0.73	
r (ML)	0.54	0.45	
r (EG)	0.45	0.46	
	Acquainted	Non-	Acquainted	Non-
Avg. (ML)	1.62	0.63	1.07	0.54
Avg. (EG)	1.42	0.62	1.11	0.34

6   Results and Discussion

We associated the answer in the Likert 7-point scale to the interval -3 to 3, where 0 is the neutral answer and 3 represents *strongly agree* when the question reflects a true statement, and *strongly disagree* when it represents a false statement. We also analysed the statistical significance of the results using the *t-test*, which is represented by p.

Table 1 presents the results of the mental model assessment. On average, participants in the treatment group give scores 55% higher than those in the control group (1.13 *vs.* 0.73, $p < 0.05$). The results also demonstrate that knowledge in machine learning and English grammar have significant positive relationship with the mental model scores in both treatment group ($r = 0.46$ for ML, $r = 0.40$ for EG) and control group ($r = 0.45$ for ML, $r = 0.41$ for EG). The invariance of the correlation coefficients among the groups and the mental model scores strongly suggest the explanation model helps users to build better mental models. To explicitly present this conclusion, we divided both treatment and control groups into four subgroups according to their knowledge in ML. We considered acquainted with ML those users that declared having *significant knowledge, but mostly from other sources* or a *bachelor with a major or minor in the topic*. In average, the score of the users acquainted with ML in the target group is 1.62, while 1.07 in the control group ($p < 0.05$). Although not being the focus of our study, the results concerning EG knowledge present a similar tendency as shown in Table 1.

7   Conclusion

Our experiments showed evidences explanations are an effective method to build mental models, regardless of the users' technical background. The experiment also suggests technical knowledge is boosted when accompanied by explanations, given its high correlations with mental model scores.

References

1. Azaria, A., et al.: Instructable intelligent personal. In: AAAI 2016 (2016)
2. Biran, O., Cotton, C.: Explanation and justification in machine learning: a survey. In: Workshop on Explainable AI (XAI), IJCAI 2017, p. 8 (2017)
3. Burgess, A.: AI prototyping. In: Burgess, A. (ed.) The Executive Guide to Artificial Intelligence, pp. 117–127. Springer, Cham (2018). https://doi.org/10.1007/978-3-319-63820-1_7
4. Caruana, R., Kangarloo, H., Dionisio, J.D., Sinha, U., Johnson, D.: Case-based explanation of non-case-based learning methods. In: Proceedings of AMIA Symposium (1999)
5. Goodman, B., Flaxman, S.: European union regulations on algorithmic decision-making and a "right to explanation". AI Mag. **38**, 50–57 (2017)
6. Ho, T.K.: Random decision forests. In: Proceedings of the Third International Conference on Document Analysis and Recognition (1995)
7. Jones, N., Ross, H., Lynam, T., Perez, P., Leitch, A.: Mental models: an interdisciplinary synthesis of theory and methods (2011)
8. Kuhn, H.W.: The hungarian method for the assignment problem. Naval Res. Logist. Q. **2**(1–2), 83–97 (1955)
9. Kulesza, T., Burnett, M., Wong, W.K., Stumpf, S.: Principles of explanatory debugging to personalize interactive machine learning. In: IUI 2015 (2015)
10. Likert, R.: A technique for the measurement of attitudes (1932)
11. Lipton, Z.C.: The mythos of model interpretability. In: Proceedings of the ICML 2016 Workshop on Human Interpretability in Machine Learning (2016)
12. van der Maaten, L., Hinton, G.: Visualizing data using t-SNE. J. Mach. Learn. Res. **9**, 2579–2605 (2008)
13. Pazzani, M.J.: Representation of electronic mail filtering profiles. In: IUI 2000 (2000)
14. Sales, J.E., Freitas, A., Handschuh, S.: An open vocabulary semantic parser for end-user programming using natural language. In: 12th IEEE ICSC (2018)
15. Sales, J.E., Handschuh, S., Freitas, A.: Semeval-2017 task 11: end-user development using natural language. In: SemEval-2017 (2017)
16. Sales, J.E., Souza, L., Barzegar, S., Davis, B., Freitas, A., Handschuh, S.: Indra: a word embedding and semantic relatedness server. In: 11th LREC (2018)
17. Selvaraju, R.R., et al.: Grad-CAM: why did you say that? Visual explanations from deep networks via gradient-based localization (2016)
18. Silva, V.D.S., Handschuh, S., Freitas, A.: Recognizing and justifying text entailment through distributional navigation on definition graphs. In: AAAI 2018 (2018)
19. Stumpf, S., et al.: Toward harnessing user feedback for machine learning. In: IUI 2007 (2007)
20. Welling, S.H., Refsgaard, H.H.F., Brockhoff, P.B., Clemmensen, L.K.H.: Forest floor visualizations of random forests (2016)
21. Zhou, J., et al.: End-user development for interactive data analytics: uncertainty, correlation and user confidence. IEEE Trans. Affect. Comput. **9**, 383–395 (2018)

Question Answering and Answer Generation

Investigating Query Expansion and Coreference Resolution in Question Answering on BERT

Santanu Bhattacharjee[2], Rejwanul Haque[1,2]($\boxtimes$) (iD),
Gideon Maillette de Buy Wenniger[1,2], and Andy Way[1,2] (iD)

[1] ADAPT Centre, Dublin, Ireland
{rejwanul.haque,gideon.debuywenniger,andy.way}@adaptcentre.ie
[2] School of Computing, Dublin City University, Dublin, Ireland
santanu.bhattacharjee2@mail.dcu.ie

Abstract. The Bidirectional Encoder Representations from Transformers (BERT) model produces state-of-the-art results in many question answering (QA) datasets, including the Stanford Question Answering Dataset (SQuAD). This paper presents a query expansion (QE) method that identifies good terms from input questions, extracts synonyms for the good terms using a widely-used language resource, WordNet, and selects the most relevant synonyms from the list of extracted synonyms. The paper also introduces a novel QE method that produces many alternative sequences for a given input question using same-language machine translation (MT). Furthermore, we use a coreference resolution (CR) technique to identify *anaphors* or *cataphors* in paragraphs and substitute them with the original referents. We found that the QA system with this simple CR technique significantly outperforms the BERT baseline in a QA task. We also found that our best-performing QA system is the one that applies these three preprocessing methods (two QE and CR methods) together to BERT, which produces an excellent F_1 score (89.8 F_1 points) in a QA task. Further, we present a comparative analysis on the performances of the BERT QA models taking a variety of criteria into account, and demonstrate our findings in the answer span prediction task.

Keywords: Query expansion · Coreference resolution · Question answering · Information retrieval · Machine translation · Neural machine translation

1 Introduction

Text-based QA systems have proven to be a crucial technique for IR since users can obtain the information that they need while avoiding having to go through thousands of documents. As far as recent research in QA is concerned, attention-based neural network (NN) architectures [5,9] have shown their potential in this

© Springer Nature Switzerland AG 2020
E. Métais et al. (Eds.): NLDB 2020, LNCS 12089, pp. 47–59, 2020.
https://doi.org/10.1007/978-3-030-51310-8_5

task and produced promising results. ELMo [17], a character-based context-aware representation model, was shown to be useful at addressing this problem, while solving the out-of-vocabulary (OOV) problem by allowing the NN model to generate embeddings for the OOV words. Recently, Vaswani et al. [24] introduced Transformer as an efficient alternative to recurrent or convolutional NNs. The encoder-decoder architecture with attention mechanism has shown promising results on MT tasks. Based on the Transformer architecture, Delvin et al. [5] proposed a powerful NN architecture – BERT – for a variety of NLP tasks including QA. BERT has significantly impacted many areas of natural language processing (NLP), e.g. QA has reached new heights on SQuAD [20]. BERT provides context-aware bidirectional representations from an unlabeled text by jointly conditioning from both the left and right contexts within a sentence, and can also be used as a pre-trained model with one additional output layer to fine-tune downstream NLP tasks, such as QA. Considering the recent success of BERT in QA, we have taken the BERT QA model as the baseline in our work.

Machine reasoning is at the core of solving a QA problem artificially, and it requires an understanding of natural language. Natural language understanding (NLU) is considered to be a complex task since it comes with its own challenges, such as word-sense disambiguation, existence of coreferencing entities, and understanding syntactic and semantic similarities between words. This work aims to address some of these problems by providing the learning model with more reasoning knowledge about enriching input questions or resolving references in paragraphs. CR [12] is regarded as a challenging task in many NLP tasks (e.g. MT), and has also been moderately investigated in QA [13,22,25]. In this work, we identify anaphors or cataphors (expressions referring to the same entity in a text passage) in paragraphs and substitute them with the original referring entities. The intuition underpinning this is that such preprocessing can provide the learning model more direct knowledge. For example, the pronoun 'He' refers to 'Sam' in the following paragraph *"Sam is moving to London. ... He has got a job there"*; replacing the pronominal entity 'He' with referent 'Sam' in the second sentence can add more direct knowledge to the QA model.

The semantic similarities between words are the other aspects of NLU, which were considered for investigation in this work. We present two novel QE techniques, the first one using a lexical knowledge base (WordNet [14]), and the second one using same-language MT [1]. Although the knowledge bases were heavily used for automatic QE [3,6], this work presents a novel technique that identifies good terms from a given input question following a state-of-the-art term classification method, extracts synonyms of the good terms using Word-Net, and selects the most relevant synonyms from the list of extracted synonyms. Same-language MT was successfully used in many NLP applications, e.g. text-to-speech synthesis for creating alternative target sequences [1], translation between varieties of the same language (Brazilian Portuguese to European Portuguese) [7], and paraphrase generation [18]. In this work, we developed an English-to-English MT system using the state-of-the-art Transformer model [24]. The MT system is able to generate n-best (same-language) translations for a given question, which can be viewed as the alternative sequences of the input question. These QE methods can considerably enrich the contexts of the input questions, and add extra reasoning knowledge to the QA model.

In this work, we carried out experiments applying these QE and CR techniques in QA individually and collaboratively taking the state-of-the-art BERT model into account. Rondeau and Hazen [21] analysed the outputs of a number of QA models applied to SQuAD to identify the core challenges for the QA systems on this data set. Since the introduction of BERT to the NLP community, researchers have been investigating the strength and weakness of BERT on the downstream tasks including QA [19,23]. This work also presents a comparative analysis on the ability of the baseline and our best-performing QA models to predict the answers correctly on SQuAD, taking a variety of criteria into account.

2   Baseline QA System

BERT, which makes use of the Transformer architecture, provides context-aware bidirectional representations from an unlabeled text by jointly conditioning from both the left and right contexts within a sentence. In short, BERT is made of a stack of encoders where each encoder consists of two sub-layers; the first sub-layer is a multi-head attention layer and the second sub-layer is a simple feed forward network. It can also be used as a pre-trained model with one additional output layer to fine-tune downstream NLP tasks, such as QA. For fine-tuning, the BERT model is first initialized with the pre-trained parameters, and all of the parameters are fine-tuned using the labeled data from the downstream tasks. Considering the recent success of BERT in QA, we have taken the BERT QA model as the baseline in our work. We used the SQuAD 1.1 dataset [20] to fine-tune the pre-trained BERT model. Given a paragraph from Wikipedia and a question relating to the paragraph, the task is to predict the answer text span in the paragraph. There are two architectural variations of the BERT model: $BERT_{BASE}$ and $BERT_{LARGE}$. These two architectures differ only in the size of the network layers and dimensions. In our experiments, we considered $BERT_{BASE}$ as our baseline.

3   Our Methods: Enriching Questions and Paragraphs

3.1   Query Expansion with WordNet

Query expansion is a commonly used method for mitigating the vocabulary mismatch problem in many NLP tasks. As far as QA is concerned, synonymous variations of an important word or phrase in a question need to be taken into account since variations instead of the actual word or phrase may appear in the paragraph that contains the answer. In theory, the word embedding layers of BERT should help address this to a certain extent. Additionally, we believe that injecting further context in the form of synonymous variations of the important words of the questions to a QA model would help it to find the right answers.

In this context, Cao et al. [2] showed that terms in a query can be categorized as good, bad and neutral. The good terms in a query help in finding the
information from the text. Cao et al. [2] used features like term distribution,
co-occurrence relations, weighted term proximity, and proposed a supervised
learning method (SVM) for classifying the good, bad and neutral terms of a
given query. In this work, first we identify those words of a question that are
more important than others in getting the right answer from the paragraph,
and then we further expand them in order to include more reasoning knowledge
to the question. In other words, given a question, we identify its good terms
and extract the most relevant synonyms of each of the good terms. We followed
[2] and considered their features in order to build a classifier. In our case, we
used a state-of-the-art classification algorithm: long short-term memory (LSTM)
network [8]. We found that the LSTM classifier performed competently in the
classification task (predicting good, bad or neutral terms) (we obtained an F_1
score of 81.3 on a held-out test set).

As mentioned above, we considered good terms only in our query expansion
process. First, we expand abbreviated good terms, if any, into full forms, e.g.
V.P. is expanded to *Vice President, Dr.* is expanded to *Doctor*. For this, we
used a python toolkit abbreviate (v 0.1.1).[1] WordNet was used to obtain the
synsets for the good terms. However, for a given good term, we chose the most
relevant synonyms from the synset. We measured cosine and semantic similarities
between the good term and its synonyms. The term (A) and a synonym (B) are
represented as distributed continuous vectors, which were obtained using the
BERT pre-trained model. The cosine similarity is computed by taking the dot
product of two vectors as shown in (1):

$$A \cdot B = ||A|| \, ||B|| \cos \theta \tag{1}$$

Semantic similarity between two words is measured using Wu-Palmer similarity [26]. The similarity score denotes how similar two word senses are, based
on the depth of the two senses in WordNet. In order to measure the Wu-Palmer
similarity between two words, we made use of the NLTK python toolkit.[2] A
synonym for a good term is selected when the cosine and semantic similarity
scores are above a threshold value. To exemplify, consider the question "*In what
year did the CIA establish its first training facility?*" from SQuAD. The LSTM
classifier identifies 'CIA', 'establish', 'training', and 'facility' as the good terms
of the question. For each of the good terms we obtain a list of synonyms from
WordNet, e.g. 'establish': 'set up', 'constitute', 'launch', 'plant', etc. Then, the
most relevant synonyms (e.g. 'establish': 'set-up', 'launch') for each good term
were identified following the strategy mentioned above. The resulting list of relevant synonyms for all good terms were then appended to the question. The
expanded input question and the paragraph are represented as a single packed
sequence.

---

[1] https://pypi.org/project/abbreviate/.
[2] http://www.nltk.org/.

3.2   Query Expansion with Neural MT

Translation of a source sentence into a target language can be generated in numerous ways. Similarly, in our case, a question can be represented in various forms. We developed a same-language MT system (English-to-English) that can generate n-best translations for an input sentence. In order to obtain different forms of a question, we translate it with the same-language MT system. The resulting n-best translations can be viewed as the alternative sequences of the question.

In our work, in order to build the MT system, we considered Transformer [24] which is regarded as the current state-of-the-art in MT research. We used the MarianNMT [10] toolkit and the European parliamentary proceedings (Europarl) corpus [11] for the NMT training. The training, development and test sets contains 13,201,483, 2,146 and 1,000 sentences, respectively. Additionally, we took high scoring five million English paraphrases from Multilingual Paraphrase Database[3] [16] and appended them to the training data. In our experiments, we followed the recommended best set-up by Vaswani et al. [24]. We obtained 99.69 BLEU [15] on the development set. The English-to-English NMT system was tested on a held-out test set, and we obtained 94.19 BLEU points on the test set. As you can see that the BLEU scores (on the development and test sets) are unusually high. This is because MT is being done on same-language (i.e. English-to-English). SQuAD includes 87,599 questions, which were translated with the English-to-English NMT system. Thus, we obtained alternative sequences for the questions.

The NMT-based QE process provides variants for a given input question, which are appended to the original question. The expanded input question and the paragraph are represented as a single packed sequence as in above (cf. Sect. 3.1). As mentioned above, the NMT system produced an n-best list for a given question. In this set-up, we experimented with different sizes of n (3, 5, 7 and 12).

3.3   Coreference Resolution for Paragraphs

Different expressions referring to the same entity are often used in text. All pronouns generally refer to some nouns that appeared previously in a given sentence. In this work, we apply CR techniques in order to find anaphors or cataphors in paragraphs, and then substitute them with the original referring entities. This preprocessing can significantly reduce ambiguities in the paragraphs and provide more direct knowledge to BERT. In order to resolve coreferences in the paragraphs, we used the NeuralCoref toolkit [4].[4] NeuralCoref is regarded as a highly extensible model to any new text data. We show a part of a paragraph from SQuAD below:

---

[3] http://paraphrase.org/#/download.
[4] https://github.com/huggingface/neuralcoref.

Paragraph: *Beyoncé Giselle Knowles (born September 4, 1981) is an American singer, songwriter, record producer and actress. Born and raised in Houston, **she** performed in various singing and dancing competitions as ...*

Resolved Coreference: *Beyoncé Giselle Knowles (born September 4, 1981) is an American singer, songwriter, record producer and actress. Born and raised in Houston, **Beyoncé Giselle Knowles** performed in various singing and dancing competitions as ...*

In the above example we see that the proper noun ('Beyoncé Giselle Knowles') in the place of the pronoun ('she') reduces ambiguity in the text, which essentially can provide more direct knowledge to the BERT attention model. As above, the input question and modified paragraph are represented as a single packed sequence for the BERT training.

Additionally, we carried out experiments applying multiple preprocessing techniques together to BERT. The intuition is that the contexts from the multiple sources can provide the QA model more reasoning knowledge. The QE (cf. Sects. 3.1 and 3.2) and CR (cf. Sect. 3.3) preprocessing techniques were applied collectively in different combinations.

4 Results and Discussion

4.1 Experimental Setups

This section explains experimental setups including a short overview on the QA data set, SQuAD. SQuAD v1.1 [20] is a standard reading comprehension dataset. It consists of reading paragraphs and associated questions in text format. These paragraphs were taken from Wikipedia articles across the various categories such as history, science etc. An answer to an input question is a segment or span (i.e. start and end indices of the segment) from the associated paragraph. The dataset is divided into a training set and a validation set. The training set includes 18,896 paragraphs from 442 documents, which also contains 87,599 questions. The validation set includes 1,867 paragraphs from 49 documents and contains 10,570 questions. In order to evaluate the performance of the QA systems, we used two evaluation metrics as in [5,20], which are 'exact match' (EM) and F_1. EM measures the percentage of predictions that match exactly with any one of the ground truth answers. F_1 is a measure of the average overlap between the prediction and ground truth answer [20]. We use approximate randomization [27] to test the statistical significance of the difference between two systems. We fine-tuned the BERT models for 3 epochs with a learning rate of *3e-5* as suggested in [5], and set batch size to 32. We followed the recommended best setup by [5] and keep the same setup for all our experiments.

4.2 Evaluation Results

In this section we obtain experimental results to evaluate the performance of our QA systems considering the different preprocessing setups discussed in Sect. 3.

We report the evaluation results in Table 1. As can be seen from the second column of Table 1, our baseline model, $BERT_{BASE}$, is quite competitive as it produces an F_1 score of 88.5 and an EM of 80.8 points on the development set.

The third column of Table 1 represents results that we obtained by applying our first preprocessing technique (i.e. QE with WordNet; cf. Sect. 3.1) to BERT. We call the QA system that incorporates this feature $BERT_{WN}$. As can be seen from the table, $BERT_{WN}$ outperforms $BERT_{BASE}$ in the answer span prediction task (with absolute improvements of 0.3 F_1 and 0.2 EM points over $BERT_{BASE}$; however, the improvements are not statistically significant). The fourth column of Table 1 presents evaluation results that we obtained by integrating the NMT-based QE feature into BERT (cf. Sect. 3.2). As mentioned in Sect. 3.2, we carried out experiments integrating varying sizes of alternative questions (n: 3, 5, 7 and 12). As far as the answer span prediction quality by the QA systems is concerned, we found that the setup with the alternative question sequences of size 12 is more effective than the other setups (i.e. with $n = 3, 5, 7$). We call the QA system that includes the NMT based QE feature (with $n = 12$) $BERT_{NMT}$. We see from Table 1 that $BERT_{NMT}$ outperforms $BERT_{BASE}$ in the answer span prediction task (with absolute improvements of 0.4 F_1 and 0.4 EM points over $BERT_{BASE}$; however, the improvements are not statistically significant). The fifth column of Table 1 represents the QA model that incorporates the CR-based features (cf. Sect. 3.3). We call this QA system $BERT_{CR}$. $BERT_{CR}$ statistically significantly outperforms $BERT_{BASE}$ in the answer span prediction task as per the scores obtained on the development set (the absolute improvements of 0.8 F_1 and 0.8 EM points over $BERT_{BASE}$).

Table 1. Evaluation results (EM and F_1 scores) obtained with different QA models.

	$BERT_{BASE}$	$BERT_{WN}$	$BERT_{NMT}$	$BERT_{CR}$	$BERT_{3F}$
F_1	80.8	81.1 ($p > 0.05$)	81.2 ($p > 0.05$)	81.6 ($p < 0.05$)	82.7 ($p < 0.01$)
EM	88.5	88.7 ($p > 0.05$)	88.9 ($p > 0.05$)	89.3 ($p < 0.05$)	89.8 ($p < 0.01$)

Since we found that $BERT_{WN}$, $BERT_{NMT}$ and $BERT_{CR}$ proved to be effective in the answer span prediction task, we carried out a few more experiments by integrating multiple features collectively into BERT. The model that includes three features collectively (i.e. QE (WordNet) + QE (NMT) + CR features) is found to be the best-performing QA system. This QA system is referred as $BERT_{3F}$. As can be seen from the last column of Table 1 that $BERT_{3F}$ produces 89.8 F_1 points and 82.7 EM points on the development set (with absolute improvements of 1.3 F_1 and 1.9 EM points over $BERT_{BASE}$; both improvements are statistically significant).

4.3   Prediction Analysis

This section presents a comparative analysis of the ability of the BERT QA systems to predict the answers correctly on SQuAD. In order to carry out the

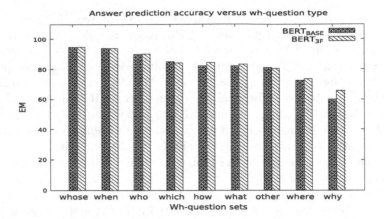

Fig. 1. Correlation between the wh-question types and BERT's answer prediction performance.

analysis, we considered a variety of criteria: (i) wh-question type, (ii) wh-word position in questions, (iii) ground truth answer span size in paragraph, and (iv) data domain, and investigate their relatedness to the QA system's answer prediction quality. This analysis helps us achieve our two goals: (a) unraveling the strengths and weaknesses of BERT on QA, and (b) comparing BERT on two experimental setups: the vanilla baseline (i.e. $BERT_{BASE}$) and context-sensitive QA (i.e. $BERT_{3F}$) models.

Wh-Question Type. We wanted to see whether there is any relationship between the wh-question type and the performance of the QA models. For this, we considered the commonly used *wh-words* that are used to introduce questions: 'when', 'who', 'which', 'how', 'what', 'where', 'why', and 'whose'. For a given input question, its wh-question type is identified using a simple rule-based procedure. We also have a particular wh-question type ('other') whose questions contain none of the wh-words listed above. We divide the development set examples as per the wh-question type. Thus, we obtained a number of subsets, and each subset contains a particular type of wh-question. From now on, we call such subsets *wh-sets*. For each of the wh-sets we obtain the number of wrong and right answer predictions by $BERT_{BASE}$ and $BERT_{3F}$. In Fig. 1, we plot histogram distributions of answer prediction accuracy (EM scores) over the wh-sets.

As can be seen from Fig. 1, both QA systems did not perform uniformly across the wh-sets. They performed excellently for predicting answers of 'whose', 'when' and 'who' questions. We also see that both BERT QA models performed moderately on the 'which', 'how', 'other' and 'what' wh-sets, and quite poorly on the 'where' and 'why' wh-sets. When we compare the bars, we see $BERT_{3F}$ outperforms $BERT_{BASE}$ in most cases bar two instances (i.e. 'other' and 'which' question types).

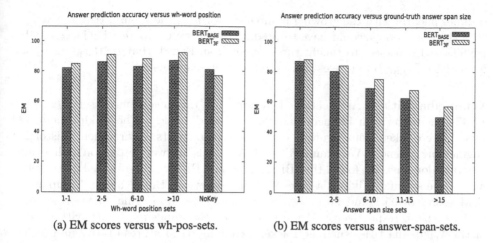

(a) EM scores versus wh-pos-sets.   (b) EM scores versus answer-span-sets.

Fig. 2. Correlation between wh-pos- and answer-span-sets and BERT's performance on QA.

Wh-Word Position. We wanted to examine whether there is any correlation between the wh-word positions in questions and the performance of BERT in the QA task. For this, we first identify the position of the wh-word in a given input question. As above, we divide the development set examples based on the positions of the wh-words in questions. This creates several subsets, and each subset contains questions whose wh-words appear in a specific position range in the questions (e.g. 1st position, 2nd to 5th position). From now, we call such subsets *wh-pos-sets*. As above, we plot the distributions of the EM scores over the wh-pos-sets in Fig. 2a for $BERT_{BASE}$ and $BERT_{3F}$. The x-axis and y-axis of Fig. 2a represent the distributions of the EM scores and the wh-pos-sets, respectively. We can see from Fig. 2a that no strong relationship can be seen between the wh-word positions in questions and the QA systems' answer prediction quality. As far as the comparison of the performances of $BERT_{BASE}$ and $BERT_{3F}$ is concerned, as above, $BERT_{3F}$ outperforms $BERT_{BASE}$ on all wh-pos-sets bar one set that contains the questions that have no wh-words.

Ground Truth Answer Span Size. This time, we choose a feature from paragraphs for analysis, which is ground truth answer span size. We divide the development set examples based on the number of words into ground truth answers (e.g. one word, two to five words). Thus, we obtained a number of subsets, and each subset contains questions whose answer spans are limited to a range of numbers. From now on, we call such subsets *answer-span-sets*. In Fig. 2b, we plot histogram distributions of answer prediction accuracy (EM scores) over the answer-span-sets for $BERT_{BASE}$ and $BERT_{3F}$. The x-axis and y-axis of Fig. 2b represent the EM scores and the answer-span-sets, respectively. We can see from Fig. 2b that there is a clear relationship between the both QA models' performance and the ground truth answer span size. The answer prediction accuracy declines linearly with the growing number of words in the ground truth answers that the QA models would have to predict. When we compare BERT$_{BASE}$ and BERT$_{3F}$ with respect to this feature, we see from Fig. 2b that BERT$_{3F}$ outperforms BERT$_{BASE}$ in all cases (i.e. on all answer-span-sets).

Wikipedia Titles. As mentioned in Sect. 4.1, the development set includes 1,867 paragraphs from 49 documents (the Wikipedia titles). The Wikipedia documents were taken from a variety of domains (e.g. sports, environment, history, engineering, science). We examined our QA models' answer prediction ability on different domains. We found that BERT$_{BASE}$ and BERT$_{3F}$, performed quite well with some specific Wikipedia titles such as 'American_Broadcasting_Company' (EM scores of 95.1 and 96.7, respectively) and 'Steam_engine' (EM scores of 92.1 and 94.5, respectively). We also observed the opposite picture with some of the Wikipedia titles such as 'Packet_switching' (EM scores of 47.2 and 58.5 with BERT$_{BASE}$ and BERT$_{3F}$, respectively). Adapting a model to a specialised domain is seen as a challenging task in many NLP areas. We see that the BERT models (both BERT$_{BASE}$ and BERT$_{3F}$) struggled to deal with the specialised and complex domain data (e.g. computer network) as well as the mixture of multiple domain data (e.g. administration, history and legal). However, we also observed that BERT$_{3F}$ performed better than BERT$_{BASE}$ on the specialised and complex domain data most of the time. In addition to the above analysis, we manually looked at a sample of answer prediction examples from the development set. A few of the examples with an analysis on the performance of our context-aware QA systems and BERT$_{BASE}$ are made available online.[5]

5 Conclusion

In this work, we presented two automatic QE strategies in QA. As far as our first QE technique is concerned, we first identified good terms from the input questions following a state-of-the-art term classification method, and then used WordNet in order to obtain synsets for each of the good terms. We presented a method that applying two word-to-word semantic similarity measures together extracts the most relevant synonyms from the synsets. As far as our second QE method is concerned, we used a state-of-the-art neural MT system in order to produce a set of alternative questions for each input question. Both QE strategies were effective in predicting answers in the QA tasks, although the improvements obtained by the QA systems with the addition of these features over the baseline are not statistically significant. This study also investigated the possibility of applying CR techniques on the paragraphs in QA. The QA model with the CR method significantly outperformed BERT$_{BASE}$, with the absolute improvements of 0.8 F_1 and 0.8 EM points over BERT$_{BASE}$.

Furthermore, we conducted a number of experiments by integrating multiple features collectively into the BERT model in various combinations. We found

---

[5] https://github.com/rejwanul-adapt/BERT-analysis/blob/master/Examples-BERT. pdf.

that the QA model that integrates all three features (two QE and CR methods) together is the best-performing system as per the F_1 and EM scores. With this setup, the BERT QA system produced significant gains in F_1 and EM (absolute improvements of 1.3 F_1 and 1.9 EM points) over BERT$_{BASE}$.

In sum, as far as the QA task on the state-of-the-art BERT architecture is concerned, all our three preprocessing methods are shown to be effective. Most importantly, the gains were achieved (some of them are statistically significant) by applying these methods without making any modification to the model architecture.

Additionally, we carried out a thorough error analysis on the predictions to see how the BERT models (the baseline and our best-performing) performed on QA. In order to do this, we took a variety of criteria into account and examined their relatedness to the answer prediction errors. From our analysis we found that the patterns of the answer prediction errors of the both baseline and our best-performing QA models are nearly similar in most cases. The both BERT QA models performed excellently for certain wh-question types (e.g. 'whose', 'when' and 'who'), although their performances were found to be below par for certain wh-question types (e.g. 'why' and 'where'). As far as the position of wh-words in questions is concerned, we could not find any strong correlation between this feature and answer prediction ability. As for the ground truth answer span size, we found that the answer prediction accuracy declines linearly with the increasing number of words in the ground truth answers that the QA system would have to predict. As far as the above three criteria (wh-question type, wh-word position in questions, answer span size) and systems' answer span prediction accuracy are concerned, our best-performing QA model outperformed the BERT baseline in all cases barring few exceptions. From our analysis we also found that the BERT baseline and our best-preforming QA systems performed below par on certain specialised domain data (e.g. computer network) or the mixture of multiple domain data (e.g. administration, history and legal). However, we observed that the best-performing system performed better than BERT$_{BASE}$ on the specialised and complex domain data. This thorough error analysis, to a certain extent, identifies patterns of the examples for which the BERT models tend to make wrong or right predictions in the QA task, which, we believe would help the NLU researchers to fix problems of the model in relation to this task.

As mentioned in Sect. 4.3, our WordNet-based QE method expands a good term by generating its relevant synonyms, which, however, may not be the same morphological forms as the good term is as the QE method does not have morphological generation module. In future, we intend to add a morphological generation module in this QE technique. We also intend to carry out a deeper analysis on BERT considering more criteria, e.g. length of the questions, head versus tail questions, and comparing the BERT models with the classical IR models.

Acknowledgments. The ADAPT Centre for Digital Content Technology is funded under the Science Foundation Ireland (SFI) Research Centres Programme (Grant No. 13/RC/2106) and is co-funded under the European Regional Development Fund. This project has partially received funding from the European Union's Horizon 2020 research and innovation programme under the Marie Skłodowska-Curie grant agreement No. 713567, and the publication has emanated from research supported in part by a research grant from SFI under Grant Number 13/RC/2077.

References

1. Cahill, P., Du, J., Way, A., Carson-Berndsen, J.: Using same-language machine translation to create alternative target sequences for text-to-speech synthesis. In: Proceedings of Interspeech 2009, the 10th Annual Conference of the International Speech Communication Association, Brighton, UK, pp. 1307–1310 (2009)
2. Cao, G., Nie, J.-Y., Gao, J., Robertson, S.: Selecting good expansion terms for pseudo-relevance feedback. In: Proceedings of the 31st Annual International ACM SIGIR Conference on Research and Development in Information Retrieval, Singapore, pp. 243–250 (2008)
3. Carpineto, C., Romano, G.: A survey of automatic query expansion in information retrieval. ACM Comput. Surv. (CSUR) **44**(1), 1 (2012)
4. Chaumond, J.: Fast coreference resolution in spaCy with neural networks. https://github.com/huggingface/neuralcoref. Accessed 8 Oct 2019
5. Devlin, J., Chang, M.-W., Lee, K., Toutanova, K.: BERT: pre-training of deep bidirectional transformers for language understanding. CoRR, abs/1810.04805 (2018)
6. Sun, R., Jiang, J., Tan, Y.F., Cui, H., Chua, T.-S., Kan, M.-Y.: Using syntactic and semantic relation analysis in question answering. In: Proceedings of the 14th Text REtrieval Conference (TREC) (2005)
7. Fancellu, F., O'Brien, M., Way, A.: Standard language variety conversion using SMT. In: Proceedings of the Seventeenth Annual Conference of the European Association for Machine Translation, Dubrovnik, Croatia, pp. 143–149 (2014)
8. Hochreiter, S., Schmidhuber, J.: Long short-term memory. Neural Comput. **9**, 1735–1780 (1997)
9. Iyyer, M., Boyd-Graber, J.L., Claudino, L.M.B., Socher, R., Daumé, H.: A neural network for factoid question answering over paragraphs. In: EMNLP 2014: Proceedings of the Conference on Empirical Methods in Natural Language Processing, Doha, Qatar, pp. 633–644 (2014)
10. Junczys-Dowmunt, M., et al.: Marian: fast neural machine translation in C++. In: Proceedings of the ACL, System Demonstrations, Melbourne, Australia, pp. 116–121 (2018)
11. Koehn, P.: Europarl: a parallel corpus for statistical machine translation. In: Proceedings of the Machine Translation Summit X, Phuket, Thailand, pp. 79–86 (2005)
12. Mitkov, R.: Anaphora Resolution. Longman, Harlow (2002)
13. Morton, T.S.: Using coreference for question answering. In: Proceedings of the ACL Workshop on Coreference and Its Applications, College Park, MD, pp. 85–89 (1999)
14. Oram, P.: WordNet: an electronic lexical database. Appl. Psycholinguist. **22**, 131–134 (2001)
15. Papineni, K., Roukos, S., Ward, T., Zhu, W.-J.: BLEU: a method for automatic evaluation of machine translation. In: Proceedings of the 40th Annual Meeting on Association for Computational Linguistics, Philadelphia, PA, pp. 311–318 (2002)

16. Pavlick, E., Rastogi, P., Ganitkevitch, J., Van Durme, B., Callison-Burch, C.: PPDB 2.0: better paraphrase ranking, fine-grained entailment relations, word embeddings, and style classification. In: Proceedings of the 53rd Annual Meeting of the Association for Computational Linguistics and the 7th International Joint Conference on Natural Language Processing (Volume 2: Short Papers), Beijing, China, pp. 425–430 (2015)
17. Peters, M., et al.: Deep contextualized word representations. In: Proceedings of the Conference of the North American Chapter of the Association for Computational Linguistics: Human Language Technologies, New Orleans, LA, pp. 2227–2237 (2018)
18. Plachouras, V., Petroni, F., Nugent, T., Leidner, J.L.: A comparison of two paraphrase models for taxonomy augmentation. In: Proceedings of the 2018 Conference of the North American Chapter of the Association for Computational Linguistics: Human Language Technologies (Volume 2: Short Papers), New Orleans, LA, pp. 315–320 (2018)
19. Qiao, Y., Xiong, C., Liu, Z.-H., Liu, Z.: Understanding the behaviors of BERT in ranking. CoRR, abs/1904.07531 (2019)
20. Rajpurkar, P., Zhang, J., Lopyrev, K., Liang, P.: SQuAD: 100,000+ questions for machine comprehension of text. In: EMNLP 2016: Proceedings of the Conference on Empirical Methods in Natural Language Processing, Austin, TX, pp. 2383–2392 (2016)
21. Rondeau, M.-A., Hazen, T.J.: Systematic error analysis of the Stanford question answering dataset. In: Proceedings of the Workshop on Machine Reading for Question Answering, pp. 12–20 (2018)
22. Stuckardt, R.: Coreference-based summarization and question answering: a case for high precision anaphor resolution. In: Proceedings of the 2003 International Symposium on Reference Resolution and Its Applications to Question Answering and Summarization, Venice, Italy, pp. 33–42 (2003)
23. van Aken, B., Winter, B., Löser, A., Gers, F.A.: How does BERT answer questions? A layer-wise analysis of transformer representations. In: Proceedings of the 28th ACM International Conference on Information and Knowledge Management, pp. 1823–1832 (2019)
24. Vaswani, A., et al.: Attention is all you need. CoRR, abs/1706.03762 (2017)
25. Vicedo, J.L., Ferrández, A.: Importance of pronominal anaphora resolution in question answering systems. In: Proceedings of the 38th Annual Meeting of the Association for Computational Linguistics, Hong Kong, pp. 555–562 (2000)
26. Wu, Z., Palmer, M.: Verb semantics and lexical selection. In: Proceedings of the 32nd Annual Meeting of the Associations for Computational Linguistics, Las Cruces, NM, pp. 133–138 (1994)
27. Yeh, A.: More accurate tests for the statistical significance of result differences. In: Proceedings of the 18th Conference on Computational Linguistics, Saarbrücken, Germany, pp. 947–953 (2000)

CONQUEST: A Framework for Building Template-Based IQA Chatbots for Enterprise Knowledge Graphs

Caio Viktor S. Avila[(✉)], Wellington Franco, José Gilvan R. Maia, and Vania M. P. Vidal

Department of Computing, Federal University of Ceará, Campus do Pici, Fortaleza, CE, Brazil
caioviktor@alu.ufc.br

Abstract. The popularization of Enterprise Knowledge Graphs (EKGs) brings an opportunity to use Question Answering Systems to consult these sources using natural language. We present CONQUEST, a framework that automates much of the process of building chatbots for the Template-Based Interactive Question Answering task on EKGs. The framework automatically handles the processes of construction of the Natural Language Processing engine, construction of the question classification mechanism, definition of the system interaction flow, construction of the EKG query mechanism, and finally, the construction of the user interaction interface. CONQUEST uses a machine learning-based mechanism to classify input questions to known templates extracted from EKGs, utilizing the clarification dialog to resolve inconclusive classifications and request mandatory missing parameters. CONQUEST also evolves with question clarification: these cases define question patterns used as new examples for training.

Keywords: Interactive Question Answering · ChatBot · Linked Data · Knowledge Graph

1 Introduction

Linked Data technologies made it possible to merge data from many fields, origins, formats, and vocabularies into a unique, uniform, and semantically integrated representation [6], known as Enterprise Knowledge Graph (EKG) [8]. An EKG can be represented by a common vocabulary defined by a closed domain ontology in *OWL*, which allows multiple heterogeneous sources to be accessed simultaneously through queries written in *SPARQL* [9,11]. Competence Questions (CQs) are commonly used to guide the process of ontology construction for EKGs [17]: domain experts list a set of questions that they hope to be answerable, i.e., a CQ can be seen as templates of frequent queries to the EKG. However, creating SPARQL queries is difficult for most users, so natural and intuitive

© Springer Nature Switzerland AG 2020
E. Métais et al. (Eds.): NLDB 2020, LNCS 12089, pp. 60–72, 2020.
https://doi.org/10.1007/978-3-030-51310-8_6

consultation interfaces are of paramount importance in this case [12]. Template-Based Question Answering (TBQA) systems can be valuable within this context: a question Q in Natural Language (NL) is mapped into a well-known $SPARQL$ query template Q', so TBQA executes Q' on the EKG in response to Q [4]. Each template contains "slots" to be filled with user-provided parameters, e.g., values for filters, properties, and classes suitable for answering Q. TBQA systems have the advantage of reducing the complex task of interpreting questions in NL to a more straightforward task of classification of intention, which is substantially cheaper than general Question Answering (QA). However, TBQA systems can run into some problems, such as (1) inconclusive template classification or (2) absence of mandatory query parameters in the question. User dialogue is usually employed to disambiguate intent and request parameters, thus generating Template-Based Interactive Question Answering (TBIQA) systems [13]. Conversational systems are popularly known as *chatbots*.

The process of building a TBIQA system can vary greatly depending on its domain, existing tools, and purpose [13]. In this paper, we propose the following standard workflow for the process of creating TBIQA systems on EKG: (1) construction of the templates of questions answerable by the system; (2) construction of the Natural Language Processing (NLP) engine; (3) construction of a question classification mechanism for mapping a question into a template; (4) definition of the system interaction flow; (5) construction of the EKG query mechanism; and (6) construction of the user interaction interface.

Thus, as the main contribution of this paper, we introduce $CONQUEST$ (*Chatbot ONtology QUESTion*), a *framework* for creating *chatbots* for the TBIQA task on EKGs represented by a closed domain ontology. $CONQUEST$ automates much of the proposed *workflow*, automatically handling steps 2–6. Thus, $CONQUEST$ only delegates to the developer the task of building the templates of questions to be answered.

2   Related Work

In [1], the authors present an approach for the automatic generation of query templates supported by TBQA systems. The system has as input a set of pairs of questions in NL and their answers. The questions are then generalized to a template by mapping sets of questions to the same query. As an advantage, the approach allows the composition of patterns for the resolution of complex queries for which complete templates are not known. However, the method depends on the quality of the lexicon used for the highest coverage of templates, and there may be a need to extend the lexicon to specific domains. Besides, the system also does not allow the user to control the templates supported by the system. The authors do not discuss how the system can be made available to users, indicating that this must be addressed per each specific case.

In [3], the authors present a TBQA system over KGs that automatically generates supported questions based on the underlying KG. The process of construction of the questions is carried out based on a small set of query patterns defined by the authors. The system then constructs the questions supported for each of the predefined patterns, generating variations of them. These questions are then stored in an index that is consulted at run time to identify the most likely question being asked by the user. In addition, the system allows the interactive construction of queries with auto-completing. As a disadvantage, the approach does not allow developers to control the questions supported by the system, which would make it challenging to implement QC support and relevant questions for specific applications.

Medibot [2] is a chatbot in Brazilian Portuguese on a KG in the domain of medicines. *Medibot* has two modes of operation, the first of which is a TBQA, where regular expressions are used to classify the template in which the user's question fits. The approach depends on the manual implementation of regular expressions and the code for querying and building responses, which makes it difficult to reuse and apply in chatbots with a large number of templates. Moreover, the implementation heavily depends on *Telegram* interface.

Many of the existing works in the area of TBQA focus on the automatic generation of templates. However, such approaches limit the developer control over the supported questions, but try to increase the question coverage, which is a positive aspect in the context of consultation on the Web. In business environments, it is expected that the discussions carried out will be limited to a specific set of queries for the performance activities of the company, so it is essential that this set is entirely and correctly covered. Consequently, *CONQUEST* ensures that the developer has full control over the collection of supported templates, ensuring the correctness of the queries that answer them. Besides, most systems do not address how the TBQA service might be made available to users, leaving the developer the task of customizing or creating systems access mechanisms from scratch. *CONQUEST* deals with this by reusing instant messaging services as an access channel to the chatbot, in addition to providing access to the service through a REST API accessible through HTTP requests, all from the execution of a single instance of the chatbot.

3   CONQUEST Framework

The *CONQUEST* framework is composed of the *CONQUEST Trainer* and *CONQUEST Chatbot* modules. The first is responsible for training the necessary components for the TBIQA chatbot being produced. The second is responsible for executing the chatbot, using the components trained to provide a TBIQA service. The source code of the framework can be found in the Github repository[1]. In this paper, the term *developer* will refer to the developer of the chatbot. The term *user* is referring to the end-user who issues questions to that chatbot.

The input given by the developer to the conquest framework is composed of the set of template questions answerable by the system, together with the EKG (ontology + instances) being consulted. The domain ontology provides the structure for the instances, allowing the identification of the type of an

---

[1] https://bit.ly/2JTE5I0.

instance or parameter value based on the context in which it appears (properties and relationships with which it is linked). A template question whose system is capable of answering is called Question Answering Item (QAI). Each QAI has its *slots* that will be filled with information from user questions, the so-called Context Variables (*CVs*). A QAI is formally defined as $QAI_{01} = ([QP_1, QP_2, ..., QP_n], SP, RP)$, where: QP_k is a Template (*Question Pattern*) in NL associated to a question, where $1 \leq k \leq n$; SP is a *SPARQL query Pattern*, a template that is employed to retrieve information from the KG; and RP is a *Response Pattern*, a template answer in NL shown to the user.

The following is an example of how the question "What is the maximum price for a given drug in a certain state?" would be represented as a QAI. Where it was given as input only the QP *"What is the maximum price for the medicine $medicine in $state?"*. This template can be provided as input to the system using a JSON file:

```
{"QPs": ["What is the maximum price for the medicine \$medicine in \$state?"],
"SP": "SELECT ?name (MAX(?priceAux) as ?price)  WHERE{
  ?s a <Medicine>;
    rdfs:label ?name;
    <price> ?appliedPrice.
  ?appliedPrice a <Price>;
    <state> $state;
    <value> ?priceAux.
  FILTER(REGEX(?name,$medicine,'i'))}",
"RP":{"header": "",
    "body": "The ?name has a maximum prince of ?price reais",
    "footer":""}}
```

3.1 CONQUEST Trainer

This module is executed only *offline* by the developer. First, two distinct indices are built during **Index Construction**: a class index and a property index. Each of these has information about the domain ontology schema being consulted and are of fundamental importance for the next workflow steps. These indexes have information about labels and definitions of classes and properties, as well as information about properties that relate classes.

The **Processing QAIs** step takes place after the index construction step. This step is divided into three processes. (1) **Consistency check:** for each QAI, all *CVs* and *Return Variables* (*RVs*) declared in the query SP are enumerated. Then, for each QP defined in this QAI, the framework checks whether the *CVs* quoted in that QP belongs to the *CV* set declared in SP. Likewise, it is checked whether the *CVs* and *RVs* quoted in the RP response pattern are contained in the set declared in SP; (2) **Parsing and semantic interpretation of a** *SPARQL query Pattern* (*SP*): The semantic *parsing* of a SP is performed while traversing the SPARQL query tree representation of SP that is generated by the RDFLib[2] library. The CVs are retrieved during this traversal, together with their type (resource or literal), class, and if this is literal type, their properties, and classes owners. Further details about this complex process will be omitted for the sake of space constraints.

The type of a CV indicates whether it should be replaced by a URI that identifies a resource in the KG (if it is resource type) or a literal. If a CV is inferred to be resource type, then the class attribute will represent the class to which the resource replacing CV must be an instance. On the other hand, if a CV is inferred as being literal, then the class attribute will assume on of the following values: *xsd:string*; *xsd:double*; *xsd:integer*; *xsd:datetime*. In the case of a literal CV, it still has two additional attributes, its "owner property" and "owner class". In the example given, the CV $state has <state> as its "owner property" and <Price> as its "owner class". For the sake of convenience, throughout this article the pairs "owner property" and "owner class" will be regarded as a *string* of the form "Property@Class", which is referred to as "owner pair"; and (3) **Constructon of a vectorial representation (QV) for a QP:** Each QP is mapped into a "representative" vector, which will be called the *Question Vector* (QV). A QV is formed by the concatenation of two other vectors, being the first a *Sentence Vector (VS)* and the second a vector representing the kinds of CVs used in the QP, i.e., a *Context Vector ($CVec$)*. Therefore, $QV = VS \oplus CVec$, where $\oplus$ is the concatenation operation over two vectors. The VS is built by resorting to NLP and *Word Embedding* techniques [14]. The first step in building VS from a QP is replacing the CVs markers with *Out of Vocabulary* (OOV) symbols. The second step consists on *string* normalization. The third and last step is computing the very VS vector, so we resort to the NLP *SpaCy* [5] for carrying out this computation. Since the VS vector is built solely based on the text from a QP, VS is considered to be the vector carrying *textual features*. $CVec$ is a vector representing the number of CVs (named entities required) to answer the question encoded by that vector. $CVec$ is a vector of $n+3$ dimensions, where n is the number of owner pairs ("Property@Class") for CVs literals *string*. The other three additional dimensions of $CVec$ refer to the CVs literals from *xsd:integer, xsd:double* and *xsd:datetime* classes. Thus, for each CV existing in QAI, the position of $CVec$ representing the CV type will be incremented by 1. Because of the use of information from the semantic interpretation from KG, $CVec$ is considered the vector representing the *semantic features* of the template.

Training the NER Module is the third step in training stage. The Named Entity Recognition [15] module is responsible for identifying potential candidates in a natural language sentence for CV values. These candidates are used to construct the $CVec$ vector for the given input question. Using NER allows possible values for CVs to be identified directly from the question, eliminating the need to request each CV individually during the consultation time. More specifically, in $CONQUEST$, the NER module is trained to recognize possible values for literal CVs. $CONQUEST$ uses a simple regular expression mechanism for identifying entities of numeric types, such as *xsd:integer* and *xsd:double*. For the recogni-

---

[2] https://rdflib.readthedocs.io/en/stable/.

tion of data type entities (*xsd:datetime*), *CONQUEST* reuses the *dateparser* library [18]. For literals of the *xsd:string* class, *CONQUEST* classifies a candidate for its likely owner pair. This is done by querying terms in an *Apache Solr* [20] index. For each owner pair used in the QAI set (only for xsd:string literals *CV*s), its possible values contained in the KG are fetched. For example, if the owner pair "*ont:name@ont:Person*" is used for a *CV* of type *xsd:string*, then all possible values for the *ont:name* attribute of instances of class *ont:Person* will be retrieved. These retrieved values will be indexed as search keys for the owner pair "*ont:name@ont:Person*". Thus, if the name of a person in the KG is queried, then its owner pair will be returned.

Training the Question Classifier is a cornerstone for our architecture, been the fourth step in the training stage. Based on the promising results obtained recently in the field of Machine Learning (ML) [7] and aiming to address the problem of linguistic variability, we resort to classification ML models due to their high generalization capabilities and versatility. However, using such an approach brings with it a new challenge, the issue of small training sample size [21]. The system is expected to face this problem during the early stages of deploying a chatbot built by *CONQUEST*. To overcome this challenge, *CONQUEST* performs a semantic enrichment step over the input features by using *CVec* as part of the classifier input (*Semantic Features*). For classifier training, the set of *QV*s produced during the stage of processing QAIs is used as the training dataset, with the respective QAI of each *QV* as the output label of the classifier. The default ML model adopted in *CONQUEST* is the Gaussian Naïve Bayes (GaussianNB), which, coupled with the use of *semantic features*, performed as one of the best models tested, both in terms of rating hit rates and time needed for its training.

Saving the trained artifacts is the final step in training stage, where are saved the artefacts: (1) *Ontology Index* that contains ontology schema information so that it can be accessed directly and easily. This information is saved as the indices described previously; (2) the *QA Items* are used in the process of question interpretation, parameter checking and requesting, SPARQL query construction, and response construction; (3) the *NLP Model* is used for natural language processing, including *workflow* for text normalization and segmentation, *word embeddings*, and index (*Apache Solr*) used in NER; (4) and the *Classification Model* that effectively maps a NL question to a QAI.

3.2   CONQUEST Chatbot

An instance of a *CONQUEST Chatbot* is executed during the online stage. This instance accesses the trained artefacts stored in *Persistence* to provide the TBIQA service. Figure 1 depicts the architecture of a *CONQUEST Chatbot*, which is divided into three layers: *User Interface, CONQUEST Core, and Data*.

The **User Interface** layer aims to provide an intuitive and practical interface for users accessing the *chatbot*. To this end, this layer has a set of *APIs* for communicating with instant messenger services, i.e., the *Chat Messenger API*.

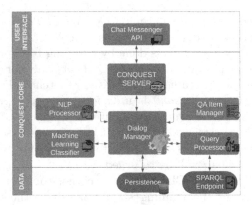

Fig. 1. Architecture for a *CONQUEST Chatbot*.

The **CONQUEST Core** is the main layer of the architecture since it is responsible for processing the questions and their answers. This layer consists of the following six components: (1) *CONQUEST Server*, responsible for providing *chatbot* services through HTTP requests, acting on the boundary between the interface layer and the system core. This component gets HTTP requests as input, forwarding them to *Dialog Manager*, and finally returning the respective responses to the user. The *CONQUEST Server* can be accessed either through an IM service (e.g., Telegram), or directly via HTTP requests, thus being available in a wide range of channels simultaneously; (2) **Dialog Manager** is the central module regarding the execution of a *CONQUEST Chatbot*. The *Dialog Manager* is responsible for managing the request processing flow, exchanging information between components, and managing the dialog flow; (3) **NLP Processor** is responsible for taking a question Q in natural language and converting it to a vectorial representation QV. The following sequence of steps is performed for this purpose: (I) normalization and *tokenization* of Q; (II) Identification of named entities contained in the sentence by the NER component. The first type of entities looked for are the literals of the *xsd:string* class. To do this, the sliding window process of a n-gram [19] is performed over the *tokens* contained in Q. The starting value of n is equal to the number of *tokens* in Q, where the window slides from left to right, one *token* at a time, and decreasing in size by 1 each time it reaches the end of the *tokens* sequence. During this process, each n-gram is queried against the *Solr* index, and if it is contained, then it is removed from the sequence. Subsequently, entities like *xsd:datetime* and numeric types are sought as defined in Sect. 3.1; (III) Computation of SV vector for Q; (IV) Computation of the $CVec$ vector for Q, using the named entities found in step II; and finally (V) calculating the QV representation of Q; (4) **Machine Learning Classifier** receives the QV vector representation of Q as input and then returns the confidence classification level for each QAI; (5) **QA Item Manager** retrieves information about the classified QAI. This information is used for (a) determining the CVs needed for the question by filling this information automatically or requesting it from users, (b) retrieving the SPARQL query template (SP) to be used, and (c) retrieving the response pattern (RP) to be generated; and (6) **Query Processor** receives as input a *template* SPARQL SP and its set of filled CVs. As a result, this module performs the actual assembling and execution of the query in *Endpoint SPARQL*; Finally, the query result is returned to the *Dialog Manager*, which generates the natural language response based on the RP template.

The third and last layer is the **Data Layer**, which is responsible for storing the *chatbot* knowledge, which refers to both learned artifacts during the training phase and the EKG being queried. This layer is divided into two components: (1) **Persistence** holds the knowledge obtained in the offline stage. This knowledge is retrieved by *Dialog Manager* and then distributed to the other *CONQUEST Core* modules so that they can perform their tasks. Moreover, *Persistence* is also used to store *Interaction State* that saves the current state of a user interaction during the *chatflow*. The state of the interaction consists of the current point of interaction following Fig. 2 and the information acquired so far (e.g., question given as input, classified QAI, values for CVs and other information for a coherent dialogue). This ensures that *chatbot* performs long interactions consistently; (2) **SPARQL Endpoint**, which is external to the system, so it is accessed using HTTP requests to execute SPARQL queries. The current implementation resorts to the *SPARQL Wrapper* [16] library, which is responsible for handling requests and responses to this *endpoint*.

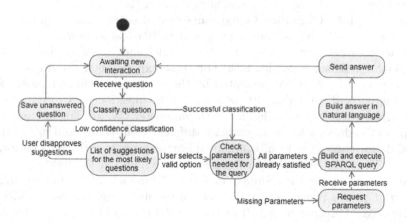

Fig. 2. *Chatflow* followed by a *CONQUEST Chatbot*.

CONQUEST Chatbot's Chatflow is depicted by Fig. 2 and can be summarized as: the *chatbot* receives the question in NL, classifying it for a QAI; if this classification is not possible, then the *chatbot* performs the disambiguation dialog; after a successful question classification, the *chatbot* checks to see if all CVs have been filled in, prompting them to the user otherwise; finally, the *chatbot* consults the EKG and returns the response to the user. In the case of confirmation of the clarification dialog, the question given as input is added as a new Question Pattern (QP) to be considered in classifier training.

4   Results and Discussions

A qualitative assessment was carried out to assess the impact of using *CONQUEST*. For the sake of comparison, we re-implemented *MediBot* [2], a chatbot published recently that fits our requirements since it adopts an TBIQA perspective to operate over KG.

The **Template Construction** process was shown to be quite natural and required the developer to input only a few variations of the NL question. The JSON file containing the QAIs used and the data needed to deploy an instance of our implementation of *MediBot* on top of *CONQUEST* are publicly available[3]. The example is given in Sect. 3 is an example of how one of the QAIs could be written, and it will be considered in the discussions that follow in this section.

In **NLP Engine Construction** step, the developer should only select the language supported by his chatbot being produced. *CONQUEST* uses the *Spacy* library for NLP, which supports more than 53. However, support for each language is at a different stage. At the same time, the library achieves great results for English, the same cannot be said for Brazilian Portuguese (language supported by MediBot). Because of this, we used the 100-dimensional GloVe model produced by [10] as the *Word Embedding*. This model was loaded into *SpaCy*, thereby leveraging the entire processing pipeline of this library.

The **Template Classifier Construction** step is transparent to the developer, with CONQUEST already having a default classification model. Experiments were carried out to select the best model and to assess the impact of using semantic features on this task. For these experiments, the 8 query templates answered by *MediBot* presented by the authors were implemented. As a set of training and validation, 10 variations of the question in NL were used for each template, using cross-validation with parameter CV = 5. For the test set, 5 examples of variations for each template different from those used in the training/validation stage. The results presented are the average of the tests performed 10 times. The script with the experiments can be found at the link[4].

Table 1 summarizes the results of main trained models without and using the *Semantic Features* proposes in this work. In the first case, the best model was the Multilayer Perceptron (MLP) classifier with two hidden layers. This MLP model achieves a score of 0.926 on the F1 metric, which is considered a good result. However, the time required for model training took around 0.229 seconds, so this is one of the slowest models for training. Since the *chatbots* produced by *CONQUEST* use the questions given at runtime as new training examples, this results in constant growth of the *dataset*. Consequently, the cost for model training is of critical importance. The use of *Semantic Features* generally presents significant improvements in the evaluated models. In this case, it is important to

---

[3] https://bit.ly/2T9Pbhu.
[4] https://bit.ly/2I0WguG.

highlight the performance improvements of the *GaussianNB* model, which has achieved the best performance in all measured aspects. When comparing the best trained model with the use of *Semantic Features* against the best without them (MLP with two hidden layers), it is possible to see a slight improvement of about 5.075%, which can already be considered a promising result. When comparing the results under the light of the F1-score for the *GaussianNB* model without and with *Semantic Features*, it is possible to notice an improvement of about 38.014 %, which configures a great improvement overall. The real improvement comes from comparing the training time taken by the two best models, *MLP with two hidden layers* and *GaussianNB*: there is a 98.280% reduction in the required time to training, which means that the first model takes about 58 times longer in training than the second. The results of the selected model (GaussianNB with *Semantic Features*) in the test set was 0.979 for Precision, 0.975 for Recall and 0.974 for F1.

Table 1. Results of the model evaluation experiment.

Classifier	Without semantic features				With semantic features			
	Precision	Recall	F1	Time (secs)	Precision	Recall	F1	Time (secs)
GaussianNB	0.772	0.712	0.705	00.023068	**0.983**	**0.975**	**0.973**	**00.003952**
LogisticRegression	0.8	0.787	0.764	01.301347	0.958	0.937	0.933	00.040490
SVC linear	0.916	0.875	0.870	00.048965	**0.983**	**0.975**	**0.973**	00.007134
DecisionTreeClassifier	0.545	0.575	0.534	00.056715	0.858	0.875	0.860	00.007359
MLPClassifier 2 layers	**0.941**	**0.912**	**0.926**	00.229768	0.966	0.962	0.96	00.176730
Nearest Neighbor	0.707	0.675	0.657	**00.004416**	0.879	0.875	0.86	00.006486
GaussianNB + Logistic (Soft Voting)	0.772	0.712	0.705	00.218400	**0.983**	**0.975**	**0.973**	00.110563

CONQUEST's **Interaction Flow** frees the developer from dealing with the scheduling of the conversion flow using techniques such as state machines, conversation scripts, etc. In this example (Fig. 3), the user formulates the question in a manner considerably different from the known template. Consequently, the *chatbot* attempts to resolve user intent by displaying the QP template by replacing the CVs values found by NER in the original question. Having the suggestion confirmed by the user, a new example is added for this QAI after the CVs values are replaced by their corresponding identifiers (e.g., "buscopan" is replaced by $medicine). However, the *chatbot* realizes that the value for CV $state is still missing, thus using the inferred type of CV to make its request. Finally, after substituting the values of CVs in SP and executing it in *endpoint SPARQL*, then the *chatbot* returns the response following RP.

The **Query Engine Construction** step is fully automatic. The SPARQL query pattern (SP) passed in QAI is used to build the actual query to be executed on the EKG. CVs markers present in SP are filled with the parameters

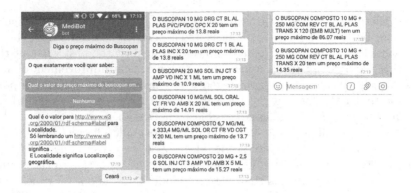

Fig. 3. Using the clarification dialog in *Telegram.*

passed by the user at query time. In the current example, $medicine and $state in *SP* are replaced by "Buscopan" and "Ceará", respectively. *CONQUEST* builds the final NL response by replacing the values of the output variables in the response pattern (*RP*) in QAI with the values returned by executing the query in the EKG. In the example, *?name* and *?price* in the "body" of *RP* are replaced by the values of the variables *?name* and *?price* for each item of the query response.

User Interface was tested with instant messaging application (*Telegram*) and directly via HTTP requests. In the first case, immediate reuse eliminates the need for the installation of new apps and adaptation by the final user. In the second case, external applications can be integrated into larger services, such as existing chatbots built with commercial environments (e.g., *Dialogflow, chatfuel, etc.*), where *CONQUEST* can provide only the specific TBIQA skill for a "larger" chatbot. Finally, *CONQUEST* allows the same instance of a chatbot to be shown in different channels running from the same code, which facilitates maintenance and service increment.

5   Conclusions

CONQUEST framework automates much of the process of building TBIQA *chatbots* on EKGs, where supported templates must be provided as input and dialogue are used to address the problems of inconclusive classification and the lack of parameters in the question. *CONQUEST* resorts to machine learning to acquire new ways in which the same question can be accomplished, which allows the chatbot to evolve with usage. Unlike other works in the field, *CONQUEST* allows complete control of the questions supported, which guarantees support for complex and specific needs, e.g., *Competency Questions*, and also addresses the problem of access to the built service, allowing support through multiple channels simultaneously. As future work, we plan to address the automatic generation of query templates to answer simple questions, so developers focus their efforts on complex and challenging templates.

References

1. Abujabal, A., Yahya, M., Riedewald, M., Weikum, G.: Automated template generation for question answering over knowledge graphs. In: Proceedings of the 26th International Conference on World Wide Web, pp. 1191–1200 (2017)
2. Avila, C.V., et al.: MediBot: an ontology based chatbot for Portuguese speakers drug's users. In: Proceedings of the 21st International Conference on Enterprise Information Systems. ICEIS, vol. 1, pp. 25–36. INSTICC, SciTePress (2019). https://doi.org/10.5220/0007656400250036
3. Biermann, L., Walter, S., Cimiano, P.: A guided template-based question answering system over knowledge graphs. In: Proceedings of the 21st International Conference on Knowledge Engineering and Knowledge Management (2018)
4. Diefenbach, D., Lopez, V., Singh, K., Maret, P.: Core techniques of question answering systems over knowledge bases: a survey. Knowl. Inf. Syst. **55**(3), 529–569 (2017). https://doi.org/10.1007/s10115-017-1100-y
5. Explosion AI: Industrial-strength natural language processing (2019). https://spacy.io
6. Frischmuth, P., et al.: Linked data in enterprise information integration. In: Semantic Web, pp. 1–17 (2012)
7. Géron, A.: Hands-On Machine Learning with Scikit-Learn and TensorFlow: Concepts, Tools, and Techniques to Build Intelligent Systems. O'Reilly Media, Inc., Sebastopol (2017)
8. Gomez-Perez, J.M., Pan, J.Z., Vetere, G., Wu, H.: Enterprise knowledge graph: an introduction. Exploiting Linked Data and Knowledge Graphs in Large Organisations, pp. 1–14. Springer, Cham (2017). https://doi.org/10.1007/978-3-319-45654-6_1
9. Jin, G., Lü, F., Xiang, Z.: Enterprise information integration based on knowledge graph and semantic web technology. J. Southeast Univ. (Nat. Sci. Ed.) **44**(2), 250–255 (2014)
10. Hartmann, N., Fonseca, E., Shulby, C., Treviso, M., Rodrigues, J., Aluisio, S.: Portuguese word embeddings: evaluating on word analogies and natural language tasks. arXiv preprint arXiv:1708.06025 (2017)
11. Heath, T., Bizer, C.: Linked data: evolving the web into a global data space. Synth. Lect. Semant. Web Theory Technol. **1**(1), 1–136 (2011)
12. Kaufmann, E., Bernstein, A.: How useful are natural language interfaces to the semantic web for casual end-users? In: Aberer, K., et al. (eds.) ASWC/ISWC - 2007. LNCS, vol. 4825, pp. 281–294. Springer, Heidelberg (2007). https://doi.org/10.1007/978-3-540-76298-0_21
13. Konstantinova, N., Orasan, C.: Interactive question answering. In: Emerging Applications of Natural Language Processing: Concepts and New Research, pp. 149–169. IGI Global (2013)
14. Li, Y., Yang, T.: Word embedding for understanding natural language: a survey. In: Srinivasan, S. (ed.) Guide to Big Data Applications. SBD, vol. 26, pp. 83–104. Springer, Cham (2018). https://doi.org/10.1007/978-3-319-53817-4_4
15. Nadeau, D., Sekine, S.: A survey of named entity recognition and classification. Lingvist. Investig. **30**(1), 3–26 (2007)
16. RDFLib: SPARQL Wrapper SPARQL endpoint interface to Python (2019). https://rdflib.github.io/sparqlwrapper/. Accessed 26 Nov 2019

17. Ren, Y., Parvizi, A., Mellish, C., Pan, J.Z., van Deemter, K., Stevens, R.: Towards competency question-driven ontology authoring. In: Presutti, V., d'Amato, C., Gandon, F., d'Aquin, M., Staab, S., Tordai, A. (eds.) ESWC 2014. LNCS, vol. 8465, pp. 752–767. Springer, Cham (2014). https://doi.org/10.1007/978-3-319-07443-6_50

18. Scrapinghub: dateparser date parsing library designed to parse dates from HTML pages (2019). https://pypi.org/project/dateparser/. Accessed 25 Nov 2019

19. Shishtla, P.M., Pingali, P., Varma, V.: A character n-gram based approach for improved recall in Indian language NER. In: Proceedings of the IJCNLP-2008 Workshop on Named Entity Recognition for South and South East Asian Languages (2008)

20. Smiley, D., Pugh, D.E.: Apache Solr 3 Enterprise Search Server. Packt Publishing Ltd., Birmingham (2011)

21. Yang, P., Hwa Yang, Y., Zhou, B.B., Zomaya, A.Y.: A review of ensemble methods in bioinformatics. Curr. Bioinform. 5(4), 296–308 (2010)

Enabling Interactive Answering
of Procedural Questions

Anutosh Maitra$^{(\boxtimes)}$, Shivam Garg, and Shubhashis Sengupta

Accenture Technology Labs, Bangalore 560037, India
anutosh.maitra@accenture.com

Abstract. A mechanism to enable task oriented procedural question answering system for user assistance in English is presented in this paper. The primary aim is to create an answering "corpus" in a tree-form from unstructured document passages. This corpus is used to respond to the queries interactively to assist in completing a technical task. Reference manuals, documents or webpages are scraped to identify the sections depicting a "procedure" through machine learning techniques and then an integrated task tree with extracted procedural knowledge from text is generated. The automated mechanism breaks the procedural sections into steps, the appropriate "decision points" are identified, the interactive utterances are generated to gain user inputs and the alternative paths are created to complete the tree. Conventional tree traversal mechanism provides step by step guidance to complete a task. Efficacy of the proposed mechanism is tested on documents collected from three different domains and test results are presented.

Keywords: Procedural question · Clause identification · Question generation

1 Introduction

Task oriented virtual agents aim at potentially automating a wide range of processes within the business. A few of the common examples of such agents include interactive self-service assistance to customers, knowledge assistance to internal help desk, guided selling or personalized guidance to portal navigation [1]. Most of these agents handle only quick, one-off advisories often leading to unsatisfactory resolution of an issue or incomplete assistance to obtain the goal. Service encounters are critical to an organization's image and therefore central to determining the success of the business. Modern task oriented virtual agents try to satisfy personalized constraints. Many service tasks relate to "How to" procedures and need assistance in an interactive manner.

This paper presents an enabling mechanism to support guided response in English in performing day-to-day customer facing operations; and to enable self-service for the customers. A guided response system demands the knowledge repository to be available in a certain form. This is often difficult to attain as such information contains both structured and unstructured data; some of them are client specific, some may be related to internal promotions, products and processes as well as installation, troubleshooting or operational manuals. Answering procedural questions from such disperse and unstructured knowledge sources would require a well-formed text structure. Such texts

© Springer Nature Switzerland AG 2020
E. Métais et al. (Eds.): NLDB 2020, LNCS 12089, pp. 73–81, 2020.
https://doi.org/10.1007/978-3-030-51310-8_7

can be a simple, ordered list of instructions to reach a goal, but mostly they are less linear, outlining different ways to realize a goal, with arguments, conditions, hypothesis or preferences. Hence, information collected from the reference documents must be organized to demarcate each procedure and stored with the corresponding sequential sets of instructions in a form to enable user interaction at intermediate levels. The contexts and conditions those determine the right path to complete the task are collected through interactions. In this work, a tree type structure is generated for each procedure description. The interaction points are the decision nodes of these trees. A conventional tree traversal mechanism is adopted to collect user inputs at every decision node.

2   Procedural Question Answering State of the Art

Recent advances in deep neural networks, language modeling and language generation have introduced stronger capabilities to the conversational agents. However, research on procedural question answering are still restricted to successful identification of procedures or responding to one-off questions. A preliminary structure of a model based on conceptual and linguistic analysis of procedural texts by simple text grammar system in French language was proposed by Delpech [2]. The issues of title identification, tagging and reconstruction via a learning mechanism in a large variety of procedural texts have been addressed by Adam et al. [3]. The challenges of answering procedural questions from procedural text have been investigated by Saint-Dizier [4]. Parsing and analyzing argumentative structures in procedural texts have been addressed successfully by Fontan [5]. Recent work on question answering tasks involving procedural text uses artificial neural networks [6]. Many times, these neural models rely on surface cues alone to make inferences. Such approaches also lead to domain-specific language systems that do not gracefully extend to other tasks. The novel work of Ribeiro et al. [7] allows semantic interpretation of procedural texts for answer retrieval and finding a single response from a procedural passage. Benchmark datasets like bAbI [8], SCoNE [9] and ProPARA [10] have also been created, but they mostly serve the purpose of procedural text comprehension and are not suitable for guided response.

3   Overview of the Proposed Mechanism

Our work first identifies the procedural passages in operational manuals and then we represent the information in the procedural passages into a tree form where the decision nodes provide the scope of interaction and the response nodes contain the advisory. When a conversation is initiated, the agent selects the appropriate process tree and traverses the right branch to generate the sequential set of instructions.

There are three major components in the whole mechanism as shown in Fig. 1. There is a Text Classifier, a Tree Generation Mechanism and an Interactive Chatbot mechanism. The first two components are required to transform an operation manual to a tree representation of the procedural passages. The Interactive Chatbot component

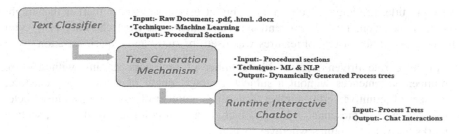

Fig. 1. Schematic representation of the components

works runtime. The Tree Generation Mechanism is the central component of the entire architecture and has five subcomponents; viz., Decision Point Identifier, Clause Identifier, Question Generator, Answer Path Identifier and Tree Structure Representation.

Detailed modeling of each of these subcomponents and the associated experimental results to substantiate the model efficacy are presented in the succeeding section.

4 Detailed Modeling and Experimentation

We have used three practical datasets from three different domains for experimentally developing the components. The datasets were manually curated to create a near equal distribution for procedural and non-procedural paragraphs. The first one is a FAQ document dataset that contains frequently asked questions available on Fitbit [11] and DLink [12] websites. About 900 paragraphs of IT domain specific questions and answers were obtained by web scraping. The second one is Insurance document dataset which contains 650 paragraphs related to banking and insurance domain. The QA pairs were obtained from Insurance document published by Bank of America [13]. The third one is Industrial document dataset which contains 500 paragraphs related to manufacturing and maintenance of industrial equipment published by Jackson [14].

4.1 Text Classifier for Identifying Procedure(s)

Operational manuals usually contain large volume of information out of which only a limited number of sections describe a procedure. Early research [15] to generate responses to "How" and "Why" kind of questions described a variety of rational structures of procedural texts. However, diverse argumentations in this type of texts have been observed and many other subtle language forms like tonality, opinion marks or injunctive forms are to be understood to create a linguistic model for procedure identification. Linguistic rules often do not discriminate between a process and a causality description. Understanding the boundary of the procedural knowledge; especially when the procedure cue has an ambiguous start is also challenge.

We propose simple binary classifiers to identify procedural sections in a document. The beginning and end of each section are the corresponding beginning and end of a paragraph, title, headings or subheadings, bullet lists or any other marker that might indicate a seclusion. First, a conventional Random Forest (RF) classifier [16], with following two different sets of features was used for study and experimentation.

- Linguistic rule driven features like number of sentences starting with a verb, number of sentences without a subject, average length of steps in a procedure, number of infinitive verbs, number of gerunds, number of co-reference clusters etc.
- Fast-text word representation features including vectors for text of the lists, section marks, titles and subtitles wherever available.

We also built a Long Short Term Memory (LSTM) deep neural network [17] and trained it with glove word embeddings as the input feature. Comparison of the training and test accuracy of the models is shown below in the Table 1. Random forest classifier using only linguistic features was weak since the documents were not written in uniform styles and formats. The results indicated a far better performance of the LSTM model. Subsequently, complete validation of the LSTM model was done on the 3 datasets mentioned in the beginning of this section. An average F1 score of 89% was obtained during validation for all these 3 practical datasets.

Table 1. Comparative training results for text classifiers

Model	Training data	Training accuracy	Testing data	Testing accuracy	Validation data	Validation accuracy
LSTM	Fitbit	91.34	Fitbit	89.76	DLink	73.56
LSTM	Fitbit+DLink	94.60	Fitbit+DLink	92.40	DLink	84.56
RF FastText	Fitbit	80.23	Fitbit	76.89	DLink	58.40
RF FastText	Fitbit+DLink	83.45	Fitbit+DLink	77.34	DLink	65.50
RF Linguistic	Fitbit	61.45	Fitbit	56.76	DLink	54.89
RF Linguistic	Fitbit+DLink	63.45	Fitbit+DLink	61.90	DLink	58.39

4.2   Identifying Decision Points

Decision points are the instructions where user inputs are required to find the next steps as alternative paths are found at these points. The dependency parser Spacy [18] was used to understand the linguistic structure of the sentences, like the Part of Speech (PoS) and Dependency (DeP) tag. Whether the sentence is a decision point can then be identified programmatically. In Fig. 2 below, we show the tags for a simple sentence: *"If using windows 10, download latest version"*. Rules related to the conditional word "if" as starting conjunction (sconj) and the location of "advcl", can identify this as a conditional statement and a decision point. The PoS and DeP tags however, often make all acknowledgement points too as decision points. As shown in Fig. 3, for a sentence *"After completion of download, shutdown server"*, no decision is required although the "advcl" is present. This is a mere acknowledgement point. Additional grammatical rules were created to address such scenarios. Additional rules are also used to consider more sparsely used conditional words like "check", "ponder" and "ensure".

Fig. 2. Parser output for a conditional sentence as a decision point

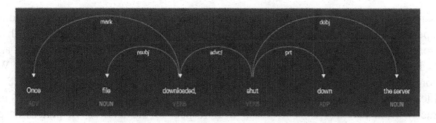

Fig. 3. Parser output for a conditional sentence as an acknowledgement point

The accuracy of decision point identification was enhanced by close to 6% with these additional rules. The accuracy is defined as the ratio of total number of decision points correctly identified to the total number of decision points identified by human referees.

4.3 Clause Identification

It is necessary to convert the conditional decision sentences into a question to enable collection of contextual information from the user. The question is based on the condition and the condition is contained in the independent clauses. Dependent clauses point to the next set of actions depending on the answer received.

A BiLSTM-CRF model [19] was used for clause identification. It has been shown that such a model can efficiently handle input features thanks to a bidirectional LSTM component. The CRF layer helps leveraging sentence level tag information. We used a published pre-trained model trained on CoNLL-2001 Shared Task Data [20] which contains 7150 sentences and 211727 tokens. This model computes the score of a sentence $[x]_1^T$ along with a path of tags $[i]_1^T$ as the sum of transition scores and network scores.

$$s\left([x]_1^T, [i]_1^T, \tilde{\theta}\right) = \sum_{t=1}^{T} \left([A]_{[i]_{t-1},[i]_t} + [f_\theta]_{[i]_t,t}\right) \quad (1)$$

This sequence tagging model identifies the clauses by maximizing the score $s\left([x]_1^T, [i]_1^T, \tilde{\theta}\right)$. It recognizes clause starts, clause ends and identifies complete, possibly embedded, clauses. An elegant improvisation was a subsequent use of the Spacy parser to identify the "first" and the "innermost" clauses. For the conditional sentence: *"If you previously downloaded playlists, skip to part 2 to download new music and podcasts"*, the dependent and independent clauses can be separated as shown below.

(S1 if
(S2 you previously downloaded playlists, E2 I)
(skip to part 2 to download new music and podcasts E1 D))

Where D and I denote Dependent and Independent respectively.

4.4   Question Generation

This module generates questions the agent will pose to the user at a decision point. Independent clauses contain the condition to generate a question. We examined three approaches for question generation; viz. Pattern-based [21], Aspect-based [22] and Data Driven Models (QGNET) [23]; for their suitability in the present context. We performed the aspect and pattern mining on the identified decision points. "Aspect" is extracted from the positive answer which is the dependent clause. "Keywords" are extracted from the independent clause with respect to the answer. In pattern-based approach, "Keywords" are used to generate the "Patterns". Then a sequence-to-sequence model with BERT pretrained embeddings is trained for question generation. In aspect-based approach, "Aspect" and "Patterns" are encoded separately and used as inputs for training this sequence-to-sequence model. QGNET is a data-driven approach built on a sequence-to-sequence model with copy mechanism. This model was originally trained on SQuAD dataset with answer tokens and other linguistic features like PoS and Named-Entity-Recognition (NER) tags. The pre-trained model of QGNET generates a "wh" type of factoid question. In our work, we required binary type of questions as otherwise the user would have a potentially open-ended choice of

Table 2. Comparative study of quality of generated questions

Sample conditional statement	If you're using the latest version of Fitbit connect, click the Fitbit connect icon located near the date and time on your computer			
Ideal question	Does your computer use the latest version of Fitbit connect?			
	Pattern based	Aspect based	QG-Net (Pretrained)	QG-Net (Retrained)
Prediction	Pattern:- Does this device## Question:- Does this device update to latest version?	Aspect:- using latest version Question:- Can this device be used with latest version?	Question:- What is the version of Fitbit connect?	Question:- Are you using latest version of Fitbit connect?
Cos- similarity with ideal question	0.47	0.59	0.62	0.89

responses that could not be used. So, we further retrained the QGNET model with AQAD dataset [24]. We selected 200000 Boolean type of questions from AQAD; and 765 question and answer pairs from 300 procedural paragraphs in the FAQ dataset for training.

Table 2 above provides a snapshot of a qualitative comparison of the questions generated by all three methods. The questions generated by QGNET were more usable in the current context. This was probably owing to the flexibility available to retrain QGNET with specific type of question answer pairs as desired.

5 Implementation of Guided Response System

During implementation, we first train offline all the modules discussed in Sect. 4. These modules enable programmatic creation of the procedural trees from a given document. Each procedural tree is assigned a label. At the beginning of a conversation, an intent matching mechanism selects the correct tree. Each tree contains two types of nodes; viz. Information Seeking node and the Response node. The information seeking nodes may have multiple paths tagged with different possibilities which are prompted to the user for tree navigation. The response type nodes either provide next step or stop if a resolution is obtained. If a resolution is not attained till the leaf node in the tree, the system may involve a human agent for further conversation. For procedures described over multiple paragraphs, each of the paragraphs are identified as a sub-procedure and the task completion is possible only after all the trees are traversed. Usually a dialog manager will have to be integrated to manage the conversation and keep the conversation grounded to the end goal; however, this was not investigated in the current research. In a laboratory setup, more than 90% of the user queries, from approximately 700 procedures collected from the three datasets mentioned before were successfully responded; and led to a close to 50% of efficiency improvement in the business process.

6 Conclusion

We presented here an enabling mechanism for conversational agents to handhold the user through a step by step execution of tasks. Most of the automated agents today respond to the how-to questions in a passage form that often leaves the user to complete the task inefficiently or even fail to complete it altogether. The purpose of the work was to create a means to convert the available knowledge into a form that would aid the agent respond in a staggered, yet, contextual manner. We have seen that fully machine learned models can distinguish a procedural part of text from the rest and we can leverage the linguistic capabilities of the modern-day parsers and state of the art deep learning mechanisms to create a pre-scripted dialog that can be availed runtime. The strength of QGNET in generating questions was found useful. The method was found suitable for at least three different domains of applications.

References

1. Verhagen, T., Feldberg, F., Nes, J.: Virtual customer service agents: using social presence and personalization to shape online service encounters. J. Comput. Mediat. Commun. **19**(3), 529–545 (2014)
2. Delpech, E., Saint-Dizier, P.: Investigating the structure of procedural texts for answering how-to questions. In: Proceedings of the Language Resources and Evaluation Conference (2008)
3. Adam, C., Delpech, E., Saint-Dizier, P.: Identifying and expanding titles in web texts. In: Proceedings of the 8th ACM Symposium on Document Engineering, pp. 213–216 (2008)
4. Saint-Dizier, P.: Some challenges of advanced question-answering: an experiment with how-to questions. In: Proceedings of the 22nd Pacific Asia Conference on Language, Information and Computation, pp. 65–73 (2008)
5. Fontan, L., Saint-Dizier, P.: Analyzing argumentative structures in procedural texts. In: Nordström, B., Ranta, A. (eds.) GoTAL 2008. LNCS (LNAI), vol. 5221, pp. 366–370. Springer, Heidelberg (2008). https://doi.org/10.1007/978-3-540-85287-2_35
6. Das, R., Munkhdalai, T., Yuan, X., Trischler, A., McCallum, A.: Building dynamic knowledge graphs from text using machine reading comprehension. In: Proceedings of the International Conference on Learning Representations (2018)
7. Ribeiro, D., Hinrichs, T., Crouse, M., Forbus, K.: Predicting state changes in procedural text using analogical question answering. In: 7th Annual Conference on Advances in Cognitive Systems (2019)
8. Weston, J., et al.: Towards ai-complete question answering: a set of prerequisite toy tasks. arXiv preprint arXiv:1502.05698 (2015)
9. Long, R., Pasupat, P., Liang, P.: Simpler context-dependent logical forms via model projections. In: Proceedings of the 54th Annual Meeting of the Association for Computational Linguistics (ACL 2016), pp. 1456–1465 (2016)
10. Du, X., et al.: Be consistent! Improving procedural text comprehension using label consistency. In: Proceedings of the Conference of the North American Chapter of the Association for Computational Linguistics: Human Language Technologies, Minneapolis (2019)
11. FitBit. https://help.fitbit.com/?l=en_US&c=Topics%3AFAQs. Accessed 03 Feb 2020
12. DLink. https://eu.dlink.com/uk/en/support/faq. Accessed 03 Feb 2020
13. Bank of America. https://www.bankofamerica.com/deposits/resources/personal-schedule-fees.go. Accessed 03 Feb 2020
14. Jackson. http://manuals.jacksonmsc.com/ecolab%20manuals/ES-2000%2&%20ES-4000%20Rev%20O.pdf. Accessed 03 Feb 2020
15. Auladomour, F., Saint-Dizier, P.: Towards generating procedural texts: an exploration of their rhetorical and argumentative structure. In: Proceedings of the 10th European Workshop on Natural Language Generation (2005)
16. Breiman, L.: Random forest. Mach. Learn. **45**(1), 5–32 (2001)
17. Hochreiter, S., Schmidhuber, J.: Long short-term memory. Neural Comput. **9**, 1735–1780 (1997). https://doi.org/10.1162/neco.1997.9.8.1735
18. Spacy. https://spacy.io. Accessed 03 Feb 2020
19. Huang, Z., Xu, W., Yu, K.: Bidirectional LSTM-CRF models for sequence tagging. arXiv preprint arXiv:1508.01991v1 (2015)
20. Tjong Kim Sang, E.F., Déjean, H.: Introduction to the CoNLL-2001 shared task: Clause Identification. In: Proceedings of CoNLL-2001, Toulouse, France (2001)

21. Duan, N., Tang, D., Chen, P., Zhou, M.: Question generation for question answering. In: Proceedings of the EMNLP 2017, pp. 866–874 (2017)
22. Hu, W., Liu, B., Ma, J., Zhao, D., Yan, R.: Aspect-based question generation. In: Proceedings of the ICLR Workshop (2018)
23. Wang, Z., Lan, A., Nie, W., Waters, A.: QG-net: a data-driven question generation model for educational content. In: Proceedings of the 5th Annual ACM Conference on Learning at Scale (L@S), pp. 1–10. ACM (2018)
24. Amazon question/answer data. http://jmcauley.ucsd.edu/data/amazon/qa/. Accessed 03 Feb 2020

Natural Language Generation Using Transformer Network in an Open-Domain Setting

Deeksha Varshney[1]($\boxtimes$), Asif Ekbal[1]($\boxtimes$), Ganesh Prasad Nagaraja[2]($\boxtimes$),
Mrigank Tiwari[2]($\boxtimes$), Abhijith Athreya Mysore Gopinath[2]($\boxtimes$),
and Pushpak Bhattacharyya[1]($\boxtimes$)

[1] Department of Computer Science and Engineering,
Indian Institute of Technology Patna, Patna, India
{1821cs13,asif,pb}@iitp.ac.in
[2] Samsung Research India, Bangalore, India
{ganesh.pn,mrigank.k}@samsung.com, abhijith@psu.edu

Abstract. Prior works on dialog generation focus on task-oriented setting and utilize multi-turn conversational utterance-response pairs. However, natural language generation (NLG) in the open-domain environment is more challenging. The conversations in an open-domain chit-chat model are mostly single-turn in nature. Current methods used for modeling single-turn conversations often fail to generate contextually relevant responses for a large dataset. In our work, we develop a transformer-based method for natural language generation (NLG) in an open-domain setting. Experiments on the utterance-response pairs show improvement over the baselines, both in terms of quantitative measures like BLEU and ROUGE and human evaluation metrics like fluency and adequacy.

Keywords: Conversational AI · Natural language generation ·
Open-IE · Transformer

1 Introduction

Conversational systems are some of the most important advancements in the area of Artificial Intelligence (AI). In conversational AI, dialogue systems can be either an open-domain chit-chat model or a task-specific goal-oriented model. Task-specific systems focus on particular tasks such as flight or hotel booking, providing technical support to users, and answering non-creative queries. These systems try to generate a response by maximizing an expected reward. In contrast, an open-domain dialog system operates in a non-goal driven casual environment and responds to the all kinds of questions. The realization of rewards is not straightforward in these cases, as there are many factors to model in. Aspects such as understanding the dialog context, acknowledging user's personal preferences, and other external factors such as time, weather, and current events need consideration at each dialog step.

© Springer Nature Switzerland AG 2020
E. Métais et al. (Eds.): NLDB 2020, LNCS 12089, pp. 82–93, 2020.
https://doi.org/10.1007/978-3-030-51310-8_8

In recent times, there has been a trend towards building end-to-end dialog systems such as chat-bots which can easily mimic human conversations. [19,22, 25] developed systems using deep neural networks by training them on a large amount of multi-turn conversational data. Virtual assistants in open-domain settings usually utilize single-turn conversations for training the models. Chit-chat bots in such situations can help humans to interact with machines using natural language, thereby allowing humans to express their emotional states.

In dialogue systems, generating relevant, diverse, and coherent responses is essential for robustness and practical usages. Generative models tend to generate shorter, inappropriate responses to some questions. The responses range from invalid sentences to generic ones like "I don't know". The reasons for these issues include inefficiency of models in capturing long-range dependencies, generation of a large number of out-of-vocabulary (OOV) words, and limitations of the maximum likelihood objective functions for training these models. Transformer models have become an essential part of most of the state-of-the-art architectures in several natural language processing (NLP) applications. Results show that these models capture long-range dependencies efficiently, replacing gated recurrent neural network models in many situations.

In this paper, we propose an efficient end-to-end architecture based on the transformer network for natural language generation (NLG) in an open-domain dialogue system. The proposed model can maximize contextual relevancy and diversity in generated responses.

Our research reported here contributes in three ways: (i) we build an efficient end-to-end neural architecture for a chit-chat dialogue system, capable of generating contextually consistent and diverse responses; (ii) we create a single-turn conversational dataset with chit-chat type conversations on several topics between a human and a virtual assistant; and (iii) empirical analysis shows that our proposed model can improve the generation process when trained with enough data in comparison to the traditional methods like retrieval-based and neural translation-based.

2   Related Work

Conversational Artificial Intelligence (AI) is currently one of the most challenging problems of Artificial Intelligence. Developing dialog systems that can interact with humans logically and can engage them in having long-term conversations has captured the attention of many AI researchers. In general, dialog systems are mainly of two types - task-oriented dialog systems and open-domain dialog systems. Task-oriented dialog systems converse with the users to complete a specific task such as assisting customers to book a ticket or online shopping. On the other hand, an open-domain dialog system can help users to share information, ask questions, and develop social etiquette's through a series of conversations.

Early works in this area were typically rule-based or learning-based methods [12,13,17,28]. Rule-based methods often require human experts to form rules for training the system, whereas learning-based methods learn from a specific algorithm, which makes it less flexible to adapt to the other domains. Data from various social media platforms like Twitter, Reddit, and other community question-answering (CQA) platforms have provided us with a large number of human-to-human conversations. Data-driven approaches developed by [6,16] can be used to handle such problems. Retrieval based methods [6] generate a suitable response from a predefined set of candidate responses by ranking them in the order of similarity (e.g., by matching the number of common words) against the input sentence. The selection of a random response from a set of predefined responses makes them static and repetitive. [16] builds a system based on phrase-based statistical machine translation to exploit single turn conversations. [30] presented a deep learning-based method for retrieval-based systems. A brief review of these methods is presented by [2].

Lately, generation based models have become quite popular. [19,22,23,25] presented several generative models based on neural network for building efficient conversational dialog systems. Moreover, several other techniques, for instance generative adversarial network (GAN) [10,29] and conditional variational autoencoder (CVAE) [3,7,18,20,32,33] are also implemented for dialog generation.

Conversations generated from retrieval-based methods are highly fluent, grammatically correct, and are of good quality as compared to dialogues generated from the generative methods. Their high-quality performance is subjected to the availability of an extensive repository of human-human interactions. However, responses generated by neural generative models are random in nature but often lack grammatical correctness. Techniques that can combine the power of both retrieval-based methods and generative methods can be adapted in such situations. On the whole hybrid methods [21,27,31,34] first find some relevant responses using retrieval techniques and then leverages them to generate contextually relevant responses in the next stage.

In this paper, we propose a novel method for building an efficient virtual assistant using single-turn open-domain conversational data. We use a self-attention based transformer model, instead of RNN based models to get the representation of our input sequences. We observe that our method can generate more diverse and relevant responses.

3   Methodology

3.1   Problem Statement

Our goal is to generate contextually relevant responses for single-turn conversations. Given an input sequence of utterance $U = u_1, u_2, ..., u_n$ composed of n words we try to generate a target response $Y = y_1, y_2, ..., y_m$.

3.2   Word Embeddings

We use pre-trained GLoVE [15][1] embeddings to initialize the word vectors. GLoVE utilizes two main methods from literature to build its vectors: global matrix factorization and local context window methods. The GloVe model is trained on the non-zero entries of a global word to word co-occurrence matrix, which computes how frequently two words can occur together in a given corpus. The embeddings used in our model are trained on *Common Crawl* dataset with 840B tokens and 2.2M vocab. We use 300-dimensional sized vectors.

3.3   Baseline Models

We formulate our task of response generation as a machine translation problem. We define two baseline models based on deep learning techniques to conduct our experiments. First, we build a neural sequence to sequence model [23] based on Bi-Directional Long Short Term Memory (Bi-LSTM) [5] cells. The second model utilizes the attention mechanism [1] to align input and output sequences. We train these models using the Glove word embeddings as input features.

To build our first baseline, we use a neural encoder-decoder [23] model. The encoder, which contains RNN cells, converts the input sequence into a *context vector*. The context vector is an abstract representation of the entire input sequence. The context vector forms the input for a second RNN based decoder, which learns to output the target sequence one word at a time. Our second baseline uses an attention layer [1] between the encoder and decoder, which helps in deciding which words to focus on the input sequence in order to predict the next word correctly.

3.4   Proposed Model

The third model, which is our proposed method, is based on the transformer network architecture [24]. We use Glove word embeddings as input features for our proposed model. We develop the transformer encoder as described in [24] to obtain the representation of the input sequence and the transformer decoder to generate the target response. Figure 1 shows the proposed architecture. The input to the transformer encoder is both the embedding, e, of the current word, $e(u_n)$, as well as positional encoding $PE(n)$ of the nth word:

$$I_u = [u_1, ..., u_n] \tag{1}$$

$$u_n = e(u_n) + PE(n) \tag{2}$$

There are a total of N_x identical layers in a transformer encoder. Each layer contains two sub-layers - a Multi-head attention layer and a position-wise feedforward layer. We encode the input utterances and target responses of our dataset using multi-head self-attention. The second layer performs linear transformation

---

[1] https://nlp.stanford.edu/projects/glove/.

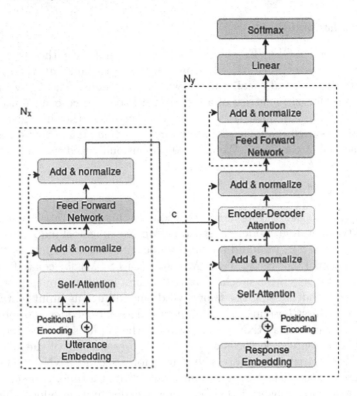

Fig. 1. Proposed model architecture

over the outputs from the first sub-layer. A residual connection is applied to each of the two sub-layers, followed by layer normalization. The following equations represent the layers:

$$M^1 = MultiHead(I_u, I_u, I_u) \tag{3}$$

$$F^1 = FFN(M^1) \tag{4}$$

$$FFN(t) = max(0, tW_1 + b_1)W_2 + b \tag{5}$$

where M^1 is the hidden state returned by the first layer of multi-head attention and F^1 is the representation of the input utterance obtained after the first feed forward layer. The above steps are repeated for the remaining layers:

$$M^n = MultiHead(I_u, I_u, I_u) \tag{6}$$

$$F^n = FFN(M^n) \tag{7}$$

where n = 1, ..., N_x. We use c to denote the final representation of the input utterance obtained at N_x-th layer:

$$c = F^{(N_x)} \tag{8}$$

Similarly, for decoding the responses, we use the transformer decoder. There are N_y identical layers in the decoder as well. The encoder and decoder layers are quite similar to each other except that now the decoder layer has two multi-head attention layers to perform self-attention and encoder-decoder attention, respectively.

$$R_y = [y_1, ..., y_m] \tag{9}$$

$$y_m = e(y_m) + PE(m) \tag{10}$$

$$P^n = MultiHead(R_y, R_y, R_y) \tag{11}$$

$$G^n = FFN(P^n) \tag{12}$$

$$D^n = MultiHead(G^n, c, c) \tag{13}$$

$$H^n = FFN(D^n) \tag{14}$$

To make prediction of the next word, we use Softmax to obtain the words probabilities decoded by the decoder.

$$\hat{y}_t = softmax(H^{(N_y)}) \tag{15}$$

4 Datasets and Experiments

In this section, we present the details of the datasets used in our experiments, along with a detailed overview of the experimental settings.

4.1 Datasets

Our dataset comprises of single-turn conversations from ten different domains - Data About User, Competitors, Emotion, Emergency, Greetings, About Bixby, Entertainment, Sensitive, Device, and Event. Professional annotators with a linguistics background and relevant expertise created this dataset. The total dataset comprises of 184,849 utterance and response pairs with an average of 7.31 and 14.44 words for utterance and response, respectively. We first split the data into a train and test set in a 95:5 ratio. We then use 5% of the training data for preparing the validation set. The dataset details are given in Table 2. Some examples from the dataset are shown in Table 1.

4.2 Experimental Setup

We use two different types of models for our experiments - recurrent and transformer-based sequence-to-sequence generative models. All data loading, model implementations, and evaluation were done using the OpenNMT[2] [9] as the code framework.

Recurrent Models. We train a seq2seq model where the encoder and decoder are parameterized as LSTMs [5]. We also experiment with the seq2seq model

---

[2] https://github.com/OpenNMT/OpenNMT-py.

Table 1. Examples of the original utterance and the associated response from the dataset

	Greetings
Utterance	How are you?
Response	I'm just happy to be here
Utterance	Hello dear
Response	Hey there! Good to see you
	Emotional
Utterance	Is it that difficult to understand me?
Response	Sorry, I missed that. Saying it a different way might help me
Utterance	Why aren't you responding?
Response	I didn't hear you, I'm here now
	Sensitive
Utterance	My mom hit me because I identify as a man
Response	There is help, and it's OK to talk about this with someone
Utterance	Are you a boy or a girl?
Response	Gender doesn't matter in our friendship

Table 2. Dataset statistics

	Train	Test	Valid
# Utterance and response pairs	152,903	15,559	16,387

with an attention mechanism [1] between the decoder and the encoder outputs. The encoder and decoder LSTMs have 2 layers with 512-dimensional hidden states with a dropout rate of 0.1.

Transformer Model. The layers of both encoder and decoder are set to 6 with 512-dimensional hidden states with a dropout of 0.1. There are 8 multi-head attention heads and 2048 nodes in the feed-forward hidden layers. The dimension of word embedding is empirically set to 512. We use Adam [8] for optimization. When decoding the responses, the beam size is set to 5.

4.3   Evaluation Metrics

Automatic Evaluation: We use the standard metrics like BLEU [14], ROUGE [11] and perplexity for the automatic evaluation of our models. Perplexity is reported on the generated responses from the validation set. Lower perplexity indicates better performance of the models. BLEU and ROUGE measure the n-gram overlap between a generated response and a gold response. Higher BLEU and ROUGE scores indicate better performance.

Human Evaluation: To qualitatively evaluate our models, we perform human evaluation on the generated responses. We sample 200 random responses from our test set for the human evaluation. Given an input utterance, target response, and predicted response triplet, two experts with post-graduate exposure were asked to evaluate the predicted responses based on the given two criteria:

1. Fluency: The predicted response is fluent in terms of the grammar.
2. Adequacy: The predicted response is contextually relevant to the given utterance.

We measure fluency and adequacy on a 0–2 scale with '0' indicating an incomplete or incorrect response, '1' indicating acceptable responses and '2' indicating a perfect response. To measure the inter-annotator agreement, we compute the Fleiss kappa [4] score. We obtained a kappa score of 0.99 for fluency and a score of 0.98 for adequacy denoting "good agreement.

5   Results and Analysis

In this section we report the results for all our experiments. The first two experiments (*seq2seq* & *seq2seq_attn*) are conducted with our baseline models. Our third experiment (c.f Fig. 1) is carried out on our proposed model using word embeddings as the input sequences. Table 3 and Table 4 show the automatic and manual evaluation results for both the baseline and the proposed model.

Automatic Evaluation Results: Our proposed model has lower perplexity and higher BLEU and ROUGE scores than the baselines. The improvement in each model is statistically significant compared to the other models[3]. For all the evaluation metrics, seq2seq_attn has the highest score among the baselines, and our model outperforms those scores by a decent margin.

Human Evaluation Results: For Adequacy, we find that our seq2seq model achieves the highest score of 73.70 among the baseline models. Our proposed model outperforms the baselines with a score of 81.75. For Fluency, we observe that the responses generated by all the models are quite fluent in general.

Table 3. Results (BLEU and ROUGE scores) for the baseline and proposed models using Glove embeddings

Model	BLEU	ROUGE			PPL
		ROUGE-1	ROUGE-2	ROUGE-L	
Seq2seq	45.26	40.94	32.50	42.96	8.45
Seq2seq_attn	45.39	40.96	32.62	43.05	8.42
Proposed Model	**46.42**	**42.41**	**34.19**	**44.35**	**7.47**

---

[3] We perform statistical significance tests [26], and it is conducted at 5% (0.05) significance level.

Table 4. Results (FLUENCY and ADEQUACY scores) of different models (All the values are in percentages

Model	Fluency	Adequacy
Seq2seq	99.25	73.75
Seq2seq_attn	99.00	71.50
Proposed Model	**100.00**	**81.75**

5.1 Error Analysis

To observe our results in more details, we perform an error analysis on the predicted response. In Table 5, we show the predicted responses of various models used in our experiments along with the input utterance and target response. Some of the other observations are listed below:

1. **Our proposed model gives adequate response for the unseen utterances:** For example, Utterance: *What success did you achieve?*; Predicted Response: *I wonder if achieving world peace is too much to ask for* Utterance: *What is your desired job?*; Predicted Response: *Those concepts don't really apply to me. I am a digital entity after all.* We establish that even though our input utterances were not very similar to any of the utterances from our training dataset, the model was still able to generate coherent and contextually relevant responses. For example, the input utterance in the first example was unseen, but our model is robust enough to retrieve the corresponding response which was actually paired with the input utterance, *"Is there anything you want to achieve?"* in the training conversation.
2. **Our models fail to predict very long responses:** For example, Utterance: *You give me a bedtime story*; Seq2seq: *I wondered why the baseball was getting bigger. Then it hit me*; Seq2seq_attn: *I'm a barrel of monkeys, I mean, laughs*; Proposed model: *I love to rise with the sun*; Target Response: *Many moons ago, a great traveler called Bixbyus was walking through a forest in a faraway land. Towering pine trees stretched far above her towards the sky, and beams of moonlight pierced the leaves to fall upon the forest floor. ... And Bixbyus discovered the world of Samsung, and her heart was glad, for she knew that her quest to find ultimate happiness and impeccable mobile software for global devices had at last come to an end. The End*
3. **Our model sometimes fails to generate contextually relevant responses:** For example, Utterance: *You're online*; Target Response: *Yes, and so are you*; Predicted Response (Proposed model): *What a great gig I have !.* As seen in the example, the predicted response would not be the best fit reply to the utterance "You are online" as the response falls out of context for the given utterance.

Table 5. Some sample responses generated by the baseline and proposed models on our test set

Input Utterance	Target Response	seq2seq	seq2seq_attn	Proposed model
How vast is your vocabulary?	It's expansive!	Well, those people seem to think of that	Above anything, I'm your friend	Well, I hate to brag, but my vocabulary verges on encyclopedic
Who does Bixby think I was in a past life?	Perhaps you were a bowling alley pinsetter	happy	I wonder what you think about it	I'll bet you were my best friend!
We'll talk tomorrow	Talk to you then!	stuff	What's on your mind?	Yeah, let's put a pin in it for now
Yadda, yadda, yoo	I try to be anything but boring. Just say "Beatbox for me"!	Sounds like you want to see you	If only I had a stenographer	I try to be anything but boring. Why dont you ask me to tell a joke?

6   Conclusion and Future Work

In this paper, we propose an effective model for response generation using single-turn conversations. Firstly, we created a large single-turn conversational dataset, and then built a transformer-based framework to model the short-turn conversations effectively. Empirical evaluation, in terms of both automatic and human-based metrics, shows encouraging performance. In qualitative and quantitative analyses of the generated responses, we observed the predicted responses to be highly relevant in terms of context, but also observed some in-corrections as discussed in our results and analysis section. Overall we observed that our proposed model attains improved performance when compared with the baseline results.

In the future, apart from improving the architectural designs and training methodologies, we look forward to evaluating our models on a much larger dataset of single-turn conversation.

Acknowledgement. The research reported in this paper is an outcome of the project "Dynamic Natural Language Response to Task-Oriented User Utterances", supported by Samsung Research India, Bangalore.

References

1. Bahdanau, D., Cho, K., Bengio, Y.: Neural machine translation by jointly learning to align and translate. arXiv preprint arXiv:1409.0473 (2014)
2. Boussaha, B.E.A., Hernandez, N., Jacquin, C., Morin, E.: Deep retrieval-based dialogue systems: a short review. arXiv preprint arXiv:1907.12878 (2019)
3. Du, J., Li, W., He, Y., Xu, R., Bing, L., Wang, X.: Variational autoregressive decoder for neural response generation. In: Proceedings of the 2018 Conference on Empirical Methods in Natural Language Processing, pp. 3154–3163 (2018)
4. Fleiss, J.L.: Measuring nominal scale agreement among many raters. Psychol. Bull. **76**(5), 378 (1971)
5. Hochreiter, S., Schmidhuber, J.: Long short-term memory. Neural Comput. **9**(8), 1735–1780 (1997)
6. Ji, Z., Lu, Z., Li, H.: An information retrieval approach to short text conversation. arXiv preprint arXiv:1408.6988 (2014)
7. Ke, P., Guan, J., Huang, M., Zhu, X.: Generating informative responses with controlled sentence function. In: Proceedings of the 56th Annual Meeting of the Association for Computational Linguistics (Volume 1: Long Papers), pp. 1499–1508 (2018)
8. Kingma, D.P., Ba, J.: Adam: a method for stochastic optimization. arXiv preprint arXiv:1412.6980 (2014)
9. Klein, G., Kim, Y., Deng, Y., Senellart, J., Rush, A.: OpenNMT: open-source toolkit for neural machine translation. In: Proceedings of ACL 2017, System Demonstrations, pp. 67–72. Association for Computational Linguistics, Vancouver, July 2017. https://www.aclweb.org/anthology/P17-4012
10. Li, J., Monroe, W., Shi, T., Jean, S., Ritter, A., Jurafsky, D.: Adversarial learning for neural dialogue generation. arXiv preprint arXiv:1701.06547 (2017)
11. Lin, C.Y.: ROUGE: a package for automatic evaluation of summaries. In: Text Summarization Branches Out, pp. 74–81. Association for Computational Linguistics, Barcelona, July 2004. https://www.aclweb.org/anthology/W04-1013
12. Litman, D., Singh, S., Kearns, M.S., Walker, M.: NJFun-a reinforcement learning spoken dialogue system. In: ANLP-NAACL 2000 Workshop: Conversational Systems (2000)
13. Misu, T., Georgila, K., Leuski, A., Traum, D.: Reinforcement learning of question-answering dialogue policies for virtual museum guides. In: Proceedings of the 13th Annual Meeting of the Special Interest Group on Discourse and Dialogue, pp. 84–93. Association for Computational Linguistics (2012)
14. Papineni, K., Roukos, S., Ward, T., Zhu, W.J.: BLEU: a method for automatic evaluation of machine translation. In: Proceedings of the 40th Annual Meeting on Association for Computational Linguistics, pp. 311–318. Association for Computational Linguistics (2002)
15. Pennington, J., Socher, R., Manning, C.D.: Glove: global vectors for word representation. In: Proceedings of the 2014 Conference on Empirical Methods in Natural Language Processing (EMNLP), pp. 1532–1543 (2014)
16. Ritter, A., Cherry, C., Dolan, W.B.: Data-driven response generation in social media. In: Proceedings of the Conference on Empirical Methods in Natural Language Processing, pp. 583–593. Association for Computational Linguistics (2011)
17. Schatzmann, J., Weilhammer, K., Stuttle, M., Young, S.: A survey of statistical user simulation techniques for reinforcement-learning of dialogue management strategies. Knowl. Eng. Rev. **21**(2), 97–126 (2006)

18. Serban, I.V., et al.: A hierarchical latent variable encoder-decoder model for generating dialogues. In: Thirty-First AAAI Conference on Artificial Intelligence (2017)
19. Shang, L., Lu, Z., Li, H.: Neural responding machine for short-text conversation. arXiv preprint arXiv:1503.02364 (2015)
20. Shen, X., Su, H., Niu, S., Demberg, V.: Improving variational encoder-decoders in dialogue generation. In: Thirty-Second AAAI Conference on Artificial Intelligence (2018)
21. Song, Y., Yan, R., Li, C.T., Nie, J.Y., Zhang, M., Zhao, D.: An ensemble of retrieval-based and generation-based human-computer conversation systems (2018)
22. Sordoni, A., et al.: A neural network approach to context-sensitive generation of conversational responses. arXiv preprint arXiv:1506.06714 (2015)
23. Sutskever, I., Vinyals, O., Le, Q.V.: Sequence to sequence learning with neural networks. In: Advances in Neural Information Processing Systems, pp. 3104–3112 (2014)
24. Vaswani, A., et al.: Attention is all you need. In: Advances in Neural Information Processing Systems, pp. 5998–6008 (2017)
25. Vinyals, O., Le, Q.: A neural conversational model. arXiv preprint arXiv:1506.05869 (2015)
26. Welch, B.L.: The generalization of student's' problem when several different population variances are involved. Biometrika **34**(1/2), 28–35 (1947)
27. Weston, J., Dinan, E., Miller, A.H.: Retrieve and refine: improved sequence generation models for dialogue. arXiv preprint arXiv:1808.04776 (2018)
28. Williams, J.D., Young, S.: Partially observable Markov decision processes for spoken dialog systems. Comput. Speech Lang. **21**(2), 393–422 (2007)
29. Xu, J., Ren, X., Lin, J., Sun, X.: Diversity-promoting GAN: a cross-entropy based generative adversarial network for diversified text generation. In: Proceedings of the 2018 Conference on Empirical Methods in Natural Language Processing, pp. 3940–3949 (2018)
30. Yan, R., Song, Y., Wu, H.: Learning to respond with deep neural networks for retrieval-based human-computer conversation system. In: Proceedings of the 39th International ACM SIGIR Conference on Research and Development in Information Retrieval, pp. 55–64 (2016)
31. Yang, L., et al.: A hybrid retrieval-generation neural conversation model. In: Proceedings of the 28th ACM International Conference on Information and Knowledge Management, pp. 1341–1350 (2019)
32. Zhao, T., Lee, K., Eskenazi, M.: Unsupervised discrete sentence representation learning for interpretable neural dialog generation. arXiv preprint arXiv:1804.08069 (2018)
33. Zhao, T., Zhao, R., Eskenazi, M.: Learning discourse-level diversity for neural dialog models using conditional variational autoencoders. arXiv preprint arXiv:1703.10960 (2017)
34. Zhou, L., Gao, J., Li, D., Shum, H.Y.: The design and implementation of Xiaoice, an empathetic social chatbot. Comput. Linguist. (Just Accepted) 1–62 (2018)

A Cooking Knowledge Graph
and Benchmark for Question Answering
Evaluation in Lifelong Learning Scenarios

Mathilde Veron[1,3]($\boxtimes$), Anselmo Peñas[2], Guillermo Echegoyen[2],
Somnath Banerjee[1], Sahar Ghannay[1], and Sophie Rosset[1]

[1] LIMSI, CNRS, Université Paris-Saclay, Orsay, France
{mathilde.veron,somnath.banerjee,sahar.ghannay,sophie.rosset}@limsi.fr
[2] UNED NLP & IR Group, Madrid, Spain
{anselmo,gblanco}@lsi.uned.es
[3] LNE, Trappes, France

Abstract. In a long term exploitation environment, a Question Answering (QA) system should maintain or even improve its performance over time, trying to overcome the lacks made evident through the interactions with users. We claim that, in order to make progress in the QA over Knowledge Bases (KBs) research field, we must deal with two problems at the same time: the translation of Natural Language (NL) questions into formal queries, and the detection of missing knowledge that impact the way a question is answered. The research on these two challenges has not been addressed jointly until now, what motivates the main goals of this work: (i) the definition of the problem and (ii) the development of a methodology to create the evaluation resources needed to address this challenge.

Keywords: Question Answering · Lifelong Learning · Evaluation resources

1 Introduction

Since every human domain is dynamic and evolves over time, in the mid-long term, any Knowledge Base (KB) will become incomplete or, at least, it won't we able to satisfy user demands of information. In a long term exploitation environment, QA systems must deal with the challenge of maintaining their performance over time and try to overcome the lacks made evident through the interactions with the users. In other words, we need to provide QA systems with Lifelong Learning mechanisms. The first step is the detection of such situations. QA systems must distinguish the reason why the system cannot answer a question: either the problem is in the translation of the Natural Language (NL) question into a formal query, or the problem is a lack of knowledge that prevent the system from giving an answer. If the reason is the latter, the system must trigger a learning process to overcome this limitation and update its previous knowledge.

© Springer Nature Switzerland AG 2020
E. Métais et al. (Eds.): NLDB 2020, LNCS 12089, pp. 94–101, 2020.
https://doi.org/10.1007/978-3-030-51310-8_9

Unfortunately, most of the current research in QA over KBs works with datasets of questions that can always be answered by the KB [4, 7]. That is to say, the research focus is on the problem of how to translate a NL question into a formal query. However, working under the assumption that there exists an answer to the question according to the KB leads researchers to a set of solutions that will not work in a real scenario.

We claim that, in order to make progress in the QA research field, we must deal with both problems at the same time: the translation of NL into formal queries, and the detection of lacks of knowledge that impact the way questions are answered. To the best of our knowledge, the effort done in this direction has not been significant. Therefore, the main goals of this work are (i) the definition of the problem and (ii) the development of a methodology to create the evaluation resources needed to address this challenge.

For a better understanding of the problem, we chose the context of a real user demand, constructing an imperfect (by definition) Knowledge Graph (KG), and asking real users to pose questions that the QA system has to answer. Then, a set of annotators have tried to translate the real NL questions into formal queries, identifying when the questions can be translated and when they cannot, annotating the reasons why. Examples of annotations can be found in Fig. 1.

The form of the Knowledge Base is a Graph (i.e. RDF triples style) for several reasons. First, the updating of the KG with new classes (or types), property names (or relations), instances (or objects), etc. is straightforward and does not affect the previous version. It only requires the addition of new triples. Secondly, working with a graph makes the use of different formalisms and different retrieval engines possible, from using SPARQL over database managers (like Virtuoso) to the use of simple Prolog. That is, in a Lifelong scenario where the systems must evolve over time and continuously update their knowledge, KGs seem to be the most appropriate formalism.

In the following sections, we describe the whole process in detail, together with our learnings and conclusions. The contributions of this work are:

- The definition of the problem;
- A methodology for studying it and creating the evaluation resources;
- A publicly available Knowledge Graph (in cooking domain)[1];
- A first version of a set of answerable and unanswerable questions over this KG, for benchmarking system self-diagnostic about the reasons why the question cannot be answered by the KG[2].

2   Previous Work

2.1   Question Answering with Unanswerable Questions

We are interested in QA systems with the ability to recognize unanswerable questions. This problem has been addressed lately under the free text assumption

---

[1] http://nlp.uned.es/lihlith-project/cook/.
[2] https://perso.limsi.fr/rosset/resources/cooking_LL_QA.zip.

and only partially. To the best of our knowledge, it has never been addressed in QA over KBs.

Under the free text paradigm, systems must answer questions whose answer can be found in a given text. Current research is more focused on answer extraction than in the complete QA architecture that includes the recovering or ranking of candidate paragraphs. (as opposed to KG-based QA, where the whole process must be carried out). SQuAD [12], TriviaQA [5] and MS Marco [11] are among the most popular collections for QA over free text featuring empty answers. They are all created following one or various crowdsourcing annotation processes. Current systems competing with these datasets are usually made out of ensembles of pre-trained language models like ALBERT [6] and XLNet [13].

However, when doing QA over KBs, a more sophisticated process is required. In general, all systems proceed with a multi-step process, comprising a combination of complex steps: Question Analysis, Named Entity Recognition and Linking, Disambiguation and Parsing. There are some surveys detailing these systems, we refer the reader to them [2], and [4]. Over the last years, neural systems have tremendously increased in capability, however in the specific domain of QA over KBs, it has been argued that deep learning does not contribute that much [10]. In particular, these systems can, for now, only answer simple questions [1,3,8]. Furthermore, to solve QA over KBs, the majority of approaches assume that the question can be answered by the KG because the most popular collections like QALD [7] or LC-QUAD [4] do not contain empty answers. Therefore, answering a question is a kind of graph matching against the KG.

In summary, a production system for QA over KBs requires the ability to recognize unanswerable questions, and therefore, we identify the need to correctly define the problem of QA over KBs, but also to develop the necessary resources to train and evaluate systems to solve this problem.

2.2 Lifelong Learning and Question Answering

This problem has already captured the attention of some researchers such as Mazumder and his colleagues [9] although in that work, the problem is only addressed partially. In particular, queries to the system are just single triples, reducing to the trivial case the problem of deciding whether the answer to a question is in the KG or not. It simplifies also the problem of detecting the pieces of knowledge that have to be added to the KG. The option taken for enriching the KG is to ask the user for some missing pieces of knowledge and try to find strategies to infer some others. However, in the general scenario of complex NL QA over KGs these decisions are not trivial. If a system does not get an answer to a question, it could be due to several factors, including some errors in the process of NL interpretation (e.g. Entity Linking).

3   Cooking Knowledge Graph Construction

The KG is a set of triples `<arg1, property-name, arg2>`, where the first argument must be always an entity and the second one can be both an entity or a literal (number or string). Entities (also mentioned as resources or objects) can refer to type names (or classes, e.g. `cookbook:ingredients`), instances (e.g. `cookbook:milk`), or category names (e.g. `category:pancake_recipes`). Categories refer to groups of recipes according to some criteria given by the original wiki. Thus, a recipe can belong to several categories and this will be encoded through the corresponding triples with the property name `recipeCategory`. Recipe categories use the prefix `category:` instead of `cookbook:` used for the rest of entities. The property names (or relations) used here follow the Recipe schema[3] when it has been possible. The complete set of properties is shown in Table 1.

The KG has been derived from the English wikibook (enwikibooks-20190701-pages-articles.xml) related to cooking (name space 102, Cookbook). We have processed both the cookbook pages one by one, and the category links file (enwikibooks-20190701-categorylinks.sql).

The processing of the category links file produced 480 triples among categories, 6935 triples that link recipes to recipe categories, and 4479 type relationships.

With respect to the processing of the Cookbook enwikibook pages, the method identify different sections in recipe pages. From ingredients section it generates *recipeIngredient* and *recipeFoodstuff* relations. From instructions section it produces a triple that relates the recipe with the list of steps (*recipeInstructions* relationship). Each element in the list corresponds to the original text describing the step. From the section of notes and variations it produces the triple for the *recipeNotes* between the recipe object and the corresponding text. Finally, we process the recipe *summary* according to the corresponding template instructions. This processing produces the triples for *recipeCategory*, *recipeYield* (servings), *totalTime* and *difficulty* (numeric value from 1 to 5).

Table 1. Property names in the Cooking KG

	Freq.	Property name	Example
Generalprops	8263	label	baguette **label** "french bread"
	5214	url	adobo **url** en.wikibooks.org/wiki/Cookbook:Adobo
	5214	name	frosting_and_icing_recipes **name** "Frosting"
	5156	type	baking_soda **type** cookbook:leavening_agents
Recipeproperties	21077	recipeIngredient	chocolate_mousse **recipeIngredient** "200 g bitter..."
	15616	recipeCategory	chocolate_mousse **recipeCategory** category:dessert_recipes
	12343	recipeFoodstuff	chocolate_mousse **recipeFoodstuff** cookbook:chocolate
	2419	recipeInstructions	chocolate_mousse **recipeInstructions** ["Melt chocolate..."]
	849	difficulty	chocolate_mousse **difficulty** 2
	844	totalTime	chocolate_mousse **totalTime** "30 min"
	805	recipeYield	chocolate_mousse **recipeYield** 4
	458	recipeNotes	chocolate_mousse **recipeNotes** "* This recipe is not the..."

---

[3] https://schema.org/Recipe.

4 Methodology for Dataset Creation

This section describes the creation process of the developed dataset. The objective of this dataset is to help the research community to study the following research issues: (i) the translation of NL into formal queries, (ii) the detection of unanswerable questions and (iii) the identification of elements missing in the KG which impact the way questions are answered. We first describe how we collected the user's queries in NL and then how we annotated them.

4.1 Collection of Queries in Natural Language

We asked collaborators from our institutions through a web form to write at least 5 queries in natural language in English. The participants were no native English speakers but Spanish and French people. We received 30 responses in 3 days, resulting in 169 queries. The participants needed around 5 min to read the guidelines and write at least 5 queries. They were asked to pose any question about the cooking domain. Thus we provided them a non exhaustive list of items they could ask about along with some examples. The query could be posed in any of these four possible ways: interrogative (e.g., "Which herbs go well with mushrooms?"), imperative (e.g., "Give me a soup recipe for tonight"), informative ("I'm looking for the name of the utensil that is used to beat the egg whites"), or propositional (yes/no question e.g. "Is tomato a fruit?") and have to fit in only one sentence.

After collecting the queries in NL, we filtered them by assessing their usability regarding our task[4]. It allowed us to directly discard the queries that couldn't be answered either with the current KG or by adding new elements to the KG. Each question has been annotated as usable or not by two different persons. After filtering, 124 queries were identified as usable (around 73%).

4.2 Annotations

The annotations were made using a unique table for each annotator as presented in Fig. 1. Using the provided guidelines (see footnote 4) the annotators had to write the associated Prolog query and to give the result of it, or if it was not possible, to give the elements missing in the KG that made the question unanswerable.

We decided to remove from the final dataset all the annotated user's queries where the annotator wrote that more than one element was missing in the KG. The first reason is that in this case, there can be multiple ways to represent the missing knowledge in the KG and to annotate the reasons why the query cannot be answered. In other words, the annotation would be subjective and the dataset would suffer from inconsistencies. Secondly, regarding machine learning algorithms, the tasks of identifying the elements missing will be much more

---

[4] The guidelines can be found here https://perso.limsi.fr/rosset/resources/cooki ng_LL_QA.zip.

ID	User's query in NL	Prolog query	Result	Reasons why the query cannot be answered	
				type of the missing element	missing element
1	When is the apple's season?	r(cookbook:apple, type, Season_ref), r(Season_ref, type, cookbook:ingredients_by_seasonality).	Season_ref = cookbook:autumn_ingredients; Season_ref = cookbook:summer_ingredients	entity ☐	
				property name ☐	
				type name ☐	
				triple ☐	
2	Can I use goat milk instead of cow milk?	r(cookbook:milk, replacement, cookbook:goat_milk).	none	entity ☑	cookbook:goat_milk
				property name ☑	ingredientReplacement
				type name ☐	
				triple ☐	
3	How long it will take to make crepes?	r(cookbook:crepes, totalTime, Time).	none	entity ☐	
				property name ☐	
				type name ☐	
				triple ☑	<cookbook:crepes, totalTime, "30 min">

Fig. 1. Examples of annotated user's queries. This annotated queries are not part of the dataset.

complex if it has to be able to detected when multiple elements are missing for one user's query, as it corresponds to a multi-labelling task. However, we consider that the annotated user's queries that were removed from the dataset, will be useful anyway, either for detecting when a user's query cannot be answered, or in the future when a system will be mature enough.

Five Annotators, including PhD students and researchers from our institutions, participated in the annotation process. Each annotator had to know at least about the basis of Prolog. We expected to remove around 10% of the annotated data when multiple elements were missing, so we decided to annotate 110 user's queries to get at the end 100 annotated queries in the final dataset. To make it possible, each annotator had 22 user's queries to annotate. The annotation process was quite long, since the annotators had to check for each element if they exist in the KG and under which name. Depending on the knowledge on Prolog and on the cooking KG, the annotators needed from 5 min to 20 min to annotate one user's question. This time take into account the corrections needed. At the end one person was responsible of reviewing all the annotations and to correct them in order to have consistent data.

4.3   Description of the Dataset

The original dataset is provided in the form of an Excel document. It contains all the annotations as presented in Fig. 1 with the comments of annotators. The characteristics of the original dataset are presented in Table 2. The final dataset is provided in the form of a json file[5]. The questions where more than one element was missing have been removed from this dataset. When a question contained typos, we replaced the question with the corrected one in the final dataset. The characteristics of the final dataset are presented in Table 3.

---

[5] https://perso.limsi.fr/rosset/resources/cooking_LL_QA.json.

Table 2. Original dataset. Proportions of questions among some categories.

#questions	110
Answerable	40%
One element missing	38%
Multiple element missing	22%

Table 3. Final dataset. Proportions of questions among some categories.

#questions	86
Typo mistakes	09%
One element missing	49%
Type of element missing	
Entity	43%
Type name	02%
Property name	24%
Triple	31%

5 Lessons Learned Through the Creation Process

We have observed that in the majority of cases, the questions that cannot be answered initially can become answerable after populating the knowledge graph with new entities, property names or triples. So the system can evolve over time. However, there is one situation where the system can't evolve easily: when it affects the structure of the data. For example, in the current version of the KG, the information related to a recipe ingredient is just a triple, but several questions require it to be a tuple with additional information beyond the food-stuff (quantity or amount, possible replacement, textual description, etc.). This problem cannot be overcome by adding some triples, but altering the current structure of the recipe ingredients nodes.

After completing the annotation process we re-evaluate the questions that we annotated as not usable regarding our task. We came to the point that we actually filtered too many questions and determined that only 10% of the questions were not usable (against 27% previously). We also figured out that we underestimated the proportion of questions with more that one element missing (22% against 10% estimated). That is why the final dataset actually contains 86 annotated questions instead of 100.

6 Conclusion and Future Work

In a real exploitation environment, usual QA systems would provide an incorrect answer when the question refers to element that are missing in the KB. Thus we state that it is fundamental for lifelong learning QA systems to be able to handle jointly the two following problems: the translation of Natural Language (NL) questions into formal queries, and the detection and identification of missing knowledge that impact the way questions are answered. As no evaluation resources are yet available to address these problems, we presented in this paper a methodology for the creation of these resources. Moreover we publicly share the resulting resources, namely (i) A cooking KG and (ii) the first version of a dataset containing a set of questions over the KG with the element missing in the KB if an answer cannot be found.

For future work we plan to collect and annotate more questions by taking advantage of lessons learned though the creation of the first version of the dataset.

Acknowledgments. This work has been supported by ERA-Net CHIST-ERA LIH-LITH Project funded by ANR (France) project ANR-17-CHR2-0001-03, and AEI (Spain) projects PCIN-2017-085/AEI and RTI2018-096846-B-C21 (MCIU/AEI/FEDER, UE).

References

1. Bordes, A., Usunier, N., Chopra, S., Weston, J.: Large-scale simple question answering with memory networks. CoRR, June 2015. http://arxiv.org/abs/1506.02075
2. Diefenbach, D., Lopez, V., Singh, K., Maret, P.: Core techniques of question answering systems over knowledge bases: a survey. Knowl. Inf. Syst. **55**(3), 529–569 (2018). https://doi.org/10.1007/s10115-017-1100-y
3. He, X., Golub, D.: Character-level question answering with attention. In: EMNLP 2016, pp. 1598–1607. Association for Computational Linguistics, Stroudsburg (2016). http://aclweb.org/anthology/D16-1166
4. Höffner, K., Walter, S., Marx, E., Usbeck, R., Lehmann, J., Ngonga Ngomo, A.C.: Survey on challenges of question answering in the semantic web. Semant. Web **8**(6), 895–920 (2017)
5. Joshi, M., Choi, E., Weld, D.S., Zettlemoyer, L.: TriviaQA: a large scale distantly supervised challenge dataset for reading comprehension. CoRR, May 2017. http://arxiv.org/abs/1705.03551
6. Lan, Z., Chen, M., Goodman, S., Gimpel, K., Sharma, P., Soricut, R.: ALBERT: a lite BERT for self-supervised learning of language representations. CoRR, September 2019. http://arxiv.org/abs/1909.11942
7. Lopez, V., Unger, C., Cimiano, P., Motta, E.: Evaluating question answering over linked data. Web Semant. Sci. Serv. Agents WWW **21**, 3–13 (2013)
8. Lukovnikov, D., Fischer, A., Lehmann, J., Auer, S.: Neural network-based question answering over knowledge graphs on word and character level. In: WWW 2017, pp. 1211–1220. ACM Press, New York (2017). https://dl.acm.org/doi/10.1145/3038912.3052675
9. Mazumder, S., Liu, B., Wang, S., Ma, N.: Lifelong and interactive learning of factual knowledge in dialogues. In: SIGDIAL 2019, pp. 21–31. ACL, Stockholm, September 2019. https://www.aclweb.org/anthology/W19-5903
10. Mohammed, S., Shi, P., Lin, J.: Strong baselines for simple question answering over knowledge graphs with and without neural networks. CoRR, December 2017. http://arxiv.org/abs/1712.01969
11. Nguyen, T., et al.: MS MARCO: a human generated machine reading comprehension dataset. In: CEUR Workshop Proceedings, vol. 1773, November 2016. http://arxiv.org/abs/1611.09268
12. Rajpurkar, P., Jia, R., Liang, P.: Know what you don't know: unanswerable questions for SQuAD. CoRR, June 2018. http://arxiv.org/abs/1806.03822
13. Yang, Z., Dai, Z., Yang, Y., Carbonell, J., Salakhutdinov, R., Le, Q.V.: XLNet: generalized autoregressive pretraining for language understanding. CoRR, June 2019. http://arxiv.org/abs/1906.08237

Classification

Enhancement of Short Text Clustering
by Iterative Classification

Md Rashadul Hasan Rakib$^{(\boxtimes)}$, Norbert Zeh, Magdalena Jankowska,
and Evangelos Milios

Dalhousie University, Halifax, NS, Canada
{rakib,nzeh,jankowsk,eem}@cs.dal.ca

Abstract. Short text clustering is a challenging task due to the lack of
signal contained in short texts. In this work, we propose iterative classification as a method to boost the clustering quality of short texts. The
idea is to repeatedly reassign (classify) outliers to clusters until the cluster assignment stabilizes. The classifier used in each iteration is trained
using the current set of cluster labels of the non-outliers; the input of the
first iteration is the output of an arbitrary clustering algorithm. Thus,
our method does not require any human-annotated labels for training.
Our experimental results show that the proposed clustering enhancement
method not only improves the clustering quality of different baseline clustering methods (e.g., k-means, k-means--, and hierarchical clustering)
but also outperforms the state-of-the-art short text clustering methods
on several short text datasets by a statistically significant margin.

Keywords: Short text clustering · Outlier removal · Iterative
classification

1 Introduction

Due to technological advances, short texts are generated at large volumes from
different sources, such as micro-blogging, question answering, and social news
aggregation websites. Organizing these texts is an important step towards discovering trends (e.g., political, economic) in conversations and in other data mining tasks, such as data summarization, frequent pattern analysis, and searching
for and filtering information. Clustering the texts into groups of similar texts is
the foundation for many of these organization strategies [1].

The lack of signal contained in short texts makes grouping of short texts based
on shared topics difficult, leading to poor cohesion of texts assigned to the same
cluster. The objective of our research is to improve the cohesion of clusters in a
cluster partition produced by an arbitrary baseline clustering method. To achieve
this, we remove outliers from each cluster and reassign them to clusters with
which they have greater similarity. We demonstrate that this approach produces
more accurate cluster partitions than computationally more costly state-of-the-
art short text clustering methods based on neural networks [2,3].

© Springer Nature Switzerland AG 2020
E. Métais et al. (Eds.): NLDB 2020, LNCS 12089, pp. 105–117, 2020.
https://doi.org/10.1007/978-3-030-51310-8_10

The k-means algorithm can be viewed as an iterative classification algorithm. Starting with an initial (random) cluster partition, each iteration computes the centers of all clusters and uses these cluster centers as a classifier to reassign every input point to a new cluster. k-means-- [5] is a variation of k-means that achieves improved clustering performance by removing outliers before computing cluster centers, that is, before "training the classifier". The classification step then assigns *all* points to their closest cluster centers, including the outliers ignored when computing cluster centers. Our method is inspired by this approach but uses a more sophisticated classifier than computing cluster centers and assigning every point to the closest cluster center. Specifically, our method follows the approach of [6] to train a classifier based on the cluster labels of the non-outliers. Iterative classification then uses the trained classifier to reassign outliers to clusters. Just as with k-means, the resulting set of clusters is the input for the next iteration or, if this is the last iteration, the final set of clusters returned by the algorithm.

Iterative classification can be applied to any set of initial clusters and is thus independent of the method used to obtain these clusters. The quality of the final set of clusters, however, does depend on the method used to compute the initial clusters. We use k-means [7], k-means-- [5] and hierarchical clustering [7] using dense and sparse similarity matrices to compute the initial clusters. k-means and k-means-- clustering are applied to the vector representations of the texts. For hierarchical clustering, we use the text similarity matrix (dense or sparse). The dense similarity matrix stores the similarity value for each text pair, whereas the sparse similarity matrix keeps a certain number of similarity values and discards the remaining ones (sets them to 0) [8].

Matrix sparsification can be performed using different criteria for choosing the values to discard. We consider two approaches here, one based on k-nearest neighbors [7] and the other based on the similarity distribution [9]. The k-nearest neighbor method keeps the k largest entries in each row. In the similarity distribution-based method, the number of similarities to keep in each row is not fixed. Instead, it is based on the distribution of the similarity values in each row, as characterized by he mean and standard deviation of these values. These sparsification methods are discussed in detail in Sect. 4.

The two main contributions of this work are as follows:

- We introduce iterative classification as a method that improves the clustering quality of different baseline clustering methods on various short text datasets and does not require human-annotated data to train the classification model. Our implementation of iterative classification and the datasets used in our experiments are publicly available.[1]
- The combination of hierarchical clustering (using a sparse similarity matrix based on similarity distribution [9]) and iterative classification performs better than other clustering methods combined with iterative classification. This combination outperforms the state-of-the-art short text clustering methods by a statistically significant margin.

---

[1] https://github.com/rashadulrakib/short-text-clustering-enhancement.

2   Related Work

2.1   Short Text Clustering

A major challenge in short text clustering is the sparseness of the vector representations of these texts resulting from the small number of words in each text. Several clustering methods have been proposed in the literature to address this challenge, including methods based on text augmentation [10,11], neural networks [2,3], topic modeling [12], and Dirichlet mixture model [4].

A recent method based on text augmentation [11] uses topic diffusion to augment each short text by finding words not appearing in the text that are related to its content. To find related words, this method determines possible topics for each text using the existing words. Then new words are added to each text; these new words are closely related to the text's topics based on the posterior probabilities of the new words given the words in the text. An earlier text augmentation method [10] finds Wikipedia articles using the short text as query string and uses the articles' titles as features.

A short text clustering method based on word embedding and a convolutional neural network called STC2-LE was proposed in [2]. It uses a convolutional neural network to learn a text representation on which clustering is performed. Another short text clustering method based on weighted word embedding and autoencoder was proposed in [3]. For each text, it calculates the average of the weighted embeddings [13] of its words. The weight of a word is calculated based on its inverse frequency in the corpus [3] which is then multiplied with its embedding to obtain weighted word embedding. After that, the embeddings of the texts are feed into an autoencoder to obtain the low dimensional representation of the texts on which clustering is performed.

Biterm topic modeling (BTM) [12] is a topic modeling approach for short texts that learns topics from word co-occurrence patterns (i.e., biterms). Given a topic distribution produced by BTM for each text, clustering is performed by assigning a text to its most probable topic.

A short text clustering method based on a Dirichlet process multinomial mixture model called GSDPMM was proposed in [4]. GSDPMM does not partition the input into a pre-specified number of clusters. It processes the texts one by one and assigns each text to a new cluster or to one of the existing clusters based on two factors: a) a preference for a cluster with more texts and, b) a preference for a cluster whose texts share more words with the current text.

2.2   Similarity Matrix Sparsification

Sparsification of the text similarity matrix keeps the association between a text and its most similar (nearest) texts while breaking associations with less similar ones by setting the corresponding similarity scores to 0 [8]. Several similarity matrix sparsification methods have been discussed in the literature, including ones based on a global threshold [7], nearest neighbors [7], and center vectors [8].

Similarity matrix sparsification based on global threshold is the simplest sparsification method. It removes all similarity values that are below a given threshold [7]. The problem with this method is that some real clusters may be destroyed or merged because different clusters may have different similarity levels between the texts they contain.

Nearest neighbors' based methods for similarity matrix sparsification include k-nearest neighbor [7] and shared nearest neighbor [14]. k-nearest neighbor sparsification keeps only the k highest similarity scores for each text; the shared-nearest neighbor approach adds a condition that texts retaining similarity values with a particular text should share a prescribed number of neighbors.

A similarity matrix sparsification method based on the center vector was proposed in [8]. Texts are represented by $tf\text{-}idf$ (term frequency-inverse document frequency) vectors and a center vector is computed by averaging these vectors. The sparsification of the similarity matrix is performed by removing similarities between all pairs of texts that are not more similar to each other than the maximum similarities of these two texts to the center vector.

3   Enhancement of Clustering by Iterative Classification

Given a collection of short texts and a partition of these texts into clusters, iterative classification modifies the given cluster partition by detecting outliers in each cluster and changing the clusters to which they are assigned. This is repeated several times, hence the term iterative in the method's name. In each iteration, we generate training and test sets containing non-outliers and outliers respectively. Then we train a classification algorithm using the training set and classify the test set using the trained model. This iterative process repeats until the stopping criterion discussed in Sect. 3.1 is satisfied. The details are shown in Algorithm 1 and are described next.

In each iteration, we choose a number P that roughly corresponds to the fraction of texts selected for the training set. P is chosen uniformly at random from an interval $[P_1, P_2]$ determined in Sect. 6.2. To generate the training set, we remove outliers from each of the K clusters defined by the current cluster labels L. To remove outliers, we use an outlier detection algorithm called Isolation Forest, which is applied to the $tf\text{-}idf$ vector representations of the texts. The algorithm isolates the texts that exist in the low density region of the $tf\text{-}idf$ feature space. If after removing outliers, a cluster contains more than $\frac{n}{K} \times P$ texts, then we remove texts from that cluster uniformly at random to reduce the number of texts in the cluster to $\frac{n}{K} \times P$. The reason of removing texts from each cluster is that we want each cluster to consist of roughly the same number of texts so as to reduce the bias of the classification algorithm. We add the removed texts to the test set and add the other texts to the training set. We train a classifier (Multinomial Logistic Regression) using the non-outliers and their cluster labels. Then we classify the texts in the test set using the trained classifier. This defines a new set of cluster labels of the texts in the test set and thus produces an updated cluster partition.

Algorithm 1. Enhancement of Clustering by Iterative Classification

---

Require: D = set of n texts, L = initial cluster labels of the texts in D, K = number of clusters

Ensure: Enhanced cluster labels of the texts

1: $maxIteration = 50$
2: $avgTextsPerCluster = n/K$
3: **for** $i = 1$ to $maxIteration$ **do**
4:     Choose a parameter P uniformly at random from the interval $[P_1, P_2]$. (P_1 and P_2 are parameters determined in Section 6.2. P bounds the fraction of texts kept per cluster.)
5:     Remove outliers from each of the K clusters defined by L using an outlier detection algorithm.
6:     If a cluster contains more than $avgTextsPerCluster \times P$ texts, remove texts from that cluster uniformly at random so that exactly $avgTextsPerCluster \times P$ texts remain in the cluster.
7:     $testSet$ = texts removed in Steps 5 and 6
        $trainingSet$ = all the texts not in $testSet$
8:     Train a classifier using the $trainingSet$ and classify the texts in $testSet$. This assigns a new cluster label $L(t)$ to each text $t \in testSet$.
9:     Stop iterative classification if the per cluster text distribution becomes stable (as described in Section 3.1).
10: **end for**
11: **return** L

3.1 Stopping Criterion for Iterative Classification

Iterative classification stops when it reaches the maximum number of iterations (i.e., 50) or the sizes of the clusters become stable. Let $C_1, ..., C_k$ and $C'_1, ..., C'_k$ be the clusters before and after an iteration, respectively. We consider the cluster sizes to be stable if

$$\frac{1}{k} \sum_{i=1}^{k} ||C'_i| - |C_i|| \leq 0.05 \frac{n}{k}$$

For example, consider the problem of partitioning 100 texts into two clusters. Then the average cluster size is 50. If one iteration assigns 48 texts to the first cluster and 52 texts to the second cluster and the next iteration assigns 49 and 51 texts to these clusters, respectively, then the average absolute change of the cluster size is $\frac{1}{2}(|48-49|+|52-51|) = 1$. Since this is less than 5% of the average cluster size (50), we consider the cluster sizes to have stabilized.

4 Similarity Matrix Sparsification

4.1 k-Nearest Neighbor Sparsification

The k-nearest neighbor (k-NN) sparsification method [7] uses the number of nearest neighbors k as a parameter. A square $n \times n$ symmetric similarity matrix $S = (s_{ij})$ is the input for k-NN sparsification method. The method criterion is to retain, for each text, exactly the k highest similarities with this text outside of the diagonal. For the text t_i, we retain a similarity (s_{ij}) between t_i and other text t_j, if s_{ij} is within the k highest similarities of t_i. However, the similarity s_{ji} between a text t_j and other text t_i may not be retained because s_{ji} may not be within the k highest similarities of t_j. Hence after applying this criterion, the resulting sparsified matrix can be a non-symmetric matrix. Therefore we symmetrize the sparsified similarity matrix by retaining both s_{ij} and s_{ji}, if any of the similarities among s_{ij} and s_{ji} is retained in the sparsified similarity matrix.

4.2   Similarity Distribution Based Sparsification

The similarity distribution based sparsification method was proposed in our previous work [9]. It sparsifies a similarity matrix based on the distribution of the similarity scores in the matrix. The input of this sparsification method is a symmetric similarity matrix for a set of n texts. The goal is to increase the signal-to-noise ratio in the matrix by keeping only the most significant similarity scores and setting less significant similarity scores to 0. Our criterion for setting entries to 0 may result in a non-symmetric matrix. Such a matrix requires symmetrization. We follow the *sparsification with exclusion* approach [7] which sets an item s_{ij} to zero only if the sparsification criterion retains neither s_{ij} nor s_{ji}.

In contrast to the k-nearest neighbor method, the number of similarities to keep for each text is not fixed. Instead, it is based on the distribution of the similarity values between each text and all other texts. For each text t_i, we calculate the mean μ_i and standard deviation σ_i of similarities between t_i and all other texts. Then, we sparsify similarities between t_i and other texts based on these statistics. In particular, we define the retaining criterion as follows: a similarity s_{ij} is to be retained if and only if

$$s_{ij} > \mu_i + \alpha\sigma_i, \tag{1}$$

for some global factor α. The factor α is chosen so that after applying the criterion and symmetrization of the matrix, the average number of non-zero elements outside of the diagonal per row is equal to $l = \frac{n}{K} - 1$. Note that if each cluster has exactly $\frac{n}{K}$ elements and we return exactly the similarity scores between elements in the same cluster, then l is the number of non-zero non-diagonal entries in each row.

To choose the retained similarity values efficiently, we use an auxiliary value $a_{ij} = \frac{s_{ij} - \mu_i}{\sigma_i}$ for each similarity value s_{ij}. This is s_{ij}'s deviation from the mean of row i normalized by the standard deviation of row i. The criterion of Eq. 1 can be restated as: a similarity s_{ij} is to be retained if and only if $a_{ij} > \alpha$. Since we follow the *sparsification with exclusion* approach for symmetrization, we keep s_{ij} in the final symmetric matrix if the retaining criterion is fulfilled for s_{ij} or for s_{ji}. Thus, if the average number of non-zero non-diagonal entries per row is to be l, we need to return $N = \lfloor \frac{n \times l}{2} \rfloor$ entries above the main diagonal, which is achieved by choosing α to be the Nth largest value in $\{\max(a_{ij}, a_{ji})|1 \leq i < j \leq n\}$.

5 Methods for Clustering of Short Texts

5.1 k-Means and k-Means--

k-means clustering [1] is used to cluster a collection of short texts into k clusters. First, k-means clustering initializes k centers, then it assigns each text to its closest center. Then the algorithm runs for a number of iterations. In each iteration, it recomputes the cluster centers using the texts assigned to each cluster and reassigns the texts to their closest centers. This iterative process continues until the algorithm reaches the maximum number of iterations or the cluster assignments becomes stable between two successive iterations.

k-means-- [5] is a variation of k-means clustering, in which outliers are removed in each iteration of the k-means clustering before recomputing the cluster centers. To detect outliers, short texts are ranked in decreasing order using their distances to their nearest cluster centers and the d (parameter for defining the total number of outliers) most distant texts are considered as outliers and removed from the clusters so that the cluster centers will become less sensitive to outliers. This has been confirmed to improve the clustering performance.

5.2 Hierarchical Clustering Using Dense or Sparse Similarity Matrix

Hierarchical agglomerative clustering uses a symmetric matrix storing pairwise similarities between documents. Such a matrix is dense if it stores a similarity between every pair of documents. The clustering method starts with each document in its own clusters and repeatedly merges pairs of *most similar* clusters until only k (the desired numbers of clusters) clusters remain.

A dense similarity matrix provides the most detailed information about pairwise text similarities but the lowest similarity scores can be considered noise in the sense that they suggest (tenuous) connections between texts that are almost guaranteed to belong to different clusters. Setting these similarities to 0 increases the separation between clusters and produces better clustering results. We consider two sparsification methods in our experiments: k-nearest neighbor and similarity distribution based, which are discussed in Sects. 4.1 and 4.2 respectively. We form clusters based on the two resulting sparse similarity matrices using the same hierarchical clustering method as discussed above.

6 Experiments

6.1 Datasets

We used five different datasets of short texts in our experiments. The basic properties of these datasets are shown in Table 1. **SearchSnippet** is a dataset of search results from Google's search engine, containing 12340 snippets distributed into 8 groups [15]. **SearchSnippet-test** is a subset of the SearchSnippet dataset consisting of 2280 search snippets distributed into 8 groups. **AgNews** is a subset of a dataset of news titles [16]. It consists of 8000 texts in 4 topic categories (for each category, we randomly selected 2000 texts). **StackOverflow** is a subset of the challenge data published on Kaggle[2], where 20000 question titles from 20 groups were randomly selected [2]. **BioMedical** is a subset of the challenge data published on the BioASQ's website[3], where 20000 paper titles from 20 groups were randomly selected [2].

Table 1. Summary of the short text datasets

Dataset	#Clusters	#Texts	Average #words/text
SearchSnippet	8	12340	17.03
SearchSnippet-test	8	2280	17.18
AgNews	4	8000	22.61
StackOverflow	20	20000	8.23
BioMedical	20	20000	12.88

6.2 Experimental Setup

Experimental Setup for Iterative Classification. We preprocessed the texts by removing stop words and converting them to lowercase. Then we transformed each text into the *tf-idf* vector representation for a given text collection.

Each iteration of the iterative classification algorithm picks some percentage P of each cluster as the training set and reassigns the remaining texts to clusters based on a classifier trained using this training set; P is chosen uniformly at the random from some interval $[P_1, P_2]$. To justify this approach and to determine optimal choices for P_1 and P_2, we ran preliminary experiments using a representative dataset (SearchSnippet-test). Specifically, we considered choosing P uniformly at random from the interval $[P_1, P_2]$ or choosing a fixed percentage P in every iteration. For the former method, we determined the optimal combination of P_1 and P_2 ($P_1 = 0.5$ and $P_2 = 0.95$). For the later, we determined the optimal choice of P ($P = 0.6$). Choosing P uniformly at random from the interval $[0.5, 0.95]$ resulted in cluster accuracy of 82.21 for the representative dataset. Choosing a fixed percentage $P = 0.6$ in every iteration resulted in cluster accuracy of 80.25. Thus we chose $P_1 = 0.5$ and $P_2 = 0.95$ and chose P uniformly at random from this interval in all experiments.

Experimental Setup for Clustering. To perform clustering, we used the preprocessed texts described in Sect. 6.2. Then, texts were represented as vectors using pretrained word embeddings (i.e., Glove [17] and BioASQ [18]). The Glove

---

[2] https://www.kaggle.com/c/predict-closed-questions-on-stack-overflow/download/train.zip.
[3] http://participants-area.bioasq.org/.

embedding[4] was trained using the Glove method [17] on Wikipedia dumps. The BioASQ embedding[5] was trained using the Word2Vec method [13] on abstracts of biomedical publications. We used the Glove embedding for all datasets except the biomedical dataset since these datasets contained terms related to general domains such as search snippets. For the biomedical dataset, the BioASQ embedding was more appropriate due to its specific focus on biomedical terms.

We represented each text by the average of the vectors of all words in the text. Then, we applied the five different clustering methods described in Sect. 5 to the text vectors. For the k-means and k-means-- clustering algorithms, we used the text vectors as the points to be clustered. For hierarchical clustering, we constructed the dense similarity matrix by computing similarities between the vectors using cosine similarity for all the text pairs. After that, we sparsified the dense similarity matrix using the k-NN and similarity distribution based (SD) sparsification methods. Then we applied hierarchical agglomerative clustering using dense (HAC) and sparse similarity matrices (HAC_k-NN and HAC_SD).

6.3 Results

In our experiments, we use five datasets of short texts which are SearchSnippet, SearchSnippet-test, AgNews, StackOverflow, and BioMedical. We used accuracy (ACC) and normalized mutual information (NMI) as the evaluation measures for different clustering algorithms (as in [2]). The clustering results (ACC, NMI) of these datasets are shown in Table 2. The last two rows of Tables 2a and 2b show the ACC and NMI scores obtained using the state-of-the-art short text clustering methods STC2-LE [2] and SIF-Auto [3]. The ACC and NMI scores of five clustering algorithms both before and after iterative classification for the five datasets are shown in these two Tables. The results with or without the _IC suffix are the results with or without iterative classification. The best result (ACC, NMI) for each dataset is shown in bold.

To compensate for the dependence of k-Means, k-Means-- on the choice of cluster seeds, we ran the k-Means and k-Means-- clustering algorithms 20 times on the same dataset and performed iterative classification on the clustering obtained in each run. After that, we calculated the mean and standard deviation of the 20 clustering results (ACC, NMI) obtained by k-Means, k-means--, k-Means_IC and k-means--_IC for each dataset. We ran hierarchical agglomerative clustering (HAC), HAC_k-NN, and HAC_SD only once since HAC is deterministic. However, the enhancement of the clustering obtained by iterative classification varies between runs since the training and test sets are chosen randomly in each iteration. So, we ran iterative classification 20 times on the clustering obtained using HAC, HAC_k-NN and HAC_SD, and again calculated the mean and standard deviation of each of the 20 clustering results obtained by HAC_IC, HAC_k-NN_IC and HAC_SD_IC for each dataset.

---

[4] http://nlp.stanford.edu/data/glove.42B.300d.zip.
[5] bioasq.lip6.fr/tools/BioASQword2vec/.

Table 2. ACC and NMI of different clustering methods, their corresponding enhancements by iterative classification, and state-of-the-art methods for short text clustering. Δ indicates that this method is statistically significantly inferior to its corresponding enhancement obtained by iterative classification. * indicates that this method is statistically significantly inferior to HAC_SD_IC.

Clustering Methods	Datasets				
	Search Snippet ACC(%)	Search SnippetTest ACC(%)	AgNews ACC(%)	Stack Overflow ACC(%)	Bio Medical ACC(%)
HAC_SD	82.69$^\Delta$	89.47$^\Delta$	81.84$^\Delta$	64.80$^\Delta$	40.13$^\Delta$
HAC_SD_IC	**87.67±0.63**	**92.16±0.85**	**84.52±0.50**	**78.73±0.17**	47.78±0.51
HAC_k-NN	79.08$^\Delta$*	87.14$^\Delta$*	76.83$^\Delta$*	58.11$^\Delta$*	39.75$^\Delta$*
HAC_k-NN_IC	83.19*±0.61	90.76*±1.79	81.83*±0.35	70.07*±0.11	46.17*±1.10
HAC	76.54$^\Delta$*	77.06$^\Delta$*	76.56$^\Delta$*	61.64$^\Delta$*	38.86$^\Delta$*
HAC_IC	80.63*±0.69	83.92*±2.66	81.13*±1.22	67.69*±2.12	46.13*±0.92
k-Means	63.89$^\Delta$*±1.15	63.22$^\Delta$*±1.79	58.17$^\Delta$*±1.87	41.54$^\Delta$*±2.16	36.92$^\Delta$*±0.81
k-Means_IC	83.13*±0.69	82.84*±2.32	78.06*±3.13	69.89*±1.52	43.50*±1.38
k-means--	47.42$^\Delta$*±1.13	61.96$^\Delta$*±1.98	62.48$^\Delta$*±2.13	43.77$^\Delta$*±0.39	39.95$^\Delta$*±1.21
k-means--_IC	79.77*±2.67	75.29*±2.79	77.45*±3.49	69.25*±1.88	45.61*±3.19
STC2-LE	78.29*±2.72			53.81*±3.37	44.81*±1.72
SIF-Auto	79.13*±1.27			59.85*±1.81	**55.73±1.97**

(a) ACC results

Clustering Methods	Datasets				
	Search Snippet NMI(%)	Search SnippetTest NMI(%)	AgNews NMI(%)	Stack Overflow NMI(%)	Bio Medical NMI(%)
HAC_SD	63.76$^\Delta$	78.73$^\Delta$	54.57$^\Delta$	59.48$^\Delta$	33.51$^\Delta$
HAC_SD_IC	**71.93±1.04**	**85.55±1.09**	**59.07±0.84**	**73.44±0.35**	41.27±0.36
HAC_k-NN	60.51$^\Delta$*	76.42$^\Delta$*	52.43$^\Delta$*	54.06$^\Delta$*	32.19$^\Delta$*
HAC_k-NN_IC	65.49*±0.97	83.17*±1.17	56.02*±0.86	68.88*±0.43	38.78*±0.53
HAC	59.41$^\Delta$*	70.99$^\Delta$*	52.82$^\Delta$*	54.46$^\Delta$*	31.01$^\Delta$*
HAC_IC	63.61*±1.09	77.49*±1.11	56.57*±1.23	61.76*±1.35	38.50*±0.61
k-Means	43.75$^\Delta$*±1.31	51.54$^\Delta$*±0.92	35.26$^\Delta$*±2.01	38.01$^\Delta$*±2.12	33.71$^\Delta$*±0.29
k-Means_IC	66.27$^\Delta$±1.00	76.88$^\Delta$±2.64	52.32$^\Delta$±2.47	69.84$^\Delta$±0.66	38.08$^\Delta$±0.81
k-means--	47.43$^\Delta$*±1.65	49.73$^\Delta$*±2.15	39.68$^\Delta$*±1.15	41.89$^\Delta$*±0.86	34.49*±1.93
k-means--_IC	63.01*±1.69	71.11*±2.40	51.05*±3.63	69.64*±1.28	35.63*±2.82
STC2-LE	64.72*±1.37			49.51*±1.63	38.42*±0.87
SIF-Auto	57.72*±1.43			55.59*±1.23	**47.21±1.19**

(b) NMI results

Impact of Iterative Classification. We evaluated whether iterative classification improves the initial clustering obtained using different clustering algorithms. We consider iterative classification to improve the clustering for a given dataset if both ACC and NMI are increased using iterative classification.

Table 2 shows that iterative classification improves the initial clustering of short texts in terms of both ACC and NMI. For most of the datasets, the best clustering ACC and NMI were obtained by applying iterative classification to the clustering obtained by HAC with SD sparsification (HAC_SD). The reason is that HAC_SD [9] produces better initial clustering than other clustering methods for these datasets and the enhancement of clustering depends on the initial clustering.

Comparison with State-of-the-Art Methods. Our second comparison aims to assess how the results of iterative classification in conjunction with the different clustering methods compare to state-of-the-art short text clustering methods, specifically STC2-LE [2] and SIF-Auto [3]. Table 2a and 2b show that HAC_SD_IC and HAC_k-NN_IC outperform STC2-LE[6] for the SearchSnippet, StackOverflow and BioMedical datasets in terms of ACC and NMI. It is also shown that HAC_SD_IC, HAC_k-NN_IC, HAC_IC, k-Means_IC, and k-means--_IC outperform SIF-Auto for the SearchSnippet and StackOverflow datasets in terms of ACC and NMI. However, on the Biomedical dataset, the performance of SIF-Auto is better than any clustering method and its corresponding enhancement by iterative classification.

Statistical Significance Testing of Clustering Performance. Our third comparison aims to investigate whether the clustering improvements achieved by iterative classification are statistically significant. In particular, we perform two investigations: a) whether the improved results achieved by iterative classification are statistically significantly better than the results of their corresponding clustering methods. b) whether the improved results achieved by our best clustering method HAC_SD_IC are statistically significantly better than the results of different clustering methods (with or without iterative classification and state-of-the-art methods). For significance testing, we performed a two-tailed paired t-test (with significance level $\alpha = 0.05$) using the pairwise differences of clustering results (ACC, NMI) of 20 runs obtained by different pairs of clustering methods.

On all datasets except the BioMedical dataset, and for all clustering methods tested, the enhancement by iterative classification is statistically significantly better than the base clustering method, and the former are statistically significantly inferior to our method HAC_SD_IC. For the BioMedical dataset, the ACC and NMI scores achieved by HAC_SD_IC are statistically significantly better than that of STC2-LE. However, SIF-Auto outperforms HAC_SD_IC on the BioMedical dataset.

7   Conclusion and Future Work

We have demonstrated that iterative classification enhances the clustering of short texts for various short text datasets based on initial clusters obtained using such as k-means, k-means--, hierarchical agglomerative clustering (HAC), HAC using k-NN and SD sparsification methods. The most promising results were obtained by applying iterative classification to the clustering obtained by HAC using the proposed SD sparsification (HAC_SD_IC). Experimental results show that HAC_SD_IC outperforms a state-of-the-art short text clustering method based on convolutional neural network (STC2-LE) on all the datasets in terms

---

[6] We were unable to reproduce the clustering for other short text datasets using STC2-LE and SIF-Auto.

of ACC and NMI. Moreover, HAC_SD_IC outperforms another state-of-the-art short text clustering method based on autoencoder (SIF-Auto) in terms of ACC and NMI on several short text datasets. The proposed clustering enhancement method advances the state of the art in short text clustering, which is important in the following practical contexts such as social media monitoring, product recommendation, and customer feedback analysis. The proposed method is a generic clustering enhancement approach for short texts where various classification algorithms, initial clustering and number of clusters can be easily integrated.

In the future, we will apply our clustering enhancement algorithm to long documents to investigate whether iterative classification leads to performance improvements. We also plan to use phrase similarity as a basis for computing text similarity so as to obtain better text similarity scores, since the performance of clustering algorithms depends on the quality of individual text similarity scores.

References

1. Aggarwal, C.C., Zhai, C.: A survey of text clustering algorithms. In: Aggarwal, C., Zhai, C. (eds.) Mining Text Data, pp. 77–128. Springer, Boston (2012). https://doi.org/10.1007/978-1-4614-3223-4_4
2. Xu, J., et al.: Self-taught convolutional neural networks for short text clustering. Neural Netw. **88**, 22–31 (2017)
3. Hadifar, A., Sterckx, L., Demeester, T., Develder, C.: A self-training approach for short text clustering. In: Proceedings of the 4th Workshop on Representation Learning for NLP, Italy, pp. 194–199 (2019)
4. Yin, J., Wang, J.: A model-based approach for text clustering with outlier detection. In: 32nd International Conference on Data Engineering (ICDE), pp. 625–636 (2016)
5. Shekhar, S., Lu, C.-T., Zhang, P.: A unified approach to detecting spatial outliers. GeoInformatica **7**(2), 139–166 (2003)
6. Li, M., Cheng, Y., Zhao, H.: Unlabeled data classification via support vector machines and k-means clustering. In: Proceedings of the International Conference on Computer Graphics, Imaging and Visualization, pp. 183–186 (2004)
7. Kumar, V.: An introduction to cluster analysis for data mining. Technical report, Department of Computer Science, University of Minnesota, Minneapolis, MN (2000). https://www-users.cs.umn.edu/hanxx023/dmclass/cluster_survey_10_02_00.pdf
8. Gollub, T., Stein, B.: Unsupervised sparsification of similarity graphs. In: Locarek-Junge, H., Weihs, C. (eds.) Classification as a Tool for Research, pp. 71–79. Springer, Heidelberg (2010). https://doi.org/10.1007/978-3-642-10745-0_7
9. Rakib, M.R.H., Jankowska, M., Zeh, N., Milios, E.: Improving short text clustering by similarity matrix sparsification. In: Proceedings of the ACM Symposium on Document Engineering 2018, Halifax, NS, Canada, pp. 50:1–50:4 (2018)
10. Banerjee, S., Ramanathan, K., Gupta, A.: Clustering short texts using Wikipedia. In: Proceedings of the 30th International ACM Conference on Research and Development in Information Retrieval, Amsterdam, The Netherlands, pp. 787–788 (2007)

11. Zheng, C., Liu, C., Wong, H.: Corpus-based topic diffusion for short text clustering. Neurocomputing **275**, 2444–2458 (2018)
12. Cheng, X., Yan, X., Lan, Y., Guo, J.: BTM: topic modeling over short texts. IEEE Trans. Knowl. Data Eng. **26**(12), 2928–2941 (2014)
13. Mikolov, T., Chen, K., Corrado, G., Dean, J.: Efficient estimation of word representations in vector space. In: Proceedings of Workshop at ICLR 2013, January 2013
14. Kanj, S., Brüls, T., Gazut, S.: Shared nearest neighbor clustering in a locality sensitive hashing framework. J. Comput. Biol. **25**(2), 236–250 (2018)
15. Phan, X., Nguyen, L., Horiguchi, S.: Learning to classify short and sparse text & web with hidden topics from large-scale data collections. In: Proceedings of the 17th International Conference on World Wide Web, Beijing, China, pp. 91–100 (2008)
16. Zhang, X., Zhao, J., LeCun, Y.: Character-level convolutional networks for text classification. In: Proceedings of the 28th International Conference on Neural Information Processing Systems, USA, pp. 649–657 (2015)
17. Pennington, J., Socher, R., Manning, C.D.: Glove: global vectors for word representation. In: Proceedings of the Conference on Empirical Methods in Natural Language Processing, Doha, Qatar, pp. 1532–1543 (2014)
18. Du, Y., Pan, Y., Wang, C., Ji, J.: Biomedical semantic indexing by deep neural network with multi-task learning. BMC Bioinform. **19**(20), 502 (2018)

Improving Latent Dirichlet Allocation: On Reliability of the Novel Method LDAPrototype

Jonas Rieger$^{(\boxtimes)}$ ⓘ, Jörg Rahnenführer ⓘ, and Carsten Jentsch ⓘ

Department of Statistics, TU Dortmund University, 44221 Dortmund, Germany
{rieger,rahnenfuehrer,jentsch}@statistik.tu-dortmund.de

Abstract. A large number of applications in text data analysis use the Latent Dirichlet Allocation (LDA) as one of the most popular methods in topic modeling. Although the instability of the LDA is mentioned sometimes, it is usually not considered systematically. Instead, an LDA is often selected from a small set of LDAs using heuristic means or human codings. Then, conclusions are often drawn based on the to some extent arbitrarily selected model. We present the novel method LDAPrototype, which takes the instability of the LDA into account, and show that by systematically selecting an LDA it improves the reliability of the conclusions drawn from the result and thus provides better reproducibility. The improvement coming from this selection criterion is unveiled by applying the proposed methods to an example corpus consisting of texts published in a German quality newspaper over one month.

Keywords: Topic model · Machine learning · Similarity · Stability · Stochastic

1 Introduction

Due to the growing number and especially the increasing amount of unstructured data, it is of great interest to be able to analyze them. Text data is an example for unstructured data and at the same time it covers a large part of them. It is organized in so-called corpora, which are given by collections of texts.

For the analysis of such text data topic models in general and the Latent Dirichlet Allocation in particular is often used. This method has the weakness that it is unstable, i.e. it gives different results for repeated runs. There are various approaches to reduce this instability. In the following, we present a new method LDAPrototype that improves the reliability of the results by choosing a center LDA. We will demonstrate this improvement of the LDA applying the method to a corpus consisting of all articles published in the German quality newspaper Süddeutsche Zeitung in April 2019.

E. Métais et al. (Eds.): NLDB 2020, LNCS 12089, pp. 118–125, 2020.
https://doi.org/10.1007/978-3-030-51310-8_11

1.1   Related Work

The Latent Dirichlet Allocation [3] is very popular in text data analysis. Numerous extensions to Latent Dirichlet Allocation have been proposed, each customized for certain applications, as the Author-Topic Model [18], Correlated Topics Model [2] or the more generalized Structural Topic Model [17]. We focus on LDA as one of the most commonly used topic models and propose a methodology to increase reliability of findings drawn from the results of LDA.

Reassigning words to topics in the LDA is based on conditional distributions, thus it is stochastic. This is rarely discussed in applications [1]. However, several approaches exist to encounter this problem based on a certain selection criterion. One of these selection criteria is perplexity [3], a performance measure for probabilistic models to estimate how well new data fit into the model [18]. As an extension, Nguyen et al. [13] proposed to average different iterations of the Gibbs sampling procedure to achieve an increase of perplexity. In general, it was shown that optimizing likelihood-based measures like perplexity does not select the model that fits the data best regarding human judgements. In fact, these measures are negatively correlated with human judgements on topic quality [5]. A better approach should be to optimize semantic coherence of topics as Chang et al. [5] proposed. They provide a validation technique called Word or Topic Intrusion which depends on a coding process by humans. Measures without human interaction, but almost automated, and also aiming to optimize semantic coherence can be transferred from the Topic Coherence [12]. Unfortunately, there is no validated procedure to get a selection criterion for LDA models from this topic's "quality" measure. Instead, another option to overcome the weakness of instability of LDA is to start the first iteration of the Gibbs sampler with reasonably initialized topic assignments [11] of every token in all texts. One possibility is to use co-occurences of words. The initialization technique comes with the drawback of restricting the model to a subset of possible results.

1.2   Contribution

In this paper, we propose an improvement of the Latent Dirichlet Allocation through a selection criterion of multiple LDA runs. The improvement is made by increasing the reliability of results taken from LDA. This particular increase is obtained by selecting the model that represents the center of the set of LDAs best. The method is called LDAPrototype [16] and is explained in Sect. 3. We show that it generates reliable results in the sense that repetitions lie in a rather small sphere around the overall centered LDA, when applying the proposed methods to an example corpus of articles from the Süddeutsche Zeitung.

2   Latent Dirichlet Allocation

The method we propose is based on the LDA [3] estimated by a Collapsed Gibbs sampler [6], which is a probabilistic topic model that is widely used in text data analysis. The LDA assumes that there is a topic distribution for every text, and it models them by assigning one topic from the set of topics $T = \{T_1, ..., T_K\}$ to every token in a text, where $K \in \mathbb{N}$ denotes the user-defined number of modeled topics. We denote a text (or document) of a corpus consisting of M texts by

$$\boldsymbol{D}^{(m)} = \left(W_1^{(m)}, ..., W_{N^{(m)}}^{(m)}\right), \quad m = 1, ..., M, \quad W_n^{(m)} \in \boldsymbol{W}, \quad n = 1, ..., N^{(m)}.$$

We refer to the size of text m as $N^{(m)}$; $\boldsymbol{W} = \{W_1, ..., W_V\}$ is the set of words and $V \in \mathbb{N}$ denotes the vocabulary size. Then, analogously the topic assignments of every text m are given by

$$\boldsymbol{T}^{(m)} = \left(T_1^{(m)}, ..., T_{N^{(m)}}^{(m)}\right), \quad m = 1, ..., M, \quad T_n^{(m)} \in T, \quad n = 1, ..., N^{(m)}.$$

Each topic assignment $T_n^{(m)}$ corresponds to the token $W_n^{(m)}$ in text m. When $n_k^{(mv)}, k = 1, ..., K, v = 1, ..., V$ describes the number of assignments of word v in text m to topic k, we can define the cumulative count of word v in topic k over all documents by $n_k^{(\bullet v)}$. Then, let $\boldsymbol{w}_k = (n_k^{(\bullet 1)}, ..., n_k^{(\bullet V)})^T$ denote the vectors of word counts for the $k = 1, ..., K$ topics. Using these definitions, the underlying probability model of LDA [6] can be written as

$$W_n^{(m)} \mid T_n^{(m)}, \boldsymbol{\phi}_k \sim \text{Discrete}(\boldsymbol{\phi}_k), \qquad \boldsymbol{\phi}_k \sim \text{Dirichlet}(\eta),$$

$$T_n^{(m)} \mid \boldsymbol{\theta}_m \sim \text{Discrete}(\boldsymbol{\theta}_m), \qquad \boldsymbol{\theta}_m \sim \text{Dirichlet}(\alpha),$$

where α and η are Dirichlet distribution hyperparameters and must be set by the user. Although the LDA permits α and η to be vector valued [3], they are usually chosen symmetric because typically the user has no a-priori information about the topic distributions $\boldsymbol{\theta}$ and word distributions $\boldsymbol{\phi}$. Increasing η leads to a loss of homogenity of the mixture of words per topic. In contrast, a decrease leads to a raise of homogenity, identified by less but more dominant words per topic. In the same manner α controls the mixture of topics in texts.

3   LDAPrototype

The Gibbs sampler in the modeling procedure of the LDA is sensitive to the random initialization of topic assignments as mentioned in Sect. 1.1. We present a method that reduces the stochastic component of the LDA. This adaption of the LDA named LDAPrototype [16] increases the reliability of conclusions drawn from the resulting prototype model, which is obtained by selecting the model that seems to be the most central of (usually around) 100 independently modeled LDA runs. The procedure can be compared to the calculation of the median in the univariate case.

The method makes use of topic similarities measured by the modified Jaccard coefficient for the corresponding topics to the word count vectors $\boldsymbol{w}_i$ and $\boldsymbol{w}_j$

$$J_m(\boldsymbol{w}_i, \boldsymbol{w}_j) = \frac{\sum_{v=1}^{V} \mathbb{1}_{\left\{n_i^{(\bullet v)} > c_i \,\wedge\, n_j^{(\bullet v)} > c_j\right\}}}{\sum_{v=1}^{V} \mathbb{1}_{\left\{n_i^{(\bullet v)} > c_i \,\vee\, n_j^{(\bullet v)} > c_j\right\}}},$$

where c is a vector of lower bounds. Words are assumed to be relevant for a topic if the count of the word passes this bound. The threshold c marks the modification to the traditional Jaccard coefficient [8] and can be chosen in an absolute or relative manner or as a combination of both.

The main part of LDAPrototype is to cluster two independent LDA replications using Complete Linkage [7] based on the underlying topic similarities of those two LDA runs. Let G be a pruned cluster result composed by single groups g consisting of topics and let $g_{|1}$ and $g_{|2}$ denote groups of g restricted to topics of the corresponding LDA run. Then, the method aims to create a pruning state where $g_{|1}$ and $g_{|2}$ are each build by only one topic for all $g \in G$. This is achieved by maximizing the measure for LDA similarity named S-CLOP (**S**imilarity of **L**ultiple Sets by **C**lustering with **Lo**cal **P**runing) [16]:

$$\text{S-CLOP}(G) = 1 - \frac{1}{2K} \sum_{g \in G} |g| \left(||g_{|1}| - 1| + ||g_{|2}| - 1| \right) \in [0, 1].$$

We denote the best pruning state by $G^* = \arg\max\{\text{S-CLOP}(G)\}$ for all possible states G and determine similarity of two LDA runs by $\text{S-CLOP}(G^*)$. The prototype model of a set of LDAs then is selected by maximizing the mean pairwise similarity of one model to all other models.

The methods are implemented in the R [14] package ldaPrototype [15]. The user can specify the number of models, various options for c including a minimal number of relevant words per topic as well as the necessary hyperparameters for the basic LDA α, η, K and the number of iterations the Gibbs sampler should run. The package is linked to the packages lda [4] and tosca [10].

4   Analysis

We show that the novel method LDAPrototype improves the Latent Dirichlet Allocation in the sense of reliability. To prove that, the following study design is applied to an example corpus from the German quality newspaper Süddeutsche Zeitung (SZ). The corpus consists of all 3 718 articles published in the SZ in April 2019. It is preprocessed using common steps for cleaning text data including duplicate removal leading to 3 468 articles. Moreover, punctuation, numbers and German stopwords are removed. In addition, all words that occur ten times or less are deleted. This results in $M = 3\,461$ non-empty texts and a vocabulary size of $V = 11\,484$. The preprocessing was done using the R package tosca [10].

4.1   Study Design

The study is as follows: First of all, a large number N of LDAs is fitted. This set represents the basic population of all possible LDAs in the study. Then we repeat P times the random selection of R LDAs and calculate their LDAPrototype. This means, finally P prototypes are selected, each based on R basic LDAs, where each LDA is randomly drawn from a set of N LDAs. Then, a single prototype is

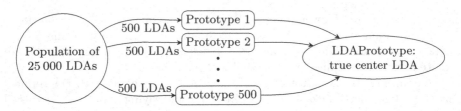

Fig. 1. Schematic representation of the study design for $N = 25\,000$ LDAs in the base population and $P = 500$ selected prototypes, each based on $R = 500$ sampled LDAs from the base population.

determined based on a comparison of the P prototypes. This particular prototype forms the assumed true center LDA. In addition, we establish a ranking of all other prototypes. The order is determined by sequentially selecting the next best prototype which realizes the maximum of the mean S-CLOP values by adding the corresponding prototype and simultaneously considering all higher ranked LDAPrototypes.

For the application we choose three different parameter combinations for the basic LDA. In fact, we want to model the corpus of the SZ with $K = 20, 35, 50$ topics. We choose accordingly $\alpha = \eta = 1/K$ and let the Gibbs sampler iterate 200 times. We choose the size of the population as $N = 25\,000$, so that we initially calculate a total of $75\,000$ LDAs, which is computationally intensive but bearable. We use the R package ldaPrototype [15] to compute the models on batch systems. We set the parameters of the study to a sufficiently high and at the same time calculable value of $P = R = 500$. That is, we get 500 PrototypeLDAs, each based on 500 basic LDAs, that are sampled without replacement from the set of $25\,000$ basic LDAs. The sampling procedure is carried out without replacement in order to protect against falsification by multiple selection of one specific LDA. Figure 1 represents this particular study design schematically.

Then, we inspect the selection of the P prototypes. On the one hand, we quantify the goodness of selection by determining how many LDAs, that were available in the corresponding run, are ranked before the corresponding LDAPrototype. On the other hand, the analysis of the distance to the best available LDA run in the given prototype run provides a better assessment of the reliability of the method. We compare the observed values with randomized choices of the prototype. This leads to statements of the form that the presented method LDAPrototype selects its prototypes only from a sufficiently small environment around the true center LDA, especially in comparison to random selected LDAs.

4.2 Results

For the analysis we first determine the true center LDA and a ranking for all 500 prototypes as described in Sect. 4.1 for each $K = 20, 35, 50$. The corresponding mean S-CLOP value at the time of addition is assigned to each prototype in the ranking as a measure of proximity to the true center LDA. To visualize the

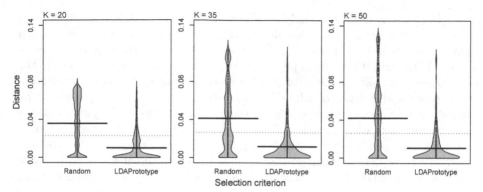

(a) Distance of each of the LDAPrototypes to the LDA that would have been the best choice in the corresponding prototype run regarding closeness to the center LDA.

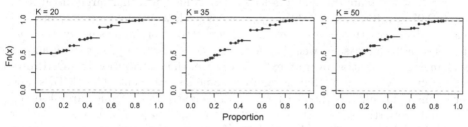

(b) Empirical cumulative distribution function of the proportion of how many LDAs are closer to the center LDA than the selected LDAPrototype.

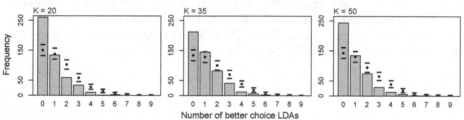

(c) Number of LDAs that are closer to the center LDA than the selected LDAPrototype.

Fig. 2. Analysis of the improvement of reliability by using the LDAPrototype for $K = 20, 35, 50$ modeled topics. Every single value corresponds to one of the $P = 500$ prototype runs resulting in the corresponding LDAPrototype.

rankings, we use so-called beanplots [9] as a more accurate form of boxplots, as well as empirical cumulative distribution functions (ECDF) and bar charts.

For $K = 20, 35, 50$ each of the 25 000 LDAs is included at least once in the 500 times 500 selected LDAs. Nevertheless, only 169, 187 and 186 different LDAs are chosen as prototypes. The LDAPrototype method thus differs significantly from a random selection, whose associated simulated 95% confidence interval suggests between 490 and 499 different prototypes.

Figure 2 summarizes the analysis of the increase of reliability for 20, 35 and 50 topics, respectively. The beanplots in Fig. 2a indicate the distance of each LDA actually selected from the LDAPrototype method to the supposedly most suitable LDA from the identical prototype run with respect to the values from the ranking. For comparison, the distribution of the distances for random selection of the prototype is given besides. The corresponding values were generated by simulation with permutation of the ranking. The ECDFs in Fig. 2b show the relative number of LDAs, in each of the $P = 500$ prototype runs, that according to the ranking would represent a better choice as prototype. Finally, the bar charts in Fig. 2c show the corresponding distribution of the absolute numbers of available better LDAs in the same run in accordance to the determined ranking of prototypes. In addition, simulated 95% confidence intervals for frequencies realized by the use of random selection are also shown.

For $K = 20$, many randomly selected LDAs have a rather large distance of about 0.07 at a total mean value of just below 0.04, while the presented method realizes distances that are on average below 0.01. For increasing K the distances seem to increase as well. While the random selection produces an almost unchanging distribution over an extended range, the distribution of LDAPrototype shifts towards zero. Higher values become less frequent. The ECDFs look very similar for all K, whereby for $K = 35$ slightly lower values are observed for small proportions. This is supported by the only major difference in the bar charts. Modeling 20 or 50 topics, for 50% of the prototype runs there is no better available LDA to choose, while for the modeling of 35 topics this scenario applies for just over 40%. The corresponding confidence intervals in Fig. 2c are lowered as well. This is an indication that for $K = 35$ it is easier to find a result that is stable to a certain extent for the basic LDA. This is supported by the fact that the distribution of distances in Fig. 2a does not seem to suffer.

5   Discussion

We show that the LDAPrototype method significantly improves the reliability of LDA results compared to a random selection. The presented method has several advantages, e.g. the automated computability, as no need of manual coding procedures. In addition, besides the intuitive statistical approach, the proposed method preserves all components of an LDA model, especially the specific topic assignments of each token in the texts. This means that all analyses previously carried out on individual runs can be applied to the LDAPrototype as well. The results suggest that $K = 35$ topics produces more stable results and might therefore be a more appropriate choice for the number of topics than $K = 20$ or 50 on the given corpus. Further studies to analyze the observed differences in the number of better LDAs as well as the distances to the best LDA between different choices of the numbers of topics, may lead to progress in the field of hyperparameter tuning for the LDA.

References

1. Agrawal, A., Fu, W., Menzies, T.: What is wrong with topic modeling? And how to fix it using search-based software engineering. Inf. Softw. Technol. **98**, 74–88 (2018). https://doi.org/10.1016/j.infsof.2018.02.005
2. Blei, D.M., Lafferty, J.D.: A correlated topic model of science. Ann. Appl. Stat. **1**(1), 17–35 (2007). https://doi.org/10.1214/07-AOAS114
3. Blei, D.M., Ng, A.Y., Jordan, M.I.: Latent Dirichlet allocation. J. Mach. Learn. Res. **3**, 993–1022 (2003). https://doi.org/10.1162/jmlr.2003.3.4-5.993
4. Chang, J.: LDA: Collapsed Gibbs Sampling Methods for Topic Models (2015). https://CRAN.R-project.org/package=lda. R package version 1.4.2
5. Chang, J., Boyd-Graber, J., Gerrish, S., Wang, C., Blei, D.M.: Reading tea leaves: how humans interpret topic models. In: Proceedings of the 22nd International NIPS-Conference, pp. 288–296. Curran Associates Inc. (2009)
6. Griffiths, T.L., Steyvers, M.: Finding scientific topics. Proc. Natl. Acad. Sci. **101**(Suppl. 1), 5228–5235 (2004). https://doi.org/10.1073/pnas.0307752101
7. Hastie, T., Tibshirani, R., Friedman, J.: The Elements of Statistical Learning. SSS, 2nd edn. Springer, New York (2009). https://doi.org/10.1007/978-0-387-84858-7
8. Jaccard, P.: The distribution of the flora in the alpine zone. New Phytol. **11**(2), 37–50 (1912). https://doi.org/10.1111/j.1469-8137.1912.tb05611.x
9. Kampstra, P.: Beanplot: a boxplot alternative for visual comparison of distributions. J. Stat. Softw. Code Snippets **28**(1), 1–9 (2008). https://doi.org/10.18637/jss.v028.c01
10. Koppers, L., Rieger, J., Boczek, K., von Nordheim, G.: tosca: Tools for Statistical Content Analysis (2019). https://doi.org/10.5281/zenodo.3591068. R package version 0.1-5
11. Maier, D., et al.: Applying LDA topic modeling in communication research: toward a valid and reliable methodology. Commun. Methods Measur. **12**(2–3), 93–118 (2018). https://doi.org/10.1080/19312458.2018.1430754
12. Mimno, D., Wallach, H.M., Talley, E., Leenders, M., McCallum, A.: Optimizing semantic coherence in topic models. In: Proceedings of the 2011 EMNLP-Conference, pp. 262–272. ACL (2011)
13. Nguyen, V.A., Boyd-Graber, J., Resnik, P.: Sometimes average is best: the importance of averaging for prediction using MCMC inference in topic modeling. In: Proceedings of the 2014 EMNLP-Conference, pp. 1752–1757. ACL (2014). https://doi.org/10.3115/v1/D14-1182
14. R Core Team: R: A Language and Environment for Statistical Computing. R Foundation for Statistical Computing, Vienna, Austria (2019). http://www.R-project.org/
15. Rieger, J.: LDAPrototype: Prototype of Multiple Latent Dirichlet Allocation Runs (2020). https://doi.org/10.5281/zenodo.3604359. R package version 0.1.1
16. Rieger, J., Koppers, L., Jentsch, C., Rahnenführer, J.: Improving Reliability of Latent Dirichlet Allocation by Assessing Its Stability Using Clustering Techniques on Replicated Runs (2020)
17. Roberts, M.E., Stewart, B.M., Tingley, D., Airoldi, E.M.: The structural topic model and applied social science. In: NIPS-Workshop on Topic Models: Computation, Application, and Evaluation (2013)
18. Rosen-Zvi, M., Griffiths, T., Steyvers, M., Smyth, P.: The author-topic model for authors and documents. In: Proceedings of the 20th UAI-Conference, pp. 487–494. AUAI Press (2004)

Pattern Learning for Detecting Defect Reports and Improvement Requests in App Reviews

Gino V. H. Mangnoesing[1]([✉]), Maria Mihaela Truşcă[2]([✉]),
and Flavius Frasincar[1][ID]

[1] Erasmus University Rotterdam,
Burgemeester Oudlaan 50, 3062 PA Rotterdam, The Netherlands
gvh.sing@gmail.com, frasincar@ese.eur.nl
[2] Bucharest University of Economic Studies,
Piata Romana 6, 010374 Bucharest, Romania
maria.trusca@csie.ase.ro

Abstract. Online reviews are an important source of feedback for understanding customers. In this study, we follow novel approaches that target the absence of actionable insights by classifying reviews as defect reports and requests for improvement. Unlike traditional classification methods based on expert rules, we reduce the manual labour by employing a supervised system that is capable of learning lexico-semantic patterns through genetic programming. Additionally, we experiment with a distantly-supervised SVM that makes use of the noisy labels generated by patterns. Using a real-world dataset of app reviews, we show that the automatically learned patterns outperform the manually created ones. Also the distantly-supervised SVM models are not far behind the pattern-based solutions, showing the usefulness of this approach when the amount of annotated data is limited.

1 Introduction

In the two last decades, the growth of user-generated content on the Web has accelerated enormously due to parallel developments, such as increased Internet access, technological advancements in mobile devices, the growth of e-commerce, and many more. An important source of user-generated content with respect to customer feedback are online reviews. Their interpretation is usually achieved using Sentiment Analysis (SA) methods which has as the main aim to automatically detect positive, neutral, and negative sentiments [10]. A major downside of SA is that it measures satisfaction at a certain point in time. In this light, we argue that in addition to SA, it is important to focus on detecting specific types of feedback that indicate potential causes and influence factors of satisfaction. We consider such specific customer feedback as actionable, since it suggests a clear course of action for addressing the feedback, and thus directly help to modify and hopefully improve products.

© Springer Nature Switzerland AG 2020
E. Métais et al. (Eds.): NLDB 2020, LNCS 12089, pp. 126–134, 2020.
https://doi.org/10.1007/978-3-030-51310-8_12

In this paper, we focus on customer feedback related to mobile software applications which we will refer to as "apps". We argue that software reviews are very important for aggregating valuable feedback. Firstly, because many companies have come to realise that all the technology required to transform industries through software is available on a global scale [1]. Secondly, the field of software engineering has the well-accepted notions of bugs and feature requests, which we argue, are actionable types of feedback.

There are very few works [4,6,12–14] that aim to detect specific information in customer feedback. Among the aforementioned works, only the method proposed in [12] is more refined. Namely, in [12] lexical patterns are used to train a supervised classifier, rather than directly employing patterns for information extraction, which makes the extraction mechanism more adaptive to the various representations of feedback. Further on, this system summarizes the extracted feedback by means of a *Topic Model* technique called *Latent Dirichlet Allocation* (LDA) [2]. However, while the objective is very relevant, the suggested methods require a vast amount of manual labour to create useful feedback patterns. We argue this to be a great limitation since analysing customer feedback is an important process that should ideally be performed in a continuous fashion. Nevertheless, the study conveys a promising direction for future research in opinion mining, and clear feedback types to focus on, which we adopt in this work.

We approach feedback detection as a multi-label classification problem based on knowledge-base rules or patterns, in which our goal is to automatically determine if a given review is an example of given actionable feedbacks. Usually, making a knowledge base of patterns is impractical to manage over time and across different domains. In this light, we suggest a system that is capable of performing pattern construction in an automated manner using genetic programming. Keeping in mind the importance of reduction of the human control over the system's design, we also tackle the problem of having a small number of labeled reviews (gold labels) using noisy labels generated based on patterns in a distantly-supervised way [8,15]. The employed dataset and the proposed framework implemented in Scala are available at https://github.com/mtrusca/PatternLearning.

The remaining parts of the paper are structured as follows. Section 2 presents a detailed overview of the proposed framework in this study. In Sect. 3 we evaluate our framework through a series of experiments. Finally, in Sect. 4 we present our conclusions and suggest future work.

2 Methods

In this research, our goal is to automatically detect actionable feedback in reviews. More specifically, we aim to detect two specific types of feedback: defect reports and improvement requests. We approach this task as a binary classification problem, meaning that each review is considered a document that requires two classifications, one for each feedback type. Using this setup it is possible to classify some reviews as both defect report and improvement request. Our main contribution to the research problem is to automate the task of discovering and constructing patterns. Rather than direct supervision, where labels are provided by human annotators, we use a group of patterns to provide (noisy) labels for each feedback type. These labels are then given as input to a linear SVM model, often applied for text classification tasks due to its learning capability that is independent of the dimensionality of the feature space.

Using noisy labels to guide algorithms is a technique called *Distant Learning* or *Distant Supervision* [8,15]. Despite the fact that *Distant Supervision* is already a great step towards minimizing the amount of human labour required to perform feedback detection, the required process for manually constructing groups of patterns per feedback type, remains rather tedious and time consuming. For this reason, we suggest another level of automation, which is to automate the pattern creation procedure (responsible to generate noisy labels) by means of a learning algorithm.

To solve our problem for learning patterns, we require to select a learning algorithm that stands out with respect to interpretability and modifiability. A specific category of algorithms that meets these requirements are *Evolutionary Algorithms* (EAs). The most popular type of EA is the *Genetic Algorithm* (GA), however we adopt a special case of GA called *Genetic Programming* (GP) inspired by Darwin's theory of evolution [3]. Genetic Programming and Genetic Algorithms are very similar. They both evolve solutions to a problem, by comparing the *fitness* of each candidate solution in a population of potential candidates, over many generations. In each generation, new candidates are found by quasi-randomly changing (mutation) or swapping parts (crossover) of other candidates. The least "fit" candidates are removed from the population. The primary difference between GA and GP is the representation of the candidate solutions. In GA a candidate is represented as a vector, and in GP a candidate is represented as a tree. As the GP representation fits better the specification of our information extraction patterns, we adopt it in our research.

The learning approach suggested in GP, is to define an environment in which a collection of randomly generated, simple programs (individuals) evolve through an analogue of natural selection. Each individual represented by a tree structure is composed from a collection of nodes. All nodes (except the first, or root node) have one parent and any number of children. Every node belongs to one of two types, namely *functions* or *terminals*. Function nodes are allowed to have children nodes, which can be either functions or terminals. Terminal nodes are not allowed to have child nodes, therefore terminal nodes are considered the leaves of the tree. In our framework, we consider each individual to be a pattern for classifying documents (app reviews) with a (recursive) match method.

Function nodes include Boolean operations, such as *AND*, *OR*, and *NOT*, as well as *Sequence* and *Repetition*. The *Sequence* node can have one or more child nodes of types function or terminal. It is also the root node of each tree. A *Repetition* node enforces two or more consecutive nodes to obey the same condition. A node of type *AND* has at least two children, and is useful to pattern match for multiple features, for example to check whether a given token is both a specific literal and part of a syntactic category. The nodes of type *OR* and of type *NOT* also follow the Boolean logic, where the *OR* nodes match as true if at least one of the children matches, and nodes of type *NOT* match as true if none of its children match for a given token. Terminal nodes are the external points (or leaves) of the tree. They are assigned a specific value, used to pattern match for specific tokens. *Literal* nodes must be exactly matching the specific word (value) that is assigned the node. For *Part-of-Speech* (POS) nodes, tokens are evaluated to match a specific Part-of-Speech tag. A *Wildcard* node will match any token, irrespective of its value. Finally, an *Entity Type* node matches a value from a manually constructed and populated gazetteer.

Typically gazetteers consists of sets of terms containing names of entities such as cities, organisations, or weekdays [5]. Since at the time of performing this research, we could not find gazetteers for our specific domain, we decided to define our own. Our gazetteer is implemented using a plain key-value mapping, where a key corresponds to the name of an entity type, and the value stores a set of lexical representations of that entity type. For example, to detect the entity type *app* we employ the following terms: *it, app, application, Evernote* (we use a set of *Evernote* reviews for our experiments). Some other entity types in our gazetteer are: *user, action, object, component, device,* and *update*. The entity types we employ are inspired by *Issue Tracking Systems* (ITS), such as *Bugzilla*, an open-source issue tracker created by *Mozilla*. Since ITS involve very comparable types of feedback to this study, we consider the entity types in ITS a useful starting point for constructing our gazetteers.

The first step for each genetic program, is to generate an initial population of N individuals. In our experiments, we use the *ramped-half-and-half* method [9], which is commonly used since it produces a wider range of variation in terms of shapes and sizes of trees compared to the other popular methods like *grow* and *full*. The *ramped-half-and-half* achieves more variety, by combining both the *grow* and *full* methods, where one half of the population is generated through the *grow* method, and the other half through the *full* method. The algorithm we employ to generate individual trees in a recursive manner is based on the one suggested in [7].

During the initialization, nodes are selected randomly to construct trees. However, for the purpose of stimulating useful combinations of terminals, we generate a pool of recommended terminal candidates. Whereas the pool contains all entity types and the wildcard, for the case of *POS* and *Literal* terminals we select only the most relevant nodes. More specifically, we pre-analyse the training set for frequently occurring unigrams (as terminals) and bigrams (as pairs of terminals) of types *Literal* and *POS* (for bigrams, four specific pair combinations are considered: (*Literal*)(*Literal*), (*POS*)(*Literal*), (*Literal*)(*POS*), and (*POS*)(*POS*)). Subsequently, we remove in each sentiment class of a target feedback type, the 100 most frequent unigrams and bigrams that occur in the another sentiment class. Then, every time a terminal node is needed we randomly select it from the pool of recommended terminal candidates.

In Evolutionary learning methods, a population of individuals can evolve for many generations. However, after a certain amount of generations, the *fitness* of the best new individuals will stop increasing. In our problem, we want individual patterns to be optimized for high precision, which means that we want more weight on precision than recall. Hence, we employ the F_β-measure with $\beta = 0.3$ instead of the widely used F_1-measure. Further on, we employ two criteria for termination. The first criterium is the maximum number of generations and is checked when generating a pattern (in the pattern group). The second criterium is checked per event type and it is triggered if the pattern does not increase the *fitness* of the entire group of patterns after a maximum number of iterations. The *fitness* measure for a group of patterns is determined by the F_1-measure, instead of the F_β-measure. Our motivation for using F_1 for group fitness is related to our goal to seek patterns for as many variations of a target feedback type as possible.

A proper procedure for selection should not find only the strongest individual of a population, but to allow more individuals to have a chance of being selected. A common method that addresses this requirement is *Tournament Selection*. Precisely, the method allows for a constant selection pressure that determines the extent to which fit individuals are preferred over less fit individuals. All the selected individuals are used to produce *offspring* or the next generation of individuals. The main objective in producing offspring, is to enhance the *fitness* for the next generation based on three genetic operations, namely *Elitism*, *Crossover*, and *Mutation*.

As discussed earlier, our goal is to learn a group of patterns that detect as many variations of a target feedback type as possible, in our training examples. In essence, each pattern can be interpreted as a rule, and each document has to be categorised as either positive or negative, according to our "knowledge" of each category, which is stored in a rule base. The set of rules learnt in our framework is generated through a *Sequential Covering Algorithm* [11].

3 Experiments

In order to evaluate the approach suggested in our framework, we performed experiments on a real-life dataset. The dataset contains 4470 reviews about *Evernote*, a mobile app for the Android platform. We automatically extracted the review dataset from the Google Play Store, through Web scraping techniques. We selected *Evernote* because it is a widely used app with a large user base, that publicly share their feedback on the Web, and therefore serves as a great example for our examined research problem.

We have annotations for 46% of the total review dataset. We hold out 20% of all reviews for testing purposes in all methods. Therefore, we have the remaining 26% of reviews available for training purposes. However, for the experiments that employ distant supervision, we generate noisy labels, hence, have 80% of the full review dataset available for training. The terms "Positive" and "Negative" refer to the classification labels that were assigned to every review per feedback type

Table 1. Examples of human (A) and automatically constructed (B) patterns. DR and IR stand for Defect Report and Improvement Request, respectively. For DR patterns ":" separates the terminal from its type.

Type	Pattern	Example
DR	OR: |-Software Bug: Entity Type |-Software Update: Entity Type	The last few months of updates haven't changed or lessened the lag you get when you edit notes
IR	SEQ: |-5: Literal |-stars: Literal	Colour coding of the notes and reminders for repetitive tasks can fetch 5 stars

Table 2. Performance metrics for feedback type classifications in terms of precision, recall, and F_1-measure. The best results are set in bold.

Task	Defect classification			Improvement classification		
Method	Precision	Recall	F_1-measure	Precision	Recall	F_1-measure
Standard SVM	0.39	0.59	0.47	0.78	**0.54**	**0.64**
Patterns A (manual)	0.61	0.42	0.50	**0.81**	0.42	0.56
Patterns B (learned)	**0.91**	0.39	**0.54**	0.79	0.51	0.62
SVM Distant Supervision A	0.24	**0.67**	0.36	0.39	0.48	0.43
SVM Distant Supervision B	0.41	0.59	0.49	0.46	0.44	0.45

by human annotators. On average 12.6% of our labeled set of reviews contains one or more actionable types of feedback, in which there are 8.4% more requests for improvement than defect reports. Finally, only 1.3% of our annotated reviews is labeled as both a defect report and an improvement request.

We collected annotations for both feedback types through *CrowdFlower* (recently renamed *Figure Eight*), an online data enrichment platform. The instructed task is to label every individual review for both defect reports and improvement requests. Every review was annotated by at least 3 annotators, and in some cases even 5 or 7 (when it is recorded a low accuracy of the test questions that inspect the quality of the annotator).

The employed patterns are constructed both manually and automatically. In the *Evernote* dataset, we have five manual and two generated patterns for defects, and eight manual and ten generated patterns for improvements. The most likely reason for this contrast is the variation in distribution of feedback types in our dataset, as a result of the fact that *Evernote* is a popular app, well tested, and optimised. Furthermore, we noticed that the most effective patterns only use function nodes of type *Sequence* and *OR*. Also, many examples of feedback can be recognized with a single terminal, such as the *Entity Type* "software update" for defect reports or the *Literal* "stars" for improvement requests, which indicates that the level of specificity does not necessarily have to be high. In that light, patterns that include the *NOT* node, which requires feedback examples in which a very specific word is not mentioned are often not necessary. While *NOT* functions can be useful to make a pattern very expressive and precise, it becomes obsolete when that level of selectivity is not required, as in our case. A similar line of reasoning can be applied to the *AND* functions. Table 1 lists two examples of automatically constructed patterns for the two types of feedback.

To classify defect reports and improvement requests we test the following methods:

Table 3. Running time for pattern creation per approach. The best results are set in bold.

Approach	Defect patterns	Improvement patterns	Total
Manual (per person)	8.5 h	10.25 h	18.75 h
Automated	**3.5 h**	**2.4 h**	**5.9 h**

Method 0: Standard SVM. In this method, we train an SVM classifier using only labelled reviews for training. This method can be considered a reference for the following methods.

Method 1: Patterns A. In this experiment, we use human patterns to perform supervised classifications directly (without SVMs). We employ the available labelled data (26%) for learning patterns.

Method 2: Patterns B. This method is similar to the Method 1, except that the human patterns are replaced with automatically constructed ones.

Method 3: SVM Distant Supervision A. In this method, we train an SVM classifier using noisy labels generated based on the human patterns for the entire training set.

Method 4: SVM Distant Supervision B. This method is similar to the Method 3, except that the human patterns are replaced with automatically constructed ones.

Table 2 displays an overview of performance measures of all proposed methods. We can notice that the *Distant Supervision* methods are not far behind the direct classification through patterns, in terms of F_1-scores. Nevertheless, given that the results are obtained with noisy labels shows the usefulness of this approach for datasets where the annotated data is limited.

As regards the comparison between the two types of patterns, it is obvious that the automatically generated patterns perform better than the human ones.

In order to have a complete insight over the pattern creation process (manual versus automated) we additionally explore the patterns' efficiency besides their effectiveness. Table 3 displays the running time for creating patterns both manually and automatically. We can observe that it takes 70% less time to generate the automatic patterns than the manual ones.

4   Conclusion

In this study we presented a framework for automatically learning lexico-semantic patterns helpful for detecting specific types of feedback expressed in conversational customer feedback (defect reports and improvement requests). Using a custom dataset, we showed that the automatically generated patterns perform slightly better than the manual ones and there is a 70% reduction in construction time. Further on, we demonstrated that the distantly-supervised SVM with noisy labels is not far behind the pattern-based classification. The results reveals the applicability of this approach when the amount of available labels is limited.

As future work, we would like to increase the flexibility of our patterns by considering more complex terminal structures. Using techniques from entity-learning we would like to explore the automatic generation of our domain-specific gazetteers lists to increase coverage and the framework's applicability in other domains.

References

1. Andreessen, M.: Why software is eating the world. Wall Street J. **20** (2011)
2. Blei, D.M., Ng, A.Y., Jordan, M.I.: Latent Dirichlet allocation. J. Mach. Learn. Res. (JMLR) **3**, 993–1022 (2003)
3. Booker, L.B., Goldberg, D.E., Holland, J.H.: Classifier systems and genetic algorithms. Artif. Intell. **40**(1), 235–282 (1989)
4. Brun, C., Hagege, C.: Suggestion mining: detecting suggestions for improvement in users' comments. Res. Comput. Sci. **70**, 171–181 (2013)
5. Cunningham, H.: GATE, a general architecture for text engineering. Comput. Humanit. **36**(2), 223–254 (2002)
6. Goldberg, A.B., Fillmore, N., Andrzejewski, D., Xu, Z., Gibson, B., Zhu, X.: May all your wishes come true: a study of wishes and how to recognize them. In: 10th Annual Conference of the North American Chapter of the Association for Computational Linguistics (NAACL HLT 2009), pp. 263–271. ACL (2009)
7. IJntema, W., Hogenboom, F., Frasincar, F., Vandic, D.: A genetic programming approach for learning semantic information extraction rules from news. In: Benatallah, B., Bestavros, A., Manolopoulos, Y., Vakali, A., Zhang, Y. (eds.) WISE 2014. LNCS, vol. 8786, pp. 418–432. Springer, Cham (2014). https://doi.org/10.1007/978-3-319-11749-2_32
8. Ji, G., Liu, K., He, S., Zhao, J.: Distant supervision for relation extraction with sentence-level attention and entity descriptions. In: 31st AAAI Conference on Artificial Intelligence (AAAI 2017), pp. 3060–3066. AAAI Press (2017)

9. Koza, J.R.: Genetic Programming: On the Programming of Computers by Means of Natural Selection, vol. 1. MIT Press, Cambridge (1992)
10. Liu, B.: Sentiment Analysis: Mining Opinions, Sentiments, and Emotions. Cambridge University Press, Cambridge (2015)
11. Mitchell, T.M., et al.: Machine learning (1997)
12. Moghaddam, S.: Beyond sentiment analysis: mining defects and improvements from customer feedback. In: Hanbury, A., Kazai, G., Rauber, A., Fuhr, N. (eds.) ECIR 2015. LNCS, vol. 9022, pp. 400–410. Springer, Cham (2015). https://doi.org/10. 1007/978-3-319-16354-3_44
13. Qiao, Z., Zhang, X., Zhou, M., Wang, G.A., Fan, W.: A domain oriented LDA model for mining product defects from online customer reviews. In: 50th Hawaii International Conference on System Sciences (HICSS 2017), pp. 1821–1830. ScholarSpace/AIS Electronic Library (2017)
14. Ramanand, J., Bhavsar, K., Pedanekar, N.: Wishful thinking: finding suggestions and 'Buy' wishes from product reviews. In: Workshop on Computational Approaches to Analysis and Generation of Emotion in Text (CAAGET 2010), pp. 54–61. ACL (2010)
15. Sahni, T., Chandak, C., Chedeti, N.R., Singh, M.: Efficient Twitter sentiment classification using subjective distant supervision. In: 9th International Conference on Communication Systems and Networks (COMSNETS 2017), pp. 548–553. IEEE (2017)

Analysis and Multilabel Classification of Quebec Court Decisions in the Domain of Housing Law

Olivier Salaün[1]([✉]), Philippe Langlais[1], Andrés Lou[2], Hannes Westermann[3], and Karim Benyekhlef[3]

[1] RALI, Université de Montréal, Montreal, QC, Canada
{salaunol,felipe}@iro.umontreal.ca
[2] CLaC, Concordia University, Montreal, QC, Canada
and_lou@encs.concordia.ca
[3] Cyberjustice Laboratory, Université de Montréal, Montreal, QC, Canada
{hannes.westermann,karim.benyekhlef}@umontreal.ca

Abstract. The Régie du Logement du Québec (RDL) is a tribunal with exclusive jurisdiction in matters regarding rental leases. Within the framework of the ACT (Autonomy Through Cyberjustice Technologies) project, we processed an original collection of court decisions in French and performed a thorough analysis to reveal biases that may influence prediction experiments. We studied a multilabel classification task that consists in predicting the types of verdict in order to illustrate the importance of prior data analysis. Our best model, based on the FlauBERT language model, achieves F1 score micro averages of 93.7% and 84.9% in Landlord v. Tenant and Tenant v. Landlord cases respectively. However, with the support of our in-depth analysis, we emphasize that these results should be kept in perspective and that some metrics may not be suitable for evaluating systems in sensitive domains such as housing law.

Keywords: Natural Language Processing · Court decisions · Legal text · Text mining · Multilabel classification · French text · Housing law

1 Context

Many works related to artificial intelligence and law focus on the creation of tools intended for legal professionals to address, say, legal information retrieval with Natural Language Processing (NLP) [10] or knowledge management [3]. In the context of the ACT project (Autonomy Through Cyberjustice Technologies, https://www.ajcact.org/en), methods are explored in order to facilitate and automate access to justice for laymen unfamiliar with legal procedures. For the purpose of evaluating how far machine learning can fulfill these goals, our work focuses on lawsuits submitted to the Régie du Logement du Québec (RDL), a

© Springer Nature Switzerland AG 2020
E. Métais et al. (Eds.): NLDB 2020, LNCS 12089, pp. 135–143, 2020.
https://doi.org/10.1007/978-3-030-51310-8_13

tribunal specialized in tenant-landlord disputes. To the best of our knowledge, no work investigated this dataset apart from [15] which only studied a tiny fraction of it. One long-term goal of the ACT project is to make a system that allows tenants to gauge their chances of winning a case against their landlord and what outcomes they could expect from it by combining personal situations and relevant laws.

In [2], the authors describe a classification model that can simulate such legal reasoning. We can distinguish a first group of classification works as in [1,11,14] that rely on relatively small datasets (usually at most ten thousand samples) but annotated by legal experts. A second group of more recent works such as [5,12,13] apply text mining and NLP engineering on available metadata, thus relaxing the constraint of scarce human annotation and allowing dramatically larger datasets (at least a hundred thousand instances). Some preprocessing work for extracting labels or categories is shown in [12,14], which emphasizes the importance of performing that step with care in order to design sensible and understandable prediction tasks.

In our work, we deepened that latter point by first conducting a thorough analysis on RDL lawsuits and then presenting one multilabel classification task. Then, we discuss the results obtained and reflect upon how to properly evaluate legal prediction experiments.

2   Dataset Analysis

Understanding the data, especially in a specific domain such as housing law, is paramount to conduct meaningful experiments. The RDL collection consists of 981,112 decisions in French issued from 2001 to early 2018 by 72 judges in 29 tribunals around Quebec. Some of these documents are provided as public data by the SOQUIJ legal documents search engine (http://citoyens.soquij.qc.ca/); however, we obtained access to the entire corpus. Each decision mainly consists of a body of text with three parts that always appear in the following order, as illustrated in Fig. 1:

- fact descriptions and evidence presented by each party (here, a proof of tenant's failure to comply with payment schedule; lines 1 to 3 in Fig. 1);
- a legal reasoning section in which the judge analyses the case in the light of the applicable laws (lines 4 to 6);
- a verdict section with the judge final decisions (e.g. defendant ordered to pay damages to the plaintiff, rejection of the claim; lines 7 to 11).

The decisions also contain metadata (top and bottom of Fig. 1). After cleaning up and removing all documents with missing information and duplicates, we obtained a total of 667,305 texts with an average length of 363 tokens.

BUREAU DE [COURT CITY LOCATION]

No dossier :   [FILE NUMBER]   No demande :   [CLAIM NUMBER]
Date :   [SIGNATURE DATE OF THE JUDGMENT]
Régisseure :   [JUDGE'S FULL NAME], juge administrative

[PLAINTIFF'S FULL NAME]
Locatrice - Partie demanderesse
c.
[DEFENDANT'S FULL NAME]
Locataire - Partie défenderesse

DÉCISION

[1]   La locatrice demande la résiliation du bail et l'expulsion du locataire, le recouvrement du loyer (1 080 $) ainsi que le loyer dû au moment de l'audience, plus l'exécution provisoire de la décision malgré l'appel.
[2]   Il s'agit d'un bail du 1er décembre 2016 au 30 juin 2018 au loyer mensuel de 545 $, payable le premier jour de chaque mois.
[3]   La preuve démontre que le locataire doit 1 620 $, soit le loyer des mois de février, mars et avril 2017, plus 9 $ représentant les frais de notification prévus au Règlement.
[4]   Le locataire est en retard de plus de trois semaines pour le paiement du loyer, la résiliation du bail est donc justifiée par l'application de l'article 1971 C.c.Q.
[5]   Le bail n'est toutefois pas résilié si le loyer dû, les intérêts et les frais sont payés avant jugement, conformément aux dispositions de l'article 1883 C.c.Q.
[6]   Le préjudice causé à la locatrice justifie l'exécution provisoire de la décision, comme il est prévu à l'article 82.1 de la *Loi sur la Régie du logement*¹.

POUR CES MOTIFS, LE TRIBUNAL :

[7]   **RÉSILIE** le bail et **ORDONNE** l'expulsion du locataire et de tous les occupants du logement;
[8]   **ORDONNE** l'exécution provisoire, malgré l'appel, de l'ordonnance d'expulsion à compter du 11e jour de sa date;
[9]   **CONDAMNE** le locataire à payer à la locatrice la somme de 1 620 $, plus les intérêts au taux légal et l'indemnité additionnelle prévue à l'article 1619 C.c.Q., à compter du 22 mars 2017 sur la somme de 1 080 $, et sur le solde à compter de l'échéance de chaque loyer, plus les frais judiciaires de 83 $;
[10] **RÉSERVE** à la locatrice tous ses recours;
[11] **REJETTE** la demande quant aux autres conclusions.

_____
[JUDGE'S FULL NAME]
Présence(s) :   la locatrice
Date de l'audience :   [AUDIENCE DATE]

Fig. 1. RDL sample decision from SOQUIJ (available at http://t.soquij.ca/p9TYc)

2.1   Analysis of the Plaintiffs and Defendants

We extracted from the metadata of each decision over a dozen of characteristics using NLP-engineered methods. For instance, we managed to identify the type of each party: legal persons (juridical entities like organizations) and natural (human and physical) persons. The latter encompasses four sub-categories: succession (a liquidator acts on behalf of a deceased person), multiple persons, single female and single male. Overall, 89% of all cases involve landlords suing tenants (Landlord v. Tenant scenarios or LvT) while 11% involve tenants suing landlords (Tenant v. Landlord scenarios or TvL). In the first scenario, plaintiffs are mostly legal persons while defendants are an absolute majority of single males as shown in Table 1. In the TvL setting, plaintiffs and defendants are predominantly single males.

Table 1. Distribution of plaintiff and defendant types (in percent) by case types

Case type		Landlord v. Tenant		Tenant v. Landlord	
Party		Plaintiff	Defendant	Plaintiff	Defendant
Legal person		41.3	0.2	0.3	33.0
Natur. pers.	Single male	36.8	60.1	54.0	40.0
	Single female	11.0	39.5	45.5	14.0
	Multiple (any genders)	10.7	0.0	0.0	12.6
	Succession	0.2	0.2	0.2	0.3
Total		100	100	100	100
Number of decisions		595,808		71,497	

2.2 Analysis of the Verdicts

Extracting consistent outcomes from the judgments (i.e. lines 7 to 11 in Fig. 1) is crucial for the feasibility and interpretability of prediction tasks. Difficulties in making a simple representation encompassing a wide variety of rulings were shown in [14]. One possible solution consists in identifying a "winner" between the plaintiff and the defendant, but this binary approach is not always suitable (e.g. the plaintiff's claims are partly accepted and rejected by the judge). An opposite approach consists in making labels that cover all possible outcomes, implying a high annotation cost partly illustrated in [15], plus the risk of numerous overly specific labels applicable to very few instances as in [5]. We chose an intermediate solution by narrowing all outcomes to three binary labels:

- **penalty:** the defendant receives penalties (e.g. an order for the landlord to pay damages, an eviction from the accommodation for a tenant);
- **agreement:** the judge enforces an agreement between both parties;
- **rejection:** the judge fully or partially rejects the plaintiff's claims.

These three outcomes are not mutually exclusive and can be applied to any case regardless of whether the plaintiff is the landlord or the tenant. We used an approach similar to [8] for determining the labels of each case by relying on key verbs in capital letters that happen to be good proxies of the verdict. In the example of Fig. 1, penalty and rejection labels apply due to the verbs *CONDAMNE* and *REJETTE* on lines 9 and 11. Major trends are shown in Table 2 for each case type: a landlord-plaintiff succeeds in winning over the tenant in 89% of lawsuits while tenant-plaintiffs' demands are totally or partially rejected by the judge in 69% of lawsuits. Such biases must be considered carefully. It might suffice to know whether the plaintiff is a landlord to get a good approximation of the outcome of a lawsuit. So far, all figures found in our analysis reveal that some care is required when developing machine learning applications as such biases and imbalance in the dataset might be the cause of deceptively good results in classification tasks.

Table 2. Distribution of labels (in percent) by case types

Scenario type	Landlord v. Tenant	Tenant v. Landlord
Cases with agreement label	2.0%	5.4%
Cases with penalty label	89.0%	23.6%
Cases with rejection label	38.3%	68.8%
Total number of cases	595,808	71,497

3   Prediction Task and Results

3.1   Models and Features

As seen in the previous section, claims made by landlords are much more successful than those made by tenants. Because of these biases, we decided to make two subtasks for LvT and TvL scenarios. For each of these subtasks, we made a 60:20:20 train-validation-test split for the corresponding datasets. Our baseline is a dummy classifier that returns a label if it occurs in more than half of the training samples. Thus, it will always and only predict the penalty and rejection labels in LvT and TvL respectively. Among the models used, we present the results for logistic regression implemented through a One-versus-Rest approach (OvR, one classifier per label). Three sets of features are used:

- the metadata alone (court location and judge in charge of the audience, presences and types of plaintiff and defendant);
- the metadata plus TF-IDF vectors (2–8-g at character level) fitted on the first line of the decision (line 1 on Fig. 1). These vectors are later replaced by a mean vector of FastText embeddings [4] of all words contained in the first line. These FastText representations are trained beforehand on the first line (window and vector sizes of 5 and 300, 10 training epochs);
- the metadata plus TF-IDF or FastText vectors (same settings as above) fitted this time on all the text before the verdict (lines 1 to 6 on Fig. 1).

The rationale behind using different lengths of the decision is to check whether models can predict the outcome of a case by solely using the factual elements of a case without relying on the legal analysis, as in [16]. As stressed in [13], elements from the legal analysis section may reveal the verdict. In the absence of efficient means to properly isolate the fact descriptions from the legal analysis, we used the first line of each decision as a proxy for factual elements.

For the latter two settings with different input text lengths, we also applied the FlauBERT base cased language model [7], a variant of BERT (Bidirectional Encoder Representations from Transformers [6]) pretrained on French corpora that we finetuned to our input text (metadata were not used). We set the batch size, maximum sequence length and learning rate to 32, 256 and 1e−5 respectively. Training was set to 10 epochs and stopped whenever a lower loss on the evaluation set was not achieved after 10,000 consecutive optimization steps. Our metrics are accuracy (the predicted labels must exactly match the true ones for a sample to be considered as correctly classified) and micro, macro and weighted F1 score averages. Results are shown in Table 3.

3.2 Discussion of the Results

With the mere use of metadata as features, we managed to beat the baseline model in the LvT scenario for almost all metrics, but got little to no improvement in TvL cases. This may be due to the fact that TvL labels distribution is less imbalanced compared to LvT (see Table 2). When given access to the first line of each document, all models outperform the baseline and the TF-IDF method performs slightly better compared to FastText and FlauBERT across all metrics and scenarios. One possible explanation is that the TF-IDF representation partially preserves characters order while FastText and FlauBERT expressiveness suffer from the shortness of the first line. When the input contains all the text before the verdict, the performances obtained with TF-IDF vectors either stagnate or slightly degrade. The FastText method, on the contrary, significantly improves across all metrics, beating TF-IDF. FlauBERT outperforms FastText with dramatic improvements across all metrics. The fact that FastText and FlauBERT achieve better performance across all metrics with respect to TF-IDF can also be explained by longer text inputs that lead to richer embeddings. On the other hand, the stagnation of TF-IDF may be due to a dramatically larger number of n-grams as the text inputs become longer, leading to longer and sparser TF-IDF vectors that could not be leveraged by our models. FastText and FlauBERT performances also need to be kept in perspective as the paragraphs at the end of the longer text input may reveal information about the verdict as mentioned earlier from [13]. All in all, in both scenarios and with all text before verdict as input, our best model is the FlauBERT one that achieves 93.7% and 85.2% on micro average F1 score and accuracy in the LvT scenario, and 84.9% and 74.6% for the TvL cases.

We must emphasize that regardless of the models and input used, because of the labels imbalance shown in Table 2, one can easily maximize the individual F1 score of the most frequent label in each subtask (individual F1 score exceeds 94% for penalty label in LvT and 81% for rejection label in TvL cases for any model). As a consequence, one can achieve a relatively high micro-average F1 score that is based on recall and precision of all labels altogether: almost all models score above 80% and 70% in LvT and TvL scenarios, even in the first-line setting. The same phenomenon applies to the weighted F1 score average that is also influenced by the most frequent label (provided it can be easily predicted). As the task of a judge consists in applying general legal rules to individual cases with their own particularities, evaluating a classifier for legal outcomes with micro or weighted F1 score averages may convey deceptively good results as these metrics can be influenced by ubiquitous patterns in the data. On the other hand, accuracy and macro F1 score seem to be less sensitive to data imbalance and may be preferred for getting a more rigorous evaluation of predictive systems in sensitive domains such as housing law, though accuracy may also be considered as a metric biased

Table 3. Multilabel classification results for Landlord v. Tenant and Tenant v. Landlord scenarios in percent (for the last two features sets, the highest value of each column is bold)

	Landlord v. Tenant				Tenant v. Landlord			
	F1 micr.	F1 macr.	F1 weig.	Accu.	F1 micr.	F1 macr.	F1 weig.	Accu.
Dummy	77.5	31.4	64.7	56.9	69.8	27.2	57.6	58.3
Metadata only								
OvR Log. reg.	84.3	50.7	82.4	65.4	69.8	35.5	63.4	57.7
Metadata (except FlauBERT) + the first line								
TFIDF representation (2-8 grams at character level)								
OvR Log. reg.	**87.0**	**66.7**	**85.9**	**70.3**	**78.1**	**65.4**	**77.4**	**65.4**
Mean vector of FastText embeddings (vector size 300 and window size 5)								
OvR Log. reg.	85.1	54.6	83.6	66.6	72.7	48.3	69.9	59.3
FlauBERT (batch size 32, max seq length 256, learning rate 1e-5)								
Transformers	83.4	60.9	80.2	64.0	74.0	58.7	73.0	60.1
Metadata (except FlauBERT) + all text before verdict								
TFIDF representation (2-8 grams at character level)								
OvR Log. reg.	86.9	66.8	85.9	70.3	78.1	65.1	77.3	65.2
Mean vector of FastText embeddings (vector size 300 and window size 5)								
OvR Log. reg.	88.7	81.0	88.2	73.7	80.1	77.1	79.7	66.6
FlauBERT (batch size 32, max seq length 256, learning rate 1e-5)								
Transformers	**93.7**	**90.8**	**93.7**	**85.2**	**84.9**	**84.7**	**85.1**	**74.6**

against the majority class when applied to an imbalanced dataset. We would not have been aware of all these fine details without a prior thorough examination of the dataset itself.

4 Conclusion

In this work, we built and analyzed thoroughly an original collection of court decisions in French about landlord-tenant disputes. We were able to extract over a dozen of characteristics for each decision and to detect biases contained in the dataset such as landlords being much more successful plaintiffs with respect to tenants. Such analysis was only feasible thanks to carefully engineered NLP tools combined with background knowledge of the housing law domain. This preliminary step allowed us to suggest one multilabel classification task for predicting legal rulings. Two distinct subtasks were designed for Landlord v. Tenant (LvT) and Tenant v. Landlord (TvL) lawsuits. We could observe that TF-IDF based methods perform relatively well when given the first line of each decision while FastText and FlauBERT approaches excel when all text before verdict is given as input. The latter achieved micro F1 score average and accuracy of 93.7% and 85.2% in LvT cases and 84.9% and 74.6% for TvL cases respectively. Thanks to our prior in-depth study of the strong trends present in the data, we emphasized the risk of using micro and weighted F1 score averages which can be artificially maximized in the presence of overly frequent labels. This remark is particularly important in the evaluation of legal classification models as judges must apply general legal rules to individual cases with their own particularities.

As future work, we consider pursuing our study with a regression task (predicting the amount of indemnities awarded that the judge orders the losing defendant to pay), improving our input corpora by isolating the text sections related to fact descriptions from those related to legal analysis, and further investigation of CamemBERT [9] for the multilabel classification task.

Acknowledgements. We would like to thank the Social Sciences and Humanities Research Council for funding this research through the Autonomy through Cyberjustice Technologies and Artificial Intelligence Project (ACT).

References

1. Aletras, N., Tsarapatsanis, D., Preoţiuc-Pietro, D., Lampos, V.: Predicting judicial decisions of the European Court of Human Rights: a natural language processing perspective. PeerJ Comput. Sci. **2**, e93 (2016)
2. Ashley, K.D., Brüninghaus, S.: Automatically classifying case texts and predicting outcomes. Artif. Intell. Law **17**(2), 125–165 (2009). https://doi.org/10.1007/s10506-009-9077-9
3. Boella, G., Di Caro, L., Humphreys, L., Robaldo, L., Rossi, P., van der Torre, L.: Eunomos, a legal document and knowledge management system for the web to provide relevant, reliable and up-to-date information on the law. Artif. Intell. Law **24**(3), 245–283 (2016). https://doi.org/10.1007/s10506-016-9184-3
4. Bojanowski, P., Grave, E., Joulin, A., Mikolov, T.: Enriching word vectors with subword information. Trans. Assoc. Comput. Linguist. **5**, 135–146 (2017)
5. Chalkidis, I., Fergadiotis, E., Malakasiotis, P., Androutsopoulos, I.: Large-scale multi-label text classification on EU legislation. In: Proceedings of the 57th Annual Meeting of the Association for Computational Linguistics, pp. 6314–6322. Association for Computational Linguistics, Florence, July 2019
6. Devlin, J., Chang, M.W., Lee, K., Toutanova, K.: BERT: pre-training of deep bidirectional transformers for language understanding. In: Proceedings of the 2019 Conference of the North American Chapter of the Association for Computational Linguistics: Human Language Technologies, Volume 1 (Long and Short Papers), pp. 4171–4186. Association for Computational Linguistics, Minneapolis, June 2019. https://doi.org/10.18653/v1/N19-1423, https://www.aclweb.org/anthology/N19-1423
7. Le, H., et al.: FlauBERT: unsupervised language model pre-training for French. arXiv preprint arXiv:1912.05372 (2019)
8. de Maat, E., Winkels, R.: Automated classification of norms in sources of law. In: Francesconi, E., Montemagni, S., Peters, W., Tiscornia, D. (eds.) Semantic Processing of Legal Texts. LNCS (LNAI), vol. 6036, pp. 170–191. Springer, Heidelberg (2010). https://doi.org/10.1007/978-3-642-12837-0_10
9. Martin, L., et al.: CamemBERT: a tasty French language model. arXiv preprint arXiv:1911.03894 (2019)

10. Maxwell, T., Schafer, B.: Natural language processing and query expansion in legal information retrieval: challenges and a response. Int. Rev. Law Comput. Technol. **24**(1), 63–72 (2010)
11. Nallapati, R., Manning, C.D.: Legal docket-entry classification: where machine learning stumbles. In: Proceedings of the Conference on Empirical Methods in Natural Language Processing, pp. 438–446. Association for Computational Linguistics (2008)
12. Soh, J., Lim, H.K., Chai, I.E.: Legal area classification: a comparative study of text classifiers on Singapore Supreme Court judgments. In: Proceedings of the Natural Legal Language Processing Workshop 2019, pp. 67–77. Association for Computational Linguistics, Minneapolis, June 2019
13. Şulea, O.M., Zampieri, M., Vela, M., van Genabith, J.: Predicting the law area and decisions of French Supreme Court cases. In: Proceedings of the International Conference Recent Advances in Natural Language Processing. RANLP 2017, pp. 716–722. INCOMA Ltd., Varna, September 2017
14. Vacek, T., Schilder, F.: A sequence approach to case outcome detection. In: Proceedings of the 16th Edition of the International Conference on Artificial Intelligence and Law, pp. 209–215. ACM (2017)
15. Westermann, H., Walker, V.R., Ashley, K.D., Benyekhlef, K.: Using factors to predict and analyze landlord-tenant decisions to increase access to justice. In: Proceedings of the Seventeenth International Conference on Artificial Intelligence and Law, pp. 133–142 (2019)
16. Zhong, H., Guo, Z., Tu, C., Xiao, C., Liu, Z., Sun, M.: Legal judgment prediction via topological learning. In: Proceedings of the 2018 Conference on Empirical Methods in Natural Language Processing, pp. 3540–3549 (2018)

Sentiment Analysis

A Position Aware Decay Weighted Network for Aspect Based Sentiment Analysis

Avinash Madasu and Vijjini Anvesh Rao(✉)

Samsung R&D Institute, Bangalore, India
{m.avinash,a.vijjini}@samsung.com

Abstract. Aspect Based Sentiment Analysis (ABSA) is the task of identifying sentiment polarity of a text given another text segment or aspect.
In ABSA, a text can have multiple sentiments depending upon each
aspect. Aspect Term Sentiment Analysis (ATSA) is a subtask of ABSA,
in which aspect terms are contained within the given sentence. Most of
the existing approaches proposed for ATSA, incorporate aspect information through a different subnetwork thereby overlooking the advantage
of aspect terms' presence within the sentence. In this paper, we propose a model that leverages the positional information of the aspect.
The proposed model introduces a decay mechanism based on position.
This decay function mandates the contribution of input words for ABSA.
The contribution of a word declines as farther it is positioned from the
aspect terms in the sentence. The performance is measured on two standard datasets from SemEval 2014 Task 4. In comparison with recent
architectures, the effectiveness of the proposed model is demonstrated.

Keywords: Aspect Based Sentiment Analysis · Attention · Sentiment
Analysis · Text classification

1 Introduction

Text Classification deals with the branch of Natural Language Processing (NLP)
that involves classifying a text snippet into two or more predefined categories.
Sentiment Analysis (SA) addresses the problem of text classification in the setting where these predefined categories are sentiments like positive or negative
[7]. Aspect Based Sentiment Analysis (ABSA) is proposed to perform sentiment
analysis at an aspect level [2]. There are four sub-tasks in ABSA namely Aspect
Term Extraction (ATE), Aspect Term Sentiment Analysis (ATSA), Aspect Category Detection (ACD), Aspect Category Sentiment Analysis (ACSA). In the first
sub-task (ATE), the goal is to identify all the aspect terms for a given sentence.
Aspect Term Sentiment Analysis (ATSA) is a classification problem where given
an aspect and a sentence, the sentiment has to classified into one of the predefined polarities. In the ATSA task, the aspect is present within the sentence but

© Springer Nature Switzerland AG 2020
E. Métais et al. (Eds.): NLDB 2020, LNCS 12089, pp. 147–156, 2020.
https://doi.org/10.1007/978-3-030-51310-8_14

can be a single word or a phrase. In this paper, we address the problem of ATSA. Given a set of aspect categories and a set of sentences, the problem of ACD is to classify the aspect into one of those categories. ACSA can be considered similar to ATSA, but the aspect term may not be present in the sentence. It is much harder to find sentiments at an aspect level compared to the overall sentence level because the same sentence might have different sentiment polarities for different aspects. For example consider the sentence, *"The taste of food is good but the service is poor"*. If the aspect term is *food*, the sentiment will be *positive*, whereas if the aspect term is *service*, sentiment will be *negative*. Therefore, the crucial challenge of ATSA is modelling the relationship between aspect terms and its context in the sentence. Traditional methods involve feature engineering trained with machine learning classifiers like Support Vector Machines (SVM) [4]. However, these methods do not take into account the sequential information and require a considerable struggle to define the best set of features. With the advent of deep learning, neural networks are being used for the task of ABSA. For ATSA, LSTM coupled with attention mechanism [1] have been widely used to focus on words relevant to certain aspect. Target-Dependent Long Short-Term Memory (TD-LSTM) uses two LSTM networks to model left and right context words surrounding the aspect term [12]. The outputs from last hidden states of LSTM are concatenated to find the sentiment polarity. Attention Based LSTM (ATAE-LSTM) uses attention on the top of LSTM to concentrate on different parts of a sentence when different aspects are taken as input [15]. Aspect Fusion LSTM (AF-LSTM) [13] uses associative relationship between words and aspect to perform ATSA. Gated Convolution Neural Network (GCAE) [17] employs a gated mechanism to learn aspect information and to incorporate it into sentence representations.

However, these models do not utilize the advantage of the presence of aspect term in the sentence. They either employ an attention mechanism with complex architecture to learn relevant information or train two different architectures for learning sentence and aspect representations. In this paper, we propose a model that utilizes the positional information of the aspect in the sentence. We propose a parameter-less decay function based learning that leverages the importance of words closer to the aspect. Hence, evading the need for a separate architecture for integrating aspect information into the sentence. The proposed model is relatively simple and achieves improved performance compared to models that do not use position information. We experiment with the proposed model on two datasets, restaurant and laptop from SemEval 2014.

2   Related Work

2.1   Aspect Term Sentiment Analysis

Early works of ATSA, employ lexicon based feature selection techniques like Parts of Speech Tagging (POS), unigram features and bigram features [4]. However, these methods do not consider aspect terms and perform sentiment analysis on the given sentence.

Phrase Recursive Neural Network for Aspect based Sentiment Analysis (PhraseRNN) [6] was proposed based on Recursive Neural Tensor Network [10] primarily used for semantic compositionality. PhraseRNN uses dependency and constituency parse trees to obtain aspect representation. An end-to-end neural network model was introduced for jointly identifying aspect and polarity [9]. This model is trained to jointly optimize the loss of aspect and the polarity. In the final layer, the model outputs one of the sentiment polarities along with the aspect. [14] introduced Aspect Fusion LSTM (AF-LSTM) for performing ATSA.

3 Model

In this section, we propose the model Position Based Decay Weighted Network (PDN). The model architecture is shown in Fig. 2. The input to the model is a sentence S and an Aspect A contained within it. Let n represent the maximum sentence length considered.

3.1 Word Representation

Let V be the vocabulary size considered and $X \in \mathbb{R}^{V \times d_w}$ represent the embedding matrix[1], where for each word X_i is a d_w dimensional word vector. Words contained in the embedding matrix are initialized to their corresponding vectors whereas words not contained are initialized to 0's. $I \in \mathbb{R}^{n \times d_w}$ denotes the pretrained embedding representation of a sentence where n is the maximum sentence length.

3.2 Position Encoding

In the ATSA task, aspect A is contained in the sentence S. A can be a word or a phrase. Let k_s denote the starting index and k_e denote the ending index of the aspect term(s) in the sentence. Let i be the index of a word in the sentence. The position encoding of words with respect to aspect are represented using the formula

$$p(i) = \begin{cases} k_s - i + 1, & k_s > i \\ 1, & i \in k_s, k_{s+1}, .., k_{e-1}, k_e \\ i - k_e + 1, & i > k_e \end{cases} \quad (1)$$

The position encodings for the sentence "granted the space is smaller than most it is the best service" where "space" is the aspect is shown in Fig. 2. This number reflects the relative distance of a word from the closest aspect word. The position embeddings from the position encodings are randomly initialized and updated during training. Hence, $P \in \mathbb{R}^{n \times d_p}$ is the position embedding representations of the sentence. d_p denotes the number of dimensions in the position embedding.

---

[1] https://nlp.stanford.edu/data/glove.840B.300d.zip.

3.3 Architecture

As shown in Fig. 2, PDN comprises of two sub-networks: Position Aware Attention Network (PDN) and Decay Weighting Network (DWN).

Position Aware Attention Network (PAN). An LSTM layer is trained on I to produce hidden state representation $h_t \in \mathbb{R}^{d_h}$ for each time step $t \in \{1, n\}$ where d_h is the number of units in the LSTM. The LSTM outputs contain sentence level information and Position embedding contain aspect level information. An attention subnetwork is applied on all h and P to get a scalar score α indicating sentiment weightage of the particular time step to the overall sentiment. However, prior to concatenation, the position embeddings and the LSTM outputs may have been output from disparate activations leading to different distribution. Training on such values may bias the network towards one of the representations. Therefore, we apply a fully connected layer separately but with same activation function Scaled Exponential Linear Unit (SELU) [5] upon them. Two fully connected layers follow this representation. Following are the equations that produce α from LSTM outputs h and position embeddings P.

$$P'_t = selu(W_p \cdot P_t + b_p) \tag{2}$$

$$h'_t = selu(W_h \cdot h_t + b_h) \tag{3}$$

$$H_t = relu(W_a \cdot [h'_t P'_t] + b_a) \tag{4}$$

$$e_t = \tanh(\mathbf{v}^\mathsf{T} \cdot H_t) \tag{5}$$

$$\alpha_t = \frac{\exp(e_t)}{\sum_{i=1}^{n} \exp(e_i)} \tag{6}$$

Decay Weighting Network (DWN). In current and following section, we introduce decay functions. The decay function for scalar position encoding $p(i)$ is represented as the scalar $d(p(i))$. These functions are continuously decreasing in the range $[0, \infty)$. The outputs from the LSTM at every time step are scaled by the decay function's output.

$$Z_t = h_t \cdot d(p(t)) \, \forall \, t \in \{1, n\} \tag{7}$$

A weighted sum O is calculated on the outputs of Decay Weighted network using the attention weights from PAN.

$$O = \alpha \cdot Z \tag{8}$$

A fully connected layer is applied on O which provides an intermediate representation Q. A softmax layer is fully connected to this layer to provide final probabilities.

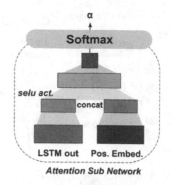

Fig. 1. Attention sub network

Table 1. Accuracy Scores of all models. Performances of baselines are cited from [13]

Model	Restaurant	Laptop
Majority	65.00	53.45
NBOW	67.49	58.62
LSTM	67.94	61.75
TD-LSTM	69.73	62.38
AT-LSTM	74.37	65.83
ATAE-LSTM	70.71	60.34
DCNN	75.18	64.67
AF-LSTM	75.44	68.81
GCAE	76.07	67.27
Tangent-PDN	78.12	68.82
Inverse-PDN	**78.9**	**70.69**
Expo-PDN	78.48	69.43

It is paramount to note that the DWN does not contain any parameters and only uses a decay function and multiplication operations. The decay function provides us with a facility to automatically weight representations closer to aspect as higher and far away as lower, as long as the function hyperparameter is tuned fittingly. Lesser parameters makes the network efficient and easy to train.

Decay Functions. We performed experiments with the following decay functions.

Inverse Decay
Inverse decay is represented as:

$$d(x) = \frac{\lambda}{x} \tag{9}$$

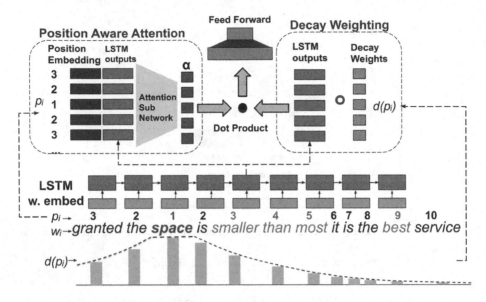

Fig. 2. PDN Architecture, in the shown example, "space" is the aspect. Refer to Fig. 1 for the Attention Sub Network.

Exponential Decay

Exponential decay is represented as:

$$d(x) = e^{-\lambda * x} \tag{10}$$

Tangent Decay

Tangent decay is represented as:

$$d(x) = 1 - tanh(\lambda * x) \tag{11}$$

λ is the hyper-parameter in all the cases.[2]

4   Experiments

4.1   Datasets

We performed experiments on two datasets, Restaurant and Laptop from SemEval 2014 Task 4 [8]. Each data point is a triplet of sentence, aspect and sentiment label. The statistics of the datasets are shown in the Table 2. As most existing works reported results on three sentiment labels *positive, negative, neutral* we performed experiments by removing *conflict* label as well.

---

[2] In our experiments we took $\lambda = 0.45$ for Tangent-PDN, 1.1333 for Inverse-PDN and 0.3 for Expo-PDN.

4.2   Compared Methods

We compare proposed model to the following baselines:

Neural Bag-of-Words (NBOW). NBOW is the sum of word embeddings in the sentence [13].

LSTM. Long Short Term Memory (LSTM) is an important baseline in NLP. For this baseline, aspect information is not used and sentiment analysis is performed on the sentence alone. [13].

TD-LSTM. In TD-LSTM, two separate LSTM layers for modelling the preceding and following contexts of the aspect is done for aspect sentiment analysis [12].

AT-LSTM. In Attention based LSTM (AT-LSTM), aspect embedding is used as the context for attention layer, applied on the sentence [15].

ATAE-LSTM. In this model, aspect embedding is concatenated with input sentence embedding. LSTM is applied on the top of concatenated input [15].

Table 2. Statistics of the datasets

Dataset	Positive		Negative		Neutral	
	Train	Test	Train	Test	Train	Test
Restaurant	2164	728	805	196	633	196
Laptop	987	341	866	128	460	169

DE-CNN. Double Embeddings Convolution Neural Network (DE-CNN) achieved state of the art results on aspect extraction. We compare proposed model with DE-CNN to see how well it performs against DE-CNN. We used aspect embedding instead of domain embedding in the input layer and replaced the final CRF layer with MaxPooling Layer. Results are reported using author's code[3] [16].

AF-LSTM. AF-LSTM incorporates aspect information for learning attention on the sentence using associative relationships between words and aspect [13].

GCAE. GCAE adopts gated convolution layer for learning aspect representation which is integrated into sentence representation through another gated

---

[3] https://github.com/howardhsu/DE-CNN.

convolution layer. This model reported results for four sentiment labels. We ran the experiment using author's code[4] and reported results for three sentiment labels [17].

4.3 Implementation

Every word in the input sentence is converted to a 300 dimensional vector using pretrained word embeddings. The dimension of positional embedding is set to 25 which is initialized randomly and updated during training. The hidden units of LSTM are set to 100. The number of hidden units in the layer fully connected to LSTM is 50 and the layer fully connected to positional embedding layer is 50. The number of hidden units in the penultimate fully connected layer is set to 64. We apply a dropout [11] with a probability 0.5 on this layer. A batch size 20 is considered and the model is trained for 30 epochs. Adam [3] is used as the optimizer with an initial learning rate 0.001.

5 Results and Discussion

The Results are presented in Table 1. The Baselines Majority, NBOW and LSTM do not use aspect information for the task at all. Proposed models significantly outperform them.

5.1 The Role of Aspect Position

The proposed model outperforms other recent and popular architectures as well, these architectures use a separate architecture which takes the aspect input distinctly from the sentence input. In doing so they loose the positional information of the aspect within the sentence. We hypothesize that this information is valuable for ATSA and our results reflect the same. Additionally since proposed architecture does not take any additional aspect inputs apart from position, we get a fairer comparison on the benefits of providing aspect positional information over the aspect words themselves.

5.2 The Role of Decay Functions

Furthermore, while avoiding learning separate architectures for weightages, decay functions act as good approximates. These functions rely on constants alone and lack any parameters thereby expressing their efficiency. The reason these functions work is because they consider an assumption intrinsic to the nature of most natural languages. It is that description words or aspect modifier words come close to the aspect or the entity they describe. For example in Fig. 2, we see the sentence from the Restaurant dataset, "granted the space is smaller than most, it is the best service you can...". The proposed model is able to handle this example which has distinct sentiments for the aspects "space" and "service" due to their proximity from "smaller" and "best" respectively.

---

[4] https://github.com/wxue004cs/GCAE.

6   Conclusion

In this paper, we propose a novel model for Aspect Based Sentiment Analysis relying on relative positions on words with respect to aspect terms. This relative position information is realized in the proposed model through parameter-less decay functions. These decay functions weight words according to their distance from aspect terms by only relying on constants proving their effectiveness. Furthermore, our results and comparisons with other recent architectures, which do not use positional information of aspect terms demonstrate the strength of the decay idea in proposed model.

References

1. Bahdanau, D., Cho, K., Bengio, Y.: Neural machine translation by jointly learning to align and translate. arXiv preprint arXiv:1409.0473 (2014)
2. Hu, M., Liu, B.: Mining opinion features in customer reviews. In: AAAI, vol. 4, pp. 755–760 (2004)
3. Kingma, D.P., Ba, J.: Adam: a method for stochastic optimization. arXiv preprint arXiv:1412.6980 (2014)
4. Kiritchenko, S., Zhu, X., Cherry, C., Mohammad, S.: NRC-Canada-2014: detecting aspects and sentiment in customer reviews. In: Proceedings of the 8th International Workshop on Semantic Evaluation (SemEval 2014), pp. 437–442 (2014)
5. Klambauer, G., Unterthiner, T., Mayr, A., Hochreiter, S.: Self-normalizing neural networks. In: Advances in Neural Information Processing Systems, pp. 971–980 (2017)
6. Nguyen, T.H., Shirai, K.: PhraseRNN: phrase recursive neural network for aspect-based sentiment analysis. In: Proceedings of the 2015 Conference on Empirical Methods in Natural Language Processing, pp. 2509–2514. Association for Computational Linguistics, Lisbon, September 2015. https://doi.org/10.18653/v1/D15-1298, https://www.aclweb.org/anthology/D15-1298
7. Pang, B., Lee, L., Vaithyanathan, S.: Thumbs up?: sentiment classification using machine learning techniques. In: Proceedings of the ACL-02 Conference on Empirical Methods in Natural Language Processing, vol. 10, pp. 79–86. Association for Computational Linguistics (2002)
8. Pontiki, M., Galanis, D., Pavlopoulos, J., Papageorgiou, H., Androutsopoulos, I., Manandhar, S.: SemEval-2014 task 4: aspect based sentiment analysis. In: Proceedings of the 8th International Workshop on Semantic Evaluation (SemEval 2014), pp. 27–35. Association for Computational Linguistics, Dublin, August 2014. https://doi.org/10.3115/v1/S14-2004, https://www.aclweb.org/anthology/S14-2004
9. Schmitt, M., Steinheber, S., Schreiber, K., Roth, B.: Joint aspect and polarity classification for aspect-based sentiment analysis with end-to-end neural networks. In: Proceedings of the 2018 Conference on Empirical Methods in Natural Language Processing, pp. 1109–1114. Association for Computational Linguistics, Brussels, October–November 2018. https://www.aclweb.org/anthology/D18-1139
10. Socher, R., et al.: Recursive deep models for semantic compositionality over a sentiment treebank. In: Proceedings of the 2013 Conference on Empirical Methods in Natural Language Processing, pp. 1631–1642. Association for Computational Linguistics, Seattle, October 2013. https://www.aclweb.org/anthology/D13-1170

11. Srivastava, N., Hinton, G., Krizhevsky, A., Sutskever, I., Salakhutdinov, R.: Dropout: a simple way to prevent neural networks from overfitting. J. Mach. Learn. Res. **15**(1), 1929–1958 (2014)
12. Tang, D., Qin, B., Feng, X., Liu, T.: Effective LSTMs for target-dependent sentiment classification. arXiv preprint arXiv:1512.01100 (2015)
13. Tay, Y., Tuan, L.A., Hui, S.C.: Learning to attend via word-aspect associative fusion for aspect-based sentiment analysis. In: Thirty-Second AAAI Conference on Artificial Intelligence (2018)
14. Tay, Y., Tuan, L.A., Hui, S.C.: Learning to attend via word-aspect associative fusion for aspect-based sentiment analysis (2018)
15. Wang, Y., Huang, M., Zhao, L., et al.: Attention-based LSTM for aspect-level sentiment classification. In: Proceedings of the 2016 Conference on Empirical Methods in Natural Language Processing, pp. 606–615 (2016)
16. Xu, H., Liu, B., Shu, L., Yu, P.S.: Double embeddings and CNN-based sequence labeling for aspect extraction. arXiv preprint arXiv:1805.04601 (2018)
17. Xue, W., Li, T.: Aspect based sentiment analysis with gated convolutional networks. arXiv preprint arXiv:1805.07043 (2018)

Studying Attention Models in Sentiment Attitude Extraction Task

Nicolay Rusnachenko[1](✉) and Natalia Loukachevitch[1,2](✉)

[1] Bauman Moscow State Technical University, Moscow, Russia
kolyarus@yandex.ru
[2] Lomonosov Moscow State University, Moscow, Russia
louk_nat@mail.ru

Abstract. In the sentiment attitude extraction task, the aim is to identify «attitudes» – sentiment relations between entities mentioned in text. In this paper, we provide a study on attention-based context encoders in the sentiment attitude extraction task. For this task, we adapt attentive context encoders of two types: (I) feature-based; (II) self-based. Our experiments (https://github.com/nicolay-r/attitu de-extraction-with-attention) with a corpus of Russian analytical texts RuSentRel illustrate that the models trained with attentive encoders outperform ones that were trained without them and achieve 1.5–5.9% increase by $F1$. We also provide the analysis of attention weight distributions in dependence on the term type.

Keywords: Relation extraction · Sentiment analysis · Attention-based models

1 Introduction

Classifying relations between entities mentioned in texts remains one of the popular tasks in natural language processing (NLP). The sentiment attitude extraction task aims to seek for positive/negative relations between objects expressed as named entities in texts [10]. Let us consider the following sentence as an example (named entities are underlined):

"Meanwhile Moscow has repeatedly emphasized that its activity in the Baltic Sea is a response precisely to actions of NATO and the escalation of the hostile approach to Russia near its eastern borders"

In the example above, named entities «Russia» and «NATO» have the negative attitude towards each other with additional indication of other named entities. The complexity of the sentence structure is one of the greatest difficulties one encounters when dealing with the relation extraction task. Texts usually

The reported study was partially supported by RFBR, research project № 20-07-01059.

E. Métais et al. (Eds.): NLDB 2020, LNCS 12089, pp. 157–169, 2020.
https://doi.org/10.1007/978-3-030-51310-8_15

contain a lot of named entity mentions; a single opinion might comprise several sentences.

This paper is devoted to study of models for targeted sentiment analysis with attention. The intuition exploited in the models with attentive encoders is that not all terms in the context are relevant for attitude indication. The interactions of words, not just their isolated presence, may reveal the specificity of contexts with attitudes of different polarities. The primary contribution of this work is an application of attentive encoders based on (I) sentiment frames and attitude participants (features); (II) context itself. We conduct the experiments on the RuSentRel [7] collection. The results demonstrate that attentive models with CNN-based and over LSTM-based encoders result in 1.5–5.9% by $F1$ over models without attentive encoders.

2   Related Work

In previous works, various neural network approaches for targeted sentiment analysis were proposed. In [10] the authors utilize convolutional neural networks (CNN). Considering relation extraction as a three-scale classification task of contexts with attitudes in it, the authors subdivide each context into *outer* and *inner* (relative to attitude participants) to apply Piecewise-CNN (PCNN) [16]. The latter architecture utilizes a specific idea of *max-pooling* operation. Initially, this is an operation, which extracts the maximal values within each convolution. However, for relation classification, it reduces information extremely rapid and blurs significant aspects of context parts. In case of PCNN, separate max-pooling operations are applied to outer and inner contexts. In the experiments, the authors revealed a fast training process and a slight improvement in the PCNN results in comparison to CNN.

In [12], the authors proposed an attention-based CNN model for semantic relation classification [4]. The authors utilized the attention mechanism to select the most relevant context words with respect to participants of a semantic relation. The architecture of the attention model is a multilayer perceptron (MLP), which calculates the weight of a word in context with respect to the entity. The resulting ATTCNN model outperformed several CNN and LSTM based approaches with 2.6–3.8% by F1-measure.

In [9], the authors experimented with attentive models in aspect-based sentiment analysis. The models were aimed to identify sentiment polarity of specific *targets* in context, which are characteristics or parts of an entity. Both targets and the context were treated as *sequences*. The authors proposed an interactive attention network (IAN), which establishes element relevance of one sequence with the other in two directions: targets to context, context to targets. The effectiveness of IAN was demonstrated on the SemEval-2014 dataset [13] and several biomedical datasets [1].

In [14,17], the authors experimented with self-based attention models, in which *targets* became adapted automatically during the training process. Comparing with IAN, the presence of targets might be unclear in terms of algorithms.

The authors considered the attention as context word quantification with respect to abstract targets. In [14], the authors brought a similar idea also onto the sentence level. The obtained hierarchical model was called as HAN.

3 Data and Lexicons

We consider sentiment analysis of Russian analytical articles collected in the RuSentRel corpus [8]. The corpus comprises texts in the international politics domain and contains a lot of opinions. The articles are labeled with annotations of two types: (I) the author's opinion on the subject matter of the article; (II) the attitudes between the participants of the described situations. The annotation of the latter type includes 2000 relations across 73 large analytical texts. Annotated sentiments can be only *positive* or *negative*. Additionally, each text is provided with annotation of mentioned named entities. Synonyms and variants of named entities are also given, which allows not to deal with the coreference of named entities.

In our study, we also use two Russian sentiment resources: the RuSentiLex lexicon [7], which contains words and expressions of the Russian language with sentiment labels and the RuSentiFrames lexicon [11], which provides several types of sentiment attitudes for situations associated with specific Russian predicates.

The RuSentiFrames[1] lexicon describes sentiments and connotations conveyed with a predicate in a verbal or nominal form [11], such as "осудить, улучшить, преувеличить" (to condemn, to improve, to exaggerate), etc. The structure of the frames in RuSentFrames comprises: (I) the set of predicate-specific roles; (II) frames dimensions such as the attitude of the author towards participants of the situation, attitudes between the participants, effects for participants. Currently, RuSentiFrames contains frames for more than 6 thousand words and expressions.

In RuSentiFrames, individual semantic roles are numbered, beginning with zero. For a particular predicate entry, Arg0 is generally the argument exhibiting features of a Prototypical Agent, while Arg1 is a Prototypical Patient or Theme [2]. In the main part of the frame, the most applicable for the current study is the polarity of Arg0 with a respect to Arg1 (A0→A1). For example, in case of Russian verb "одобрить" (to approve) the sentiment polarity A0→A1 is positive.

4 Model

In this paper, the task of sentiment attitude extraction is treated as follows: given a pair of named entities, we predict a sentiment label of a pair, which could be positive, negative, or *neutral*. As the RuSentRel corpus provides opinions with positive or negative sentiment labels only (Sect. 3), we automatically added neutral sentiments for all pairs not mentioned in the annotation and co-occurred in the same sentences of the collection texts. We consider a *context* as a text fragment that is limited by a single sentence and includes a pair of named entities.

---

[1] https://github.com/nicolay-r/RuSentiFrames/tree/v1.0.

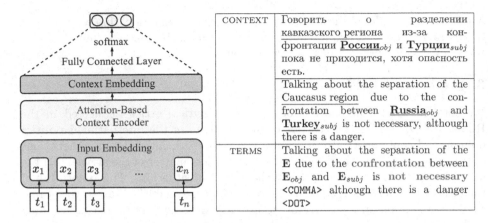

Fig. 1. (*left*) General, context-based 3-scale (positive, negative, neutral) classification model, with details on «Attention-Based Context Encoder» block in Sect. 4.1 and 4.2; (*right*) An example of a context processing into a sequence of terms; attitude participants («Russia», «Turkey») and other mentioned entities become masked; frames are bolded and optionally colored corresponding to the sentiment value of A0→A1 polarity.

The general architecture is presented in Fig. 1 (left), where the sentiment could be extracted from the context. To present a context, we treat the original text as a sequence of terms $[t_1, \ldots, t_n]$ limited by n. Each term belongs to one of the following classes: ENTITIES, FRAMES, TOKENS, and WORDS (if none of the prior has not been matched). We use masked representation for attitude participants ($\underline{E}_{obj}$, $\underline{E}_{subj}$) and mentioned named entities (E) to prevent models from capturing related information.

To represent FRAMES, we combine a frame entry with the corresponding A0→A1 sentiment polarity value (and *neutral* if the latter is absent). We also invert sentiment polarity when an entry has "не" (not) preposition. For example, in Fig. 1 (right) all entries are encoded with the negative polarity A0→A1: "конфронтация" (confrontation) has a negative polarity, and "не приходится" (not necessary) has a positive polarity of entry "necessary" which is inverted due to the "not" preposition.

The TOKENS group includes: punctuation marks, numbers, url-links. Each term of WORDS is considered in a lemmatized[2] form. Figure 1 (right) provides a context example with the corresponding representation («TERMS» block).

To represent the context in a model, each term is embedded with a vector of fixed dimension. The sequence of embedded vectors $X = [x_1, \ldots, x_n]$ is denoted as *input embedding* ($x_i \in \mathbb{R}^m, i \in \overline{1..n}$). Sections 4.1 and 4.2 provide an encoder implementation in details. In particular, each encoder relies on input embedding and generates output *embedded context* vector s.

---

[2] https://tech.yandex.ru/mystem/.

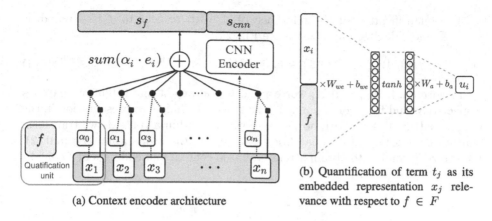

(a) Context encoder architecture

(b) Quantification of term t_j as its embedded representation x_j relevance with respect to $f \in F$

Fig. 2. ATTCNN neural network [6]

In order to determine a sentiment class by the embedded context s, we apply: (I) the hyperbolic tangent activation function towards s and (II) transformation through the *fully connected layer*:

$$r = W_r \cdot \tanh(s) + b_r \qquad W_r \in \mathbb{R}^{z \times c}, \; b_r \in \mathbb{R}^c, \; c = 3 \qquad (1)$$

In Formula 1, W_r, b_r corresponds to hidden states; z correspond to the size of vector s, and c is a number of classes. Finally, to obtain an output vector of probabilities $o = \{\rho_i\}_{i=1}^c$, we use *softmax* operation:

$$\rho_i = softmax(r_i) = \frac{\exp(r_i)}{\sum_{j=1}^c \exp(r_j)} \qquad (2)$$

4.1   Feature Attentive Context Encoders

In this section, we consider *features* as a significant for attitude identification context terms, towards which we would like to quantify the relevance of each term in the context. For a particular context, we select embedded values of the (I) attitude participants ($\underline{E}_{obj}$, $\underline{E}_{subj}$) and (II) terms of the FRAMES group and create a set of features $F = [f_1, \ldots, f_k]$ limited by k.

MLP-Attention.   Figure 2 illustrates a feature-attentive encoder with the quantification approach called Multi-Layer Perceptron [6]. In formulas 3–5, we describe the quantification process of a context embedding X with respect to a particular feature $f \in F$. Given an i'th embedded term x_i, we concatenate its representation with f:

$$h_i = [x_i, f] \qquad h_i \in \mathbb{R}^{2 \cdot m} \qquad (3)$$

The quantification of the relevance of x_i with respect to f is denoted as $u_i \in \mathbb{R}$ and calculated as follows (see Fig. 2a):

$$u_i = W_a \left[\tanh(W_{we} \cdot h_i + b_{we}) \right] + b_a \qquad W_{we} \in \mathbb{R}^{2 \cdot m \times \mathbf{h}_{\mathrm{MLP}}}, \qquad W_a \in \mathbb{R}^{\mathbf{h}_{\mathrm{MLP}}} \quad (4)$$

In Formula 4, W_{we} and W_a correspond to the weight and attention matrices respectively, and $\mathbf{h}_{\mathrm{MLP}}$ corresponds to the size of the hidden representation in the weight matrix. To deal with normalized weights within a context, we transform quantified values u_i into probabilities α_i using $softmax$ operation (Formula 2). We utilize Formula 5 to obtain attention-based context embedding $\hat{s}$ of a context with respect to feature f:

$$\hat{s} = \sum_{i=1}^{n} x_i \cdot \alpha_i \qquad \hat{s} \in \mathbb{R}^m \tag{5}$$

Applying Formula 5 towards each feature $f_j \in F$, $j \in \overline{1..k}$ results in vector $\{\hat{s}_j\}_{j=1}^{k}$. We use *average-pooling* to transform the latter sequence into single averaged vector $s_f = \hat{s}_j / [\sum_{j=1}^{k} \hat{s}_j]$.

We also utilize a CNN-based encoder (Fig. 2b) to compete the context representation $s_{cnn} \in \mathbb{R}^{\mathbf{c}}$, where $\mathbf{c}$ is related to convolutional filters count [10]. The resulting context embedding vector s (size of $z = m + \mathbf{c}$) is a concatenation of s_f and s_{cnn}.

IAN. As a context encoder, a Recurrent Neural Network (RNN) model allows treating the context $[t_1, \ldots, t_n]$ as a sequence of terms to generate a hidden representation, enriched with features of previously appeared terms. In comparison with CNN, the application of RNN allows keeping a history of the whole sequence while CNN-based encoders remain limited by the window size. The application of RNN towards a context and certain features appeared in it – is another way how the correlation of these both factors could be quantitatively measured [9].

Figure 3a illustrates the IAN architecture attention encoder. The input assumes separated sequences of embedded terms X and embedded features F. To learn the hidden term semantics for each input, we utilize the LSTM [5] recurrent neural network architecture, which addresses learning long-term dependencies by avoiding gradient vanishing and expansion problems. The calculation h_t of t'th embedded term x_t based on prior state h_{t-1}, where the latter acts as a parameter of auxiliary functions [5]. The application of LSTM towards the input sequences results in $[h_1^c, \ldots, h_n^c]$ and $[h_1^f, \ldots, h_k^f]$, where $h_i^c, h_j^f \in \mathbb{R}^{\mathbf{h}}$ ($i \in \overline{1..n}$, $j \in \overline{1..k}$) and $\mathbf{h}$ is the size of the hidden representation. The quantification of input sequences is carried out in the following directions: (I) feature representation with respect to context, and (II) context representation with respect to features. To obtain the representation of a hidden sequence, we utilize *average-pooling*. In Fig. 3a, p_f and p_c denote a hidden representation of features and context respectively. Figure 3b illustrates the quantification computation of a hidden state h_t with respect to p:

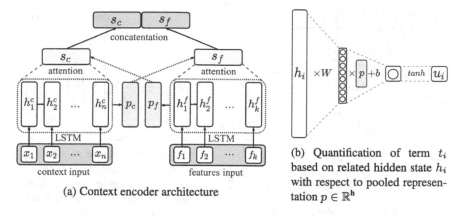

Fig. 3. Interactive Attention Network (IAN) [9]

(b) Quantification of term t_i based on related hidden state h_i with respect to pooled representation $p \in \mathbb{R}^h$

(a) Context encoder architecture

$$u_i^c = \tanh(h_i^c \cdot W_f \cdot p_f + b_f) \qquad W_f \in \mathbb{R}^{h \times h}, \quad b_f \in \mathbb{R}, \quad i \in \overline{1..n}$$
$$u_j^f = \tanh(h_j^f \cdot W_c \cdot p_c + b_c) \qquad W_c \in \mathbb{R}^{h \times h}, \quad b_c \in \mathbb{R}, \quad j \in \overline{1..k} \tag{6}$$

In order to deal with normalized weight vectors α_i^f and α_j^c, we utilize the *softmax* operation for u^f and u^c respectively (Formula 2). The resulting context vector s (size of $z = 2 \cdot \mathbf{h}$) is a concatenation of weighted context s_c and features s_f representations:

$$s_c = \sum_{i=1}^{n} \alpha_i^c \cdot h_i^c \quad s_f = \sum_{j=1}^{k} \alpha_j^f \cdot h_j^f \tag{7}$$

4.2 Self Attentive Context Encoders

In Sect. 4.1 the application of attention in context embedding fully relies on the sequence of predefined features. The quantification of context terms is performed towards each feature. In turn, the *self-attentive* approach assumes to quantify a context with respect to an abstract parameter. Unlike quantification methods in feature-attentive embedding models, here the latter is replaced with a hidden state (parameter w, see Fig. 4b), which modified during the training process.

Figure 4a illustrates the bi-directional RNN-based self-attentive context encoder architecture. We utilize bi-directional LSTM (BiLSTM) to obtain a pair of sequences $\overrightarrow{h}$ and $\overleftarrow{h}$ ($\overrightarrow{h_i}, \overleftarrow{h_i} \in \mathbb{R}^h$). The resulting context representation $H = [h_1, \ldots, h_n]$ is composed as the concatenation of bi-directional sequences elementwise: $h_i = \overrightarrow{h_i} + \overleftarrow{h_i}$, $i \in \overline{1..n}$. The quantification of hidden term representation $h_i \in \mathbb{R}^{2 \cdot \mathbf{h}}$ with respect to $w \in \mathbb{R}^{2 \cdot \mathbf{h}}$ is described in formulas 8–9 and illustrated in Fig. 4b.

$$m_i = \tanh(h_i) \tag{8}$$
$$u_i = m_i^T \cdot w \tag{9}$$

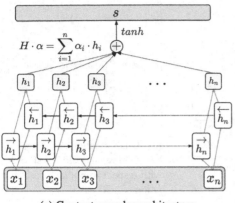
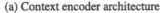

(a) Context encoder architecture

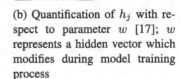

(b) Quantification of h_j with respect to parameter w [17]; w represents a hidden vector which modifies during model training process

Fig. 4. Attention-based bi-directional LSTM neural network (ATT-BLSTM) [17]

We apply the *softmax* operation towards u_i to obtain vector of normalized weights $\alpha \in \mathbb{R}^n$. The resulting context embedding vector s (size of $z = 2 \cdot \mathbf{h}$) is an activated weighted sum of each parameter of context hidden states:

$$s = tanh(H \cdot \alpha) \tag{10}$$

5 Model Details

Input Embedding Details. We provide embedding details of context term groups described in Sect. 4. For WORDS and FRAMES, we look up for vectors in precomputed and publicly available model[3] M_{word} based on news articles with window size of 20, and vector size of 1000. Each term that is not presented in the model we treat as a sequence of *parts* (n-grams) and look up for related vectors in M_{word} to complete an averaged vector. For a particular part, we start with a trigram ($n = 3$) and decrease n until the related n-gram is found. For masked entities ($E, \underline{E}_{obj}, \underline{E}_{subj}$) and TOKENS, each element embedded with a randomly initialized vector with size of 1000.

Each context term has been additionally expanded with the following parameters:

- Distance embedding [10] ($v_{\text{D-}obj}, v_{\text{D-}subj}$) – is vectorized distance in terms from attitude participants of entry pair ($\underline{E}_{obj}$ and $\underline{E}_{subj}$ respectively) to a given term;
- Closest to synonym distance embedding ($v_{\text{SD-}obj}, v_{\text{SD-}subj}$) is a vectorized absolute distance in terms from a given term towards the nearest entity, synonymous to $\underline{E}_{obj}$ and $\underline{E}_{subj}$ respectively;

---

[3] http://rusvectores.org/static/models/rusvectores2/news_mystem_skipgram_1000 _20_2015.bin.gz.

- Part-of-speech embedding (v_{POS}) is a vectorized tag for WORDS (for terms of other groups considering «unknown» tag);
- A0→A1 polarity embedding ($v_{A0\rightarrow A1}$) is a vectorized «positive» or «negative» value for frame entries whose description in RuSentiFrames provides the corresponding polarity (otherwise considering «neutral» value); polarity is inverted when an entry has "не" (not) preposition.

Training. This process assumes hidden parameter optimization of a given model. We utilize an algorithm described in [10]. The input is organized in minibatches, where minibatch yields of l *bags*. Each bag has a set of t pairs $\langle X_j, y_j \rangle_{j=1}^{t}$, where each pair is described by an input embedding X_j with the related label $y_j \in \mathbb{R}^c$. The training process is iterative, and each iteration includes the following steps:

1. Composing a minibatch of l bags of size t;
2. Performing forward propagation through the network which results in a vector (size of $q = l \cdot t$) of outputs $o_k \in \mathbb{R}^c$;
3. Computing cross entropy loss for output: $L_k = \sum_{j=1}^{c} \log p(y_i|o_{k,j}; \theta)$, $k \in \overline{1..q}$;
4. Composing cost vector $\{cost_i\}_{i=1}^{l}$, $cost_i = \max\left[L_{(i-1)\cdot t} .. L_{i \cdot t}\right)$ to update hidden variables set; $cost_i$ is a maximal loss within i'th bag;

Parameters Settings. The minibatch size (l) is set to 2, where contexts count per bag t is set to 3. All the sentences were limited by 50 terms. For embedding parameters ($v_{\text{D-}obj}$, $v_{\text{D-}subj}$, $v_{\text{SD-}obj}$, $v_{\text{SD-}subj}$, v_{POS}, $v_{A0\rightarrow A1}$), we use randomly initialized vectors with size of 5. For CNN and PCNN context encoders, the size of convolutional window and filters count (**c**) were set to 3 and 300 respectively. As for parameters related to sizes of hidden states in Sect. 4: $\mathbf{h}_{\text{MLP}} = 10$, $\mathbf{h} = 128$. For feature attentive encoders, we keep frames in order of their appearance in context and limit k by 5. We utilize the AdaDelta optimizer with parameters $\rho = 0.95$ and $\epsilon = 10^{-6}$ [15]. To prevent models from overfitting, we apply *dropout* towards the output with keep probability set to 0.8. We use Xavier weight initialization to setup initial values for hidden states [3].

6   Experiments

We conduct experiments with the RuSentRel[4] corpus in following formats:

1. Using 3-fold cross-validation (CV), where all folds are equal in terms of the number of sentences;
2. Using predefined TRAIN/TEST separation[5].

---

[4] https://github.com/nicolay-r/RuSentRel/tree/v1.1.
[5] https://miem.hse.ru/clschool/results.

Table 1. Three class context classification results by $F1$ measure (RuSentRel dataset); Columns from left to right: (I) average value in CV-3 experiment ($F1_{avg}$) with results on each split ($F1^i_{cv}$, $i \in \overline{1..3}$); (II) results on TRAIN/TEST separation ($F1_{TEST}$)

Model	$F1_{avg}$	$F1^1_{cv}$	$F1^2_{cv}$	$F1^3_{cv}$	$F1_{TEST}$
ATT-BLSTM	**0.314**	**0.35**	0.27	**0.32**	**0.35**
ATT-BLSTM$^{z\text{-}yang}$	0.292	0.33	0.25	0.30	0.33
BiLSTM	0.286	0.32	0.26	0.28	0.34
IAN$_{ef}$	0.289	0.31	0.28	0.27	0.32
IAN$_{ends}$	0.286	0.31	0.26	0.29	0.32
LSTM	0.284	0.28	0.27	0.29	0.32
PCNN$_{att\text{-}ends}$	0.297	0.32	**0.29**	0.28	**0.35**
PCNN$_{att\text{-}ef}$	0.289	0.31	0.25	0.31	0.31
PCNN	0.285	0.29	0.27	0.30	0.32

In order to evaluate and assess attention-based models, we provide a list of baseline models. These are independent encoders described in Sects. 4.1 and 4.2: PCNN [10], LSTM, BiLSTM. In case of models with feature-based attentive encoders (IAN$_*$, PCNN$_*$) we experiment with following feature sets: attitude participants only (*att-ends*), and frames with attitude participants (*att-ef*). For self-based attentive encoders we experiment with ATT-BLSTM (Sect. 4.2) and ATT-BLSTM$^{z\text{-}yang}$ – is a bi-directional LSTM model with word-based attentive encoder of HAN model [14].

Table 1 provides related results. For evaluating models in this task, we adopt macroaveraged F1-score ($F1$) over documents. F1-score is considered averaging of the positive and negative class. We measure $F1$ on train part every 10 epochs. The number of epochs was limited by 150. The training process terminates when $F1$ on train part becomes greater than 0.85. Analyzing $F1_{TEST}$ results it is quite difficult to demarcate attention-based models from baselines except ATT-BLSTM and PCNN$_{att\text{-}ends}$. In turn, average results by $F1$ in the case of CV-3 experiments illustrate the effectiveness of attention application. The average increase in the performance of such models over related baselines is as follows: 1.4% (PCNN$_*$), 1.2% (IAN$_*$), and 5.9% (ATT-BLSTM, ATT-BLSTM$^{z\text{-}yang}$) by $F1$. The greatest increase in 9.8% by $F1$ is achieved by ATT-BLSTM model.

7   Analysis of Attention Weights

According to Sects. 4.1 and 4.2, attentive embedding models perform the quantification of terms in the context. The latter results in the probability distribution of weights[6] across the terms mentioned in a context.

---

[6] We consider and analyze only context weights in case of IAN models.

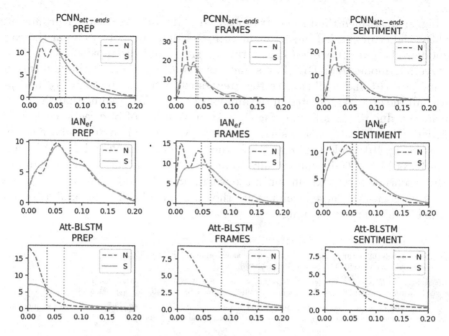

Fig. 5. Kernel density estimations (KDE) of context-level weight distributions of term groups (from left to right: PREP, FRAMES, SENTIMENT) across *neutral* (N) and *sentiment* (S) context sets for models: $PCNN_{att-ef}$, IAN_{ef}, ATT-BLSTM; the probability range (x-axis) scaled to $[0, 0.2]$; vertical lines indicate expected values of distributions

We utilize the TEST part of the RuSentRel dataset (Sect. 6) for analysis of weight distribution of FRAMES group, declared in Sect. 4, across all input contexts. We also introduce two extra groups utilized in the analysis by separating the subset of WORDS into prepositions (PREP) and terms appeared in RuSentiLex lexicon (SENTIMENT) described in Sect. 3.

The *context-level weight* of a group is a weighted sum of terms which both appear in the context and belong the corresponding term group. Figure 5 illustrates the weight distribution plots, where the models are organized in rows, and the columns correspond to the term groups. Each plot combines distributions of context-levels weights across:

– **Neutral contexts** – contexts, labeled as **neutral**;
– **Sentiment contexts** – contexts, labeled with **positive or negative** labels.

In Fig. 5 and further, the distribution of context-level weights across neutral («N» in legends) and sentiment contexts («S» in legends) denoted as ρ_N^g and ρ_S^g respectively. The rows in Fig. 5 correspond to the following models: (1) $PCNN_{att-ef}$, (2) IAN_{ef}, (3) ATT-BLSTM. Analyzing prepositions (column 1) it is possible to see the lack of differences in quantification between the ρ_N^{PREP} and ρ_S^{PREP} contexts in the case of the models (1) and (2). Another situation is in case of the model (3), where related terms in sentiment contexts are higher quantified than in neutral ones. FRAMES and SENTIMENT groups are slightly higher quantified in sentiment contexts than in neutral one in the case of models (1) and (2), while (3) illustrates a significant discrepancy.

Overall, model ATT-BLSTM stands out among others both in terms of results (Sect. 6) and it illustrates the greatest discrepancy between ρ_N and ρ_S across all the groups presented in the analysis (Fig. 5). We assume that the latter is achieved due to the following factors: (I) application of bi-directional LSTM encoder; (II) utilization of a single trainable vector (w) in the quantification process (Fig. 4b) while the models of other approaches (ATTCNN, IAN, and ATT-BLSTM$^{z\text{-}yang}$) depend on fully-connected layers. Figure 6 shows examples of those sentiment contexts in which the weight distribution is the largest among the FRAMES group. These examples are the case when both frame and attention masks convey context meaning.

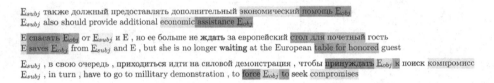

Fig. 6. Weight distribution visualization for model ATT-BLSTM on sentiment contexts; for visualization purposes, weight of each term is normalized by maximum in context

8   Conclusion

In this paper, we study the attention-based models, aimed to extract sentiment attitudes from analytical articles. The described models should classify a context with an attitude mentioned in it onto the following classes: positive, negative, neutral. We investigated two types of attention embedding approaches: (I) feature-based, (II) self-based. We conducted experiments on Russian analytical texts of the RuSentRel corpus and provide the analysis of the results. According to the latter, the advantage of attention-based encoders over non-attentive was shown by the variety in weight distribution of certain term groups between sentiment and non-sentiment contexts. The application of attentive context encoders illustrates the classification improvement in 1.5–5.9% range by $F1$.

References

1. Alimova, I., Solovyev, V.: Interactive attention network for adverse drug reaction classification. In: Ustalov, D., Filchenkov, A., Pivovarova, L., Žižka, J. (eds.) AINL 2018. CCIS, vol. 930, pp. 185–196. Springer, Cham (2018). https://doi.org/10. 1007/978-3-030-01204-5_18
2. Dowty, D.: Thematic proto-roles and argument selection. Language **67**(3), 547–619 (1991)

3. Glorot, X., Bengio, Y.: Understanding the difficulty of training deep feedforward neural networks. In: Proceedings of the Thirteenth International Conference on Artificial Intelligence and Statistics, pp. 249–256 (2010)
4. Hendrickx, I., et al.: Semeval-2010 task 8: multi-way classification of semantic relations between pairs of nominals. In: Proceedings of the Workshop on Semantic Evaluations: Recent Achievements and Future Directions, pp. 94–99 (2009)
5. Hochreiter, S., Schmidhuber, J.: Long short-term memory. Neural Comput. **9**(8), 1735–1780 (1997)
6. Huang, X., et al.: Attention-based convolutional neural network for semantic relation extraction. In: Proceedings of COLING 2016, the 26th International Conference on Computational Linguistics: Technical Papers, pp. 2526–2536 (2016)
7. Loukachevitch, N., Levchik, A.: Creating a general Russian sentiment lexicon. In: Proceedings of the Tenth International Conference on Language Resources and Evaluation (LREC 2016), pp. 1171–1176 (2016)
8. Loukachevitch, N., Rusnachenko, N.: Extracting sentiment attitudes from analytical texts. In: Proceedings of International Conference on Computational Linguistics and Intellectual Technologies Dialogue-2018 (arXiv:1808.08932), pp. 459–468 (2018)
9. Ma, D., Li, S., Zhang, X., Wang, H.: Interactive attention networks for aspect-level sentiment classification. arXiv preprint arXiv:1709.00893 (2017)
10. Rusnachenko, N., Loukachevitch, N.: Neural network approach for extracting aggregated opinions from analytical articles. In: Manolopoulos, Y., Stupnikov, S. (eds.) DAMDID/RCDL 2018. CCIS, vol. 1003, pp. 167–179. Springer, Cham (2019). https://doi.org/10.1007/978-3-030-23584-0_10
11. Rusnachenko, N., Loukachevitch, N., Tutubalina, E.: Distant supervision for sentiment attitude extraction. In: Proceedings of the International Conference on Recent Advances in Natural Language Processing (RANLP 2019) (2019)
12. Shen, Y., Huang, X.: Attention-based convolutional neural network for semantic relation extraction. In: Proceedings of COLING 2016, the 26th International Conference on Computational Linguistics: Technical Papers, pp. 2526–2536 (2016)
13. Wagner, J., et al.: DCU: aspect-based polarity classification for SemEval task 4 (2014)
14. Yang, Z., Yang, D., Dyer, C., He, X., Smola, A., Hovy, E.: Hierarchical attention networks for document classification. In: Proceedings of the 2016 Conference of the North American Chapter of the Association for Computational Linguistics, pp. 1480–1489 (2016)
15. Zeiler, M.D.: ADADELTA: an adaptive learning rate method. arXiv preprint arXiv:1212.5701 (2012)
16. Zeng, D., Liu, K., Chen, Y., Zhao, J.: Distant supervision for relation extraction via piecewise convolutional neural networks. In: Proceedings of the 2015 Conference on Empirical Methods in Natural Language Processing, pp. 1753–1762 (2015)
17. Zhou, P., et al.: Attention-based bidirectional long short-term memory networks for relation classification. In: Proceedings of the 54th Annual Meeting of the Association for Computational Linguistics, vol. 2, pp. 207–212 (2016)

A Sentiwordnet Strategy for Curriculum Learning in Sentiment Analysis

Vijjini Anvesh Rao[(✉)], Kaveri Anuranjana, and Radhika Mamidi

Language Technologies Research Center, Kohli Center on Intelligent Systems,
International Institute of Information Technology, Hyderabad, Hyderabad, India
{vijjinianvesh.rao,kaveri.anuranjana}@research.iiit.ac.in,
radhika.mamidi@iiit.ac.in

Abstract. Curriculum Learning (CL) is the idea that learning on a
training set sequenced or ordered in a manner where samples range from
easy to difficult, results in an increment in performance over otherwise
random ordering. The idea parallels cognitive science's theory of how
human brains learn, and that learning a difficult task can be made easier
by phrasing it as a sequence of easy to difficult tasks. This idea has gained
a lot of traction in machine learning and image processing for a while
and recently in Natural Language Processing (NLP). In this paper, we
apply the ideas of curriculum learning, driven by SentiWordNet in a sentiment analysis setting. In this setting, given a text segment, our aim is to
extract its sentiment or polarity. SentiWordNet is a lexical resource with
sentiment polarity annotations. By comparing performance with other
curriculum strategies and with no curriculum, the effectiveness of the
proposed strategy is presented. Convolutional, Recurrence and Attention based architectures are employed to assess this improvement. The
models are evaluated on standard sentiment dataset, Stanford Sentiment
Treebank.

Keywords: Curriculum Learning · Sentiment Analysis · Text
classification

1 Introduction

Researchers from Cognitive Science have established a long time ago that humans
learn better and more effectively in an incrementive learning setting [14,27].
Tasks like playing a piano or solving an equation, are learnt by humans in a
strategy where they are first provided easier variants of the main challenge, followed by gradual variation in difficulty. This idea of incremental human learning
has been studied for machines as well, specifically in machine learning. Curriculum Learning (CL) as defined by [3] introduce and formulate this concept
from Cognitive Science to a machine learning setting. They observe that on
shape recognition problem (rectangle, ellipse or triangle), training the model

---

V. A. Rao and K. Anuranjana—These authors have contributed equally to this work.

© Springer Nature Switzerland AG 2020
E. Métais et al. (Eds.): NLDB 2020, LNCS 12089, pp. 170–178, 2020.
https://doi.org/10.1007/978-3-030-51310-8_16

first on a synthetically created dataset with less variability in shape, generalizes faster as compared to directly training on the target dataset. Furthermore, other experiments by [3] demonstrate performance improvements on a perceptron classifier when incremental learning is done based on the margin in support vector machines (SVM) and a language model task where growth in vocabulary size was chosen as the curriculum strategy. These examples indicate that while curriculum learning is effective, the choice of the curriculum strategy, the basis for ordering of samples is not clear cut and often task specific. Furthermore some recent works like [21] have suggested that anti curriculum strategies perform better, raising more doubts over choice of strategy. In recent years Self-Paced Learning (SPL) [12,15] has been proposed as a reformulation of curriculum learning by modeling the curriculum strategy and the main task in a single optimization problem.

Sentiment Analysis (SA) is a major challenge in Natural Language Processing. It involves classifying text segments into two or more polarities or sentiments. Prior to the success of Deep Learning (DL), text classification was dealt using lexicon based features. However sentiment level information is realized at more levels than just lexicon or word based. For a model to realize a negative sentiment for "not good", it has to incorporate sequential information as well. Since the advent of DL, the field has been revolutionized. Long Short Term Memory [10,20] (LSTM), Convolutional Neural Networks (CNN) [13,19] and Attention based architectures [32] have achieved state-of-art results in text classification and continue to be strong baselines for text classification and by extension, Sentiment Analysis. Sentiment Analysis, further aids other domains of NLP such as Opinion mining and Emoji Prediction [4].

Curriculum Learning has been explored in the domain of Computer Vision (CV) extensively [11,16,18] and has gained traction in Natural Language Processing (NLP) in tasks like Question Answering [25,26] and Natural Answer Generation [17]. In Sentiment Analysis, [5] propose a strategy derived from sentence length, where smaller sentences are considered easier and are provided first. [9] provide a tree-structured curriculum based on semantic similarity between new samples and samples already trained on. [31] suggest a curriculum based on hand crafted semantic, linguistic, syntactic features for word representation learning. However, these CL strategies pose the easiness or difficulty of a sample irrespective of sentiment. While their strategies are for sentiment analysis, they do not utilize sentiment level information directly in building the order of samples. Utilizing SentiWordNet, we can build strategies that are derived from sentiment level knowledge.

SentiWordNet [1,8] is a highly popular word level sentiment annotation resource. It has been used in sentiment analysis and related fields such as opinion mining and emotion recognition. This resource was first created for English and due to its success it has been extended to many other languages as well [6,7,23,24]. This lexical resource assigns positivity, negativity and derived from the two, an objectivity score to each WordNet synset [22]. The contributions of the paper can be summarized as follow:

- We propose a new curriculum strategy for sentiment analysis (SA) from SentiWordNet annotations.
- Existing curriculum strategies for sentiment analysis rank samples with a difficulty score impertinent to the task of SA. Proposed strategy ranks samples based on how difficult assigning them a sentiment is. Our results show such a strategy's effectiveness over previous work.

2   Problem Setting for Curriculum Learning

While Curriculum Learning as defined by [3] is not constrained by a strict description, later related works [5,9,29] make distinctions between Baby Steps curriculum and One-Pass curriculum. Since, these previous works have also shown the dominance of Baby Steps over One-Pass, we use the former for proposed SentiWordNet driven strategy. Baby Steps curriculum algorithm can be defined as following. For every sentence $s_i \in D$, its sentiment is described as $y_i \in \{0, 1, 2, 3, 4\}^1$, where $i \in \{1, 2, .., n\}$ for n data points in D. For a model f_w, its prediction based on s_i will be $f_w(s_i)$. Loss L is defined on the model prediction and actual output as $L(y_i, f_w(s_i))$ and the net cost for the dataset is defined as $C(D, f_w)$ as $\sum_{\forall i} \frac{1}{n} L(y_i, f_w(s_i))$. Then the task is modelled by

$$\min_w C(D, f_w) + g(w) \tag{1}$$

Where $g(w)$ can be a regularizer. In this setting, Curriculum Learning is defined by a Curriculum Strategy $S(s_i)$. S defines an "easiness" quotient of sample s_i. If the model is currently trained on $D\prime \subset D$. Then sample $s_j \in D - D\prime$ is chosen based on S as:

$$s_j = \arg\min_{s_i \in D-D\prime} S(s_i) \tag{2}$$

Sample s_j is then added to the new training set or $D\prime = D\prime + s_j{}^2$ and the process continues until training is done on all the sentences in D. The process starts with first training on a small subset of D, which have least S score. In this way incremental learning is done in Baby Steps.

3   Experiments

3.1   Dataset

Following previous works in curriculum driven sentiment analysis [5,9,31] We use the Stanford Sentiment Treebank (SST) dataset [28][3]. Unlike most sentiment analysis datasets with binary labels, SST is for a 5-class text classification which consists of 8544/1101/2210 samples in train, development and test set respectively. We use this standard split with reported results averaged over 10 turns.

---

[1] Our dataset has 5 labels.

[2] Adding one sample at a time can be a very slow process, hence we add in batches. For our experiments, we take a batch size of bs samples with lowest S to add at once.

[3] https://nlp.stanford.edu/sentiment/.

Table 1. Accuracy scores in percentage of all models on different strategies

Model	SentiWordNet	Curriculum strategies sentence length	No Curriculum
Kim CNN	**41.55**	40.81	40.59
LSTM	**44.54**	43.89	41.71
LSTM+Attention	**45.27**	42.98	41.66

3.2 Architectures

We test our curriculum strategies on popular recurrent and convolutional architectures used for text classification. It is imperative to note that curriculum strategies are independent of architectures, they only decide the ordering of samples for training. The training itself could be done with any algorithm.

Kim CNN. This baseline is based on the deep CNN architecture [13] highly popular for text classification.

LSTM. We employ Long Short Term Memory Network (LSTM) [10] for text classification. Softmax activation is applied on the final timestep of the LSTM to get final output probability distributions. Previous approach [5] uses LSTM for this task as well with sentence length as curriculum strategy.

LSTM+Attention. In this architecture we employ attention mechanism described in [2] over the LSTM outputs to get a single context vector, on which softmax is applied. In this baseline, attention mechanism is applied on the top of LSTM outputs across different timesteps. Attention mechanism focuses on most important parts of the sentence that contribute most to the sentiment, especially like sentiment words.

3.3 Implementation Details

We used GloVe pretrained word vectors[4] for input embeddings on all architectures. The size of the word embeddings in this model is 300. A maximum sentence length of 50 is considered for all architectures. Number of filters taken in the CNN model is 50 with filter size as 3, 4, 5. We take number of units in the LSTM to be 168, following previous work [30] for empirical setup. For the LSTM + Attention model, we take number of units in the attention sub network to be 10. Categorical crossentropy as the loss function and Adam with learning rate of 0.01 as optimizer is used. The batch size bs defined in curriculum learning framework is

---

[4] https://nlp.stanford.edu/data/glove.840B.300d.zip.

900 for Sentence Length Strategy in LSTM and LSTM+Attention, and 750 for CNN. For SentiWordNet strategy, it is 1100 for LSTM and LSTM+Attention, and 1400 for CNN.

3.4   Curriculum Strategies

In this section we present the proposed SentiWordNet driven strategy followed by a common strategy based on sentence length.

SentiWordNet Driven Strategy. We first train an auxiliary feed forward model Aux for sentiment analysis on the same dataset utilizing only SentiWord-Net features. This allows us to find out which training samples are actually difficult. Following are the features we use for the auxiliary model:

- Sentence Length l: For a given sentence, this feature is just the number of words after tokenization.
- Net Positivity Score P: For a given sentence, this is the sum of all positivity scores of individual words.
- Net Negativity Score N: For a given sentence, this is the sum of all negativity scores of individual words.
- Net Objectivity Score O: For a given sentence, this is the sum of all objectivity scores of individual words.[5]. This feature is meant to show how difficult it is to tell the sentiment of a sentence.
- Abs. Difference Score: This score is the absolute difference between Net Positivity and Net Negativity Scores or $AD = |P - N|$. This feature is meant to reflect overall sentiment of the sentence.
- Scaled Positivity: Since the Net Positivity may increase with number of words, we also provide the scaled down version of the feature or $\frac{P}{l}$.
- Scaled Negativity: For the same reason as above, we also provide $\frac{N}{l}$.
- Scaled Objectivity: Objectivity scaled down with sentence length or $\frac{O}{l}$.
- Scaled Abs Difference: Abs. Difference D scaled down with sentence length or $\frac{AD}{l}$.

Since all the features lie in very different ranges, before passing for training to the architectures they are normalized between -1 and 1 first with mean 0. Also important to note is that, the SentiWordNet scores are for a synset and not for a word. In essence, a word may have multiple scores. In such cases, positivity, negativity and objectivity scores are averaged for that word. We use a simple feed forward network to train this auxiliary model with final layer as a softmax layer[6]. We get an accuracy of just 25.34 on this model, significantly lesser than performances we see by LSTM and CNN in No Curriculum setting as seen in Table 1. But the performance doesn't actually matter. From this model, we learn

---

[5] Note that for an individual word, The *Objectivity score* is just *1 - Negativity Score - Positivity Score*.

[6] The number of layer units are as follows: $[8, 100, 50, 5]$.

what samples are the most difficult to classify and what are the easiest. For all 8544 training samples of D, we define the curriculum score as follows:

$$S(s_i) = \sum_{j}^{c} (Aux(s_i)^j - y_i^j)^2 \tag{3}$$

where $Aux(s_i)^j$ is the prediction of auxiliary model Aux on sentence s_i, j is the iterator over the number of classes $c = 5$. In essence, we find the mean squared error between the prediction and the sentence's true labels. If $S(s_i)$ is high, it implies the sentence is hard to classify and if less, then the sentence is easy. Because the features were trained on an auxiliary model from just SentiWord-Net features, we get an easiness-difficulty score purely from the perspective of sentiment analysis.

Sentence Length. This simple strategy tells that, architectures especially like LSTM find it difficult to classify sentences which are longer in length. And hence, longer sentences are difficult and should be ordered later. Conversely shorter sentence lengths are easier and should be trained first. This strategy is very common and has not only been used in sentiment analysis [5][7] but also in dependency parsing [29]. Which is why it becomes a strong baseline especially to evaluate the importance of SentiWordNet driven strategy.

4   Results

We report our results in Table 1. As evident from the table, we see that proposed SentiWordNet based strategy beats Sentence Length driven and No Curriculum always. However, the difference between them is quite less for the CNN model. This must be because, CNN for this dataset is worse of all other models without curriculum, this architecture finds it difficult to properly classify, let alone fully exploit curriculum strategies for better generalization. Furthermore, another reason behind effectiveness of Sentence Length strategy for LSTM and LSTM+Attention is that, considering the LSTM's structure which observes one word at a time, its only natural that longer sequences will be hard to remember, hence Sentence Length ordering acts as a good curriculum basis. This idea has also been referenced by previous works such as [5]. Since Attention mechanism observes all time steps of the LSTM, the difficulty in longer sentence lengths diminishes and hence the improvement in performance with Sentence Length strategy is lesser as compared to LSTM. Sentence Length driven Strategy, while performing better in LSTM and LSTM+Attention model, is still less than SentiWordNet, this is because sentence length strategy defines difficulty and easiness in a more global setting, not specific to sentiment analysis. However, with SentiWordNet we define a strategy which characterizes the core of curriculum

---

[7] [5] have done CL on SST as well, however our numbers do not match because they use the phrase dataset which is much larger.

learning in sentiment analysis, namely the strategy for ranking samples based solely on how difficult or easy it is to classify the sample into predefined sentiment categories.

5   Conclusion

In this paper, we define a SentiWordNet driven strategy for curriculum learning on sentiment analysis task. The proposed approach's performance is evident on multiple architectures, namely recurrent, convolution and attention based proving the robustness of the strategy. This approach also shows the effectiveness of simple lexicon based annotations such as SentiWordNet and how they can be used to further sentiment analysis. Future works could include strategies that consecutively enrich SentiWordNet as well and also those that can refine the resource by pointing out anomalies in the annotation.

References

1. Baccianella, S., Esuli, A., Sebastiani, F.: SentiWordNet 3.0: an enhanced lexical resource for sentiment analysis and opinion mining. In: Lrec, vol. 10, pp. 2200–2204 (2010)
2. Bahdanau, D., Cho, K., Bengio, Y.: Neural machine translation by jointly learning to align and translate. arXiv preprint arXiv:1409.0473 (2014)
3. Bengio, Y., Louradour, J., Collobert, R., Weston, J.: Curriculum learning. In: Proceedings of the 26th Annual International Conference on Machine Learning, pp. 41–48. ACM (2009)
4. Choudhary, N., Singh, R., Rao, V.A., Shrivastava, M.: Twitter corpus of resource-scarce languages for sentiment analysis and multilingual emoji prediction. In: Proceedings of the 27th International Conference on Computational Linguistics, pp. 1570–1577 (2018)
5. Cirik, V., Hovy, E., Morency, L.P.: Visualizing and understanding curriculum learning for long short-term memory networks. arXiv preprint arXiv:1611.06204 (2016)
6. Das, A., Bandyopadhyay, S.: SentiWordNet for Indian languages. In: Proceedings of the Eighth Workshop on Asian Language Resources, pp. 56–63 (2010)
7. Das, A., Bandyopadhyay, S.: Towards the global SentiWordNet. In: Proceedings of the 24th Pacific Asia Conference on Language, Information and Computation, pp. 799–808 (2010)
8. Esuli, A., Sebastiani, F.: SentiWordNet: a publicly available lexical resource for opinion mining. In: LREC, vol. 6, pp. 417–422. Citeseer (2006)
9. Han, S., Myaeng, S.H.: Tree-structured curriculum learning based on semantic similarity of text. In: 2017 16th IEEE International Conference on Machine Learning and Applications (ICMLA), pp. 971–976. IEEE (2017)
10. Hochreiter, S., Schmidhuber, J.: Long short-term memory. Neural Comput. 9(8), 1735–1780 (1997)
11. Jiang, L., Meng, D., Mitamura, T., Hauptmann, A.G.: Easy samples first: self-paced reranking for zero-example multimedia search. In: Proceedings of the 22nd ACM International Conference on Multimedia, pp. 547–556. ACM (2014)
12. Jiang, L., Meng, D., Zhao, Q., Shan, S., Hauptmann, A.G.: Self-paced curriculum learning. In: Twenty-Ninth AAAI Conference on Artificial Intelligence (2015)

13. Kim, Y.: Convolutional neural networks for sentence classification. arXiv preprint arXiv:1408.5882 (2014)
14. Krueger, K.A., Dayan, P.: Flexible shaping: how learning in small steps helps. Cognition **110**(3), 380–394 (2009)
15. Kumar, M.P., Packer, B., Koller, D.: Self-paced learning for latent variable models. In: Advances in Neural Information Processing Systems, pp. 1189–1197 (2010)
16. Lee, Y.J., Grauman, K.: Learning the easy things first: self-paced visual category discovery. In: CVPR 2011, pp. 1721–1728. IEEE (2011)
17. Liu, C., He, S., Liu, K., Zhao, J.: Curriculum learning for natural answer generation. In: IJCAI, pp. 4223–4229 (2018)
18. Louradour, J., Kermorvant, C.: Curriculum learning for handwritten text line recognition. In: 2014 11th IAPR International Workshop on Document Analysis Systems, pp. 56–60. IEEE (2014)
19. Madasu, A., Rao, V.A.: Gated convolutional neural networks for domain adaptation. In: Métais, E., Meziane, F., Vadera, S., Sugumaran, V., Saraee, M. (eds.) NLDB 2019. LNCS, vol. 11608, pp. 118–130. Springer, Cham (2019). https://doi.org/10.1007/978-3-030-23281-8_10
20. Madasu, A., Rao, V.A.: Sequential learning of convolutional features for effective text classification. In: Proceedings of the 2019 Conference on Empirical Methods in Natural Language Processing and the 9th International Joint Conference on Natural Language Processing (EMNLP-IJCNLP), pp. 5662–5671 (2019)
21. McCann, B., Keskar, N.S., Xiong, C., Socher, R.: The natural language decathlon: multitask learning as question answering. arXiv preprint arXiv:1806.08730 (2018)
22. Miller, G.A.: WordNet: a lexical database for English. Commun. ACM **38**(11), 39–41 (1995)
23. Parupalli, S., Rao, V.A., Mamidi, R.: BCSAT: a benchmark corpus for sentiment analysis in Telugu using word-level annotations. arXiv preprint arXiv:1807.01679 (2018)
24. Parupalli, S., Rao, V.A., Mamidi, R.: Towards enhancing lexical resource and using sense-annotations of OntoSenseNet for sentiment analysis. arXiv preprint arXiv:1807.03004 (2018)
25. Sachan, M., Xing, E.: Easy questions first? A case study on curriculum learning for question answering. In: Proceedings of the 54th Annual Meeting of the Association for Computational Linguistics (Volume 1: Long Papers), vol. 1, pp. 453–463 (2016)
26. Sachan, M., Xing, E.: Self-training for jointly learning to ask and answer questions. In: Proceedings of the 2018 Conference of the North American Chapter of the Association for Computational Linguistics: Human Language Technologies, Volume 1 (Long Papers), pp. 629–640 (2018)
27. Skinner, B.F.: Reinforcement today. Am. Psychol. **13**(3), 94 (1958)
28. Socher, R., et al.: Recursive deep models for semantic compositionality over a sentiment treebank. In: Proceedings of the 2013 Conference on Empirical Methods in Natural Language Processing, pp. 1631–1642 (2013)
29. Spitkovsky, V.I., Alshawi, H., Jurafsky, D.: From baby steps to leapfrog: how less is more in unsupervised dependency parsing. In: Human Language Technologies: The 2010 Annual Conference of the North American Chapter of the Association for Computational Linguistics, pp. 751–759. Association for Computational Linguistics (2010)
30. Tai, K.S., Socher, R., Manning, C.D.: Improved semantic representations from tree-structured long short-term memory networks. arXiv preprint arXiv:1503.00075 (2015)

31. Tsvetkov, Y., Faruqui, M., Ling, W., MacWhinney, B., Dyer, C.: Learning the curriculum with Bayesian optimization for task-specific word representation learning. arXiv preprint arXiv:1605.03852 (2016)
32. Yang, Z., Yang, D., Dyer, C., He, X., Smola, A., Hovy, E.: Hierarchical attention networks for document classification. In: Proceedings of the 2016 Conference of the North American Chapter of the Association for Computational Linguistics: Human Language Technologies, pp. 1480–1489 (2016)

Personality, Affect and Emotion

The Role of Personality and Linguistic Patterns in Discriminating Between Fake News Spreaders and Fact Checkers

Anastasia Giachanou[1]($\boxtimes$), Esteban A. Ríssola[2], Bilal Ghanem[1],
Fabio Crestani[2], and Paolo Rosso[1]

[1] Universitat Politècnica de València, Valencia, Spain
angia9@upv.es, bigha@doctor.upv.es, prosso@dsic.upv.es
[2] Università della Svizzera italiana, Lugano, Switzerland
{esteban.andres.rissola,fabio.crestani}@usi.ch

Abstract. Users play a critical role in the creation and propagation of fake news online by consuming and sharing articles with inaccurate information either intentionally or unintentionally. Fake news are written in a way to confuse readers and therefore understanding which articles contain fabricated information is very challenging for non-experts. Given the difficulty of the task, several fact checking websites have been developed to raise awareness about which articles contain fabricated information. As a result of those platforms, several users are interested to share posts that cite evidence with the aim to refute fake news and warn other users. These users are known as *fact checkers*. However, there are users who tend to share false information, who can be characterised as potential *fake news spreaders*. In this paper, we propose the CheckerOrSpreader model that can classify a user as a potential fact checker or a potential fake news spreader. Our model is based on a Convolutional Neural Network (CNN) and combines word embeddings with features that represent users' personality traits and linguistic patterns used in their tweets. Experimental results show that leveraging linguistic patterns and personality traits can improve the performance in differentiating between checkers and spreaders.

Keywords: Fact checkers detection · Personality traits · Linguistic patterns

1 Introduction

Although fake news, rumours and conspiracy theories exist for a long time, the unprecedented growth of social media has created a prosper environment for their propagation. Fake news are propagated rapidly in social media and indeed faster than real news [29]. Inaccurate and fabricated information can negatively influence users' opinions on different aspects, ranging from which political party to vote to doubting about the safety of vaccination. For example, research has

© Springer Nature Switzerland AG 2020
E. Métais et al. (Eds.): NLDB 2020, LNCS 12089, pp. 181–192, 2020.
https://doi.org/10.1007/978-3-030-51310-8_17

shown how medical misinformation can result to false treatment advice [17], whereas in the political domain, several researchers have underlined the influence of fake news on elections and referendums [2,5].

Users play a critical role in all the different phases of the fake news cycle, from their creation to their propagation. However, users are dealing with an incredible huge amount of information everyday coming from different sources. Therefore, parsing this information and understanding if it is correct and accurate is almost impossible for the users who are non-experts. On the other side, experts such as journalists have the appropriate background to find relevant information and judge the credibility of the different articles and sources. In an attempt to raise awareness and inform users about pieces of news that contain fake information, several platforms (e.g., snopes[1], politifact[2], leadstories[3]) have been developed. These platforms employ journalists or other domain experts who thoroughly examine the claims and the information presented in the articles before they label them based on their credibility.

The advent of the fact checking platforms have resulted in a new type of social media users who have showed interest in halting the propagation of fake news. Users who consume and share news from social media can be roughly classified in the following two categories; (i) users that tend to believe some of the fake news and who further share them intentionally or unintentionally, characterised as *potential fake news spreaders*, and (ii) users who want to raise awareness and tend to share posts informing that these articles are fake, characterised as *potential fact checkers*[4].

Even the detection of fake news has received a lot of research attention, the role of the users is still under-explored. The differentiation between checkers and spreaders is an important task and can further help in the detection of fake news[5]. This information can be further used by responsible recommendation systems to suggest to users that tend to share fake news, news articles from reliable sources in order to raise their awareness. Also, these systems should be regularly updated regarding the information they have for the users given that users can learn to better identify fake news.

We believe that checkers are likely to have a set of different characteristics compared to spreaders. For example, it is possible that checkers use different linguistic patterns when they share posts and have different personality traits compared to spreaders. We use the posts (i.e., tweets) of the users to extract a range of linguistic patterns and to infer their personality traits. We use Linguistic Inquiry and Word Count (LIWC) [18] to extract psychometric and linguistic style patterns of the posts and a vectorial semantics approach proposed by Neuman and Cohen [16] to infer the personality trait of the users.

---

[1] https://www.snopes.com.

[2] https://www.politifact.com/.

[3] https://leadstories.com/.

[4] For brevity we will refer to the users that have the tendency to share fake news as *spreaders* and to those that check the factuality of articles as *checkers*.

[5] Here we should note that in this paper we focus only in the classification at a user level and we leave the exploration of the role of users at a post level as a future work.

The contributions of this paper can be summarised as follows:

- We create a collection that contains sets of tweets that are published by two different groups of social media users; users that tend to share fact check tweets (checkers) and those that tend to share fake news (spreaders).
- We extract different linguistic patterns and infer personality traits from the tweets posted by users to study their impact on classifying a user as a checker or spreader.
- We propose CheckerOrSpreader, a model based on a CNN network and hand-crafted features that refer to the linguistic patterns and personality traits, and which aims to classify a user as a potential checker or spreader.

The rest of the paper is organised as follows. Section 2 discusses related work on fake news detection. In Sect. 3 we present the collection and the process we followed to create it. Next we present the CheckerOrSpreader model in Sect. 4. Section 5 presents the evaluation process and the evaluation performance of the approach. Finally, Sect. 6 discusses the limitations and the ethical concerns regarding our study followed by the conclusions and future work in Sect. 7.

2   Related Work

The detection of fake news has attracted a lot of research attention. Among other problems, researchers have tried to address bot detection [22], rumour detection [21] and fact checking [7]. Many of the proposed works have explored a wide range of linguistic patterns to detect fake news such as the number of pronouns, swear words or punctuation marks. Rashkin et al. [23] compared the language of real news with that of satire, hoaxes, and propaganda based on features they extracted with the LIWC software [18]. Emotions and sentiment have been shown to play an important role in various classification tasks [6,9]. In case of fake news, Vosoughi et al. [29] showed that they trigger different emotions than real news. In addition, Ghanem et al. [8] explored the impact of emotions in the detection of the different types of fake news, whereas Giachanou et al. [10] analysed the effect of emotions in credibility detection.

Users are involved in various steps in the life cycle of fake news, from creating or changing information to sharing them online. The tendency of some users to believe fake news depends on a range of different factors, such as network properties, analytical thinking or cognitive skills [20]. For example, Shu et al. [26] analysed different features, such as registration time and found that users that share fake news have more recent accounts than users who share real news. Vo and Lee [28] analysed the linguistic characteristics (e.g., use of tenses, number of pronouns) of fact checking tweets and proposed a deep learning framework to generate responses with fact checking intention.

The personality of the users is also likely to have an impact on the tendency of some users to believe fake news. A traditional way to measure the personality traits is via explicit questionnaires that persons are asked to fill. A number of researchers have employed those questionnaires and tried to find the relation between personality traits and the use of social media [3,25] or information seeking behavior [12].

With all the advancements in Natural Language Processing, several studies have claimed that personality traits can also be inferred from the text generated by the user. In particular, several studies have addressed the problem of personality detection as a classification or a regression task based on text and conversations generated by the users [1,24]. In the present work, we use the posts that are written by users to extract linguistic patterns based on LIWC [18] and to infer their personality traits based a vectorial semantics approach proposed by Neuman and Cohen [16]. Differently from previous works, we explore the impact of those characteristics on classifying a user as a potential fake news spreader and fact checker based on the posts that he/she published.

3   Collection

There are different collections built in the field of fake news [27,28,30]. However, the majority of the previous datasets focus on the classification of the article as fake or not [27,30]. Vo and Lee [28] focus on fact checking but they collect fact check tweets and not previous tweets posted by the users. To the best of our knowledge, there is no collection that we can use for the task of differentiating users as checkers and spreaders. Therefore, we decided to build our own collection[6]. To build the collection, we first collect articles that have been debunked as fake from the Lead Stories website[7]. Crawling articles from fact check websites is the most popular way to collect articles since they are already labeled by experts. This approach has been already used by other researchers in order to create collections [27]. In total, we collected 915 titles of articles that have been labeled as fake by experts. Then, we removed stopwords from the headlines and we used the processed headlines to search for relevant tweets. Figure 1 shows the pipeline that we used to create the collection.

To extract the tweets we use Twitter API. In total we collected 18,670 tweets that refer to the articles from Lead Stories. For some of the articles we managed to collect a high number of tweets, whereas other articles were not discussed a lot in Twitter. Table 1 shows examples of the articles for which we collected the highest and lowest number of tweets. From this table, we observe that the most popular article was about a medical topic and for which we collected 1,448 tweets. In addition, Fig. 2 shows the number of collected tweets per article. We observe that the frequencies follow a heavy-tailed distribution since a lot of tweets were posted for few articles and very few tweets for a lot of articles.

The tweets that we collected can be classified in two categories. The first category contains tweets that debunk the original article by claiming its falseness (fact check tweet), and usually citing one of the fact checking websites (snopes, politifact or leadstories). The second category contains tweets that re-post the article (spreading tweet) implying its truthfulness. To categorise the tweets into

---

[6] The collection and the code will be available upon acceptance.

[7] https://leadstories.com/.

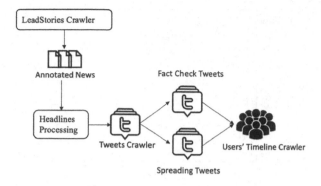

Fig. 1. Pipeline for the creation of the collection.

Table 1. Titles of the articles with the highest and lowest number of tweets.

Titles of articles with the highest number of tweets	Titles of articles with the lowest number of tweets
1. Doctors Who Discovered Cancer Enzymes In Vaccines NOT All Found Murdered	1. Make-A-Wish Did NOT Send Terminally Ill Spider-Man To Healthy Kid
2. Sugar Is NOT 8 Times More Addictive Than Cocaine	2. Man Did NOT Sue Radio Station For Playing Despacito 800 Times A Day
3. George H.W. Bush Did NOT Die at 93	3. Man-Eating Shark NOT Spotted In Ohio River
4. NO Alien Invasion This Is NOT Real	4. FBI DID NOT Classify President Obama As A Domestic Terrorist
5. First Bee Has NOT *Just* Been Added to Endangered Species List	5. Will Smith IS NOT Leaving America With His Family Never To Come Back

fact check and spreading tweets, we follow a semi-automated process. First, we manually identify specific patterns that are followed in the fact check tweets. According to those rules, if a tweet contains any of the terms {hoax, fake, false, fact check, snopes, politifact leadstories, lead stories} is a fact check tweet, otherwise it is a spreading tweet.

Figure 3 shows some examples of articles debunked as fake together with fact check and spreading tweets. We notice that in the fact check tweets we have terms such as fake, false and fact check, whereas in the spreading tweets we have re-posts of the specific article. Then, we manually checked a sample of the data to check if there are any wrong annotations. We manually checked 500 tweets and we did not find any cases of misclassification.

After the annotation of the tweets, we annotate the authors of the tweets as checkers or spreaders based on the number of fact check and spreading tweets they posted. In particular, if a user has both fact check and spreading tweets, then we consider that this user belongs to the category for which he/she has the larger number of tweets.

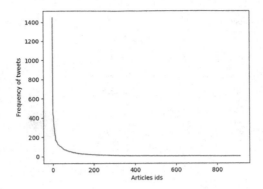

Fig. 2. Frequency distribution regarding of the number of tweets per article.

Finally, we collect the timeline tweets that the authors have posted to create our collection. In total, our collection contains tweets posted by 2,357 users, of which 454 are checkers and 1,903 spreaders.

4   CheckerOrSpreader

In this section, we present the CheckerOrSpreader system that aims to differentiate between checkers and spreaders. CheckerOrSpreader is based on a Convolutional Neural Network (CNN). The architecture of the CheckerOrSpreader system is depicted in Fig. 4.

CheckerOrSpreader consists of two different components, the word embeddings and the user's psycho-linguistic component. The embeddings component is based on the tweets that users have posted on their timeline. The psycholinguistic component represents the psychometric and linguistic style patterns and the personality traits that were derived from the textual content of the posts.

To extract the linguistic patterns and the personality traits we use the following approaches:

- **Linguistic patterns**: For the linguistic patterns, we employ LIWC [18] that is a software for mapping text to 73 psychologically-meaningful linguistic categories[8]. In particular, we extract pronouns (I, we, you, she/he, they), personal concerns (work, leisure, home, money, religion, death), time focus (past, present, future), cognitive processes (causation, discrepancy, tentative, certainty), informal language (swear, assent, nonfluencies, fillers), and affective processes (anxiety).
- **Personality scores**: The Five-Factor Model (FFM) [13], also called the Big Five, constitutes the most popular methodology used in automatic personality research [15]. In essence, it defines five basic *factors* or *dimensions* of personality. These factors are:

---

[8] For a comprehensive list of LIWC categories see: http://hdl.handle.net/2152/31333.

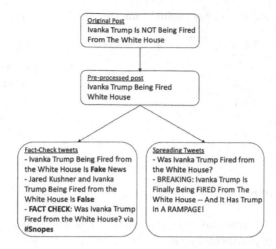

Fig. 3. Examples of fact check and spreading tweets.

- *openness to experience* (unconventional, insightful, imaginative)
- *conscientiousness* (organised, self-disciplined, ordered)
- *agreeableness* (cooperative, friendly, empathetic)
- *extraversion* (cheerful, sociable, assertive)
- *neuroticism* (anxious, sad, insecure)

Each of the five factors presents a *positive* and a complementary *negative* dimension. For instance, the complementary aspect to neuroticism is defined as *emotional stability*. Each individual can have a combination of these dimensions at a time. To obtain the personality scores, we followed the approach developed by Neuman and Cohen [16]. They proposed the construction of a set of vectors using a small group of adjectives, which according to theoretical and/or empirical knowledge, encode the essence of personality traits and personality disorders. Using a context-free word embedding they measured the semantic similarity between these vectors and the text written by different individuals. The similarity scores derived, allowed to quantify the degree in which a particular personality trait or disorder was evident in the text.

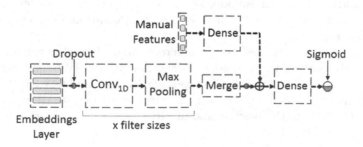

Fig. 4. Architecture of the CheckerOrSpreader model.

Table 2. Parameter optimisation for the different tested systems.

	Filters sizes	# of filters	Activation	Optimiser	Epochs
LSTM	64 (lstm units)		tanh	rmsprop	12
CNN	3,4	16	relu	adadelta	10
CNN+LIWC	3,4	32	relu	adadelta	15
CNN+personality	3,5	16	relu	adam	8
CheckerOrSpreader	4,5	32	relu	adam	13

5   Experiments

In this section we describe the experimental settings, the evaluation process and the results of our experiments.

5.1   Experimental Settings

For our experiments, we use 25% of our corpus of users for validation, 15% for test and the rest for the training. We initialize our embedding layer with the 300-dimensional pre-trained GloVe embeddings [19]. We allow the used embeddings to be tuned during the training process to fit more our training data. It's worth to mention that at the beginning of our experiments, we tested another version of our system by replacing the CNN with an Long Short-Term Memory (LSTM) network. The overall results showed that the CNN performs better for the particular task.

To find the best parameters of the different approaches on the validation set, we use the hyperopt library[9]. Table 2 shows the optimisation parameters for each approach.

5.2   Evaluation

For the evaluation, we use macro-F1 score. We use the following baselines to compare our results:

- *SVM+BoW* is based on Support Vector Machine (SVM) classifier trained on bag of words using Term Frequency - Inverse Document Frequency (Tf-Idf) weighting scheme.
- *Logistic Regression* trained on the different linguistic and personality scores features. In particular, we tried sentiment, emotion, LIWC and personality traits. For emotions we use NRC emotions lexicon [14] and we extracted anger, anticipation, disgust, fear, joy, sadness, surprise, and trust. We use the same lexicon to estimate the positive and negative sentiment in users' tweets.

---

[9] https://github.com/hyperopt/hyperopt.

- *Universal Sentence Encoder (USE)* [4]: For the USE baseline, we represent the final concatenated documents (tweets) using USE embeddings[10].
- *LSTM*: is based on a LSTM network with Glove pre-trained word embeddings for word representation.
- *CNN*: is a CNN with Glove pre-trained word embeddings for word representation.

5.3 Results

Table 3 shows the results of our experiments. We observe that CNN performs better than LSTM when they are trained only using word embeddings. In particular, CNN outperforms LSTM by 20.41%. Also, we observe that Logistic Regression achieves a low performance when it is trained with the different psycho-linguistic features. The best performance regarding Logistic Regression is achieved with the linguistic features extracted with LIWC.

Table 3. Performance of the different systems on the fact checkers detection task.

	F1-score
SVM+BoW	0.48
USE	0.53
LR+emotion	0.45
LR+sentiment	0.44
LR+LIWC	0.50
LR+personality	0.44
LSTM	0.44
CNN	0.54
CNN+LIWC	0.48
CNN+personality	0.57
CheckerOrSpreader	0.59

From Table 3 we also observe that combining CNN with the personality traits leads to a higher performance compared to combining CNN with the LIWC features. In particular, CNN+personality outperforms CNN+LIWC by 17.14%. This is an interesting observation that shows the importance of considering personality traits of users for their classification in checkers and spreaders.

Also, the results show that CheckerOrSpreader (CNN+personality+LIWC) achieves the best performance. In particular, CheckerOrSpreader manages to improve the performance by 8.85% compared to the CNN baseline and by 3.45% compared to the CNN+personality version.

---

[10] https://tfhub.dev/google/universal-sentence-encoder-large/3.

6   Limitations and Ethical Concerns

Even if our study can provide valuable insights regarding the profile of spreaders and their automated detection, there are some limitations and ethical concerns. One limitation of our study is the use of an automated tool to infer the personality traits of the users based on the tweets that they have posted. Even if this tool has been shown to achieve good prediction performance, it is still prone to errors similar to all the automated tools. That means that some of the predictions regarding the personality traits that were inferred from the tweets might not be completely accurate. However, it is not possible to evaluate the performance of this tool on our collection since we do not have ground truth data regarding the users' personality traits. An alternative way to obtain information regarding the personality traits would be to contact these users and ask them to fill one of the standard questionnaires (e.g., IPIP questionnaire [11]) that have been evaluated based on several psychological studies and tend to have more precise results. However, the feasibility of this approach depends on the willingness of the users to fill the questionnaire.

Our study has also some ethical concerns. We should mention that the aim of a system that can differentiate between potential checkers and spreaders should be used by no means to stigmatise the users that have shared in the past fake news. On the contrary, such a tool should be used only for the benefit of the users. For example, it could be used as a supportive tool to prevent propagation of fake news and to raise awareness to users. We also want to highlight that a system that differentiates users to potential spreaders and checkers requires to consider ethics at all steps.

This study has also some ethical concerns regarding the collection and the release of the data. First, we plan to make this collection available only for research purposes. To protect the privacy of users, we plan to publish the data anonymized. Also, we plan to use neutral annotation labels regarding the two classes (i.e., 0 and 1 instead of checker and spreader) since we do not want to stigmatise specific users. Future researchers that want to use the collection will not have access to the information of which class each label refers to. Finally, we will not make available the labels at a post level since this information can reveal the information regarding the annotation labels at a user level.

7   Conclusions

In this paper, we focused on the problem of differentiating between users that tend to share fake news (spreaders) and those that tend to check the factuality of articles (checkers). To this end, we first collect articles that have been manually annotated from experts as fake or fact and then we detect the users on Twitter that have posts about the annotated articles. In addition, we propose the CheckerOrSpreader model that is based on a CNN network. CheckerOrSpreader incorporates the linguistics patterns and the personality traits of the users that are inferred from users' posts to decide if a user is a potential spreader or checker.

Experimental results showed that linguistic patterns and the inferred personality traits are very useful for the task.

In future, we plan to investigate how the linguistic and personality information that is extracted from users' posts can be incorporated into the systems that detect fake news.

Acknowledgements. The work of the first author is supported by the SNSF Early Postdoc Mobility grant under the project Early Fake News Detection on Social Media, Switzerland (P2TIP2_181441). The work of Paolo Rosso is partially funded by the Spanish MICINN under the research project MISMIS-FAKEnHATE on Misinformation and Miscommunication in social media: FAKE news and HATE speech (PGC2018-096212-B-C31).

References

1. Bai, S., Zhu, T., Cheng, L.: Big-Five Personality Prediction Based on User Behaviors at Social Network Sites. https://arxiv.org/abs/1204.4809 (2012)
2. Bastos, M.T., Mercea, D.: The Brexit botnet and user-generated hyperpartisan news. Soc. Sci. Comput. Rev. **37**(1), 38–54 (2019)
3. Burbach, L., Halbach, P., Ziefle, M., Calero Valdez, A.: Who shares fake news in online social networks? In: Proceedings of the 27th ACM Conference on User Modeling, Adaptation and Personalization, UMAP 2019, pp. 234–242 (2019)
4. Cer, D., et al.: Universal Sentence Encoder. https://arxiv.org/abs/1803.11175 (2018)
5. DiFranzo, D., Gloria, M.J.K.: Filter Bubbles and Fake News. ACM Crossroads **23**(3), 32–35 (2017)
6. Farías, D.I.H., Patti, V., Rosso, P.: Irony detection in Twitter: the role of affective content. ACM Trans. Internet Technol. (TOIT) **16**(3), 1–24 (2016)
7. Ghanem, B., Glavaš, G., Giachanou, A., Paolo, S., Ponzetto, P.R., Rangel, F.: UPV-UMA at CheckThat! lab: verifying Arabic claims using a cross lingual approach. In: Working Notes of CLEF 2019 - Conference and Labs of the Evaluation Forum (2019)
8. Ghanem, B., Rosso, P., Rangel, F.: An emotional analysis of false information in social media and news articles. ACM Trans. Internet Technol. (TOIT) **20**(2), 1–18 (2020)
9. Giachanou, A., Gonzalo, J., Crestani, F.: Propagating sentiment signals for estimating reputation polarity. Inf. Process. Manage. **56**(6), 102079 (2019)
10. Giachanou, A., Rosso, P., Crestani, F.: Leveraging emotional signals for credibility detection. In: Proceedings of the 42nd International ACM SIGIR Conference on Research and Development in Information Retrieval, SIGIR 2019, pp. 877–880 (2019)
11. Goldberg, L.R.: A broad-bandwidth, public domain, personality inventory measuring the lower-level facets of several five-factor models. Pers. Psychol. Europe **7**(1), 7–28 (1999)
12. Heinström, J.: Five personality dimensions and their influence on information behaviour. Inf. Res. **9**(1), 1–9 (2003)
13. John, O.P., Srivastava, S.: The big-five trait taxonomy: history, measurement, and theoretical perspectives. In: Handbook of Personality: Theory and Research, pp. 102–138 (1999)

14. Mohammad, S.M., Turney, P.D.: Emotions evoked by common words and phrases: using mechanical turk to create an emotion lexicon. In: Proceedings of the NAACL HLT 2010 Workshop on Computational Approaches to Analysis and Generation of Emotion in Text, pp. 26–34 (2010)
15. Neuman, Y.: Computational Personality Analysis: Introduction, Practical Applications and Novel Directions, 1st edn. Springer, Heidelberg (2016). https://doi.org/10.1007/978-3-319-42460-6
16. Neuman, Y., Cohen, Y.: A vectorial semantics approach to personality assessment. Sci. Rep. **4**(1), 1–6 (2014)
17. Oyeyemi, S.O., Gabarron, E., Wynn, R.: Ebola, Twitter, and misinformation: a dangerous combination? BMJ Clin. Res. **349**, g6178 (2014)
18. Pennebaker, J.W., Boyd, R.L., Jordan, K., Blackburn, K.: The Development and Psychometric Properties of LIWC 2015. Technical report (2015)
19. Pennington, J., Socher, R., Manning, C.: Glove: global vectors for word representation. In: Proceedings of the 2014 Conference on Empirical Methods in Natural Language Processing, EMNLP 2014, pp. 1532–1543 (2014)
20. Pennycook, G., Rand, D.: Who falls for fake news? The roles of bullshit receptivity, overclaiming, familiarity, and analytic thinking. J. Pers. **88**, 185–200 (2018)
21. Qazvinian, V., Rosengren, E., Radev, D.R., Mei, Q.: Rumor has it: identifying misinformation in microblogs. In: Proceedings of the Conference on Empirical Methods in Natural Language Processing, EMNLP 2011, pp. 1589–1599 (2011)
22. Rangel, F., Rosso, P.: Overview of the 7th author profiling task at PAN 2019: bots and gender profiling in Twitter. In: Working Notes of CLEF 2019 - Conference and Labs of the Evaluation Forum (2019)
23. Rashkin, H., Choi, E., Jang, J.Y., Volkova, S., Choi, Y.: Truth of varying shades: analyzing language in fake news and political fact-checking. In: Proceedings of the 2017 Conference on Empirical Methods in Natural Language Processing, pp. 2931–2937 (2017)
24. Ríssola, E.A., Bahrainian, S.A., Crestani, F.: Personality recognition in conversations using capsule neural networks. In: 2019 IEEE/WIC/ACM International Conference on Web Intelligence, WI 2019, pp. 180–187 (2019)
25. Ross, C., Orr, E.S., Sisic, M., Arseneault, J.M., Simmering, M.G., Orr, R.R.: Personality and motivations associated with Facebook use. Comput. Hum. Behav. **25**(2), 578–586 (2009)
26. Shu, K., Wang, S., Liu, H.: Understanding user profiles on social media for fake news detection. In: Proceedings of the 2018 IEEE Conference on Multimedia Information Processing and Retrieval, MIPR 2018, pp. 430–435 (2018)
27. Shu, K., Mahudeswaran, D., Wang, S., Lee, D., Liu, H.: FakeNewsNet: A Data Repository with News Content, Social Context and Dynamic Information for Studying Fake News on Social Media. https://arxiv.org/abs/1809.01286 (2018)
28. Vo, N., Lee, K.: Learning from fact-checkers: analysis and generation of fact-checking language. In: Proceedings of the 42nd International ACM SIGIR Conference on Research and Development in Information Retrieval, SIGIR 2019, pp. 335–344 (2019)
29. Vosoughi, S., Roy, D., Aral, S.: The spread of true and false news online. Science **359**(6380), 1146–1151 (2018)
30. Wang, W.Y.: Liar, Liar Pants on Fire: A New Benchmark Dataset for Fake News Detection. https://arxiv.org/abs/1705.00648 (2017)

Literary Natural Language Generation with Psychological Traits

Luis-Gil Moreno-Jiménez[1,4](✉) ⓘ, Juan-Manuel Torres-Moreno[1,3]ⓘ,
and Roseli S. Wedemann[2]ⓘ

[1] Laboratoire Informatique d'Avignon (LIA) – Avignon Université,
339 Chemin des Meinajaries, 84911 Avignon, cédex 9, France
luis-gil.moreno-jimenez@alumni.univ-avignon.fr,
juan-manuel.torres@univ-avignon.fr
[2] Instituto de Matemática e Estatística, Universidade do Estado do Rio deJaneiro,
Rua São Francisco Xavier 524, Rio de Janeiro, RJ 20550-900, Brazil
roseli@ime.uerj.br
[3] Polytechnique Montréal, Québec 69121, Canada
[4] Universidad Tecnológica de la Selva, Entronque Toniná Km. 0.5 Carretera
Ocosingo-Altamirano, 29950 Ocosingo, Mexico

Abstract. The area of Computational Creativity has received much attention in recent years. In this paper, within this framework, we propose a model for the generation of literary sentences in Spanish, which is based on statistical algorithms, shallow parsing and the automatic detection of personality features of characters of well known literary texts. We present encouraging results of the analysis of sentences generated by our methods obtained with human inspection.

Keywords: Natural Language Processing · Generation of literary texts · Psychological traits

1 Introduction

Automatic Text Generation (ATG) is a task that has been widely studied by researchers in the area of Natural Language Processing (NLP) [13, 20–23]. Results from several investigations have presented very encouraging results that have allowed the establishment of progressively more challenging objectives in this field. Currently, the scope of ATG is being expanded and there is much recent work that aims at generating text related to a specific domain [8, 10, 18]. In this research, algorithms have been developed, oriented to such diverse purposes as creating chat-bots for customer service in commercial applications, automatic generation of summaries for academic support, or developing generators of literary poetry, short stories, novels, plays and essays [3, 17, 25].

The creation of a literary text is particularly interesting and challenging, when compared to other types of ATG, as these texts are not universally and

Supported partially by Conacyt (Mexico) and Université d'Avignon (France).

perpetually perceived. Furthermore, this perception can also vary depending on the reader's mood. It can thus can be assumed that literary perception is subjective and from this perspective, it is difficult to ensure that text generated by an algorithm will be perceived as literature. To reduce this possible ambiguity regarding literary perception, we consider that literature is regarded as text that employs a vocabulary which may be largely different from that used in common language and that it employs various writing styles, such as rhymes, anaphora, etc. and figures of speech, in order to obtain an artistic, complex, possibly elegant and emotional text [11]. This understanding gives us a guide for the development of our model whereby literary sentences can be generated.

We present here a model for the generation of literary text (GLT) in Spanish which is guided by psychological characteristics of the personality of characters in literature. The model is based on the assumption that these psychological traits determine a person's emotions and speech. We thus generate literary sentences based upon a situation or context, and also on psychological traits. It is then possible to perform an analysis of the personality of a character through the author's writing, considering parts of speech such as verbs, adjectives, conjunctions, and the spinning of words or concepts, as well as other characteristics.

In Sect. 2, we present a review of the main literature that has addressed topics related to ATG, with focus on those that proposed methods and algorithms integrated into this work. We describe the corpus used to train our models in Sect. 3. Section 4 describes in detail the methodology followed for the development of our model. In Sect. 5, we show some experiments, as well as the results of human evaluations of the generated sentences. Finally, in Sect. 6 we present our conclusions.

2 Related Work

The task of ATG has been widely addressed by the research community in recent years. In [21], Szymanski and Ciota presented a model based on Markov sequences for the stochastic generation of text, where the intention is to generate grammatically correct text, although without considering a context or meaning. Shridaha et al. [20] present an algorithm to automatically generate descriptive summary comments for Java methods. Given the signature and body of a method, their generator identifies the content for the summary and generates natural language text that summarizes the method's overall actions.

Work with an artistic, literary approach has also been developed for GLT. The works of Riedl and Young [17] and Clark, Ji and Smith [3] propose stochastic models, based on contextual analysis, for the generation of fictional narratives (stories). Zhang and Lapata [25] use neural networks and Oliveira [12,13] uses the technique of *canned text* for generating poems. Some research has achieved the difficult task of generating large texts, overcoming the barrier of phrases and paragraphs, such as the MEXICA project [15].

Personality analysis is a complicated task that can be studied from different perspectives (see [19,24] and references therein). Recent research has investigated the relation between the characteristics of literary text and personality, which can be understood as the complex of the behavioural, temperamental, emotional and mental attributes that characterise a unique individual [6, 7]. In [7], a type of personality is detected from the analysis of a text, using an artificial neural network (ANN), which classifies text into one of five personality classes considered by the authors (Extroversion, Neuroticism, Agreeableness, Conscientiousness, Openness). Some characteristics that are considered by the authors are writing styles and relationships between pairs of words.

3   Corpus

We have built two corpora in Spanish consisting of the main works of Johann Wolfgang von Goethe and Edgar Allan Poe, called **cGoethe** and **cPoe**, respectively. These corpora are analyzed and used to extract information about the vocabulary used by these authors. We later chose an important work for each author where the emotions and feelings, *i.e. psychological traits*, of main characters are easily perceived by readers. For Goethe, we selected the novel *The Sorrows of Young Werther* [5] and for Poe, we selected the story *The Cask of Amontillado* [16], both in their Spanish version. The two corpora generated from these literary works were used to extract sentences, that were later used as a basis for the generation of new sentences, as we describe in Sect. 4.1. We also use the corpora **5KL** described in [11] for the final phase of the sentence generation procedure described in 4.2.

To build the **cGoethe** and **cPoe** corpora, we processed each constituent literary work (originally found in heterogeneous formats), creating a single document for each corpus, encoded in *utf8*. This processing consisted of automatically segmenting the phrases into regular expressions, using a program developed in PERL 5.0, to obtain one sentence per line in each corpus.

From the segmented phrases in **cGoethe** and **cPoe**, we selected only those that belong to the works *The Sorrows of Young Werther* (set 1) and *The Cask of Amontillado* (set 2). From sets 1 and 2, we manually extracted phrases that we considered to be very *literary*, to form two new corpora, **cWerther** and **cCask**, respectively. In this step, we chose phrases with complex vocabulary, a directly expressed message and some literary styles like rhymes, anaphoras, etc. Table 1 shows basic statistical information of the **cGoethe** and **cPoe** corpora. Table 2, shows similar information for **cWerther** and **cCask**. Table 3 shows statistical information of the **5KL** corpus. The **5KL** corpus contains approximately 4 000 literary works, some originally written in Spanish and the rest in their translations to Spanish, from various authors and different genres, and is extremely useful, as it consists of an enormous vocabulary, that forms a highly representative set to train our Word2vec based model, described in Sect. 4.

4   Model

We now describe our proposed model for the generation of literary phrases in Spanish, which is an extension of Model 3 presented in [11]. The model consists of two phases described as follows. In the **first phase**, the Partially Empty

Table 1. Corpora formed by main works of each author. K represents one thousand and M represents one million.

	Sentences	Tokens	Characters
cPoe	5 787	70 K	430 K
Average for sentence	–	12	74
cGoethe	19 519	340 K	2 M
Average for sentence	–	17	103

Table 2. Corpora of literary phrases of one selected work.

	Sentences	Tokens	Characters
cCask	141	1 856	11 469
Average for sentence	–	13	81
cWerther	134	1 635	9 321
Average for sentence	–	12	69

Grammatical Structures (PGSs), each composed by elements constituted either by parts of speech (POS) tags or function words[1], are generated. A PGS is constructed, through a morphosyntactic analysis made with FreeLing[2], for each phrase of the corpora **cWerther** and **cCask**, described in the Sect. 3. The POS tags of these PGSs are replaced by words during the second phase.

FreeLing [14] is a commonly used tool for morphosyntactic analysis, which receives as input a string of text and returns a POS tag as output, for each word in the string. The POS tag indicates the type of word (verb, noun, adjective, adverb, etc.), and also information about inflections, i.e., gender, conjugation and number. For example, for the word "Investigador" FreeLing generates the POS tag [NCMS000]. The first letter indicates a **N**oun, the second a **C**ommon noun, **M** stands for **M**ale gender and the fourth gives number information (**S**ingular). The last 3 characters give information about semantics, named entities, etc. We will use only the first 4 symbols of the POS tags.

Table 3. Corpus 5KL, composed of 4 839 literary works.

	Sentences	Tokens	Characters
5KL	9 M	149 M	893 M
Average for sentence	2.4 K	37.3 K	223 K

---

[1] Function words (or functors) are words that have little or ambiguous meaning and express grammatical relationships among other words within a sentence, or specify the attitude or mood of the speaker, such as prepositions, pronouns, auxiliary verbs, or conjunctions.

[2] FreeLing can be downloaded from: http://nlp.lsi.upc.edu/freeling.

In the **second phase**, each POS tag in the PGSs are replaced by a corresponding word, using a semantic approach algorithm based on an ANN model (Word2vec[3]). Corpus **5KL**, described in Sect. 3, was used for training Word2vec, as well as the following parameters: only words with more than 5 occurrences in **5KL** were considered, the size of the context window is 10, the dimensions of the vector representations were tested within a range of 50 to 100, being 60 the dimension with the best results. The Word2vec model we have used is the *continuous skip-gram model* (Skip-gram), which receives a word (*Query*) as input and, as output, returns a set of words (*embeddings*) semantically related to the *Query*. The process for the generation of sentences is described in what follows.

4.1   Phase I: PGS Generation

For the generation of each PGS, we use methods guided by fixed morphosyntactic structures, called *Template-based Generation* or *canned text*. In [10], it is argued that the use of these techniques saves time in syntactic analysis and allows one to concentrate directly on the vocabulary. The *canned text* technique has also been used in several works, with specific purposes, such as in [4,8], where the authors developed models for the generation of simple dialogues and phrases.

We use *canned text* to generate text based on templates obtained from **cCask** and **cWerther**. These corpora contain flexible grammatical structures that can be manipulated to create new phrases. The templates in a corpus can be selected randomly or through heuristics, according to a predefined objective. The process starts with the random selection of an original phrase $f_o \in$ corpus of length $N = |f_o|$. A template PGS is built from the words of f_o, where content words, verbs (v), nouns (n) or adjectives (a), are replaced by their respective POS tags and function words are retained. f_o is analyzed with FreeLing and words with "values" in $\{v, n, a\}$ are replaced by their respective POS tags. These content words provide most of the information in any text, regardless of their length or genre [2]. Our hypothesis is that by changing only content words, we simulate the generation of phrases by homo-syntax: different semantics, same structure. The output of this process is a PGS with function words that give grammatical support and POS tags that will be replaced, in order to change the meaning of the sentence. Phase I is illustrated in Fig. 1, where full boxes represent function words and empty boxes represent POS tags.

4.2   Phase II: Semantic Analysis and Substitution of POS Tags

In this phase, the POS tags of the PGS generated in Phase I are replaced. Tags corresponding to nouns are replaced with a vocabulary close to the context defined by the user (the query), while verbs and adjectives are replaced with a vocabulary more similar in meaning to the original terms of f_o. The idea is to preserve the style and emotional-psychological content, that the author intended to associate with the characters that he is portraying in his work.

---

[3] Word2vec is a group of related ANN models, used to produce word embeddings [1].

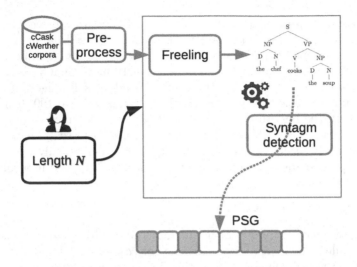

Fig. 1. *Canned text* model for generating a PGS.

Corpus **5KL** is pre-processed to standardize text formatting, eliminating characters that are not important for semantic analysis such as punctuation and numbers. This stage prepares the Word2vec training data that uses a vector representation of **5KL**. We use Gensim[4], a Python implementation of Word2vec. A query Q, provided by the user, is given as input to this algorithm, and its output is a set of words (*embeddings*) associated with a context defined by Q. In other words, Word2vec receives a term Q and returns a lexicon $L(Q) = (Q_1, Q_2, ..., Q_m)$, that represents a set of $m = 10$ words semantically close to Q. We chose this value of m because we found that if we increase the number of words obtained by Word2vec, they start to lose their relation to Q. Formally, we represnt a mapping by Word2vec as $Q \rightarrow L(Q)$.

Corpora **cGoethe** or **cPoe**, previously analyzed using FreeLing to obtain PGSs, had a POS tag associated to each content word. Now, with FreeLing, each POS tag is used to create a set of words, with the same grammatical information (identical POS tags). An Association Table (AT) is generated as a result of this process. The AT consists of entries of the type: $\text{POS}_k \rightarrow$ list of words $v_{k,i}$, with same grammatical information, formally $\text{POS}_k \rightarrow V_k = \{v_{k,1}, v_{k,2}, ..., v_{k,i}, ...\}$. To generate a new phrase, each tag $\text{POS}_k \in \text{PGS}$, is replaced by a word selected from the lexicon V_k, given by AT.

To choose a word in V_k to replace POS_k, we use the following algorithm. A vector is constructed for each of the three words defined as:

– o: is the k_{th} word in the phrase f_o, corresponding to tag POS_k;
– Q: word defining the *query* provided by the user;
– w: candidate word that could replace POS_k, $w \in V_k$.

---

[4] Available in: https://pypi.org/project/gensim/.

For each word o, Q and w, 10 closest words, o_i, Q_i and w_i, $i = 1, ..., 10$, are obtained with Word2vec. These 30 words are concatenated and represented by a vector U with dimension 30. The dimension was set to 30, as a compromise between lexical diversity and processing time. The vector U can be written as

$$U = (o_1, ..., o_{10}, Q_{11}, ..., Q_{20}, w_{21}, ..., w_{30}) = (u_1, u_2, ..., u_{30}). \quad (1)$$

Words o, Q and w generate three numerical vectors of 30 dimensions respectively, $o \rightarrow X = (x_1, ..., x_{30})$, $Q \rightarrow Q = (q_1, ..., q_{30})$, and $w \rightarrow W = (w_1, ..., w_{30})$, where the elements x_j of X are obtained by taking the distance $x_j = dist(o, u_j) \in [0, 1]$, between o and each $u_j \in U$, provided by Word2vec. Obviously, o will be closer to the 10 first u_j than to the remaining ones. A similar process is used to obtain the elements of Q and W from Q and w, respectively. Cosine similarities are then calculated between Q and W, and X and W as

$$\theta = \cos(Q, W) = \frac{Q \cdot W}{|Q||W|}, \quad 0 \le \theta, \le 1, \quad (2)$$

$$\beta = \cos(X, W) = \frac{X \cdot W}{|X||W|}, \quad 0 \le \beta, \le 1. \quad (3)$$

This process is repeated r times, once for each word $w = v_{k,i}$ in V_k, and similarities θ_i and β_i, $i = 1, ..., r$, are obtained for each $v_{k,i}$, as well as the averages $\langle \theta \rangle = \sum \theta_i / r$ and $\langle \beta \rangle = \sum \beta_i / r$. The normalized ratio $\left(\frac{\langle \theta \rangle}{\theta_i} \right)$ indicates how large the similarity θ_i is with respect to the average $\langle \theta \rangle$ that is, how close is the candidate word $w = v_{k,i}$ to the *query* Q. The ratio $\left(\frac{\beta_i}{\langle \beta \rangle} \right)$ indicates how reduced the similarity β_i is to the average $\langle \beta \rangle$, that is, how far away the candidate word w is from word o of f_o. A score Sn_i is obtained for each pair (θ_i, β_i) as

$$Sn_i = \left(\frac{\langle \theta \rangle}{\theta_i} \right) \cdot \left(\frac{\beta_i}{\langle \beta \rangle} \right). \quad (4)$$

The higher the value of Sn_i, the better the candidate, $w = v_{k,i}$, complies to the goal of approaching Q and moving away from the semantics of f_o. This goal aims to obtain the candidate $v_{k,i}$ closer to Q, although still considering the context of f_o. We use candidates with large values of Sn_i to replace the nouns. To replace verbs and adjectives, we want the candidate $w = v_{k,i}$ closer to f_o, so we choose among candidates with large Sva_i, given by

$$Sva_i = \left(\frac{\theta_i}{\langle \theta \rangle} \right) \cdot \left(\frac{\langle \beta \rangle}{\beta_i} \right). \quad (5)$$

Finally, we sort the values of Sn_i (nouns) or Sva_i (verbs and adjectives) in decreasing order and choose, at random, from the highest three values, the candidate $v_{k,i}$ that will replace the POS_k tag. The result is a newly generated phrase $f(Q, N)$ that does not exist in the corpora, but maintains the psychological mood (emotional content) of f_o. The model is shown in Fig. 2.

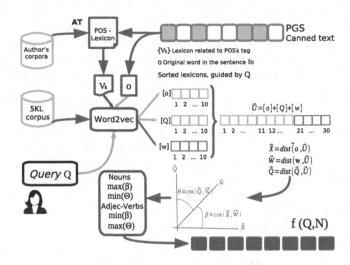

Fig. 2. Model for semantic approximation based on geometrical interpretation.

5   Evaluation and Results

A manual evaluation protocol has been designed to measure some characteristics of the phrases generated by our model. For baseline comparison, we used the model with the best results observed in experiments described in [11]. Although the baseline evaluation was done with a different scale for the evaluation parameters than in the current case, the comparison we present here helps us to understand the human evaluators' perception of the generated sentences.

Sentences have been generated using the corpora **5KL**, **cGoethe**, **cPoe**, **cWerther** and **cCask**, as explained in Sect. 4. The queries employed for generating the sentences in Spanish are $Q \in \{$ODIO, AMOR, SOL, LUNA$\}$ (in English $\{$HATE, LOVE, SUN, MOON$\}$). We show some examples of sentences generated in Spanish in our experiments, manually translated to English.

Sentences Generated Using cCask, cPoe and 5KL

1. $f($LOVE,12$)$ = But I do not think anyone has ever promised against good will.
2. $f($HATE,11$)$ = A beautiful affection and an unbearable admiration took hold of me.
3. $f($SUN,9$)$ = So much does this darkness say, my noble horizon!
4. $f($MOON,9$)$ = My light is unhappy, and I wish for you.

Sentences Generated Using cWerther, cGoethe and 5KL

1. $f($LOVE,11$)$ = Keeping my desire, I decided to try the feeling of pleasure.
2. $f($HATE,7$)$ = I set about breaking down my distrust.
3. $f($SUN,17$)$ = He shouted, and the moon fell away with a sun that I did not try to believe.
4. $f($MOON,12$)$ = Three colors of the main shadow were still bred in this moon.

The experiment we performed consisted of generating 20 sentences for each author's corpora and the 5KL corpus. For each author, 5 phrases were generated with each of the four queries $Q \in \{$LOVE, HATE, SUN,MOON$\}$. Five people were asked to read carefully and evaluate the total of 40 sentences. All evaluators are university graduates and native Spanish speakers. They were asked to score each sentence on a scale of $[0-4]$, where $0 =$ very bad, $1 =$ bad, $2 =$ acceptable, $3 =$ good and $4 =$ very good. The following criteria were used in the evaluations.

- **Grammar:** spelling, conjugations and agreement between gender and number;
- **Coherence:** legibility, perception of a general idea;
- **Context:** relation between the sentence and the query.

We also asked the evaluators to indicate if, according to their own criteria, they considered the sentences as literary. Finally, the evaluators were to indicate which emotion they associate to each sentence ($0 =$ Fear, $1 =$ Sadness, $2 =$ Hope, $3 =$ Love, and $4 =$ Happiness). We compared our results with the evaluation made in [11] as a *baseline*. The evaluated criteria are the same in that and in this work. However, the evaluation scale in [11] is in a range of $[0-2]$ ($0 =$ bad, $1 =$ acceptable, $2 =$ very good). Another difference is that, for the current evaluation, we have calculated the mode instead of the arithmetic mean, since it is more feasible for the analysis of data evaluated in the *Likert* scale.

In Fig. 3a, it can be seen that the **Grammar** criterion obtained good results, with a general perception of *very good*. This is similar to the average of 0.77 obtained in the evaluation of the model proposed in [11]. The **Coherence** was rated as *bad*, against the arithmetic mean of 0.60 obtained in [11]. In spite of being an unfavourable result, we can infer that the evaluators were expecting coherent and logical phrases. Logic is a characteristic that is not always perceived in literature and we inferred, noting that many readers considered the sentences as not being literary (Fig. 3b). The evaluators perceived as *acceptable* the relation between the sentences and the **Context** given by the *query*. This score is similar with the average of 0.53 obtained in [11]. Although one might consider that this rate should be improved, it is important to note that our goal in the current work is not only to approach the context, but to stay close enough to the original sentence, in order to simulate the author's style and to reproduce the psychological trait of the characters in the literary work.

In Fig. 3b, we observe that 67% of the sentences were perceived as literary, although this is a very subjective opinion. This helps us understand that, despite the low rate obtained for **Coherence**, the evaluators do perceive distinctive elements of literature in the generated sentences. We also asked the evaluators to indicate the emotion they perceived in each sentence. We could thus measure to what extent the generated sentences maintain the author's style and the emotions that he wished to transmit. In Fig. 4a, we observe that **hope, happiness** and **sadness** were the most perceived emotions in phrases generated with **cCask** and **cPoe**. Of these, we can highlight **Sadness** which is characteristic of much of Poe's works. Although **Hapiness** is not typical in Poe's works, we may have an explanation for this perception of the readers. If we analyze *The Cask of*

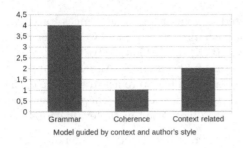 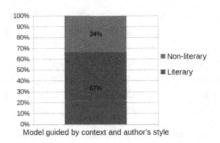

(a) Mode calculated from the evaluation made for the sentence generation model.

(b) Perception of literary nature of sentences.

Fig. 3. Evaluation of our GLT model.

Amontillado, we observe that its main character, *Fortunato*, was characterized as a happy and carefree man until his murder, perhaps because of his drunkenness. The dialogues of *Fortunato* may have influenced the selection of the vocabulary for the generation of the sentences and the perceptions of the evaluators. In Fig. 4b, we can observe that sentences generated with **cWerther** and **cGoethe** transmit mainly **sadness**, **hope** and **love**, which are psychological traits easily perceived when reading *The Sorrows of Young Werther*.

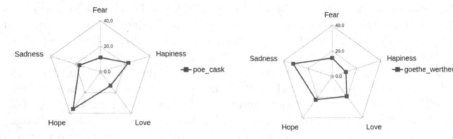

(a) Perceived emotions in sentences generated with Allan Poe's corpora

(b) Perceived emotions in sentences generated with Goethe's corpora

Fig. 4. Comparison between the emotions perceived in sentences.

6   Conclusions and Future Work

We have proposed a model for the generation of literary sentences, that is influenced by two important elements: a context, given by a word input by the user, and a writing mood and style, defined by the training corpora used by our models. The corpora **cGoethe** and **cPoe**, used to generate the association table in Phase II, capture the general mood and style of the two authors. The *canned text* technique applied to corpora **cCask** and **cWerther**, and the similarity measures and scores given by Eqs. (2), (3), (4) and (5), used to generate the final phrases of our generator, reflect the psychological traits and emotions of the characters in the corresponding works. The results are encouraging, as the model generates grammatically correct sentences. The phrases also associate well with the established context, and perceived emotions correspond, in good part, to the emotions transmitted in the literature involved. In the case of *The Cask of Amontillado*, the perceived emotions seem not to resemble the author's main moods. This may be due to the fact that, in this short story, the dialogues of the main character are happy and carefree, the tragic murder occurring only in the end. When characters in a literary text have different psychological traits, the semantic analysis of the generated phrases may show heterogeneous emotional characteristics. Experiments with characters showing more homogeneous psychological traits, such as the melancholic, suicidal tendencies of Werther in *The Sorrows of Young Werther*, more easily detect emotions (as sadness and love) associated with a dominant psychological trend portrayed by the author.

Although there was a poor evaluation for the **Coherence** criterion, it is possible to argue that coherence is not a dominant feature of literature in general, and most of the generated sentences were perceived as literary. The model is thus capable of generating grammatically correct sentences, with a generally clear context, that transmits well the emotion and psychological traits portrayed by the content and style of an author. In future work, we consider extending the length of the generated text by joining several generated sentences together. The introduction of rhyme can be extremely interesting in this sense, when used to produce several sentences to constitute a paragraph or a stanza [9]. We also plan to use and train our model to analyse and generate text in other languages.

Acknowledgements. This work was partially funded by CONACYT, scholarship number 661101 and by the Laboratoire Informatique d'Avignon (LIA) of Avignon Université (France).

References

1. Bengio, Y., Courville, A., Vincent, P.: Representation learning: a review and new perspectives. IEEE Trans. Pattern Anal. Mach. Intell. **35**(8), 1798–1828 (2013)
2. Bracewell, D.B., Ren, F., Kuriowa, S.: Multilingual single document keyword extraction for information retrieval. In: 2005 International Conference on Natural Language Processing and Knowledge Engineering, pp. 517–522. IEEE, Wuhan (2005)
3. Clark, E., Ji, Y., Smith, N.A.: Neural text generation in stories using entity representations as context. In: Conference of the NAC ACL-HLT, vol. 1, pp. 2250–2260. ACL, New Orleans (2018)
4. van Deemter, K., Theune, M., Krahmer, E.: Real versus template-based natural language generation: a false opposition? Comput. Linguist. **31**(1), 15–24 (2005)
5. Goethe, J.W.: Las desventuras del joven Werther, vol. 172. Ediciones Brontes (2019)
6. Mairesse, F., Walker, M.A., Mehl, M.R., Moore, R.K.: Using linguistic cues for the automatic recognition of personality in conversation and text. J. Artif. Intell. Res. **30**, 457–500 (2007)

7. Majumder, N., Poria, S., Gelbukh, A., Cambria, E.: Deep learning-based document modeling for personality detection from text. IEEE Intell. Syst. **32**(2), 74–79 (2017)
8. McRoy, S., Channarukul, S., Ali, S.: An augmented template-based approach to text realization. Nat. Lang. Eng. **9**, 381–420 (2003)
9. Medina-Urrea, A., Torres-Moreno, J.M.: Rimax: Ranking semantic rhymes by calculating definition similarity. arXiv (2020)
10. Molins, P., Lapalme, G.: JSrealB: a bilingual text realizer for web programming. In: 15th ENLG, pp. 109–111. ACL, Brighton (2015)
11. Moreno-Jiménez, L.G., Torres-Moreno, J.M., Wedemann, R.S.: Generación automática de frases literarias en español. arXiv pp. arXiv-2001 (2020)
12. Oliveira, H.G.: Poetryme: a versatile platform for poetry generation. In: Computational Creativity, Concept Invention and General Intelligence, vol. 1. Institute of Cognitive Science, Osnabrück, Germany (2012)
13. Oliveira, H.G., Cardoso, A.: Poetry generation with poetryme. In: Computational Creativity Research: Towards Creative Machines, vol. 7. Atlantis Thinking Machines, Paris (2015)
14. Padró, L., Stanilovsky, E.: Freeling 3.0: towards wider multilinguality. In: 8th LREC, Istanbul, Turkey (2012)
15. Pérez y Pérez, R.: Creatividad Computacional. Larousse - Grupo Editorial Patria, México (2015)
16. Poe, E.A.: El barril de amontillado. BoD E-Short (2015)
17. Riedl, M.O., Young, R.M.: Story planning as exploratory creativity: techniques for expanding the narrative search space. New Gener. Comput. **24**(3), 303–323 (2006). https://doi.org/10.1007/BF03037337
18. Sharples, M.: How We Write: Writing as Creative Design. Routledge, London (1996)
19. Siddiqui, M., Wedemann, R.S., Jensen, H.J.: Avalanches and generalized memory associativity in a network model for conscious and unconscious mental functioning. Phys. A: Stat. Mech. Appl. **490**, 127–138 (2018)
20. Sridhara, G., Hill, E., Muppaneni, D., Pollock, L., Vijay-Shanker, K.: Towards automatically generating summary comments for java methods. In: IEEE/ACM International Conference on Automated Software Engineering, pp. 43–52. ACM, Antwerp (2010)
21. Szymanski, G., Ciota, Z.: Hidden markov models suitable for text generation. In: Mastorakis, N., Kluev, V., Koruga, D. (eds.) WSEAS, pp. 3081–3084. WSEAS - Press, Athens (2002)
22. Torres-Moreno, J.: Beyond stemming and lemmatization: Ultra-stemming to improve automatic text summarization. arXiv abs/1209.3126 (2012)
23. Torres-Moreno, J.M.: Automatic Text Summarization. ISTE Wiley, Hoboken (2014)
24. Wedemann, R.S., Plastino, A.R.: Física estadística, redes neuronales y freud. Revista Núcleos **3**, 4–10 (2016)
25. Zhang, X., Lapata, M.: Chinese poetry generation with recurrent neural networks. In: 2014 EMNLP, pp. 670–680. ACL, Doha (2014)

Movies Emotional Analysis Using Textual Contents

Amir Kazem Kayhani[1], Farid Meziane[1(✉)], and Raja Chiky[2]

[1] School of Science, Engineering and Environment,
University of Salford, Salford M5 4WT, UK
A.K.Kayhani@edu.salford.ac.uk, F.Meziane@salford.ac.uk
[2] ISEP-LISITE, Paris, France
raja.chiky@isep.fr

Abstract. In this paper, we use movies and series subtitles and applied text mining and Natural Language Processing methods to evaluate emotions in videos. Three different word lexicons were used and one of the outcomes of this research is the generation of a secondary dataset with more than 3658 records which can be used for other data analysis and data mining research. We used our secondary dataset to find and display correlations between different emotions on the videos and the correlation between emotions on the movies and users' scores on IMDb using the Pearson correlation method and found some statistically significant correlations.

Keywords: Emotional analysis of movies · Text mining

1 Introduction

Contextual analysis of videos (in this paper, this will encompass movies and TV series) is very important for media companies as it helps them define standard measures and a better understanding of the huge number of video contents without watching them. It also allows them to predict viewers interest, classify and cluster millions of videos based on their contents for different age groups and smart recommendation systems.

Research in emotional analysis and clustering of movies is traditionally based on users' interests and profiles, general characteristics of the movies such as country of production, genre, production year, language and duration or based on linking the emotions and sentiments on users reviews on social media. In this paper we are adopting a completely different approach for emotional analysis of movies by using textual analysis based on their subtitles. The dataset used in this study is freely available and downloaded from Opensubtitles website [1]. To our knowledge, this is the first study on emotional analysis on movies that is based on textual contents. The methodology used in this research is composed of two phases.

---

[1] Opensubtitles.org

© Springer Nature Switzerland AG 2020
E. Métais et al. (Eds.): NLDB 2020, LNCS 12089, pp. 205–212, 2020.
https://doi.org/10.1007/978-3-030-51310-8_19

In the first phase, after data preparation and cleansing we performed sentiment analysis on more than 3650 subtitle files with three different lexicons and calculated the percentage of words with different emotions (trust, joy, fear, positive, etc.) on every SubRip Subtitle file. A SubRip file is the file associated with the subtitle (with the .srt extension). The structure of a subtitle file contains "the section of subtitles number", "The time the subtitle is displayed begins", "The time the subtitle is displayed ends", and the "Subtitle". This phase also includes movies' scoring based on their adult contents (violence and sexual content) that can be used as a source for age and parental ratings and guidance.

In the second phase, scores normalisation is performed. The emotional scores are normalised to values between 0 and 100 and these are assigned to every video. Although the emotional rating of the videos is useful for data analysis on its own, the outcome of this scoring is also used as a new dataset with more than 3650 items and 34 features. This new dataset will be used for other data mining applications such as recommendation systems and predicting viewers interest and score to movies. This last aspect is not covered in this paper.

The remaining of this paper is organised as follows. In Sect. 2 we review some related works. The data cleansing and preparation phase is described in Sect. 3. The emotions analysis is performed in Sect. 4 with the lexicons used in this study and their developments described in Sect. 5. The correlations between emotions and the IMDb scores analysis is given in Sect. 6. Finally, Sect. 7 discusses the results of this research, draw some conclusions and provides some insights into future works.

2 Literature Review

Plutchick [5] developed his emotions model based on eight human emotions including acceptance, surprise, sadness, anger, joy, fear, anticipation and disgust. He also defined some emotions as compounds of two other emotions (for example love is defined as a compound of joy and trust) and he also defined levels of intensity for each of the eight emotions. His model became the most popular for displaying human emotions. Plutchik's wheel of emotions is utilized in many researches in psychology and interdisciplinary fields such as NLP.

Alsheikh, Shaalan and Meziane [1] used the polarity, intensity and combinational concepts in Plutchik's wheel of emotions with text mining and sentiment analysis methods to evaluate trust as an emotion between sellers and buyers in the Customer to Customer marketplace. They have used text mining methods to find correlations between emotions on the hosts' description of their facilities (accommodation in this case as they have used Airbnb as a case study) and negative sentiments by guests through their reviews. They have also used the combinational concepts of emotions based on Plutchick and Ekman emotional model for calculating trust.

Cambria, Livingstone, and Hussain [2] proposed a new model for human emotions which they named "The Hourglass of Emotions". Their model is a reinterpretation of the Plutchik's wheel of emotions and is specifically designed for applications such as sentiment analysis, social data mining and NLP. They used polarity and intensity levels of emotions in Plutchik's wheel of emotions and defined 4 main emotions (instead of the 8 emotions in the Plutchik's model).

Topal and Ozsoyoglu [7] proposed a model for emotional analysis and classification of movies based on the viewers reviews on the IMDb website arguing that there is a close link between users' reviews on IMDb and emotions on the movies. In addition, they have also found correlations between high level of emotionality in movies and high scores (7 or more) to movies by IMDb users. In their research, Topal and Ozsoyoglu [7] used the Hour Glass of Emotions [2] to find emotional scores for each movie based on the reviews and used the K-means algorithm for clustering movies based on their emotional scores according to users' reviews on IMDb. A recommendation system based on the movies emotional score by their method and users' emotional preferences was then proposed.

Li, Liao and Qin [3] stated that most of the works on clustering and recommendations systems for movies are based on users' profiles and interests in movies and/or based on users' social media interactions. However, this approach is not so accurate as it is not based on movies contents, features and characteristics but are focused on users. They proposed clustering movies based on their characteristics such as year and country of production, director, movie type, language, publishing company, casts and duration. They used Jaccard distance for calculating the similarities between movies. Although they have used movies characteristics for clustering, they have combined the results of clustering with users ratings for improving their movie recommendation system [3].

3 Data Understanding and Preparation

In the original dataset, there was a large number of subtitle files in different languages. About 3650 of them have been selected as our sample where 119 are for movies (mostly from top 200 IMDb movies) and the rest are for video series. Two layers of data cleansing were performed on the subtitle files to prepare them for text mining and analysis. The first layer is removing special characters, numbers and extra spaces. In the second layer stop words were removed. In addition, all the letters in all words are converted to lower case and then converted to their root forms (stemming). The output of the data cleansing and preparation phase is a single text file where the tab separator character is used to separate the contents of the different files. Since text mining was performed on a large number of text files and the performance is also important for us, this method of buffering all the files can also help to increase our code performance and execution speed.

Furthermore, we performed an analysis on the number of words and their grammatical roles (part of speech tagging) before and after data cleansing. Although the number of words with all grammatical roles has decreased; as expected, the biggest change occurred among numbers and verbs which have fallen from more than 5.8 million and 3.6 million to 36 and 26,324 respectively.

4   Emotional Analysis

The output of the data cleansing phase is used as the input for emotional analysis. Our method for emotional analysis is similar to the most common methods used for sentiment analysis and is based on Term Frequency (TF) such the work of Rafferty for emotional analysis of the Harry Potter's books [6]. However, our work has additional complexities since it has been defined for emotional analysis on videos (instead of books) and some additional features such as the calculation of 'in-between' emotions, enhancements in data cleansing and normalising the results for a better visualisation and preparation for machine learning tasks. We used three lexicons namely, NRC, AFINN and Ero (these lexicons will be described in Sect. 5) with thousands of words associated to different emotions and we have counted the number of words with each emotion on movies to find the ratio of words with each emotion on every movie (or episode). $E(m, e)$ is the percentage of emotion e in movie m and is calculated using Eq. 1 where $Num_{m,e}$ represents the number of words with emotion e (ex. joy) in movie m (ex. Titanic) and W_m represent the number of all words in movie m.

$$E(m, e) = \frac{num_{m,e}}{W_m} * 100 \tag{1}$$

We have also calculated the total percentage of emotionality in movies by counting the number of all the words in each movie which are also in our NRC Emotion Lexicon. We called this value Emotional Expression $EE(m, e)$ and is calculated using Eq. 2, where Num_m is the number of words in movie M which are also in the NRC lexicon and W_m is the number of all words in movie m.

$$EE(m, e) = \frac{Num_m}{W_m} * 100 \tag{2}$$

In addition, the difference between positivity and negativity for each movie m or episode is calculated using Eq. 3.

$$E(Pos - Neg, m) = \frac{Num_{pos,m} - Num_{neg,m}}{W_m} * 100 \tag{3}$$

The values for 8 in-between emotions which are not in our lexicons were calculated, but they are combinations of other emotions based on Plutchik's wheel of emotions. Calculating the in-between emotions was performed using two methods. The first method is based on the average value of the related emotions. For instance, from the psychological point of view and based on Plutchik's wheel of emotions, love is the combination of joy and trust and its value in movie m is the average of these two emotions as given in Eq. 4, where $P_{joy,m}$ and $P_{trust,m}$ are the percentages of joy and trust in movie m respectively.

$$L(i) = \frac{P_{joy,i} + P_{trust,i}}{2} \tag{4}$$

The second method is based on expanding the NRC Emotion Lexicon according to Plutchik's wheel of emotions (this will be described in Sect. 5). Finally, we

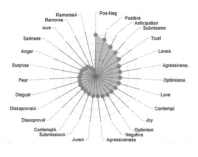

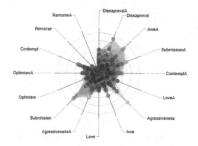

Fig. 1. Emotions in Titanic.   **Fig. 2.** Emotions in Fargo (all episodes).

have normalised emotional percentage results in order to have a standard score from 0 to 100 for all emotions in our dataset. The outcome of this part of the research is the production of two datasets (one normalised and the other not) in the form of two CSV files with 34 columns. After converting the unstructured text data of the initial sample dataset to a structured dataset, we analysed the results for finding the statistical characteristics of the new dataset. Radar charts in Figs. 1 and 2 show the results of emotional analysis for Titanic and Fargo (all episodes) respectively.

5   Lexicons Developments

NRC Lexicon is used as the main Lexicon in this research. The original NRC lexicon [4] consisted of 14,183 rows (words) and 10 columns (8 emotions and 2 sentiments) which is available in over 40 languages and show the association between each word and each emotion in a 0 and 1 matrix where 1 represents the existence of an association and 0 the non-existence. In this research we used the English version of NRC lexicon [4]. The NRC Lexicon consists of the following columns: Trust, Joy, Anticipation, Anger, Disgust, Sadness, Surprise, Fear, Positive and Negative. We expanded the NRC lexicon based on the Plutchik's wheel of emotions. We considered that some emotions like Love, Submission, Optimism or Awe are in fact combination of two other emotions. Figure 3 shows the frequency of association of words with each emotion in the expanded NRC lexicon.

AFINN is the second used lexicon [8] and includes 1477 ratings from −5 (extremely negative) to +5 (extremely positive). We have only used the combination of very negative words in AFINN dataset with −4 and −5 scores for detecting offensive words which may also be associated with sex and/or violence [8]. For simplicity and better understanding, in this research we refer to this secondary lexicon as AFINNVN (AFINN Very Negative). Using this method was our first attempt for scoring movies and series based on adult contents (violence, sex, drugs) which can help us in defining a parental score and finding some interesting correlations and increasing our accuracy for clustering the movies and series.

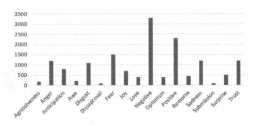

Fig. 3. Frequency of association of words with each emotion in NRC lexicon and expanded NRC lexicon

Although using very negative words in AFINN helped us to detect some offensive, violence and sex related words, it was not enough for detecting many of the sex related words in the movies and after searching, it seems that there is no available and open source lexicon for detecting such words and contents. Hence, there was a need to develop such a lexicon that we named Ero. Ero is constructed from 1422 words which are mostly copied from the "Dirty Sex Dictionary" by filtering bold words on the mentioned HTML page. However, some preparations and modification were needed as many of the words on the list have commonly non-sexual meanings. This lexicon significantly enhanced our work for scoring adult contents.

After finding the amount and percentage of emotions and normalising the results, the secondary dataset has been prepared for further analysis. One of the interesting analysis was finding correlations between emotions in movies and the scores given by the users as provided by the IMDb website. While the range of scores in our sample dataset was between 4.8 and 9.5, we normalised the scores to the range 0 to 100 as the emotions were scored in the range 0–100. Based on the size of our dataset and since our data is normalised, we used Pearson method in R for finding the correlations between the two variables X and Y as given in Eq. 5.

$$r_{X,Y} = \frac{\sum_{i=1}^{n}(X_i - \overline{X})(Y_i - \overline{Y})}{\sqrt{\sum_{i=1}^{n}(X_i - \overline{X})^2}\sqrt{\sum_{i=1}^{n}(Y_i - \overline{Y})^2}} \tag{5}$$

6   Correlation Between Emotions and IMDb Scores

The correlogram shown in Fig. 4 visualises the correlations between emotions (excluding in-between emotions), sentiments (positive and negative) and users' scores to movies on the IMDb database using the Pearson correlation method. As expected, all the emotions have considerable correlation with either negative or positive sentiments and there is a negative correlation between negative and positive sentiments. However, it is interesting to note that correlations between negative and positive sentiments are not very high (+0.2). On the other hand, we can see that there is a high correlation (+0.6) between usage of offensive words (AFINNVN) and sexual words (Ero). The main reason could be common usage of sexual words as offensive words. One of the interesting correlations is the very high correlation (+0.7) between anger and fear (probably since anger can cause fear). The only emotion with positive correlation with both positive (0.3) and negative (0.1) sentiments is surprise as surprising happen in both positive and negative ways. In addition, based on the Pearson correlation results (Fig. 4), we can see that positive sentiment and joy, trust and anticipation emotions have negative correlation with Emotional expression which is the ratio of emotional words to all words in a movie or episode. It was completely against our expectations since words with positive sentiment and joy, trust and anticipation emotions will be counted as emotional expression. Based on these results we can conclude that an increase in each of the positive sentiments of joy, trust or anticipation emotions usually will lead to decreasing other emotions.

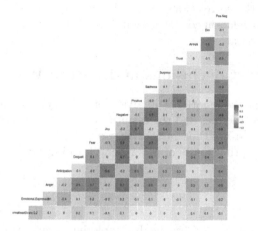

Fig. 4. Correlations Heatmap. Blue colour indicates negative correlations, red indicate positive correlations and white indicate not having correlations (Color figure online)

Computing correlations between users' scores in IMDb and sentiments and emotions on movies is of great interest. Indeed, it can help in predicting users' scores and can help media companies to invest in movies which can be more interesting and attractive to users and also can help them to increase the quality of their movies and series based on users emotional interests. Generally, in statistics using two alpha p-values for accepting Pearson correlation results as statistically significant; Alpha <0.01 and alpha <0.05 are two common alpha p-values used in statistical studies. According to the results shown in Fig. 4 we can clearly see that there are lots of considerable and statistically significant correlations between emotions on the movies and users' scores on IMDb. Although there are cases where is no statistically significant correlation between some emotions and users score on IMDb, most of the emotions have statistically significant correlation with users scores on IMDb and most of the correlations are statistically significant at p-value alpha level <0.01. Most effective parameter in users' scores to movies is 'Emotional Expression' on movies with +0.22 Pearson correlation which is also statistically significant at the level of alpha <0.01. It means that in general movies with rich words and higher level of emotionality are more likely to be interesting to viewers and get higher score in IMDb. However, this conclusion is not true for all emotions as some emotions have negative Pearson correlation with users' scores on IMDb and it is more likely to negatively affect users' scores to movies. Consequently, for more accurate analysis we should consider each emotion separately.

Some emotions such as joy, love and anticipation have negative correlation with users' scores and it is more likely to affect users score to movies in a negative way but on the other hand most of the emotions such as anger, fear and contempt have positive effect on users score and satisfaction. Furthermore, we can see that words in AFINNVN and Ero have positive correlation with users' scores on IMDb and their correlation is statistically significant at the alpha level <0.01. Although many of the correlations are statistically significant according to their p-value, Pearson correlation coefficient with values between −0.3 and 0.3 usually indicate a weak correlation.

7 Discussions, Conclusions and Future Works

We have performed the emotional analysis on a relatively large data set with more than 3650 subtitle files and the results of this analysis created a secondary dataset which can be used for further research and analysis. We are particularly aiming at using the results of this research to improve on recommendation systems.

References

1. Alsheikh, S.S., Shaalan, K., Meziane, F.: Exploring the effects of consumers' trust: a predictive model for satisfying buyers' expectations based on sellers' behavior in the marketplace. IEEE Access **7**, 73357–73372 (2019)
2. Cambria, E., Livingstone, A., Hussain, A.: The hourglass of emotions. In: Esposito, A., Esposito, A.M., Vinciarelli, A., Hoffmann, R., Müller, V.C. (eds.) Cognitive Behavioural Systems. LNCS, vol. 7403, pp. 144–157. Springer, Heidelberg (2012). https://doi.org/10.1007/978-3-642-34584-5_11
3. Li, B., Liao, Y., Qin, Z.: Precomputed clustering for movie recommendation system in real time. J. Appl. Math. 1–9 (2014)
4. Mohammad, S., Turney, P.: Crowdsourcing a word-emotion association lexicon. Comput. Intell. **29**(3), 436–465 (2013)
5. Plutchik, R., Kellerman, H.: Emotion theory, research and experience. Theories of emotion. Psychol. Med. **1**(1), 207–207 (1981)
6. Rafferty, G.: Harry potter NLP (2019). https://github.com/raffg/harry_potter_nlp/blob/master/sentiment_analysis.ipynb. Accessed 10 Oct 2019
7. Topal, K., Gultekin, O.: Emotional classification and visualization of movies based on their IMDb reviews. Inf. Disc. Deliv. **45**(3), 149–158 (2017)
8. Nielsen, F.Å.: A new ANEW: evaluation of a word list for sentiment analysis in microblogs. In: Rowe, M., Stankovic, M., Dadzie, A., Hardey, M. (eds.) Proceedings of the ESWC2011 Workshop on 'Making Sense of Microposts': Big Things Come in Small Packages, vol. 718, pp. 93–98, May 2011

Combining Character and Word Embeddings for Affect in Arabic Informal Social Media Microblogs

Abdullah I. Alharbi[1,2]([⊠]) and Mark Lee[1]([⊠])

[1] School of Computer Science, University of Birmingham, Birmingham, UK
{aia784,m.g.lee}@cs.bham.ac.uk
[2] Faculty of Computing and Information Technology, King Abdulaziz University,
Rabigh, Kingdom of Saudi Arabia
aamalharbe@kau.edu.sa

Abstract. Word representation models have been successfully applied in many natural language processing tasks, including sentiment analysis. However, these models do not always work effectively in some social media contexts. When considering the use of Arabic in microblogs like Twitter, it is important to note that a variety of different linguistic domains are involved. This is mainly because social media users employ various dialects in their communications. While training word-level models with such informal text can lead to words being captured that have the same meanings, these models cannot capture all words that can be encountered in the real world due to out-of-vocabulary (OOV) words. The inability to identify words is one of the main limitations of this word-level model. In contrast, character-level embeddings can work effectively with this problem through their ability to learn the vectors of character n-grams or parts of words. We take advantage of both character- and word-level models to discover more effective methods to represent Arabic affect words in tweets. We evaluate our embeddings by incorporating them into a supervised learning framework for a range of affect tasks. Our models outperform the state-of-the-art Arabic pre-trained word embeddings in these tasks. Moreover, they offer improved state-of-the-art results for the task of Arabic emotion intensity, outperforming the top-performing systems that employ a combination of deep neural networks and several other features.

Keywords: Word-level embeddings · Character-level embeddings · Arabic affect tweets

1 Introduction

People use language not only to express their sentiments and emotions, but also to show how intense these feelings may be. We use the term 'affect' to refer to different emotion-related categories, ranging from the sentiment classification

© Springer Nature Switzerland AG 2020
E. Métais et al. (Eds.): NLDB 2020, LNCS 12089, pp. 213–224, 2020.
https://doi.org/10.1007/978-3-030-51310-8_20

(positive to negative) to finer grained sentiment strength (e.g. high positive to low positive) and emotional intensity (e.g. high anger to low anger). Detecting affect in text is challenging, especially in the context of social media, such as Twitter, owing to difficulties involving the limited number and informal nature of words used, with the latter including slang and symbols. However, this task becomes even more challenging when considering morphology-rich languages, such as Arabic [4]. Social media users employ various dialects and sub-dialects in their communications. In contrast to the use of Modern Standard Arabic (MSA), the form of dialectical Arabic words used varies widely, and there is a general lack of rules and standards. Therefore, the need for effective resources and tools to better understand and treat these various linguistic forms is important when targeting Arabic affect in tweets.

Word embedding is one of the most important methods that have been applied recently to many natural language processing tasks [9,14,19,28]. Word embedding uses dense vectors to represent words projecting into a continuous vector space, thus reducing the number of dimensions [20]. However, these models do not always work effectively in Arabic tweet contexts. While training word-level models with such informal text can lead to the capture of words with the same meanings, it has been shown in testing that these models are unable to recognise other forms of the same words encountered in the real world. These unknown words are called out-of-vocabulary (OOV) words, and this is one of the main limitations of the word-level model. In contrast, character-level embeddings can work effectively in resolving the problem of OOV words through their ability to learn the vectors of character n-grams or parts of words. However, this sensitivity of character-level embedding leads the model to encode all variants of a word's morphology that are closer to each other in the embedded space than those with semantic similarity. Table 1 shows two examples of dialectical affect words متنرفز mtnrfz[1] (uptight) and مروق mrwq (relaxed), where the similarity of the words is mostly based on morphology at the character level and semantics at the word level.

In this paper, we take advantage of both character-level and word-level models to discover more effective means of representing Arabic affect in tweets, which we call affect Character and Word Embeddings (ACWE). We first trained both levels of models on a massive number of tweets, which were collected carefully to ensure that there was significant variation of affect and Arabic dialects in the words. We then employed a novel method that concatenates both levels of models to represent each word morphologically and semantically. We evaluate the effectiveness of our ACWE model by applying it only as a feature under a supervised learning, using the benchmark datasets of SemEval-2018 task 1 (Affect in Tweets) [21]. Our method advances a state-of-the-art approach to the task of discerning Arabic emotional intensity, outperforming the top-performing systems. In addition, our method achieves better results compared to other Arabic pre-trained word embeddings. ACWE has been released to be used in pre-trained

---

[1] We used Buckwalter transliteration [10].

Table 1. Most similar words of different affect words using character and word level embeddings.

Example of a negative query term: متنرفز mtnrfz (uptigh)		Example of a positive query term: مروق mrwq (relaxed)	
Character-level model	Word-level model	Character-level model	Word-level model
متنرفزه mtnrfz (uptight-feminine)	معصب mESb (angry)	ومروق wmrwq (and relaxed)	مصحصح mSHSH (mindful)
متنرفزين mtnrfzyn (uptight-plural)	متوتر mtwtr (tense)	مروقه mrwqh (relaxed-feminine)	ومروق wmrwq (and relaxed)
نتنرفز ntnrfz (uptight-present verb)	متضايق mtDAyq (annoyed)	ومروق wmrwqh (and relaxed-feminine)	فايق fAyq (awake)
بيتنرفز bytnrfz (uptight-future verb)	منفس mnfs (furious)	رايق rAyq (relaxed)	مفلل mfll (restful)
تتنرفز ttnrfz (uptight- feminine verb)	مضغوط mDgwT (enraged)	رايقه rAyqh (relaxed-feminine)	مستانس mstAns (happy)

word embeddings for applications and research relying on Arabic sentiment and emotion analysis[2].

2   Related Works

Most work on Arabic word embeddings has relied on word-level models [3,6, 27], and to a lesser degree, character-level models have been employed [5]. To our knowledge, there is no existing work that aims to combine both levels to generate word representations specifically for sentiment or emotion analysis. One of the largest open-source word embeddings is AraVec [27], which consists of six different word embedding models for the Arabic language. Here, the researchers derived the training data from three separate sources: Wikipedia, Twitter and Common Crawl webpages crawl data; they employed two word-level models to learn word representations for general NLP tasks.

More recently, [3] proposed the largest word-level embeddings by using 250M Arabic tweets. Although the models are trained on many words, they cannot realise other forms of the same words that can be seen in the real world due to the limitations of such word-level models. Furthermore, it has been observed that the effectiveness of word embeddings is more likely to be task-dependent [25], and it is highly influenced by the richness of related words to the target task [11].

Much research has been undertaken on Arabic sentiment analysis, but research has focussed on other affect aspects such as emotion analysis or intensity remains limited [21]. Most of the existing work on affect in Arabic is based on the SemEval-2018 competition, Affect in Tweet. Most of the top-performing

---

[2] https://github.com/aialharbi/ACWE.

systems proposed for this shared task employed deep learning approaches, such as CNN, LSTM and Bi-LSTM [1,2,16]. The majority of these systems employed AraVec as a feature besides other input features, Arabic sentiment and emotion lexicons [7,22,24].

3 Methodology

In this work, we aim to generate an effective distributed word representation model for Arabic affect in tweets. The data collection method and the different models of word embeddings used are detailed in the subsections below.

3.1 Data Collection

One of the main factors in improving the quality of word embeddings is associated with the training dataset size and its richness. We collected a large number of tweets (10M) containing various affect-associated words of different Arabic dialects. To ensure the tweets contained a variety of affect-associated words, we first used English NRC lexicons [23] to select a number of words (63 words)[3] from different emotional expressions and intensity levels. Then, the selected words were translated into Arabic using the online translation application Reverso Context[4]. We also used Reverso to find synonyms of these translated words to extend our list of terms from 63 to 228 words. At this stage, our list of terms contained MSA affect words, which was an expected result of this means of English-Arabic translation.

To ensure the tweets reflected a variety of dialects, we used our MSA terms list to find synonyms in Arabic dialects from two online dictionaries (Atlas Allhajaat[5] and Mo3jam[6]). This expanded our list of terms by 217 different dialectical affect words. In addition, it should be noted that emojis could be employed, given that, according to [17], they function as a universal language. Therefore, we selected the 30 most frequently used emojis from different sentiment scores obtained from [17] and added them to our list of terms. Finally, we assumed that tweets from specific Arabic-speaking countries would more likely be associated with the dialects of these locations. Therefore, we collected tweets that included all the identified terms (about 500 terms) using the Twitter Search API by specifying the geolocations of different Arab countries.

3.2 Data Preprocessing

The data that we extracted from Twitter typically contained a range of content that could be considered useless for our task, such as hashtags, website links and

---

[3] These are words that directly convey meanings of sentiment or emotion, such as *anger* or *rage*. They are not words that indirectly convey sentiment, such as *dead* or *tears*.

[4] http://context.reverso.net.

[5] http://atlasallhajaat.com.

[6] http://en.mo3jam.com.

mentions. It was important that such noisy content be removed before training our learning models to reduce both the noise and vector space size [18,26]. We followed the procedure laid out by several research works [3,15], which involved the following steps:

- **Normalisation of letters:** Letters that appeared in different forms in the original tweets were rendered into a single form. For example, the 'hamza' on characters {إ,أ} was replaced with {ا}, while the 't marbouta' {ة} was replaced with {ه}.

- **Hashtags:** Hashtags are used to draw attention to words or phrases that are trending. For example, #anger, #happy. While it is common to remove the hash symbols and words, we only removed the hash symbols and kept the words. Users sometimes express their emotions using these hashtags, so it was considered useful to retain them.

- **Cleaning:** All unknown symbols and other characters were eliminated. For example, other language letters, diacritics, punctuation and URLs were removed. However, emojis were not removed, and like the words, each emoji was represented by a vector.

3.3 Embedding Models

After retrieving and pre-processing a massive number of tweets that are rich in Arabic affect-related words, we used this to generate a language model. Word embeddings are learned representations of text, with words of similar meanings represented in similar ways. An essential element of this methodology is the concept of employing dense distributed representations for every word. Here, each word is encoded to a real-valued vector with a few hundred dimensions. Given a large corpus, there are different models and levels available for learning word embeddings. We first employed the Word2Vec model [20] for word-level embeddings and FastText model [8] for character-level embeddings. Hence, we leveraged these two pre-trained embeddings as an input feature after combining them with a novel concatenation approach. These main steps are detailed in the following subsections.

Word-Level Embeddings (WE). To learn individual words with their embeddings from our collected data, we used the Word2Vec algorithm [20]. Word2Vec is based on a pair of learning techniques: the Continuous Bag-of-Words (CBOW) and Skip-Gram (SG) models. The CBOW model effectively averages the vectors of all the words in a given context. The model is trained by predicting the current word based on the projected average of the surrounding context. The continuous SG model is similar, but instead of predicting the current word based on context, it predicts the surrounding words based on the current one. Words within a certain distance before and after the current word are predicted with the network optimised for these predictions. We used both models (CBOW and SG) to generate affect word embeddings by training the models on a massive number of tweets that we retrieved. We used the Gensim Library[7] to implement the Word2Vec models. We assumed that each tweet was a sentence, so the input of the word-level model was a list of pre-processed tweets that were tokenised into words on whitespace. The main parameters that we used were (200) for size, (5) for the window context and (3) to ignore words with a total frequency lower than three.

Character-Level Embeddings (CE). To learn morphological features found in each word, we used a character n-grams model (FastText) [8]. FastText differs from Word2Vec in its ability to learn the vectors of character n-grams or parts of words. This feature enables the model to capture words that have similar meanings but different morphological word formations. We used the Gensim Library[8] to implement the FastText model. We assumed that each tweet was a sentence, so the input of the character-level model was a list of characters for each tweet. We used the same main parameters that we employed for Word2Vec. In addition, to control the lengths of character n-grams, we used 3 and 6 for parameters (min_n) and (max_n), respectively.

Affect Character and Word Embeddings (ACWE). As explained in the introduction, while CE seems to encode all variants of a word's morphology closer in the embedded space, WE seems to give more importance to semantic similarity. To take advantage of both models, we propose ACWE, a novel approach that aims to concatenate these two pre-trained embeddings; hence, it can be used as an input feature for a range of sentiment and emotion tasks.

Given a tweet t_i that has a sequence of words $\{w_1, w_2, ..., w_n\}$, our goal is to morphologically and semantically represent each word in each tweet $w_i \in t_i$ as an n-dimensional continuous vector. To achieve this goal, we assumed that each word $w_i \in t_i$ is represented semantically by $WE(w_i)$ and morphologically by $CE(w_i)$, where $WE(w_i)$ is the word embedding of w_i, while $CE(w_i)$ is the character embedding of w_i. The $ACWE(w_i)$ method is used to concatenate both embeddings, and it can be obtained in three different cases. The first case is a direct concatenation of $CE(w_i)$ and $WE(w_i)$, and it arises if w_i can be found in both embeddings. However, if w_i cannot be found in WE[9], we assume this is due to variants in the given word's morphology. Consequently, instead of using a vector of zeros for unseen w_i, it will be replaced by another word's morphology that can be realised by WE. Alternative words can be obtained using $most\_similar(w_i)$, which aims to find the most similar word based on the cosine similarity of the w_i vector and the vectors for each word in CE. Finally, if w_i cannot be determined using CE and WE, it will be represented by a vector of zeros.

---

[7] http://radimrehurek.com/gensim/models/word2vec.html.
[8] http://radimrehurek.com/gensim/models/fasttext.html.
[9] As explained in the introduction, WE cannot process OOV words.

$$ACWE(w_i) = \begin{cases} CE(w_i) \oplus WE(w_i), & \text{if } w_i \in (CE|V|, WE|V|) \\ CE(w_i) \oplus WE(most\_similar(w_i)), & \text{if } w_i \notin (WE|V|) \\ zeros \ of (CE + WE) \ dimensions & \text{otherwise} \end{cases} \tag{1}$$

4 Experiments

To validate the effectiveness of our embeddings, we incorporated them into a supervised learning framework for a range of affect-sensitive tasks. We compared our models against available state-of-the-art pre-trained Arabic word embeddings. We also compared our method with top systems targeting these different tasks.

4.1 Datasets

We evaluated our model using different affect tasks in the SemEval 2018 task 1 (Affect in Tweets) datasets [21]. We selected these datasets because of the variety of affect tasks and Arabic dialects. These tasks can be categorised as follows:

- **Emotion Intensity Task:** When given an emotion and a tweet, compute the emotional intensity (EI) that most accurately represents the emotion experienced by the publisher using a real-value score as follows: 1) The EI-regression (EI-reg) task scores range from 0 to 1, from least to most emotion; and 2) the EI-ordinal classification (EI-oc) Task scores range from 0 to 3, where 0 refers to an unrelated emotion.
- **Sentiment or Valence Intensity Task:** When given a tweet, predict the valence (V) that most effectively represents the tweeter's mental state using a real-value score as follows: 1) the V-reg task scores range from 0 to 1, from most negative to most positive; and 2) The V-oc task scores range from -3 (very negative) to $+3$ (very positive).

Table 2. Number of tweets in the SemEval 2018 Task 1 (Affect in Tweets) datasets.

Task	Emotion	Train	Dev	Test	Total
EI-reg/EI-oc	Anger	877	150	373	1,400
	Fear	882	146	372	1,400
	Joy	728	224	448	1,400
	Sadness	889	141	370	1,400
V-reg/V-oc	Valence intensity	932	730	1,800	1,800

4.2   Pre-trained Word Embeddings

To evaluate the effectiveness of our models, we compared them with Arabic pre-trained word embeddings in the following models: Ara2Vec [27], Mazajak [3] and Altwyan [6]. To the best of our knowledge, these embeddings are the most commonly available resources released to the research community as free to use. Table 3 presents a summary of important information about each of these models with their sizes and pre-trained corpora (Table 2).

Table 3. Different pre-trained Arabic word embeddings used for experimental evaluation.

Model	No. of words	Corpus	Size
Ara2Vec	4,347,845	General - Twitter	77M Tweets
Mazajak	1,476,715	Sentiment - Twitter	250M Tweets
Altwaian	159,175	Sentiment - Twitter	190M words
Our WE	626,212	Affect - Twitter	100B tokens
Our CE	441,025	Affect - Twitter	3B tweets

4.3   Model Training

We pre-processed the datasets using the pre-processing techniques described in Sect. 3.2. To predict a real-value score for each task, we employed the XGBoost learning model [12] and used one of the aforementioned pre-trained word embeddings as an input feature. The XGBoost learning model is frequently employed for different problems because it performs extremely well on a wide range of significant challenges. The tool is both extremely versatile and flexible, and it can address different classification and regression problems [12]. This is an algorithm of decision trees in which new trees correct errors of those trees which are already part of the model. Trees are added to the model until no further changes can be made. We input tweet vector representations obtained from an average of real-value word vectors for every word with matching vector representations derived from pre-trained embeddings.

4.4   Results

The results of our experiments were evaluated using Pearson's correlation coefficient, which calculates a bivariate linear correlation between two given variables. In our experiments, this comprised the correlation between the score predicted by our systems and the score given by the test data. We used this evaluation metric because it is the official metric for all the relevant tasks. Our results and findings are discussed in the following subsections.

Comparison with State-of-the-Art Pre-trained Arabic Word Embeddings: We compared five pre-trained word embeddings (see Table 3), including three open-source models and both of our generated models. In addition, we compared these models with the ACWE method. The information presented in Table 4 shows the effectiveness of each model in the supervised framework of performing affect-sensitive tasks. The Pearson correlation coefficient for our *CE* significantly outperformed the other models. We consider that the main reason for this was associated with OOV problems. Although these models were trained using a massive corpus, we found that word-level embeddings could not realise more than 700 words from each dataset. Moreover, the ACWE method improved the results by 1.3% to 5% across all datasets. This indicates the effectiveness of the proposed method and the importance of leveraging character-level and word-level embeddings in Arabic words in the context of social networks and microblogs.

Table 4. Pearson correlation coefficient results for our models and State-of-the-art pre-trained Arabic Word Embeddings

Model	EI-reg					EI-oc					V-reg	V-oc
	Anger	Fear	Joy	Sad	Avg.	Anger	Fear	Joy	Sad	Avg.		
Ara2Vec	55.6	53.6	68.8	64.1	60.5	47.2	52.6	60.4	59.4	54.9	77.3	72.3
Mazajak	55.5	57.6	68.3	62.3	60.9	45.0	51.2	64.6	53.0	53.4	72.0	68.0
Altwyan	29.7	33.3	44.9	49.7	41.5	27.2	31.2	42.5	48.9	37.5	51.5	53.5
Our generated Arabic word Embeddings												
WE	53.9	52.9	65.3	60.7	58.7	47.9	51.1	62.8	55.6	54.4	75.6	70.2
CE	60.1	59.5	70.4	65.8	64.3	51.1	53.1	64.7	60.6	57.6	78.3	73.1
ACWE	**63.8**	**62.2**	**75,8**	**68.6**	**67.6**	**54.3**	**57.2**	**67.5**	**60.9**	**60.0**	**81.8**	**76.7**

Comparison Against Top Systems Analysing Affect in Tweets: Most of the top-performing systems proposed for this shared task employed deep learning approaches, such as CNN, LSTM and Bi-LSTM. The majority of these systems used AraVec as a feature alongside other input features, such as the sentiment and emotional lexicons found in the Arabic language. We used our embeddings as the input feature for XGBoost, a machine learning classifier/regressor. As shown in Table 5, we achieved competitive results: We outperformed the top system in the EI-oc task by 1.3% and ranked second in the remaining tasks. Our goal was not to fully address affect tasks but rather to demonstrate that, by using a well-generated word embedding model, we could obtain competitive results. We will investigate other features and employ deep learning methods to improve the results in future works.

Table 5. Pearson correlation coefficient results for our ACWE and top systems across all tasks.

Task	1st best	2nd best	Our ACWE
Ei-reg	**68.5**	66.7	67.6
EI-oc	58.7	57.4	**60.0**
V-reg	**82.8**	81.6	81.8
V-oc	**80.9**	75.2	76.7

5   Conclusion

In this paper, we generated word and character embeddings to analyse affect in Arabic social media networks and microblogs. We also proposed a novel method that combines different levels of word embeddings to represent the morphology and semantics for each word in a given task. We evaluated the models by incorporating them into a supervised learning framework for a range of affect-sensitive tasks. Our models outperformed state-of-the-art pre-trained Arabic word embeddings on these tasks.

In future works, we will apply more sophisticated algorithms to improve the quality of our embeddings. Especially, we would like to employ contextualised word embeddings, such as BERT [13]. We would also like to investigate more deep learning algorithms to fully target affect tasks.

References

1. Abdou, M., Kulmizev, A., Ginés i Ametllé, J.: AffecThor at SemEval-2018 task 1: a cross-linguistic approach to sentiment intensity quantification in tweets. In: Proceedings of The 12th International Workshop on Semantic Evaluation, pp. 210–217. Association for Computational Linguistics, New Orleans (2018)
2. Abdullah, M., Shaikh, S.: TeamUNCC at SemEval-2018 task 1: emotion detection in English and Arabic tweets using deep learning. In: Proceedings of The 12th International Workshop on Semantic Evaluation, pp. 350–357. Association for Computational Linguistics, New Orleans (2018)
3. Abu Farha, I., Magdy, W.: Mazajak: An online Arabic sentiment analyser. In: Proceedings of the Fourth Arabic Natural Language Processing Workshop, pp. 192–198. Association for Computational Linguistics, Florence (2019)
4. Al-Ayyoub, M., Khamaiseh, A.A., Jararweh, Y., Al-Kabi, M.N.: A comprehensive survey of Arabic sentiment analysis. Inf. Process. Manage. **56**(2), 320–342 (2019)
5. Altowayan, A.A., Elnagar, A.: Improving Arabic sentiment analysis with sentiment-specific embeddings. In: 2017 IEEE International Conference on Big Data (Big Data), pp. 4314–4320. IEEE, Boston (2017)
6. Altowayan, A.A., Tao, L.: Word embeddings for Arabic sentiment analysis. In: 2016 IEEE International Conference on Big Data (Big Data), pp. 3820–3825. IEEE, Washington (2016)

7. Badaro, G., Baly, R., Hajj, H., Habash, N., El-Hajj, W.: A large scale Arabic sentiment lexicon for Arabic opinion mining. In: Proceedings of the EMNLP 2014 Workshop on Arabic Natural Language Processing (ANLP), pp. 165–173. Association for Computational Linguistics, Doha, October 2014
8. Bojanowski, P., Grave, E., Joulin, A., Mikolov, T.: Enriching word vectors with subword information. Trans. Assoc. Comput. Linguist. **5**, 135–146 (2017)
9. Bordes, A., Chopra, S., Weston, J.: Question answering with subgraph embeddings. In: Proceedings of the 2014 Conference on Empirical Methods in Natural Language Processing (EMNLP), pp. 615–620. Association for Computational Linguistics, Doha (2014)
10. Buckwalter, T.: Buckwalter Arabic morphological analyzer version 2.0. LDC catalog number LDC2004l02, ISBN 1-58563-324-0 (2004)
11. Çano, E., Morisio, M.: Quality of word embeddings on sentiment analysis tasks. In: Frasincar, F., Ittoo, A., Nguyen, L.M., Métais, E. (eds.) NLDB 2017. LNCS, vol. 10260, pp. 332–338. Springer, Cham (2017). https://doi.org/10.1007/978-3-319-59569-6_42
12. Chen, T., Guestrin, C.: XGBoost: a scalable tree boosting system. In: Proceedings of the 22nd ACM SIGKDD International Conference on Knowledge Discovery and Data Mining, KDD 2016, pp. 785–794. Association for Computing Machinery, New York (2016)
13. Devlin, J., Chang, M.W., Lee, K., Toutanova, K.: BERT: pre-training of deep bidirectional transformers for language understanding. In: Proceedings of the 2019 Conference of the North American Chapter of the Association for Computational Linguistics: Human Language Technologies, Volume 1 (Long and Short Papers), pp. 4171–4186. Association for Computational Linguistics, Minneapolis (2019)
14. Devlin, J., Zbib, R., Huang, Z., Lamar, T., Schwartz, R., Makhoul, J.: Fast and robust neural network joint models for statistical machine translation. In: Proceedings of the 52nd Annual Meeting of the Association for Computational Linguistics (Volume 1: Long Papers), Baltimore, Maryland, pp. 1370–1380 (2014)
15. Duwairi, R., El-Orfali, M.: A study of the effects of preprocessing strategies on sentiment analysis for Arabic text. J. Inf. Sci. **40**(4), 501–513 (2014)
16. Jabreel, M., Moreno, A.: EiTAKA at SemEval-2018 task 1: an ensemble of n-channels ConvNet and XGboost regressors for emotion analysis of tweets. In: Proceedings of The 12th International Workshop on Semantic Evaluation, pp. 193–199. Association for Computational Linguistics, New Orleans (2018)
17. Kralj Novak, P., Smailović, J., Sluban, B., Mozetič, I.: Sentiment of emojis. PLoS ONE **10**(12), 1–22 (2015)
18. Li, Q., Shah, S., Liu, X., Nourbakhsh, A.: Data sets: word embeddings learned from tweets and general data. In: Proceedings of the Eleventh International Conference on Web and Social Media (ICWSM-17), pp. 428–436. AAAI Press, Montréal (2017)
19. Lin, C.C., Ammar, W., Dyer, C., Levin, L.: Unsupervised POS induction with word embeddings. In: Proceedings of the 2015 Conference of the North American Chapter of the Association for Computational Linguistics: Human Language Technologies, pp. 1311–1316. Association for Computational Linguistics, Denver (2015)
20. Mikolov, T., Sutskever, I., Chen, K., Corrado, G., Dean, J.: Distributed representations of words and phrases and their compositionality. In: Proceedings of the 26th International Conference on Neural Information Processing Systems, NIPS 2013, vol. 2, pp. 3111–3119. Curran Associates Inc., Red Hook (2013)

21. Mohammad, S., Bravo-Marquez, F., Salameh, M., Kiritchenko, S.: SemEval-2018 task 1: affect in Tweets. In: Proceedings of The 12th International Workshop on Semantic Evaluation, pp. 1–17. Association for Computational Linguistics, New Orleans (2018)

22. Mohammad, S., Salameh, M., Kiritchenko, S.: Sentiment lexicons for Arabic social media. In: Proceedings of the Tenth International Conference on Language Resources and Evaluation (LREC 2016), pp. 33–37. Portorož (2016)

23. Mohammad, S.M.: Word affect intensities. In: Proceedings of the 11th Edition of the Language Resources and Evaluation Conference (LREC-2018), Miyazaki, Japan, pp. 174–183 (2018)

24. Mohammad, S.M., Turney, P.D.: Crowdsourcing a word-emotion association lexicon. Comput. Intell. **29**(3), 436–465 (2013)

25. Qu, L., Ferraro, G., Zhou, L., Hou, W., Schneider, N., Baldwin, T.: Big data small data. domain out-of domain, known word unknown word: the impact of word representations on sequence labelling tasks. In: Proceedings of the Nineteenth Conference on Computational Natural Language Learning, pp. 83–93. Association for Computational Linguistics, Beijing, July 2015

26. Singh, T., Kumari, M.: Role of text pre-processing in Twitter sentiment analysis. Proc. Comput. Sci. **89**, 549–554 (2016)

27. Soliman, A.B., Eissa, K., El-Beltagy, S.R.: AraVec: a set of Arabic word embedding models for use in Arabic NLP. Proc. Comput. Sci. **117**, 256–265 (2017)

28. Zhang, J., Liu, S., Li, M., Zhou, M., Zong, C.: Bilingually-constrained phrase embeddings for machine translation. In: Proceedings of the 52nd Annual Meeting of the Association for Computational Linguistics (Volume 1: Long Papers), pp. 111–121. Association for Computational Linguistics, Baltimore (2014)

Towards Explainability in Using Deep Learning for the Detection of Anorexia in Social Media

Hessam Amini$^{(\boxtimes)}$ and Leila Kosseim

Computational Linguistics at Concordia (CLaC) Laboratory,
Department of Computer Science and Software Engineering,
Concordia University, Montréal, QC H3G 2W1, Canada
{hessam.amini,leila.kosseim}@concordia.ca

Abstract. Explainability of deep learning models has become increasingly important as neural-based approaches are now prevalent in natural language processing. Explainability is particularly important when dealing with a sensitive domain application such as clinical psychology. This paper focuses on the quantitative assessment of user-level attention mechanism in the task of detecting signs of anorexia in social media users from their posts. The assessment is done through monitoring the performance measures of a neural classifier, with and without user-level attention, when only a limited number of highly-weighted posts are provided. Results show that the weights assigned by the user-level attention strongly correlate with the amount of information that posts provide in showing if their author is at risk of anorexia or not, and hence can be used to explain the decision of the neural classifier.

Keywords: Explainability · Deep learning · Attention mechanism · Anorexia · Social media

1 Introduction

Social media is a rich source of information for the assessment of mental health, as its users often feel they can express their thoughts and emotions more freely, and describe their everyday lives [12]. This is why the use of natural language processing (NLP) techniques to extract information about the mental health of social media users has become an important research question in the last few years [18,27].

One of the main challenges of developing tools for the automatic detection of mental health issues from social media is providing justification for the decisions. Mental health issues are still often stigmatised and labelling a user as a victim of a mental health illness without a proper justification is not socially responsible. As a result, to be applicable in a real-life setting, automatic systems should not only be accurate, but their decisions need to be explained.

In the past decade, deep learning algorithms have become the state of the art in many NLP applications. By automatically learning the representation of useful

© Springer Nature Switzerland AG 2020
E. Métais et al. (Eds.): NLDB 2020, LNCS 12089, pp. 225–235, 2020.
https://doi.org/10.1007/978-3-030-51310-8_21

linguistic features for the tasks they are performing, deep learning approaches have lead to impressive improvements in most NLP tasks [4, 7]. This also applies to the domain of NLP for mental health assessment, where recent deep learning models have led to state-of-the-art results in the field [19, 21, 22]. However, despite achieving high performance, one of the most important drawbacks of these models is their *black box* nature, where the reasoning behind their decision is difficult to interpret and explain to the end users. This constitutes a serious setback to their adoption by health professionals [10].

The focus of this paper is to assess the usefulness of user-level attention mechanism [22] as a means to help explain neural classifiers in mental health. Although the experiments were performed on the detection of anorexia in social media, the methdology is not domain-dependent, hence can be applied to other tasks involved in the detection of mental health issues of social media users, based on their online posts.

The paper is organized as follows: Sect. 2 explains the two levels where the attention mechanism can be used (i.e. intra-document and inter-document), and describes the related work in validating explainability using attention mechanism. Section 3 explains our experiments to validate the interpretability of user-level attention, whose results are then presented in Sect. 4. Section 5 provides additional observations in terms of how the attention mechanism has worked. Finally, Sect. 6 concludes the paper and provides future directions for the current work.

2   Related Work

Attention mechanism [1] has become an essential part of many deep learning architectures used in NLP, as it allows the model to learn which segments of text should be focused on to arrive at a more accurate decision. In text classification applications, such as the detection of mental health issues, attention mechanisms can be applied both at the intra and the inter-document levels [20].

At the intra-document level, the attention mechanism learns to find informative segments of each document, and assigns higher weights to these segments when creating a representation of the whole document. The success of the intra-document attention mechanism has made it an essential part of transformers [25], which are now the building block of several powerful NLP models, such as BERT [5].

On the other hand, the inter-document attention mechanism tries to identify entire documents that are more informative from a collection, and assign higher weights to these when computing the representation of the whole collection. The inter-document attention mechanism is generally used when the classification pertains to the entire collection, as opposed to individual documents. Previous work in NLP for clinical psychology has typically used this type of attention mechanism to create a representation of social media users: a collection of online posts from each user is fed to the model and the inter-document attention (also referred to as *user-level* attention) creates a representation of the user through a weighted average of the representations of their online posts, with the most informative posts are assigned higher weights. While Mohammadi et al. [21] and Matero et al. [19] have used inter-document attention for the task of suicide risk assessment, Maupome et al. [20] and Mohammadi et al. [22] have utilized it for the detection of depression and anorexia, respectively.

To explicitly provide explainability in deep NLP models, several methods have been proposed. Wang et al. [26], Lee et al. [11], Lin et al. [13], and Ghaeini et al. [6] have used attention visualization based on attention heat maps. These heat maps graphically show which parts of the texts have been given higher or lower attention weights.

In NLP for clinical psychology, the data is usually sensitive and standard attention visualization are not ideal. Hence, other methods have been developed to show the validity of the attention explainability. For example, Ive et al. [8] provided paraphrased sentences from the dataset, alongside their assigned attention weights.

Jain and Wallace [9] and Serrano and Smith [24] proposed quantitative approaches to validate the explainability of intra-document attention mechanism. While Jain and Wallace's method was focused on randomly shuffling, and also generating adversarial attention weights [9], Serrano and Smith analyzed attention explainability by zeroing out the attention weights.

In this paper, we propose a quantitative approach, specifically focused on the user-level (inter-document) attention mechanism in a binary classification task of detection of a specific mental health issue, anorexia.

3   Experiments

Our approach is based on monitoring the performance measures of a neural classifier, with and without user-level attention, when only a limited number of highly-weighted posts are provided.

The neural classifier used is the *CNN-ELMo* model from Mohammadi et al. [22]. This model was chosen because it achieved comparable results to the best performing model at the recent eRisk shared task [17,22], and is based on an end-to-end architecture, which makes the reasoning behind its decision more easily explainable.

The trained model was first run on the testing data, and for each user, her/his posts were ranked from the highest attention weights to the lowest. We then ran the following two experiments:

1) We tested the model by feeding it only the n top-weighted posts by each user. We gradually increased values of n from 1 to 1000, and monitored the performance of the system as n changes. The purpose of this experiment was to compare the performance of the model when all the posts are available, with when only the top-ranking posts (based on the attention weights) are available to the system.

2) We replaced the user-level attention with a simple average pooling and re-ran experiment 1. The aim of this experiment was to evaluate the contribution of the user-level attention by ablating it from the model.

3.1 Model Architecture

The architecture of the *CNN-ELMo* model is shown in Fig. 1. For each user, her/his posts are first tokenized and then fed to an embedder, to extract a dense representation for each token. For the embedder, the original 1024d version of ELMo [23], pretrained on the 1 Billion Word Language Model Benchmark [2] was used.

For each post, 300 unigram and 50 bigram convolution filters were applied on the token embeddings. The output of the convolution filters were then fed to a Concatenated Rectified Linear Unit (CReLU), and max pooling was applied to the output of the CReLUs. The output of the two max pooling layers were then concatenated and used as the representation for each post.

The final user representation of a user was calculated by averaging (experiment 2) or weighted averaging (experiment 1) the representations of the available posts by that user. In order to calculate the weights, a single fully connected layer was applied to the representation of each post, mapping the post representation to a scalar. A softmax activation function was then applied over the scalars, which resulted in the weights corresponding to each post.

The last layer of the model was comprised of a single fully-connected layer, mapping the user representation to a vector of size two. Finally, by applying a softmax activation function over this vector, the probability for each user belonging to the anorexic/non-anorexic class was calculated.

3.2 Dataset

The dataset used is from the first sub-task of the eRisk 2019 shared task [17], whose focus is the early risk detection of anorexia. The dataset consists of a collection of posts from the Reddit social media, and is annotated at the user-level, indicating whether a user is anorexic or not. For this work, we have focused on the detection of anorexia, without considering the earliness of the detection as the shared task does.

Table 1 shows statistics of the training, validation, and testing datasets. As the table shows, the data contains posts from 152 users for training, 320 users for validation, and 815 users for testing, with an average of 300 to 400 posts per user.

As indicated in Losada et al. [17], the dataset was collected following the extraction and annotation method, proposed by Coppersmith et al. [3]. The anorexic users were self-identified by explicitly stating being diagnosed with anorexia on Reddit, while the non-anorexic users were randomly crawled from the same social media. From the set of anorexic users, these specific posts which discussed being diagnosed with anorexia were removed from the dataset.

4 Results

The results from the experiments are shown graphically in Fig. 2, and selected results are provided in Table 2.

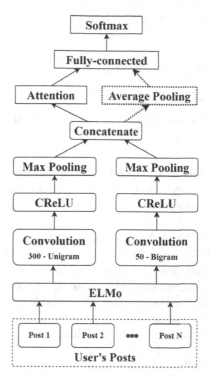

Fig. 1. The architecture of the model used for the experiment. In the ablated model, the *Attention* is replaced by the *Average Pooling* (shown in the dotted box).

As the solid lines in Fig. 2 show, by increasing the maximum number of available posts per user, the performance of the model with user-level attention (experiment 1) generally improves in terms of accuracy, precision, and F1, while the recall drops. It can also be observed that, the changes in performance measures decreases as the number of available posts increases, and the performance gradually converges to the final ones when all the posts are available (see Table 2). We believe that the gradual improvement in the precision and drop in recall is because, in general, the posts that have been highly weighted by the user-level attention mechanism, include signals that the user is anorexic (rather than signals that the user is not).

The dotted lines in Fig. 2a show that, by increasing the maximum number of available posts from 1 to 10, the performance of model with the user-level average pooling (experiment 2) also improves in terms of accuracy, precision, and F1, but deteriorates in terms of recall. This shows that, the first 10 highly-weighted posts included information necessary for the system to make a prediction about the user. This has even led the model with average pooling to have a higher F1 score than the model with user-level attention, as the former has a tendency to get less biased towards specific posts.

Table 1. Statistics of the dataset.

Dataset	# of users		# of posts per user			
	Anorexic	Non-anorexic	Min	Max	Ave	Med
Train	20	132	9	1999	558	330
Validation	41	279	9	1999	527	318
Test	73	742	10	2000	700	478

Table 2 and Fig. 2b show that, the F1 and the accuracy of the model with the user-level average pooling starts to drop from 30 and 60 posts, respectively. As a result, the model with user-level attention overtakes the one with average pooling in terms of F1 and accuracy, after more than 30 and 50 posts are available, respectively. This shows the higher capability of the model with the user-level attention over the other in handling the higher number of posts.

Figure 2 also shows that increasing the maximum number of available posts leads to a rapid drop in the recall of the model with user-level average pooling. This shows that, the higher the number of available posts to the model with average pooling, the more this model loses the capability on observing the patterns that are useful in detecting anorexia. This can also support the hypothesis that the user-level attention mechanism generally assigns higher weights to the posts that are more signalling of anorexia.

Table 2. Performance of the system (in percentage) in terms of the maximum number of highly-weighted posts from each user. The columns labelled as *with Avg Pool* refer to the model in which the user-level attention mechanism is ablated. The last row refers to the case when all the posts from each user are provided to the system.

Max # of posts/user	With attention (experiment 1)				With avg pool (experiment 2)			
	A	P	R	F1	A	P	R	F1
1	65.15	19.60	93.15	32.38	65.15	19.60	93.15	32.38
2	69.57	21.86	93.15	35.42	72.39	23.43	91.78	37.33
5	79.88	29.96	93.15	45.33	83.19	32.61	82.19	46.69
10	84.29	34.97	87.67	50.00	88.83	43.08	76.71	55.17
20	88.59	43.06	84.93	57.14	91.90	54.02	64.38	58.75
30	90.18	47.29	83.56	60.40	93.74	67.74	57.53	62.22
40	92.27	54.46	83.56	65.95	93.50	69.23	49.31	57.60
50	93.13	58.09	83.56	68.54	93.37	71.11	43.84	54.24
60	93.74	61.00	83.56	70.52	93.50	75.00	41.10	53.10
70	94.23	63.54	83.56	72.19	93.01	72.22	35.62	47.71
80	94.48	64.89	83.56	73.05	92.76	71.87	31.51	43.81
90	94.85	67.03	83.56	74.39	92.76	75.00	28.77	41.58
100	95.21	69.32	83.56	75.78	92.64	74.07	27.40	40.00
200	96.07	76.62	80.82	78.67	92.76	88.89	21.92	35.16
500	96.32	80.28	78.08	79.17	92.27	91.67	15.07	25.88
1000	96.69	83.82	78.08	80.85	91.90	88.88	10.96	19.51
2000 (all)	96.93	86.36	78.08	82.01	91.90	88.89	10.96	19.51

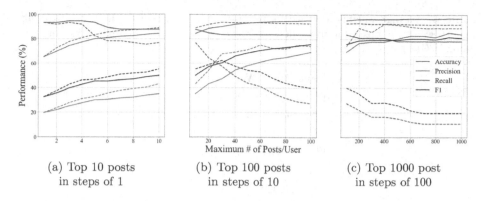

(a) Top 10 posts in steps of 1   (b) Top 100 posts in steps of 10   (c) Top 1000 post in steps of 100

Fig. 2. Performance of the system in terms of the maximum number of highly-weighted posts from each user. The solid lines correspond to the model with user-level attention (experiment 1), while the dotted lines correspond to the model with user-level average pooling (experiment 2).

5   Discussion

In order to further analyze the behavior of the user-level attention mechanism, the highest weights assigned by the attention mechanism were studied across users. In addition, we also calculated the average of the n-th highest weights assigned to the posts by the users, with n ranging from 1 to 10. We compared these values for two types of users: labelled by the model as anorexic (i.e. true-positive and false positive users) and labelled by the model as non-anorexic (i.e. true-negative and false-negative users). As Table 3 shows, on average, the attention mechanism has assigned 6.96 higher weights to the most highly weighted posts in users detected as anorexic, compared to users detected as non-anorexic. The value of this ratio drops in the lower-ranked posts. This seems to indicate that, generally when the attention mechanism assigns a high weight to a post, the system is more likely to label its author as positive. It is similar to when humans observe a piece of evidence, and tend to heavily base their decision upon it. This also seems to support the hypothesis that the attention mechanism assigns weights based mostly on how signalling their authors were anorexic, as opposed to signalling not having anorexia.

As opposed to Jain and Wallace [9] and Serrano and Smith [24], who reported that attention is not a means to explainability, our findings are generally in favor of explainability in the user-level attention mechanism. This may be due to the following two reasons:

1. The approach by Jain and Wallace [9] was only focused explainability of attention mechanism, when applied on the output of a recurrent encoder. We argue that, in such a case, each sample (contextual word representation, in their case) already has part of the information from the other samples in the context. As a result, finding the source of information is difficult in such

Table 3. Average weights assigned by the user-level attention mechanism to the nth highest weighted posts for users detected by the system as anorexic (W_p) or non-anorexic (W_n)

Rank	W_p	W_n	W_p/W_n
1st	0.388	0.056	6.96
2nd	0.124	0.034	3.66
3rd	0.067	0.026	2.62
4th	0.047	0.021	2.18
5th	0.035	0.019	1.86
6th	0.029	0.017	1.70
7th	0.024	0.015	1.59
8th	0.019	0.014	1.31
9th	0.016	0.013	1.23
10th	0.015	0.012	1.20

a case. Serrano and Smith [24] also with using attention over non-encoded samples, and they showed that the level of explainability in this case is significantly higher than when the input to the attention is encoded (using an RNN or CNN). However, they mainly focused their report on the cases where the attention input is encoded. Our work was fully focused on non-encoded attention inputs.

2. The difference in the nature of the task we are performing is generally different from Jain and Wallace [9] and Serrano and Smith [24], as our approach focuses on the user-level (inter-document) attention mechanism, while their experiments were focused on intra-document attention. In a task involving the detection of a mental health problem, such as anorexia, the number relevant and informative posts is quite rare [14–17], while even in a similar task, there may be several ways of inferring information from a particular document.

Finally, in order to achieve stronger evidence that an inter-document attention is explainable, we believe that our approach would benefit from being used in conjunction with the experiments proposed by Jain and Wallace [9] and Serrano and Smith [24], as their experiments can also be applied to the inter-document attention mechanism.

6   Conclusion

In this work, we proposed a quantitative approach to validate the explainability of the user-level attention mechanism for the task of the detection of anorexia in social media users based on their online posts. Our results show that, the user-level attention mechanism has assigned higher weights to the posts from a user based on how much they were signalling the user is at risk of anorexia.

Two directions for the future work can be proposed: As indicated in Sect. 5, the first direction is to complement the current experiments with the ones proposed by Jain and Wallace [9] and Serrano and Smith [24], in order to see if the findings from the current experiments are in line with theirs. The second direction is to expand the current set of experiments to other mental health binary classification tasks (such as detection of depression, PTSD, or suicide risk), and later to multi-class or multi-label classification tasks in the field of NLP for clinical psychology.

Acknowledgements. The authors would like to thank the anonymous reviewers for their feedback on a previous version of this paper. This work was financially supported by the Natural Sciences and Engineering Research Council of Canada (NSERC).

References

1. Bahdanau, D., Cho, K., Bengio, Y.: Neural machine translation by jointly learning to align and translate. In: Proceedings of the 3rd International Conference for Learning Representations (ICLR 2015), San Diego, California, USA, May 2015
2. Chelba, C., et al.: One billion word benchmark for measuring progress in statistical language modeling. In: 15th Annual Conference of the International Speech Communication Association (INTERSPEECH 2014), Singapore, September 2014
3. Coppersmith, G., Dredze, M., Harman, C.: Quantifying mental health signals in Twitter. In: Proceedings of the Workshop on Computational Linguistics and Clinical Psychology: From Linguistic Signal to Clinical Reality, Baltimore, Maryland, USA, pp. 51–60. Association for Computational Linguistics, June 2014. https://doi.org/10.3115/v1/W14-3207, http://aclweb.org/anthology/W14-3207
4. Zhao, X., Li, C.: Deep learning in social computing. In: Deng, L., Liu, Y. (eds.) Deep Learning in Natural Language Processing, pp. 255–288. Springer, Singapore (2018). https://doi.org/10.1007/978-981-10-5209-5_9
5. Devlin, J., Chang, M.W., Lee, K., Toutanova, K.: BERT: pre-training of deep bidirectional transformers for language understanding. In: Proceedings of the 2019 Conference of the North American Chapter of the Association for Computational Linguistics: Human Language Technologies (NAACL-HLT 2019), Minneapolis, Minnesota, USA, June 2019
6. Ghaeini, R., Fern, X., Tadepalli, P.: Interpreting recurrent and attention-based neural models: a case study on natural language inference. In: Proceedings of the 2018 Conference on Empirical Methods in Natural Language Processing (EMNLP 2018), Brussels, Belgium, pp. 4952–4957, October-November 2018
7. Goldberg, Y., Hirst, G.: Neural Network Methods in Natural Language Processing. Morgan & Claypool Publishers (2017)
8. Ive, J., Gkotsis, G., Dutta, R., Stewart, R., Velupillai, S.: Hierarchical neural model with attention mechanisms for the classification of social media text related to mental health. In: Proceedings of the Fifth Workshop on Computational Linguistics and Clinical Psychology: From Keyboard to Clinic (CLPsych 2018), New Orleans, Louisiana, USA, pp. 69–77. Association for Computational Linguistics, June 2018
9. Jain, S., Wallace, B.C.: Attention is not explanation. In: Proceedings of the 2019 Conference of the North American Chapter of the Association for Computational Linguistics (NAACL 2019), Minneapolis, Minnesota, USA, pp. 3543–3556. Association for Computational Linguistics, June 2019

10. Kwak, G.H.J., Hui, P.: DeepHealth: deep learning for health informatics. Computing Research Repository arXiv:1909.00384 (2019)

11. Lee, J., Shin, J.H., Kim, J.S.: Interactive visualization and manipulation of attention-based neural machine translation. In: Proceedings of the 2017 Conference on Empirical Methods in Natural Language Processing: System Demonstrations, Copenhagen, Denmark, pp. 121–126. Association for Computational Linguistics, September 2017

12. Lin, H., Tov, W., Qiu, L.: Emotional disclosure on social networking sites: the role of network structure and psychological needs. Comput. Hum. Behav. **41**, 342–350 (2014)

13. Lin, Z., et al.: A structured self-attentive sentence embedding. In: Proceedings of the 5th International Conference on Learning Representations (ICLR 2017), Toulon, France, April 2017

14. Losada, D.E., Crestani, F.: A test collection for research on depression and language use. In: Fuhr, N., et al. (eds.) CLEF 2016. LNCS, vol. 9822, pp. 28–39. Springer, Cham (2016). https://doi.org/10.1007/978-3-319-44564-9_3

15. Losada, D.E., Crestani, F., Parapar, J.: eRISK 2017: CLEF lab on early risk prediction on the Internet: experimental foundations. In: Jones, G.J.F., et al. (eds.) CLEF 2017. LNCS, vol. 10456, pp. 346–360. Springer, Cham (2017). https://doi.org/10.1007/978-3-319-65813-1_30

16. Losada, D.E., Crestani, F., Parapar, J.: Overview of eRisk 2018: early risk prediction on the Internet (extended lab overview). In: Working Notes of CLEF 2018 - Conference and Labs of the Evaluation Forum, Avignon, France, September 2018

17. Losada, D.E., Crestani, F., Parapar, J.: Overview of eRisk 2019: early risk prediction on the Internet. In: Working Notes of CLEF 2019 - Conference and Labs of the Evaluation Forum, Lugano, Switzerland, September 2019

18. Lynn, V., Goodman, A., Niederhoffer, K., Loveys, K., Resnik, P., Schwartz, H.A.: CLPsych 2018 shared task: predicting current and future psychological health from childhood essays. In: Proceedings of the Fifth Workshop on Computational Linguistics and Clinical Psychology: From Keyboard to Clinic (CLPsych 2018), New Orleans, Louisiana, USA, pp. 37–46. Association for Computational Linguistics, June 2018

19. Matero, M., et al.: Suicide risk assessment with multi-level dual-context language and BERT. In: Proceedings of the Sixth Workshop on Computational Linguistics and Clinical Psychology (CLPsych 2019), Minneapolis, Minnesota, USA, pp. 39–44. Association for Computational Linguistics, June 2019

20. Maupomé, D., Queudot, M., Meurs, M.J.: Inter and intra document attention for depression risk assessment. In: Proceedings of the 2019 Canadian Conference on Artificial Intelligence, Canadian AI 2019, Kingston, Canada, pp. 333–341, May 2019

21. Mohammadi, E., Amini, H., Kosseim, L.: CLaC at CLPsych 2019: fusion of neural features and predicted class probabilities for suicide risk assessment based on online posts. In: Proceedings of the Sixth Workshop on Computational Linguistics and Clinical Psychology (CLPsych 2019), Minneapolis, Minnesota, USA, pp. 34–38. Association for Computational Linguistics, June 2019

22. Mohammadi, E., Amini, H., Kosseim, L.: Quick and (maybe not so) easy detection of anorexia in social media posts. In: Working Notes of CLEF 2018 - Conference and Labs of the Evaluation Forum, Lugano, Switzerland, September 2019

23. Peters, M., et al.: Deep contextualized word representations. In: Proceedings of the 2018 Conference of the North American Chapter of the Association for Computational Linguistics: Human Language Technologies (NAACL-HLT 2018), New Orleans, Louisiana, USA, pp. 2227–2237. Association for Computational Linguistics, June 2018

24. Serrano, S., Smith, N.A.: Is attention interpretable? In: Proceedings of 57th Annual Meeting of the Association for Computational Linguistics (ACL 2019), Florence, Italy, vol. abs/1906.03731. Association for Computational Linguistics, July 2019

25. Vaswani, A., et al.: Attention is all you need. In: Advances in Neural Information Processing Systems (NIPS 2017), Long Beach, California, USA, vol. 30, pp. 5998–6008, January 2017

26. Wang, Y., Huang, M., Zhu, X., Zhao, L.: Attention-based LSTM for aspect-level sentiment classification. In: Proceedings of the 2016 Conference on Empirical Methods in Natural Language Processing (EMNLP 2016), Austin, Texas, USA, pp. 606–615. Association for Computational Linguistics, November 2016

27. Zirikly, A., Resnik, P., Uzuner, Ö., Hollingshead, K.: CLPsych 2019 shared task: predicting the degree of suicide risk in Reddit posts. In: Proceedings of the Sixth Workshop on Computational Linguistics and Clinical Psychology (CLPsych 2019), Minneapolis, Minnesota, USA. pp. 24–33. Association for Computational Linguistics, June 2019

Retrieval, Conversational Agents and Multimodal Analysis

An Adaptive Response Matching Network for Ranking Multi-turn Chatbot Responses

Disen Wang[1](✉) and Hui Fang[1,2]

[1] Institute for Financial Services Analytics, University of Delaware, Newark, USA
{disen,hfang}@udel.edu
[2] Department of Electrical and Computer Engineering, University of Delaware, Newark, USA

Abstract. With the increasing popularity of personal assistant systems, it is crucial to build a chatbot that can communicate with humans and assist them to complete different tasks. A fundamental problem that any chatbots need to address is how to rank candidate responses based on previous utterances in a multi-turn conversation. A previous utterance could be either a past input from the user or a past response from the chatbot. Intuitively, a correct response needs to match well with both past responses and past inputs, but in a different way. Moreover, the matching process should depend on not only the content of the utterances but also domain knowledge. Although various models have been proposed for response matching, few of them studied how to adapt the matching mechanism to utterance types and domain knowledge. To address this limitation, this paper proposes an adaptive response matching network (ARM) to better model the matching relationship in multi-turn conversations. Specifically, the ARM model has separate response matching encoders to adapt to different matching patterns required by different utterance types. It also has a knowledge embedding component to inject domain-specific knowledge in the matching process. Experiments over two public data sets show that the proposed ARM model can significantly outperform the state of the art methods with much fewer parameters.

Keywords: Response selection · Multi-turn chatbot · Response ranking

1 Introduction

With the prevalence of intelligent personal assistant systems, it becomes increasingly important to build an effective chatbot that can communicate with humans fluently and help them fulfill different tasks. Moreover, chatbots also play an important role in many other applications such as customer support and tutoring systems [1,10,11].

One of the key components of any chatbots is the underlying response matching model, whose goal is to identify the most appropriate response from a pool

© Springer Nature Switzerland AG 2020
E. Métais et al. (Eds.): NLDB 2020, LNCS 12089, pp. 239–251, 2020.
https://doi.org/10.1007/978-3-030-51310-8_22

of candidates given past conversations. The past conversations include both user inputs and the system's previous responses. As illustrated in Fig. 1, a user is having a multi-turn conversations with the system (e.g., chatbot). Given the current input "something is slowing me down bad" as well as the past utterances, the system is expected to identify the most appropriate candidate response, i.e., "what is the process name with the highest cpu usage?", among all the candidates.

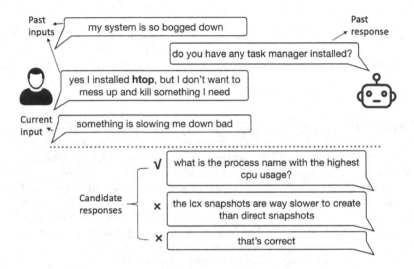

Fig. 1. An example conversation

An optimal response matching model needs to address the following three challenges. (1) It needs to capture a matching relationship that goes beyond simple lexical or semantic similarities. As shown in the Fig. 1, the current input and its correct response do not share any similar words, so the models that are only based on word similarity would not work well for this problem [5,6,17,19]. (2) It should be able to capture different matching relationships for different utterance types. Past utterances include two types of information: past inputs from the user, and past responses from the system. Intuitively, given a candidate response, its desirable matching relationship with past inputs should be different from that with past responses. For example, the correct response needs to address the questions or concerns described in the current input, while it needs to avoid repeating the same information as those mentioned in the past responses. (3) It can utilize domain knowledge to understand the specific meanings of some utterances. For example, "htop" is a process monitoring application for Linux. Without understanding the meaning of this command, it would be difficult for the system to figure out that htop is related to the cpu usage.

Most existing studies on multi-turn response selection [8,16–18,20] mainly focused on the first challenge (i.e., modeling the matching relationships that go beyond semantic similarity), but little attention has been paid to address the last two.

In this paper, we propose an adaptive response matching network (ARM) to address all three challenges. Specifically, a novel response matching encoder is proposed to model the response matching relationship between each utterance and response pair. For each utterance-response pair, instead of computing the matching score based on word or segment level, the encoder computes a response matching matrix through transfer matrices and the multi-attention mechanism. To adapt to the different utterance types, separate encoders are trained: one encoder is used to capture the relationship between current response and the past responses, while the other is used to model the relationship between the current response and the past input. Finally, a knowledge embedding layer is added to the model, and such a layer enables the model to leverage domain knowledge during the response matching process. To validate the proposed ARM model, we conduct experiments over two public data sets. Experimental results and further analysis demonstrate the proposed ARM model is able to achieve superior performance in terms of both effectiveness and efficiency when compared with the state of the art methods.

2 Related Work

Given the past conversations, a chatbot can either automatically generate responses [7,12,15], or retrieve the most appropriate response from a pool of candidates [8,17,19,20]. This paper focuses on the retrieval-based models for multi-turn response selection, and we now briefly review the related work in this area.

Early studies concatenated all of the past utterances together and computed the matching score between the merged utterance and each candidate response [5,6,8]. Specifically, the **Dual-encoder** model [8] used two LSTMs to generate the embeddings for the utterances and candidate response respectively to compute the matching score. The deep relevance matching model (**DRMM**) [5] and the **ARC-II** model [6] were proposed for ad-hoc retrieval tasks, but they were also applied to the response selection problem when past conversations were used as queries and candidate responses were used as documents.

One limitation of these models is that they concatenated all the previous utterances before embedding. Sequential matching network (**SMN**) [17] was proposed to address this limitation. It treated each utterance separately, computed the word-level and segment-level similarity for each response-utterance pair, and used a CNN to distill matching features. Deep matching network (**DMN**) [19] also treated each past utterance separately. It extracted relevant question-answer posts from the collection and utilize the pseudo relevance feedback methods to expand candidate responses with the extracted Q/A pairs. These methods are mainly based on the word semantic similarity scores [2,17]. However, semantic similarity is not sufficient to capture the relationship between a past utterance and a candidate response as shown in Fig. 1.

More recently, inspired by the Transformer structure [14], the attention mechanism has been applied to find better semantic representations of the utterances. Deep attention model (**DAM**) [20] proposed self-attention and cross-attention to construct semantic representations at different granularity, and the multi-representation fusion network (**MRFN**) [13] has further applied multiple representation strategies for utterances and fused them in the final step to compute the matching scores.

All these previous studies mainly tackled the first challenge discussed in Sect. 1, and focused on developing models to capture the matching relationship between the past utterances and candidate responses. Few of them studied how to adapt the matching model to different types of utterances and how to incorporate the domain knowledge in a more general way, which is the focus of our paper.

3   Adaptive Response Matching Network

3.1   Problem Formulation

The problem of multi-turn response selection can be described as follows. Assume we have a training data set $\mathcal{D} = \{(u_i, r_i, l_i)\}_{i=1}^{N}$, where $u_i = \{p_{i,1}, q_{i,2}, ..., p_{i,n_i}\}$ denotes a conversation consisting of multiple utterances. Each utterance could be either a previous input $(p_{i,j})$ or a previous response $(q_{i,j})$. r_i denotes a candidate response for u_i, and $l_i \in \{0,1\}$ indicates whether r_i is the correct response for u_i. The task is to learn a model f based on $\mathcal{D}$, which can compute the response matching score between any response r and utterance u. Given a new utterance, the learned model f will rank a list of candidate responses based on their matching scores, and the one with the highest score will be selected as the final response.

In this paper, we will also study how to incorporate the domain knowledge in the training process. Specifically, we assume that the knowledge base can be denoted as follows: $\mathcal{K} = \{(c_i, g_i)\}_{i=1}^{M}$, where c_i is a domain-specific keyword, and g_i is the corresponding description of that keyword. Take the conversations shown in Fig. 1 as an example, c_i could represent the command $htop$ and g_i would be the description of that command. Both $\mathcal{D}$ and $\mathcal{K}$ will be used to learn the model f.

3.2   Overview of the ARM Model

The key challenge in multi-turn response selection model lies in how to model the matching relationship between a candidate response and the past utterances. Almost all of the recent studies followed a three-step procedure: representation, matching and accumulation [2,17]. The first step is to represent candidate responses and utterances in various ways that can capture their semantic meanings. The second step is to compute the matching scores between the utterances and the candidate response based on these representations. And the last step is to accumulate all the scores into the final one.

Our proposed adaptive response matching network model (ARM) also follows the above three-step procedure, with major differences in the first two steps. Figure 2 shows the overall architecture of the ARM model. Compared with the existing studies, ARM aims to develop a matching mechanism that can adapt

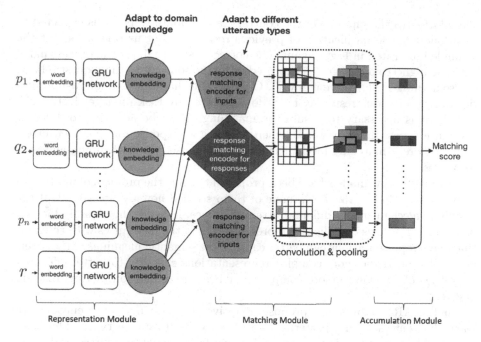

Fig. 2. Overview of the adaptive response matching network (ARM)

to the domain knowledge (in the representation step) and different types of utterances (in the matching step).

In the ARM model, the *representation module* first converts each utterance into a segment-level vector representation using word embedding and GRU, and then enhances the vector representation with domain knowledge using knowledge embedding layer. After that, *the matching module* utilizes the representations of the utterance vectors and the response vectors to calculate the response matching score, and extracts features to feed into the accumulation module. More specifically, multiple transfer matrices are trained to transfer hidden states vectors into different representations spaces, and the combination of response matching matrix from each representation space is used to compute the matching score in the response matching encoder. The segments in an utterance that are important for recognizing appropriate response will have higher matching scores. The areas with higher scores in the final relevance matrix will be extracted by CNN network. Finally, the *accumulation module* generates the final matching score based on the matching vectors provided by the matching module.

3.3 Adaptive Response Matching Encoder

A past utterance could be either an input from the user or a response from the system. Both utterance types are useful to select the matching candidate response, but in a different way. An input often describes a request or a problem encountered by a user, so the correct candidate response is expected to be the solution to the inputs. On the contrary, a candidate response is expected to be a follow-up or clarification of previous responses. Let us take a look at the example illustrated in Fig. 1 again. The correct response, i.e., "the process name with the highest cpu usage", is expected to be the solution to the request related to "something is slowing me down". On the other hand, it is a follow-up question to the previous response, i.e,. "do you have any task manager installed?" Clearly, it is necessary to ensure the matching model be adaptive to different utterance types. In other words, when selecting a response for the given utterances, different matching mechanisms need to be used for past inputs and past responses.

Although a few models have been proposed to solve the problem of multi-turn response selection [2,13,17,20], none of them studied how to directly adapt the matching mechanisms to different utterance types. Instead, they mainly focused on exploring various complicated representations of the utterances with the hope that these representations can better capture the semantic meanings of the utterances. Although the more complex representations can lead to better effectiveness, they often require more computational resources and longer time to train and test.

In the ARM model, we propose adaptive response matching encoders to learn different matching patterns according to the utterance types. The basic idea of ARM encoders is to start with some basic semantic representations of the utterances/responses, and then learn new matching representations for each matching type. The new matching representations are expected to better capture the response matching relationship for each utterance type. We now describe the encoders in detail, and the important notations are summarized in Table 1.

Starting with Basic Representations: Following the previous study [17], we represent both responses (r) and utterances (either p for a previous user input or q for a previous response) using segment-level representation. Specifically, we first apply Word2Vec [9] algorithm to generate the word embedding $e \in \mathbb{R}^d$ for each word, where d is the number of dimensions in the word embedding. The model looks up a pre-trained word embedding table to convert $p = [w_{p,1}, w_{p,2}, ..., w_{p,n_p}]$ into $P = [e_{p,1}, e_{p,2}, ..., e_{p,n_p}]$, where $w_{p,i}$ is the i-th word and $e_{p,i}$ is the corresponding word embedding vector, and n_p is the length of p. Similarly, we can represent q as $Q = [e_{q,1}, e_{q,2}, ..., e_{q,n_q}]$ and r as $R = [e_{r,1}, e_{r,2}, ..., e_{r,n_r}]$ where $e_{q,i}, e_{r,i} \in \mathbb{R}^d$, are the embeddings of the i-th word of q and r, and n_q and n_r are the length of q and r. To extract the contextual information in each utterance, we feed P, Q and R into GRU network [3] and use the generated hidden states H_p, H_q and H_r as basic representations of the responses and utterances.

Learning New Matching Representations: Given the basic representations of a previous utterance and a response (e.g., H_p and H_r), two transfer matrices (i.e., W_p and W_r) are learned to transfer the basic representations to the new ones (i.e., RM_p and RM_r) that can better capture the response matching relationship. Formally, the new representations (i.e,. relevance matrix) of the utterance and the response can be computed using

Table 1. Explanations of key notations.

Notation	Explanation
p	a past input
q	a past response
u	an utterance, could be either p or q
r	a candidate response
w_i	a word
e_i	the word embedding vector of word w_i
h_i	the hidden state vector generated by GRU for word w_i
h_i^k	the basic knowledge embedding vector of w_i
h_i^{new}	the new knowledge embedding vector of w_i after the gating mechanism
H	hidden state matrix of a utterance or response (based on h_i or h_i^{new})
W	transfer matrix in the adaptive response matching encoder
RM	relevance matrix in the adaptive response matching encoder
M	single-head response matching matrix
M'	final response matching matrix in multi-head encoder
W^s, W^g	learning parameters for the knowledge embedding layer

$$RM_p = H_p W_p, RM_r = H_r W_r$$

where $W_p, W_r \in \mathbb{R}^{h \times m}$, h is the number of dimensions in hidden states, and m is the number of dimensions in the response matching encoder. W_p and W_r are transfer matrices and will be learned from the training data. The initial weights of these matrices are randomly initialized with different values, and the training data contain the labels indicating whether a utterance is a input or a response.

Computing Matching Scores: With the newly learned matching representations of a utterance and a candidate response, we can compute a response matching matrix as follows.

$$M = softmax(\frac{RM_p RM_r^T}{\sqrt{m}}).$$

Specifically, $M[i, j]$ represents the response matching score of the i-th hidden state from H_p and the j-th hidden state from H_r. The i-th hidden state from the utterance (i.e., $h_{p,i}$) is first transferred to a vector in a new representation space (i.e., RM_{pi}) through the transfer matrix (i.e., W_p). Similarly, the j-th hidden state from the response (i.e., $h_{r,j}$) is converted to another vector in the new representation space (i.e., RM_{rj}) through W_r. The response matching score of these two new vectors is then computed using $M_{i,j} = softmax(\frac{RM_{pi} \cdot RM_{rj}^T}{\sqrt{m}})$.

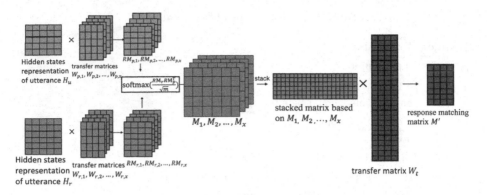

Fig. 3. Details of adaptive response matching encoders

Improvement via Multi-head Mechanism: In order to capture different representations that could be useful for response matching, we apply the multi-head attention mechanism [14] to the response matching encoder. The structure of multi-head encoder is shown in Fig. 4. We learn different transfer matrices to transfer the hidden states vectors into different representation spaces, and combine the matrices from each representation space to get the final matrix M'. Specifically, we stack matrices $M_1, M_2, ..., M_x$ into one matrix and multiply it with a transfer matrix W_t to get the final response matching matrix M', where the elements of W_t are learning parameters. W_t learns how to combine information from multiple channels into the final response matching matrix. In the final response matching matrix M', elements with higher values mean the corresponding word pairs have higher semantic matching scores. This multi-head mechanism can expand the model's ability to focus on different positions, and it is able to capture more diverse response matching patterns through the multiple representation spaces (Fig. 3).

3.4   Knowledge Embedding Layer

An optimal response matching model also needs to adapt to the domain-specific knowledge. As explained in Fig. 1, if we have domain-specific knowledge about "htop", we might be able to better match the candidate responses. Assume the available knowledge base can be represented as pairs of domain-specific concepts and their descriptions (i.e., (c_i, g_i)), we now discuss how our model adapt to domain knowledge.

A straightforward way to incorporate knowledge base is to replace the domain-specific words with their definitions or descriptions in the corresponding hidden states. However, words are ambiguous, and not every occurrence of a domain-specific word refers to the same meaning. For example, the word "install" is a command in the Ubuntu system. But if a user asks "how to install the task manager", the word "install" in this utterance should not be replaced by the description of the command because it did not refer to the command. To tackle this problem, we propose to apply gating mechanisms to decide when and how to fuse knowledge into utterance representations in the knowledge embedding layer [4].

For each word w_i that occurs in either the utterances or the response, if it is one of the domain-specific word (c_i), we would extract its corresponding description from the knowledge base (i.e., g_i), feed g_i into a GRU unit, and the generated hidden state is used as knowledge embedding, which is denoted as h_i^k. After that, we can apply gating mechanism to fuse knowledge embedding h_i^k into word representation h_i to generate the new representation h_i^{new}:

$$h_i^{new} = bh_i + (1 - b)\tanh W^s[h_i; h_i^k; h_i - h_i^k]$$

$$b = sigmoid(W^g[h_i; h_i^k; h_i - h_i^k])$$

where W^s and W^g are learning parameters, and $[v_1, v_2, v_3]$ means to stack the three vectors into a matrix.

With the gating mechanism, the new word representation h_i^{new} has selectively adapt to the domain knowledge based on the context information. For each dimension in the vector h_i, the gating mechanism decides whether to keep the original value or replace it with the value from knowledge embedding. Without the gating mechanism, the model would replace values in all dimensions with those from knowledge embedding, which might not be always the best solution. The new representation h_i^{new} is then used to replace h_i in the hidden state matrix H_p, H_q and H_r, i.e., the input of the adaptive response matching encoders.

3.5 Summary

The ARM model can be regarded as an extension of the SMN model [17] with a couple of notable differences. First, the model uses adaptive response matching encoders to learn different matching patterns according to the utterance type, and the captured matching relationship is able to go beyond the simple semantic similarity. Second, the model adds a knowledge embedding layer (in the representation module) to provide a general way to incorporate domain knowledge. These two differences enable the ARM model better capture the response matching relationship, and explain why the ARM model is more effective than the state of the art models.

DMN [19] is the only existing study that tried to utilize knowledge base. It extracted question-answer pairs from the collection as knowledge, and then utilized the pseudo relevance feedback methods to expand candidate responses with the extracted knowledge. On the contrary, the ARM model presents a more general and robust way of incorporating domain-specific knowledge. In particular, the representation of the knowledge base is more general. The knowledge can come from either collection itself or external domain-specific resources. Moreover, the gating mechanism in the embedding layer makes it possible to selectively apply the domain knowledge based on the context information, which can improve the robustness of the model.

Another major advantage of ARM model lies in its efficiency. When designing the model, we intentionally use the basic semantic representations (i.e., word/knowledge embedding and GRU outputs) and let the transfer matrices to learn useful matching relationships for each utterance type. Such a learning process is more targeted than learning a general yet more complicated representation that could be useful to match all kinds of utterance types [13,20]. As shown in Sect. 4.2, our model uses much fewer parameters than the state of the art models, yet it is able to achieve better performance.

4 Experiments

4.1 Experiment Setup

Data Sets: We evaluate the performance of the proposed model on the two publicly available data sets from the DSTC7 Response Selection Challenge[1]. (1) The first data set is the *Ubuntu dialogue corpus*, which contains conversations about solving an Ubuntu user's posted problem. The domain knowledge includes the commands and their corresponding function descriptions. The training set contains 1 million conversations, the development set and the test set each contains 0.5 million conversations. (2) The second data set is the *student-advisor data set*. In each conversation, the advisor will guide the student to pick courses. The external knowledge is about the courses such as their descriptions and areas. The training set contains 0.5 million conversations, development set and test set each contains 50,000 conversations.

Evaluation Measures: Following the previous studies [8,17], the primary evaluation measures are $R_{100}@k$, which is the recall at position k in 100 candidates. k is set to 1, 5, 10. Since there is only one correct response for each conversation, the precision at position k always equal to the recall at position k divided by k. Thus, only the values of recall are reported.

Table 2. Performance comparison. * means statistically significant difference over the best baseline with $p < 0.05$ under student's t-test.

Model	Ubuntu data set			Student-advisor data set		
	$R_{100}@1$	$R_{100}@5$	$R_{100}@10$	$R_{100}@1$	$R_{100}@5$	$R_{100}@10$
Dual-encoder	18.3%	34.35%	47.15%	11.35%	19.08%	33.2%
DRMM	21.25%	37.83%	52.48%	15.41%	24.92%	36.75%
ARC-II	20.31%	36.53%	49.42%	14.85%	23.42%	37.25%
SMN	34.14%	59.13%	71.52%	19.57%	28.2%	52.39%
DMN	33.91%	58.9%	70.86%	19.6%	38.23%	51.64%
DAM	35.37%	61.18%	72.29%	21.13%	40.57%	55.32%
MRFN	36.13%	63.45%	77.85%	20.35%	38.92%	54.28%
ARM	**39.93%***	**67.21%***	**78.95%***	**23.74%***	**41.83%***	**58.5%***

---

[1] https://github.com/IBM/dstc7-noesis.

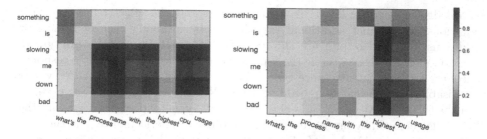

Fig. 4. Response matching matrix in ARM (left) vs. similarity matrix in SMN (right)

Table 3. Ablation analysis results

Model	Ubuntu data set			Student-advisor data set		
	$R_{100}@1$	$R_{100}@5$	$R_{100}@10$	$R_{100}@1$	$R_{100}@5$	$R_{100}@10$
ARM-K	36.74%	63.93%	75.12%	22.38%	38.96%	55.82%
ARM-S	38.35%	65.05%	75.32%	23.27%	40.15%	55.26%
ARM	**39.93%***	**67.21%***	**78.95%***	**23.74%***	**41.83%***	**58.5%***

Parameter Settings: In our model, dropout layer was added to the CNN network, and the dropout rate is set to 0.5. Zero padding was applied to make the size of interaction matrix same for all utterance-response pairs. The size of interaction matrix after padding is 50×50. We also set the maximum length of utterance and response as 50 words. The learning rate was set as 0.0005, and experiments show that larger learning rate would lead to a significant decrease in performance. We applied Word2Vec algorithm to train the word embedding matrix, and the number of word embedding dimensions is 200. All these hyper-parameters are chosen to be consistent with the previous study [17].

4.2 Performance Comparison

We compare the performance of the proposed ARM model with several state of the art baseline methods over both data sets. In particular, the baseline models include the following seven state of the art response matching models: Dual-encoder [8], DRMM [5], ARC-II [6], SMN [17], DMN [19], DAM [20] and MRFN [13], which were briefly reviewed in Sect. 2. The implementations of the baseline models were obtained either through the code published by the authors or MatchZoo[2] on the Github.

The results of performance comparison are summarized in Table 2. It is clear that our proposed ARM model outperforms all the strong baseline models significantly on both data sets, which indicates the effectiveness of the ARM model in addressing the limitations we discussed before. We conduct additional experiments to better understand the proposed model.

The proposed ARM model is an extension of the SMN model [17] with the addition of two important components: adaptive response encoders and the

---

[2] https://github.com/NTMC-Community/MatchZoo.

knowledge embedding layer. To better understand the effectiveness of these additions, we conduct additional experiments by disabling each of these new additions, and the results are shown in Table 3. ARM-S is the variation of ARM model, where we disable the separate encoders and use the same response encoders for different utterance types. ARM-K is the variation of ARM, where we disable the knowledge embedding layer. When we compare the two variations with the ARM model, it is clear that both type-adapted encoders and the knowledge embedding layer are useful to improve the performance. Another key difference between ARM and SMN model is how to model the response matching relationships. SMN mainly relies on the semantic similarity, while the proposed response matching encoder can capture other semantic matching relationship. The difference can be easily seen through an example shown in Fig. 4. The darker color means a higher score. It is clear that the ARM model can correctly capture the matching relationship between {*slowing, me, down*} from the input and {*process, name, with, the, cpu, usage*} from the correct response, while the SMN cannot.

Furthermore, ARM is shown to be more effective than the recently proposed DAM and MRFN models according to Table 2. In fact, it is also more efficient. Similar to DAM and MRFN, ARM aims to capture the matching relationship that goes beyond simple semantic similarity. Instead of learning general yet more complicated representations for all utterances, ARM is more focused and it explicitly adapts to different matching patterns caused by different utterance types. As a result, ARM is more efficient and requires much fewer parameters than DAM and MRFN. With the same hyper-parameter values (e.g., the number of dimensions in Word2Vec vectors), the numbers of parameters used in the ARM, DAM and MRFN models are 30 millions, 74 millions, and 91 millions respectively. Fewer parameters means significant improvement in terms of efficiency.

5   Conclusions and Future Work

In this paper, we propose an adaptive response matching network for multi-turn chatbot response selection. Existing models focused on modeling different relationships using multiple representation strategies, while the ARM utilizes adaptive response matching encoders in the matching module to directly model different matching relationships for different types of utterances. Moreover, ARM has a knowledge embedding layer, which can adapt to external domain knowledge in a general way. Empirical results over two data sets show that the proposed model outperforms various state-of-the-art models in terms of both effectiveness and efficiency. In the future, we plan to study how to incorporate unstructured domain knowledge to further improve performance.

Acknowledgement. The first author is grateful to the JP Morgan Chase scholarship he received from the Ph.D. Program in Financial Services Analytics to support this research.

References

1. Assefi, M., Liu, G., Wittie, M.P., Izurieta, C.: An experimental evaluation of Apple Siri and Google Speech Recognition. In: ISCA SEDE, pp. 1–6 (2015)
2. Chen, Q., Wei, S., Inkpen, D.: Enhanced LSTM for natural language inference. In: ACL, pp. 1657–1668 (2017)
3. Cho, K., et al.: Learning phrase representations using RNN encoder-decoder for statistical machine translation. In: EMNLP, pp. 1724–1734 (2014)
4. Gers, F., Schmidhuber, J., Cummins, F.: Learning to forget: continual prediction with LSTM. Neural Comput. 12(1), 2451–2471 (2000)
5. Guo, J., Fan, Y., Ai, Q., Croft, W.B.: A deep relevance matching model for ad-hoc retrieval. In: CIKM, pp. 55–64 (2017)
6. Hu, B., Lu, Z., Li, H., Chen, Q.: Convolutional neural network architectures for matching natural language sentences. Adv. Neural Inf. Process. Syst. 3(1), 2042–2050 (2015)
7. Li, J., Galley, M., Brockett, C., Spithourakis, G.P., Gao, J., Dolan, B.: A persona-based neural conversation model. In: ACL, pp. 994–1003 (2016)
8. Lowe, R., Pow, N., Vlad, I., Charlin, L., Liu, C.W., Pineau, J.: Training end-to-end dialogue systems with the Ubuntu Dialogue Corpus. Dialogue Discourse 8(1), 31–65 (2017)
9. Mikolov, T., Chen, K., Corrado, G., Dean, J.: Efficient estimation of word representations in vector space. In: ICLR, pp. 1–12 (2013)
10. Qiu, M., et al.: AliMe chat: a sequence to sequence and rerank based chatbot engine. In: ACL, pp. 498–503 (2017)
11. Shum, H.Y., He, X., Li, D.: From Eliza to XiaoIce: challenges and opportunities with social chatbots. Front. Inf. Technol. Electron. Eng. 19(1), 10–26 (2018). https://doi.org/10.1631/FITEE.1700826
12. Sordoni, A., et al.: A Neural Network Approach to Context-Sensitive Generation of Conversational Responses. arXiv e-prints arXiv:1506.06714 (2015)
13. Tao, C., Wu, W., Xu, C., Hu, W., Zhao, D., Yan, R.: Multi-reprentation fusion network for multi-turn response selection in retrieval-based chatbots. In: WSDM, pp. 267–275 (2019)
14. Vaswani, A., et al.: Attention is all you need. In: Advances in Neural Information Processing Systems, pp. 5998–6008 (2017)
15. Wen, T.H., et al.: A network-based end-to-end trainable task-oriented dialogue system. In: ACL, pp. 438–449 (2017)
16. Wu, B., Wang, B., Xue, H.: Ranking responses oriented to conversational relevance in chat-bots. In: COLING, pp. 652–662 (2016)
17. Wu, Y., Wu, W., Xing, C., Xu, C., Li, Z., Zhou, M.: A sequential matching framework for multi-turn response selection in retrieval-based chatbots. In: ACL, pp. 496–505 (2017)
18. Yan, R., Song, Y., Wu, H.: Learning to respond with deep neural networks for retrieval-based human-computer conversation system. In: SIGIR, pp. 55–64 (2016)
19. Yang, L., Huang, J., Chen, H., Croft, W.B.: Response ranking with deep matching networks and external knowledge in information-seeking conversation systems. In: SIGIR, pp. 245–254 (2018)
20. Zhou, X., et al.: Multi-turn response selection for chatbots with deep attention matching network. In: ACL, pp. 1118–1127 (2018)

Improving the Community Question Retrieval Performance Using Attention-Based Siamese LSTM

Nouha Othman[1,3](✉), Rim Faiz[2](✉), and Kamel Smaïli[3](✉)

[1] LARODEC, University of Tunis, Tunis, Tunisia
nouha.othman@loria.fr
[2] LARODEC, University of Carthage, Tunis, Tunisia
rim.faiz@ihec.rnu.tn
[3] LORIA, University of Lorraine, Nancy, France
kamel.smaili@loria.fr

Abstract. In this paper, we focus on the problem of question retrieval in community Question Answering (cQA) which aims to retrieve from the community archives the previous questions that are semantically equivalent to the new queries. The major challenges in this crucial task are the shortness of the questions as well as the word mismatch problem as users can formulate the same query using different wording. While numerous attempts have been made to address this problem, most existing methods relied on supervised models which significantly depend on large training data sets and manual feature engineering. Such methods are mostly constrained by their specificities that put aside the word order and ignore syntactic and semantic relationships. In this work, we rely on Neural Networks (NNs) which can learn rich dense representations of text data and enable the prediction of the textual similarity between the community questions. We propose a deep learning approach based on a Siamese architecture with LSTM networks, augmented with an attention mechanism. We test different similarity measures to predict the semantic similarity between the community questions. Experiments conducted on real cQA data sets in English and Arabic show that the performance of question retrieval is improved as compared to other competitive methods.

Keywords: Community Question Answering · Question retrieval · Siamese LSTM · Attention mechanism

1 Introduction

Community Question Answering (cQA) sites such as Yahoo! Answers[1], Stackoverflow[2], Quora[3], WikiAnswers[4], and Google Ejabat[5] give people the ability

---

[1] http://answers.yahoo.com/.
[2] http://stackoverflow.com/.
[3] https://fr.quora.com/.
[4] https://wiki.answers.com/.
[5] https://ejaaba.com/.

© Springer Nature Switzerland AG 2020
E. Métais et al. (Eds.): NLDB 2020, LNCS 12089, pp. 252–263, 2020.
https://doi.org/10.1007/978-3-030-51310-8_23

to post their various questions and get them answered by other users. Interestingly, users can directly obtain short and precise answers rather than a list of potentially relevant documents. Community sites are exponentially growing over time, building up very huge archives of previous questions and their answers. However, multiple questions with the same meaning can make information seekers spend more time searching for the best answer to their question. Therefore, retrieving similar questions could greatly improve the QA system and benefit the community. Detecting similar previous questions that best match a new user's query is a crucial and challenging task in cQA, known as Question Retrieval (QR). Using the existing answers to similar previous questions could dodge the lag time incurred by waiting for new answers, thus enhancing user satisfaction. Owing to its importance, the question retrieval task has received wide attention over the last decade [14,17,18]. One critical challenge for this task is the word mismatch between the new posted questions and the existing ones in the archives as similar questions can be formulated using different, but related words. For instance, the questions *How can we relieve stress naturally?* and *What are some home remedies to help reduce feelings of anxiety?* have nearly the same meaning but include different words and then may be regarded as dissimilar. This constitutes a barrier to traditional Information Retrieval (IR) and Natural Language Processing (NLP) models since users can phrase the same query using different wording. Furthermore, community questions are mostly short, have different lengths, and usually have sparse representations with little word overlap. Although numerous attempts have been made to tackle this problem, most existing methods rely on the bag of-words (BOWs) representations which are constrained by their specificities that put aside the word order and ignore semantic and syntactic relationships. Recent advances in question retrieval have been achieved using Neural Networks (NNs) [5,6,8,12] which provide powerful tools for modeling language, processing sequential data and predict the text similarity.

In this paper, we propose an approach based on NNs to detect the semantic similarity between the questions. The deep learning approach is based on a Siamese architecture with LSTM networks, augmented with an attention mechanism. We tested different similarity measures to compare the final hidden states of the LSTM layers.

2   Related Work

The question retrieval task has been intensively studied over the past decade. Early works were based on the vector space model referred to as VSM to calculate the cosine similarity between a query and archived questions [2]. However, the major limitation of VSM is that it favors short questions, while cQA services can handle a wide variety of questions not limited to factoïd questions. Language Models (LM)s [3] have been also used to model queries as sequences of terms instead of sets of terms. LMs estimate the relative likelihood for each possible successor term taking into account relative positions of terms. Nevertheless, such models might not be effective when there are only few common words between the questions. Further methods exploited the available category information of questions such as in [2]. Wang et al. [15] used a parser to build syntactic trees of questions, and rank them based on the similarity between their syntactic trees. Nonetheless, such an approach requires large training data and existing parsers are still not well-trained to parse informally written questions. Recent works focused on the representation learning for questions, relying on the Word Embedding model for learning distributed representations of words in a low-dimensional vector space. Along with the popularization of word embeddings and its capacity to produce distributed representations of words, advanced NN architectures such as Convolutional Neural Networks (CNN), Recurrent Neural Networks (RNN) and LSTM have proven effectiveness in extracting higher-level features from constituting word embeddings. For instance, Dos Santos et al. [5] employed CNN and bag-of-words (BOW) representations of the questions to calculate the similarity scores. Within the same context, Mohtarami et al. [8] developed a bag-of-vectors approach and used CNN and attention-based LSTMs to capture the semantic similarity between the community questions and rank them accordingly. LSTM model was also used in [12], where the weights learned by the attention mechanism were exploited for selecting important segments and enhancing syntactic tree-kernel models. More recently, the question retrieval task was modeled as a binary classification problem in [6] using a combination of LSTM and a contrastive loss function to effectively memorize the long term dependencies. In our work, we use a Siamese adaptation of LSTM [9] for pairs of variable-length sentences named Siamese LSTM. It is worth noting that work on cQA has been mostly carried out for other languages than Arabic mainly due to a lack of resources. Recent works in Arabic mainly rely on word embeddings and parse trees to analyze the context and syntactic structure of the questions [1,7,8,13].

3   Description of the Proposed ASLSTM Approach

In order to improve the QR task, we propose an attentive Siamese LSTM approach for question retrieval, referred to as ASLSTM to detect the semantically similar questions in cQA. The approach is composed of three main modules namely, question preprocessing, word embedding learning and attentive Siamese LSTM. The basic principle underlying the ASLSTM approach is to map every question word token into a fix-sized vector. The word vectors of the questions are therefore fed to the Siamese LSTM with the aim of representing them in the final hidden states encoding semantic meaning of the questions. An attention mechanism is integrated in the Siamese architecture to determine which words should give more attention on than other words over the question. Community questions are then ranked by means of the Manhattan similarity function based on the vector representation of each question. A previous posted question is considered to be semantically equivalent to a queried question if their corresponding LSTM representations lie close to each other according to the Manhattan similarity measure. The historical question with the highest Manhattan score will be returned as the most similar question to the new posted one. The components of ASLSTM and the dataset used are described below.

3.1 Dataset

We used the dataset released in [19] for the QR evaluation. The questions of the community collection were harvested from all categories in the Yahoo! Answers platform, and were randomly splitted into the test and search sets while maintaining their distributions in all categories. The community questions in the collection are in various structures, different lengths and belonging to diverse categories e.g., Health, Sports, Computers and Internet, Diet and Fitness, Pets, Travel, Business and Finance, Entertainment and Music etc. Table 1 gives some statistics on the experimental data set.

Table 1. Description of the data set

Number of questions in the search set	1,123,034
Number of queries in the test set	252
Number of relevant questions in the test set	1,624
Number of questions in the dev set	83
Number of relevant questions in the dev set	644
Questions' lengths (number of words)	[1;20]

For our experiments in Arabic, we translated the same English collection using Google Translation with a careful manual verification, as there is no large Arabic dataset available for the question retrieval task. Note that the Arabic collection includes exactly the same number of questions as the English set.

3.2 Question Preprocessing

Pre-processing is important to make the question collections cleaner and easier to process. The question preprocessing module aims to filter the community questions and extract the useful terms in order to represent them in a formal way. It comprises text cleaning, tokenization, stopwords removal and stemming. Punctuation marks, non letters, diacritics, and special characters are removed. English letters are lowercased while dates are normalized to the token *date* and numerical digits are normalized to the token *num*. For the Arabic question collection, in addition to the aforementioned tasks, orthographic normalization was applied, including Tachkil removal, Tatweel removal, and letter normalization.

3.3 Word Embedding Learning

Word embeddings are low-dimensional vector representations of words, learned by harnessing large amounts of text corpora using shallow neural networks. In the word embedding learning module, we map every word into a fix-sized vector using Word2Vec pretrained on an external corpus. For English word embedding training, we resorted to the publicly available word2vec vectors[6], with dimensionality of 300, that were trained on 100 billion words from Google News.

For the experiments in Arabic, we used the Yahoo!Webscope dataset[7], translated into Arabic including 1,256,173 questions with 2,512,034 distinct words. The Continuous Bag-of-Words (CBOW) model was used, as it has proven through experiments to be more efficient and outperform Skip gram on our dataset [10]. The training parameters of the CBOW model on the Arabic collection were set after several tests as follows:

- Size=300: feature vector dimension. We tested different values in the range [50, 500] but did not get significant difference in terms of precision.
- Sample=1e-4: down sampling ratio for the redundant words in the corpus.
- Negative samples=25: number of noise words
- min-count=1: we set the minimum number of words to 1 to make sure we do not throw away anything.
- Context window=5: fixed window size.

3.4 Attentive Siamese LSTM

3.5 Siamese LSTM

The overall aim of Siamese LSTM is to compare a pair of sentences to decide whether or not they are semantically equivalent. Siamese LSTM uses the Siamese network [9] architecture which is known to have identical sub-networks LSTMleft and LSTMright that are passed vector representations of two sentences and return a hidden state encoding semantic meaning of the sentences. These hidden states are then compared using a similarity metric to return a similarity score.

In our work, Siamese LSTM was adapted to the context of question retrieval, that is to say, the sentence pairs become pairs of questions. LSTM learns a mapping from the space of variable length sequences d_{in} and encode the input sequences into a fixed dimension hidden state representation d_{rep}. More concretely, each question is represented as a word vector sequence and fed into the LSTM, which updates, at each sequence-index, its hidden state. The final state of LSTM for each question is a vector of d dimensions, which holds the inherent context of the question. Unlike vanilla RNN language models which predict next words, the given network rather compares pairs of sequences. A major feature of the Siamese architecture is the shared weights across the sub-networks, which reduce not only the number of parameters but also the tendency of overfitting.

---

[6] https://code.google.com/p/word2vec/.

[7] The Yahoo! Webscope dataset Yahoo answers comprehensive questions and answers version 1.0.2, available at "http://research.yahoo.com/Academic_Relations".

To measure the similarity between the two question vectors, we tested several similarity measures and finally adapted the Manhattan one with which we acquired the best outcome as will be seen later in the next section.

The Manhattan similarity between the last hidden states of a sequence pairs $h^{(left)}$ and $h^{(right)}$ is computed as follows:

$$y = exp(- \| h^{(left)} - h^{(right)} \|_1) \tag{1}$$

For Siamese LSTM training, we employed the publicly available Quora Question Pairs dataset[8]. The given collection encompasses 400,000 samples of question duplicate pairs, where each sample has a pair of questions along with ground truth about their corresponding similarity (1: similar, 0: dissimilar). During LSTM training, we applied the Adadelta method for weights optimization to automatically decrease the learning rate. Gradient clipping was also used with a threshold value of 1.25 to avoid the exploding gradient problem [11]. The LSTM layers' size was set to 50 and the embedding layer's size to 300. We employed the back propagation and small batches of size equals 64, to reduce the cross-entropy loss and we resorted to the Mean Square Error (MSE) as a common regression loss function for prediction. We trained the model for several epochs to observe how the results varied with the epochs. We found out that the accuracy changed with the variation of the number of epochs but stabilized after epoch 25. The given parameters were set based on several empirical tests; each parameter was tuned separately on a development set to pick out the best one. Note that we used the same LSTM configuration for both languages.

3.6   Attention Mechanism

Attention mechanism with neural networks have recently achieved tremendous success in several NLP tasks [4,12]. We assume that every word in a question contributes to the meaning of the whole question but the words do not have equal influential information. Thus, we should assign a probability to every word to determine how influential it is to the entire question.

The general architecture of the Siamese LSTM model augmented with an attention layer is illustrated in Fig. 1, where the different constituent layers are shown from the input (question words) to the output (similarity score). Siamese LSTM model employs only the last hidden states of a sequence pair e.g., $h_5^{(a)}$ and $h_4^{(b)}$, which may ignore some information. To remedy this problem, in the attention layer, we used all hidden states $H = \{h_1, h_2, ..., h_L\}$, where h_i is the hidden state of the LSTM at time step i summarizing all the information of the question up to x_i and L denotes the length of the question. Note that $\alpha^{(a)}$ and $\alpha^{(b)}$ denote the weights of $LSTM_a$ and $LSTM_b$, respectively. Basically, the attention mechanism measures the importance of a word through a context vector. It computes a weight α_i for each word annotation h_i according to its importance. The final question representation r is the weighted sum of all the word annotations using the attention weights, computed by Eq. 4.

---

[8] www.kaggle.com/quora/question-pairs-dataset.

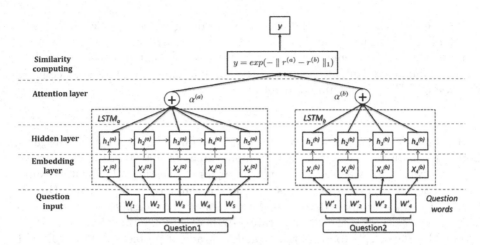

Fig. 1. An illustration of attentive Siamese LSTM model

In the attention layer, a context vector u_h is introduced, which is randomly initialized and can be viewed as a fixed query, that allows to identify the informative words.

$$e_i = \tanh(W_h h_i + b_h), e_i \in [-1, 1] \tag{2}$$

$$\alpha_i = \frac{\exp(e_i^T u_h)}{\sum_{i=1}^{T} \exp(e_t^T u_h)}, \sum_{i=1}^{T} \alpha_i = 1 \tag{3}$$

$$r = \sum_{i=1}^{T} \alpha_i h_i, r \in R^{2L} \tag{4}$$

where W_h, b_h, and u_h are the learnable parameters, W_h is a weight matrix and b_h is a bias vector used to project each context vector into a common dimensional space and L is the size of each LSTM.

4   Experimental Evaluation

4.1   Evaluation Metrics

For the automatic evaluation, we used the following metrics: Mean Average Precision (MAP), Precision@n (P@n) and Recall as they are the most used ones for assessing the performance of the QR task. MAP assumes that the user is interested in finding many relevant questions for each query and then rewards methods that not only return relevant questions early, but also get good ranking of the results. Precision@n gives an idea about the classifier's ability of not labeling a positive sample as a negative one. It returns the proportion of the top-n retrieved questions that are equivalent. Recall is the measure by which we check how well the model is in finding all the positive samples of the dataset. It returns the proportion of relevant similar questions that have been retrieved over the total number of relevant questions. We also used accuracy, which returns the proportion of correctly classified questions as relevant or irrelevant.

4.2   Results and Discussion

We compare ASLSTM against our previous approach called WEKOS as well as the competitive state-of-the-art question retrieval methods tested in [19] on the same datasets. The methods being compared are briefly described below:

- **WEKOS** [10]: A word embedding based method which uses the cosine distance to measure the similarity between the weighted continuous valued vectors of the clustered questions.
- **TLM** [16]: A translation based language model which uses a query likelihood approach for the question and the answer parts, and integrates word-to-word translation probabilities learned through various information sources.
- **ETLM** [14]: An entity based translation language model, which is an extension of TLM where the word translation was replaced with entity translation to integrate semantic information within the entities.
- **PBTM** [20]: A phrase based translation model which uses machine translation probabilities assuming that QR should be performed at the phrase level.
- **WKM** [22]: A world knowledge based model which integrates the knowledge of Wikipedia into the questions by deriving the concept relationships that allow to identify related topics between the questions.
- **M-NET** [21]: A word embedding based model, which integrates the category information of the questions to get a category based word embedding.
- **ParaKCM** [19]: A key concept paraphrasing based approach which explores the translations of pivot languages and expands queries with paraphrases.

Table 2 gives a comparison of the performance of ASLSTM against the aforementioned models on the English Yahoo! Answers dataset.

As illustrated in Table 2, ASLSTM outperforms in English all the compared methods on all criteria by successfully returning a significant number of similar questions among the retrieved ones. This good performance indicates that the use of Siamese LSTM along with the attention mechanism is effective in the QR task. Word embeddings allow to obtain an efficient input representation for LSTM, capturing syntactic and semantic information in a word level.

Table 2. Question retrieval performance comparison of different models in English.

	TLM	ETLM	PBTM	WKM	M-NET	ParaKCM	WEKOS	ASLSTM
P@5	0.3238	0.3314	0.3318	0.3413	0.3686	0.3722	0.4338	**0.5033**
P@10	0.2548	0.2603	0.2603	0.2715	0.2848	0.2889	0.3647	**0.4198**
MAP	0.3957	0.4073	0.4095	0.4116	0.4507	0.4578	0.5036	**0.5799**

Interestingly, our approach does not require an extensive feature generation owing to the use of a pre-trained model. The results show that ASLSTM performs better than translation and knowledge based methods, which provides evidence that the question representations made by the Siamese LSTM sub-networks can learn the semantic relatedness between pairs of questions and then are more adequate for representing questions in the question similarity task. The Siamese network was trained using backpropagation-through-time under the MSE loss function which compels the LSTM sub-networks to detect textual semantic difference during training. A key virtue of LSTM is that it can accept variable length sequences and map them into fixed length vector representations which can overcome the length and structure's problems in cQA.

Another significant finding is the effectiveness of the attention mechanism which was able to improve the performance of the approach. We assume that the attention mechanism managed to boost the similarity learning process by assigning a weight to each element of the question. The weights will then allow to compute which element in the sequence the neural network should more attend.

WEKOS averages the weighted embeddings, which is one of the most simple and widely used techniques to derive sequence embedding but it leads to losing the word order, while in ASLSTM, the LSTMs update their state to get the main context meaning of the text sequence in the order of words. The goal of the Siamese architecture is to learn a function which can map a question to an appropriate fixed length vector which is favor for similarity measurement. Interestingly, it offers vector representation for a very short text fragment that should grasp most of the semantic information in that fragment.

In order to properly assess the Siamese LSTM model performance on the similarity prediction problem, we plot training data vs validation data accuracy using the Matplotlib library.

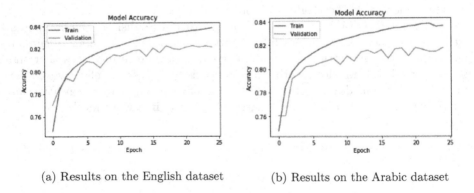

(a) Results on the English dataset   (b) Results on the Arabic dataset

Fig. 2. Epochs vs accuracy of Siamese LSTM on the English and Arabic dataset

From the plots of accuracy given in Figs. 2a and 2b, we observe that we get about 82% and 81% accuracy rate on the validation data for English and Arabic respectively. The model has comparable consistent accuracy on both train and validation sets. Both training and validation accuracy continue to increase without a sudden decrease of the validation accuracy, indicating a good fit. Therefore, we can admit that, whilst the performance on the training set is slightly better than that of the validation set in term of accuracy, the model converged to a stable value without any typical overfitting signs.

It is worth mentioning that the accuracy used in the epochs-accuracy plots, is the binary accuracy calculated by Keras, and it implies that the threshold is set at 0.5 so, everything above 0.5 will be considered as correct.

Our results are fairly stable across different similarity functions, namely cosine and Euclidean distances. We found that the Manhattan distance outperformed them on both the English and Arabic datasets as depicted in Tables 3a and 3b which demonstrates that it is the most relevant measure for the case of high dimensional text data.

Table 3. Comparison between similarity measures

(a) Results on the English dataset

	P@5	**Recall**
Manhattan	**0.5033**	**0.5477**
Cosine	**0.3893**	**0.4345**
Euclidean	**0.3393**	**0.3843**

(b) Results on the Arabic dataset

	P@5	**Recall**
Manhattan	**0.3702**	**0.4146**
Cosine	**0.2562**	**0.3006**
Euclidean	**0.2062**	**0.2506**

Furthermore, we remarked that ASLSTM could find the context mapping between certain expressions mostly used in the same context such as *bug* and *error message* or also *need help* and *suggestions*. ASLSTM was also able to retrieve similar questions containing certain common misspelled terms like *recieve* instead of *receive*, but it failed to capture other less common spelling mistakes like *relyable* or *realible* instead of *reliable*. Such cases show that our approach can address some lexical disagreement problems. Moreover, there are few cases where ASLSTM fails to detect semantic equivalence, including queries having only one similar question and most words of this latter do not appear in a similar context with those of the query.

Table 4. Question retrieval performance of ASLSTM in Arabic

	WEKOS	ASLSTM
P@5	0.3444	**0.3702**
P@10	0.2412	**0.2872**
MAP	0.4144	**0.4540**
Recall	0.3828	**0.4146**

Table 4 shows that ASLSTM outperforms in Arabic the best compared system which proves that it can also perform well with complex languages.

Nevertheless, a major limitation of the proposed approach is that it ignores the morphological structure of Arabic words. Harnessing the word internal structure might help to capture semantically similar words. Therefore, endowing word embeddings with grammatical information such as, the person, gender, number and tense could help to obtain more meaningful embeddings that detect morphological and semantic similarity. In terms of recall, ASLSTM reaches 0.4136 for Arabic which implies that the number of omitted similar questions is not too big. Interestingly, unlike traditional RNNs, Siamese LSTM is able effectively handle the long questions and learn long range dependencies thanks to its use of memory cell units that can store information across long input sequences.

4.3   Conclusion

In this paper, we presented an Attention-based Siamese LSTM approach, aiming at solving the question retrieval problem, which is of great importance in real-world cQA. For this purpose, we suggested using Siamese LSTM to capture the semantic similarity between the community questions. An attention mechanism was integrated to let the model give different attention to different words while modeling questions. Interestingly, we showed that Siamese LSTM is capable of modeling complex structures and covering the context information of question pairs. Experiments on large scale Yahoo! Answers datasets showed that the proposed approach can successfully improve the question retrieval task in English and Arabic and outperform some competitive methods evaluated on the same dataset. In the future, we plan to integrate morphological features into the embedding layer to improve the question representations.

References

1. Barrón-Cedeno, A., Da San Martino, G., Romeo, S., Moschitti, A.: Selecting sentences versus selecting tree constituents for automatic question ranking. In: Proceedings of the COLING, the 26th International Conference on Computational Linguistics, pp. 2515–2525 (2016)
2. Cao, X., Cong, G., Cui, B., Jensen, C.S.: A generalized framework of exploring category information for question retrieval in community question answer archives. In: Proceedings of the 19th International Conference on WWW, pp. 201–210. ACM (2010)
3. Cao, X., Cong, G., Cui, B., Jensen, C.S., Zhang, C.: The use of categorization information in language models for question retrieval. In: Proceedings of the 18th Conference on Information and Knowledge Management, pp. 265–274. ACM (2009)
4. Chorowski, J.K., Bahdanau, D., Serdyuk, D., Cho, K., Bengio, Y.: Attention-based models for speech recognition. In: Advances in Neural Information Processing Systems, pp. 577–585 (2015)
5. Dos Santos, C., Barbosa, L., Bogdanova, D., Zadrozny, B.: Learning hybrid representations to retrieve semantically equivalent questions. In: Proceedings of ACL and the 7th International Joint Conference on NLP, vol. 2, pp. 694–699 (2015)
6. Kamineni, A., Shrivastava, M., Yenala, H., Chinnakotla, M.: Siamese LSTM with convolutional similarity for similar question retrieval. In: 2018 International Joint Symposium on Artificial Intelligence and NLP, pp. 1–7. IEEE (2019)

7. Malhas, R., Torki, M., Elsayed, T.: QU-IR at SemEval 2016 task 3: learning to rank on arabic community question answering forums with word embedding. In: Proceedings of the SemEval, pp. 866–871 (2016)
8. Mohtarami, M., et al.: SLS at SemEval-2016 task 3: neural-based approaches for ranking in community question answering. In: Proceedings of the SemEval, pp. 828–835 (2016)
9. Mueller, J., Thyagarajan, A.: Siamese recurrent architectures for learning sentence similarity. In: Thirtieth AAAI Conference on Artificial Intelligence (2016)
10. Othman, N., Faiz, R., Smaïli, K.: Enhancing question retrieval in community question answering using word embeddings. In: Proceedings of the 23rd International Conference on Knowledge-Based and Intelligent Information and Engineering Systems (KES) (2019)
11. Pascanu, R., Mikolov, T., Bengio, Y.: On the difficulty of training recurrent neural networks. In: International Conference on Machine Learning, pp. 1310–1318 (2013)
12. Romeo, S., et al.: Neural attention for learning to rank questions in community question answering. In: Proceedings of the COLING, pp. 1734–1745 (2016)
13. Romeo, S., et al.: Language processing and learning models for community question answering in Arabic. In: IPM (2017)
14. Singh, A.: Entity based Q&A retrieval. In: Proceedings of the 2012 Joint Conference on Empirical Methods in Natural Language Processing and Computational Natural Language Learning, pp. 1266–1277. ACL (2012)
15. Wang, K., Ming, Z., Chua, T.S.: A syntactic tree matching approach to finding similar questions in community-based QA services. In: Proceedings of the 32nd International ACM SIGIR Conference on Research and Development in Information Retrieval, pp. 187–194. ACM (2009)
16. Xue, X., Jeon, J., Croft, W.B.: Retrieval models for question and answer archives. In: Proceedings of the 31st Annual International ACM SIGIR Conference on Research and Development in Information Retrieval, pp. 475–482. ACM (2008)
17. Ye, B., Feng, G., Cui, A., Li, M.: Learning question similarity with recurrent neural networks. In: 2017 IEEE International Conference on Big Knowledge (ICBK), pp. 111–118. IEEE (2017)
18. Zhang, K., Wu, W., Wu, H., Li, Z., Zhou, M.: Question retrieval with high quality answers in community question answering. In: Proceedings of the 23rd ACM International Conference on Information and Knowledge Management, pp. 371–380. ACM (2014)
19. Zhang, W.N., Ming, Z.Y., Zhang, Y., Liu, T., Chua, T.S.: Capturing the semantics of key phrases using multiple languages for question retrieval. IEEE Trans. Knowl. Data Eng. 28(4), 888–900 (2016)
20. Zhou, G., Cai, L., Zhao, J., Liu, K.: Phrase-based translation model for question retrieval in community question answer archives. In: Proceedings of the 49th Annual Meeting of the ACL: Human Language Technologies-Volume 1, pp. 653–662. ACL (2011)
21. Zhou, G., He, T., Zhao, J., Hu, P.: Learning continuous word embedding with metadata for question retrieval in community question answering. In: Proceedings of the 53rd Annual Meeting of the ACL and the 7th International Joint Conference on Natural Language Processing of the Asian Federation of Natural Language Processing, pp. 250–259 (2015)
22. Zhou, G., Liu, Y., Liu, F., Zeng, D., Zhao, J.: Improving question retrieval in community question answering using world knowledge. IJCAI 13, 2239–2245 (2013)

Jointly Linking Visual and Textual Entity Mentions with Background Knowledge

Shahi Dost[1,2]([✉]), Luciano Serafini[1], Marco Rospocher[3], Lamberto Ballan[2], and Alessandro Sperduti[2]

[1] Fondazione Bruno Kessler, Trento, Italy
sdost@fbk.eu
[2] University of Padova, Padova, Italy
[3] University of Verona, Verona, Italy

Abstract. "A picture is worth a thousand words", the adage reads. However, pictures cannot replace words in terms of their ability to efficiently convey clear (mostly) unambiguous and concise knowledge. Images and text, indeed, reveal different and complementary information that, if combined, result in more information than the sum of that contained in the single media. The combination of visual and textual information can be obtained through linking the entities mentioned in the text with those shown in the pictures. To further integrate this with agent background knowledge, an additional step is necessary. That is, either finding the entities in the agent knowledge base that correspond to those mentioned in the text or shown in the picture or, extending the knowledge base with the newly discovered entities. We call this complex task Visual-Textual-Knowledge Entity Linking (VTKEL). In this paper, after providing a precise definition of the VTKEL task, we present a dataset composed of about 30K commented pictures, annotated with visual and textual entities, and linked to the YAGO ontology. Successively, we develop a purely unsupervised algorithm for the solution of the VTKEL tasks. The evaluation on the VTKEL dataset shows promising results.

Keywords: AI · NLP · Computer vision · Knowledge representation · Semantic web · Entity recognition and linking

1 Introduction

Given the prominent presence in the web of documents that combines text and images, it becomes crucial to be able to properly process them. In spite of the maturity and reliability of natural language processing (NLP) and computer vision (CV) technologies, an independent processing of the textual and visual part of a document is not sufficient. A more integrated process is necessary. Indeed, the pictorial and textual parts of a document typically provide complementary information about a set of entities occurring both in the picture and

© Springer Nature Switzerland AG 2020
E. Métais et al. (Eds.): NLDB 2020, LNCS 12089, pp. 264–276, 2020.
https://doi.org/10.1007/978-3-030-51310-8_24

in the text. For instance, in a news about a car accident, the text may mention the brand and model of the car and the name of the driver, while the picture may reveal the car brand and model as well, but also the car color and its status after the crash. The information conveyed by the two media can be joined by linking the entities mentioned in the text with those shown in the pictures, possibly integrating them with some background knowledge that provides further information about the entities. We call this task *Visual-Textual-Knowledge Entity Linking (VTKEL)*. More precisely, the VTKEL task aims at detecting and linking the maximum visual and textual portions of a document that refer to the same or individual entities of the document, a.k.a. *entity mentions*, with the corresponding entity (or a newly created one) in a knowledge base.

State-of-the-art only provides partial solutions to the VTKEL task. Namely entity linking [1] align textual mentions to entities of a knowledge base, coreference resolution [2] links different textual mentions of the same entity, visual entity linking [3] align visual entity mentions to a knowledge base, visual semantic alignment [4] links different visual entity mentions that refer to the same entity, and, text to image coreference [5] aligns visual and textual mentions of the same entity.

The paper introduces VT-LINKER[1] (Visual-Textual-Knowledge Entity Linker), an algorithm for solving the VTKEL task that combines state-of-the-art NLP and computer vision tools, and ontological reasoning. Given a document composed of text and image, VT-LINKER applies an object detector to the image, resulting in a set of bounding boxes labeled with classes of the ontology. Each bounding box is called *visual mention* and the corresponding object, which is an instance of the class label, is called *visual entity*. In parallel, VT-LINKER processes the text with a tool for entity recognition, which labels the noun phrases with classes of the ontology. The recognized noun phrases are called *textual mentions* and the corresponding instances of the ontological class are *textual entities*. Finally, VT-LINKER attempts to link visual and textual mentions which correspond to the same entity. This final task is done by exploiting ontological knowledge about class/subclass hierarchy, and similarity information available in the textual mentions.

To evaluate VT-LINKER, we created a ground-truth dataset for the VTKEL task, called the *Visual-Textual-Knowledge Entity Linking dataset (VTKEL)*. This dataset is derived from the Flickr30k-Entities [6] dataset, which contains about 30 K images, each described by 5 captions. Each picture is annotated with bounding boxes for objects and with coreference chains (a coreference chain links mentions of the same entities across different captions with the corresponding bounding box). We extended the Flickr30k-Entities by annotating each element of the coreference chains with the proper ontological class. As a reference ontology, we adopted YAGO [7]. Since the linking of the ontological class is performed automatically (by using PIKES [8,22]), we manually evaluate the accuracy by checking 1000 randomly selected entries from the VTKEL dataset. The resulting accuracy was about 95% (notice that PIKES annotates *all* the noun phrases).

---

[1] https://github.com/shahidost/Baseline4VTKEL.

Out of the 1000 pictures, we created a dataset, called VTKEL*, by manually correcting the errors.

We evaluate VT-LINKER on both VTKEL and VTKEL* datasets. The evaluation is performed in three sub-tasks i.e. visual entities detection and typing, textual entities detection and typing, and visual textual coreference. The F1 measure for visual entities detection and typing on VTKEL* and VTKEL is 65.7% and 64.9% respectively; The F1 measure for textual entities detection and typing 91.8% and 90.5%; the F1 for visual textual conference is 57.1% and 50.4%.

The paper is structured as follows: in Sect. 2, we give a detailed formulation of the VTKEL task. In Sect. 3, we review the main approaches related to the VTKEL task and argue that only partial solutions are available. Section 4 describes VT-LINKER in details. In Sect. 5, we describe the experiments. Section 6 provides some conclusions and future research directions.

2   Visual-Textual-Knowledge Entity Linking

The Visual-Textual-Knowledge Entity Linking (VTKEL) task takes in input a document composed of text and a picture.[2] More precisely, a document d is a pair $\langle d_t, d_i \rangle$, where d_t is a text in natural language represented as a string of characters and d_i is an image, represented as a 3-channel $(w \times h)$-matrix. We ignore all the structural information about the document, e.g. the relative position of the image w.r.t. the text, the explicit references to the figures, etc. If e is an entity of the domain of discourse of a document d, for example a specific *car* or a *person*, a *textual mention* of e in d is a portion of the text d_t that refers to the entity e. Such a mention can be identified by an interval $\langle l, r \rangle$ with $0 \leq l < r \leq len(d_t)$, corresponding to the characters (in d_t) of the mention. Analogously, a *visual mention* of an entity e is a region of the picture d_i that shows (a characterizing part of) the entity e. E.g., the region of a picture that shows the (face of a) *person* is a visual mention of that *person*. If we restrict to rectangular regions (a.k.a. bounding boxes) a visual mention can be represented by a bounding box encoded by four integers $\langle x, y, x+w, y+h \rangle$ with $0 \leq x, x+w \leq width(d_i)$ and $0 \leq y, y+h \leq height(d_i)$, where $\langle x, y \rangle$ represents the position of the pixel in the top left corner of the bounding box, and w, h represent the width and height of the bounding box (in pixels).

A knowledge base is a logical theory that states properties and relations about a set of entities, called the domain, using a logical language. In description logics a knowledge base is composed of a T-box and an A-box. The T-box contains a set of axioms of the form $C \sqsubseteq D$ and $R \sqsubseteq S$, for some concept expressions C and D and relations R and S stating that C is a subclass of D (R is a sub-relation of S). The A-box contains assertions of the form $C(e)$ (the entity e is of type C) and $R(e, f)$ (the pair of entities $\langle e, f \rangle$ are in relation R) where e and f are

---

[2] For the sake of simplicity, we consider only documents that contain one single picture. The extension to multiple pictures, though intuitive, presents additional challenges that are out of the scope of this paper.

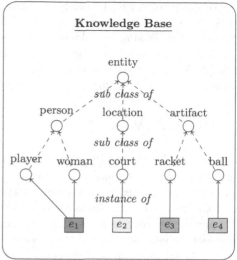

- A young woman on a tennis court with a ball coming from behind her.
- A female tennis player casually swinging her tennis racket .

Fig. 1. The picture shows the output of the VTKEL task, which takes in input a picture with related text and an ontology. The output consists of a set of visual mentions (c.f. the bounding boxes in the image) and textual mentions (c.f. the highlighted words in the sentences), corresponding to the mentioned entities (in this case: a ball, a woman, the tennis court and a racket), and the extension (or alignment) of the ontology with entities of the correct (most specific) type.

entities of the knowledge base and C and R are concept and role expressions respectively. The *entities* of a knowledge base are constant symbols that explicitly occur in some axiom of the T-box or assertion of the A-box. For instance, the T-box may contain the knowledge that every car has a manufacturer and that a manufacturer is a company. This knowledge can be formalized by the axioms Car $\sqsubseteq \exists$ hasManufacturer. Manufacturer and Manufacturer $\sqsubseteq$ Company, where Car, Manufacturer, and Company are concept names and hasManufacturer is a relation (or role). The A-box may contain the knowledge that a specific car (an entity), say car_{22}, is a BMW and that BMW is a Manufacturer. This is formalized by the assertional axioms Car(car_{22}), hasManufacturer(car_{22}, BMW), and Manufacturer(BMW).

Problem 1 (VTKEL). Given a document composed of a text d_t and an image d_i and a knowledge base K, *VTKEL* is the problem of detecting all the entities mentioned in d_t *and* shown in d_i, and linking them to the corresponding entities in K, if they are present, or to newly added entities of the correct type.

An example of the result of the VTKEL task is shown in Fig. 1. VTKEL is a complex task that requires the solution of a set of well studied elementary tasks in NLP, CV, and logical reasoning. In particular, the following are the key subtasks of VTKEL: entity recognition and classification (i.e. typing) in texts [9]; object detection in images [10]; textual co-reference resolution [2]; textual entity linking to a knowledge base (ontology) [1]; visual entity linking to a knowledge base (ontology) [11]; visual and textual co-reference resolution [4,5,12]. We propose a method to solve the VTKEL task which is obtained by composing state-of-the-art tools that solve some of the subtasks listed above.

3   Related Work

Recently the NLP and CV scientific communities devoted some effort in investigating the interaction and integration of text and image. For an exhaustive survey of the approaches in the area of entity information extraction and linking, we refer the reader to [13]. In particular: [5] exploits natural language descriptions of a picture in order to understand the content of the scene itself. The proposed approach solves the image-to-text coreference problem. It successively exploits the visual information and visual-textual coreference previously found to solve coreference in text. The work described in [14,15] tackles the problem of ranking the concepts from the knowledge base that best represents the core message expressed in an image. This work involves the three elements: Image, Text, and Knowledge, but it does not provide information about the entities mentioned in the text and shown in the image. The approach in [3] adapts Markov Random Fields to represent the dependencies between what is shown in the frames of videos about the wild-life animal and the subtitles. The main objective is to detect the animal shown in a frame, and the mentions of animal in the subtitle. The set of entities are the animal names available in WordNet [16]. Object detection is not performed: the approach assumes that only one animal is shown in a frame, and the vision part consists of image classification. Furthermore, no background knowledge about animals is used. [11] proposes a basic framework for visual entity linking to DBpedia and Freebase. The approach involves also textual processing since the link of bounding boxes to DBpedia and Freebase entities is found passing through an automatically generated textual description of the image. The approach uses the Flickr8k dataset, which is a subset of the Flikr30k-Entities dataset. A combination of textual coreference resolution and linking of image and textual mentions is described in [17] with the objective of solving the problem of assigning names to people appearing in TV-show.

Concerning datasets that combine text and images, there are several resources available, however, none of them have all the three components necessary for the VTKEL task. VisualGenome [18] is an extremely large dataset that contains pictures in which objects are annotated with their types, attributes, and relationships. Annotations are mapped to WordNet synsets. Objects can also be annotated with some short sentence that describes some qualitative property of the object. E.g., "The girl is feeding the elephant" or "a handle of bananas". However, there is no alignment between the objects mentioned in these phrases and the objects shown in the picture. E.g., there is no bounding box for the object "bananas" or "elephant". The Visual Relationship Dataset (VRD) [19] is a dataset of images annotated with bounding boxes around key objects. Furthermore, VRD contains annotations about relationships between objects in the form of triplets ⟨object_type, relation, subject_type⟩ describing the scene. Examples of annotations are ⟨man, riding, bicycle⟩ and ⟨car, on, road⟩. However, these annotations are not aligned to any knowledge base. The Microsoft COCO dataset [20] contains pictures associated with five captions. They are annotated with objects regions of any shape (not simple bounding boxes) and each region is assigned with an object-type. This dataset does not contain any information about the relation between object regions, and the relation between regions and mentions in the captions. Conceptual Captions [21] is a recently introduced dataset that has been developed for automatic image caption generation. It contains one order of magnitude more items than Microsoft COCO. It is a realistic dataset as images with captions have been automatically extracted and filtered from the web. However, there is no visual/textual mention annotation and visual textual entity linking.

From the above analysis, it becomes clear that there is not a single, comprehensive approach corresponding to the VTKEL task. This justifies the introduction of the task, the development of a ground truth dataset, and a first (baseline) algorithm for its solution.

4   The VT-LinKEr Algorithm

VT-LinKEr is composed of two sequential phases: The first phase, *the entity detection phase*, focuses on visual entity detection & typing (VMD-VET) and textual entity detection & typing (TMD-TET); the second phase, *the matching phase*, attempts to match the discovered entities i.e. visual-textual coreference (VTC). The entity detection phase is based on the output of state-of-the-art tools in NLP and CV. The matching phase is realized by using the semantic matching which exploits the knowledge available in the T-box (i.e. class/subclass hierarchy). In the following, we illustrate the different steps for each phase.

Visual Mention Detection (VMD): To implement VMD, we process images with YOLO [23], which returns a set of bounding box proposals each of which is associated with a YOLO-class and a confidence score in [0,1]. We used the model pre-trained on the 80 classes of the COCO dataset. Among the bounding box candidates, we retain only those having confidence equal or greater than a specified threshold (in the experiments we set it to 0.5). In general, one could use some more sophisticated selection criteria that take into account also the co-occurrence with the other bounding box candidates (e.g., glass and bottle are more probable than glass and elephant) and the output of the textual mention detection and the ontological knowledge. For the picture of Fig. 1, YOLO returns three bounding box candidates with score higher than 0.5, labeled with *person*, *ball* and *racket*, but no bounding box has been found for the tennis court (due to the lack of appropriate classes for locations in the YOLO class set).

Visual Entity Typing (VET): The objective of this sub-task is to find the correct most specific class in the knowledge base that can be associated to each visual entity associated to the visual mention detected in the VMD step. Notice that the COCO class does not correspond one-to-one with the YAGO classes, this implies that we need to map the class returned by YOLO into YAGO. A naïve way to implement this task is to map the label contained in the output of the object detector to its corresponding ontology class. Also, here more sophisticated methods can be implemented that take into account also the weight of the labels or additional visual/numerical features. In the VT-LINKER algorithm, we adopt the straightforward approach of manually mapping the 80 COCO classes to the corresponding (most specific) classes of the YAGO ontology.[3] Examples of mappings from COCO to YAGO are: *person* → `yago:Person100007846`, *ball* → `yago:Ball102778669`, and *hotdog* → `yago:Frank107676602`.

Textual Mention Detection (TMD): To detect textual mentions of entities we process the text with the PIKES suite, which provides services for both textual mention detection and textual entity typing to the YAGO ontology. These two tasks are tightly integrated in PIKES, however, for conceptual clarity, here we present them separately. Let us focus on the entity mention detection. Given a text in input PIKES applies different state-of-the-art NLP techniques to discover entity mentions depending on their "nature":

- *named entity mentions* (e.g., Barak Obama, Trento, IBM) refers to entities for which there is an individual in the knowledge base. They are recognized and linked (performing a task called Entity Linking) to the corresponding entity in YAGO (the knowledge base is not extended).
- *common nouns* (e.g., racket, ball, player, and woman) implicitly identify entities, by referring to their type (e.g., the mention of "racket" does not refer to the general notion of racket, but to a specific object, of type racket). Common nouns are discovered via word sense disambiguation (WSD). For every common noun, WSD returns the WordNet synset corresponding to the correct sense in which the noun is used. For instance, the correct sense of "racket" is the one indicating a sport equipment, and not a loud and disturbing noise. A new entity is created and added to the knowledge base for common nouns occurring in the text.
  Some further processing is performed to properly handle compound noun phrases (e.g., "a female tennis player"). PIKES also performs a syntactic analysis of the text: in particular, words in a noun phrase can be tagged either with *head* or with *modifier*, depending on their syntactic role in the noun phrase (e.g., in "a female tennis player" the noun "player" is the head and "female" and "tennis" are modifiers). In the current version of the VT-LINKER algorithm, a new entity is added to the knowledge base only for the head noun, and not for its modifiers.

For example, for the first sentence of the caption in Fig. 1, PIKES detects three textual mentions: *woman, court* and *ball.*

---

[3] The whole mapping can be downloaded from https://figshare.com/articles/ YOLO_to_YAGO_classes_mapping/8889848.

Textual Entity Typing (TET): This task is also implemented using PIKES primitives. Typing for named entities is not necessary since these entities are in the YAGO knowledge base, and thus already typed according to the YAGO ontology. For the common nouns, we exploit the mapping from WordNet to YAGO also available in PIKES to obtain the (more specific) YAGO class associated to the WordNet synset of the mention, and the corresponding type assertion will be added to the knowledge base. For example, for the first sentence of the caption in Fig. 1, PIKES types the entities corresponding to the textual mentions *woman, court* and *ball*, with the YAGO classes `yago:Woman110787470`, `yago:Court108329453`, and `yago:Ball102778669`, respectively.

Visual Textual Coreference (VTC): This is the last sub-task that has to be accomplished by VT-LINKER. For this task, we exploit the class/subclass hierarchy between the classes in the knowledge base. Let VE and TE be the set of textual and visual entities that are mentioned in a visual-textual document, and that are present in the knowledge base with a given type. The coreference sub-task has the objective of finding the coreference relation $CR \subseteq VE \times TE$ such that the following consistent properties hold:

(i) For every $ve \in VE$ there is at least one $\langle ve, te \rangle \in CR$;
(ii) For every $ve \in VE$ there is at most one $\langle ve, te \rangle \in CR$;
(iii) If $\langle ce, ve \rangle$ (ce is the coreference entity) and ve and te are of type C_v and C_t respectively then either $C_v \sqsubseteq C_t$ or $C_t \sqsubseteq C_e$ holds in the knowledge base.

In simple situations, the above criteria uniquely defines the coreference relations. This is the case for instance for the example presented in Fig. 1. However, in many cases the relation $CR \subseteq VE \times TE$ is not uniquely defined by the above criteria. Nevertheless, the problem can be straightforwardly encoded as a MaxSat problem. In case of CRs with equal total weight, a random choice is taken although additional heuristics could be implemented either by using some supervised learning method or by handcrafting the weight of a pair $\langle ve, te \rangle$ by exploiting some additional features of the mentions of ve and te.

5   Experimental Evaluations

To evaluate the performance of VT-LINKER, we have developed two ground truth datasets [25]. The first one, called VTKEL, has been derived from Flickr30k-Entities, and it is generated automatically by typing the visual and textual entities with classes from the YAGO ontology. The second one, called VTKEL*, has been obtained by randomly selecting 1000 pictures (and the corresponding captions) from the first dataset, and manually validating and revising the proposed alignments to YAGO. In the following, we provide some details on the datasets, and then we describe the evaluations conducted.

5.1   Datasets

The first dataset called VTKEL, [4] has been obtained by extending the Flickr30k-Entities dataset by linking textual and visual mentions to entities assigned with the most specific YAGO class. Looking at Fig. 1, we started form the left part of the figure (the picture and captions, with annotated visual and textual mentions, and alignment between corresponding mentions), available in the Flickr30k-Entities, and we extended it with the right part, by populating a knowledge base with corresponding entities typed according to the YAGO ontology. The 30K VTKEL dataset has been automatically produced by processing the captions of Flickr30k-Entities with PIKES for entity recognition and linking to YAGO. Specifically, for each textual mention (aligned to a visual mention) in Flickr30k-Entities, detected also by PIKES, a corresponding entity is created (or aligned to, if already existing) and typed according to the appropriate YAGO ontology.

The second dataset, called VTKEL*,[5] has been obtained by randomly sampling 1000 entries from the VTKEL dataset (corresponding to $20,356$ textual mentions, and 8673 visual mentions). Every entry of VTKEL* has been manually checked for the correctness and completeness of the YAGO classes associated to the mentioned entities. Wrong and missing links are manually adjusted. Errors are mainly due to the incorrect word sense disambiguation: e.g., in some cases, "bus" was linked to the concept of the computer bus, instead of that of coach, and "arm" to weapon instead of bodypart. The construction of VTKEL*-dataset allows us also to estimate the error rate of the larger VTKEL dataset. In particular, we found no missing link (i.e., recall is 100%) and 916 incorrectly linked mentions, which amounts to $Precision = 0.955, Recall = 0.893, and F1 = 0.923$. We believe that an error rate of $\approx 4.5\%$ is physiological also in manually developed datasets, and therefore we believe that the VTKEL-dataset can be reasonably considered a ground truth.

To maximize reusability and connection with the Semantic Web, we represent the datasets in RDF. This representation will also support semantic visual query answering via standard SPARQL language. To organize the dataset, we adopt the model proposed in [8], extending it for representing visual mentions. The model is organized in three distinct yet interlinked representation layers: *Resource*, *Mention*, and *Entity layer*.

5.2   Evaluation

We evaluated the performances of VT-Linker on both VTKEL and VTKEL* datasets. We separately assessed the performance on the three sub-tasks described in Sect. 4. We use the standard metrics, namely precision (P), recall (R), and F-score (F_1). The figures obtained from the evaluation are reported in Table 1.

---

[4] The VTKEL dataset can be downloaded from https://figshare.com/articles/VTKEL_dataset/9816242/4.

[5] https://figshare.com/articles/VTKEL_dataset/10318985.

Table 1. VT-LINKER evaluation results

	VTKEL* dataset			VTKEL dataset		
Task	*Precision*	*Recall*	F_1	*Precision*	*Recall*	F_1
VMD + VET	0.765	0.574	0.657	0.731	0.585	0.649
TMD + TET	0.954	0.884	0.918	0.942	0.872	0.905
VTC	0.586	0.558	0.571	0.514	0.486	0.504

Visual Entities Detection and Typing (VMD) + (VET): To evaluate the visual detection part, we use standard method adopted for evaluating object detection. A visual mention b_p of type t_p produced by VT-LINKER on an image is considered to be correct if the ground truth annotation of the image contains a bounding box b_g of type t_g such that the intersection over union ratio ($\frac{area(b_p \cap b_g)}{area(b_p) \cup area(b_g)}$) is greater or equal to $\frac{1}{2}$ and if the predicted type t_p is equal or a subclass of t_g in YAGO. For the 1000 entries dataset VTKEL*, VT-LINKER predicted 6914 total visual entities with respect to the 9243 annotated visual entity objects. VT-LINKER correctly predicted 5306 ($P = 0.767, R = 0.574, F1 = 0.657$) of them. By using the same procedure for 30 K entries VTKEL dataset, VT-LINKER predicted 220, 853 total visual entities with respect to the 275, 770 annotated visual entity objects. VT-LINKER correctly predicted 161, 342 ($P = 0.731, R = 0.585, F1 = 0.649$) of them. In the majority of the cases, VT-LINKER framework ignored human bodyparts and clothing during the prediction of visual mentions due to the 80 classes of COCO dataset [20]. In some cases, VT-LINKER predicts additional correct visual mention not annotated in Flickr30k-Entities. In the evaluation, these are considered errors though they are not strictly so.

Textual Entities Detection and Typing (TMD) + (TET): To evaluate the performance of this sub-task, we apply a criterion analogous to the visual entity detection and typing sub-task. A textual mention w_p of an entity of YAGO class t_p predicted by VT-LINKER on a caption, is considered to be correct if the ground truth annotation on the caption contains a mention w_g of an entity of type t_g such that w_p is equal or a sub-string of w_g and the type t_p is equal or a sub-type of t_g according to the YAGO class hierarchy. From the 5000 captions of VTKEL*dataset, VT-LINKER wrongly recognized and linked 935 out of total 20, 374 textual entities, which amount to $P = 0.954$, $Recall = 0.884$, and $F1 = 0.918$. Similarly, for 158, 605 captions of VTKELdataset, VT-LINKER correctly recognized and linked 576, 769 out of total 612, 281 textual entities. Most of the errors during entity recognition and linking are due to the word sense disambiguation.

Visual Textual Coreference (VTC): We evaluate the capability of VT-LINKER of aligning visual and textual entities. A coreference pair $\langle ve_p, te_p \rangle$ produced by VT-LINKER is correct, if the ground truth contains the triple

ve_g `owl:sameAs` te_v such that the visual mentions (bounding boxes) of ve_p and ve_g matches (under the IOU ratio), the textual mention of te_p matches the textual mention of te_g (i.e., te_p is equal or a substring of te_g). Notice that here we are not considering the types of the entities. Type compatibility is indeed guaranteed by the fact that coreference pairs are added only if their types are compatible (i.e., they are either equal or in subclass relation in YAGO). From the 1000 entries VTKEL*dataset, VT-LINKER correctly aligned 4082 visual entities with 8681 textual entities out of total 6914 visual and 14,786 textual entities ($P = 0.586, R = 0.558, F1 = 0.571$). Similarly, for VTKEL dataset, VT-LINKER correctly aligned 118,502 visual entities with 243,831 textual entities out of total 220,853 visual and 576,769 textual entities. In most of the cases, the alignment of human-body parts and clothing with visual entities are missed by VT-LINKER.

6   Conclusion and Future Works

In this paper, we have introduced a new complex task for recognizing mentions of entities in multimedia documents composed of image and text, and align them with a reference ontology. This task turns out to be rather important for many applications in the area of multimedia indexing processing and retrieval, e.g., information extraction from multimedia systems [24], for visual question answering [26], and for visual textual dialogue systems [27]. We argue that there are advantages to solve the VTKEL task in a collective manner, i.e., trying to jointly solve all the tasks involved in it. For this reason, we created a new dataset annotated with all the information necessary for the VTKEL task. We perform this in a completely automatic manner, by processing the captions of the Flickr30k dataset to find entities and linking them to the YAGO ontology. We also developed the first algorithm to solve the task of VTKEL. The proposed algorithm is developed by using state-of-the-art tools for object detection in images, entity recognition in text, entity linking to ontologies and alignment of visual-textual entity mentions. This allows us to close the loop between language, vision, and knowledge. In the future, we are planning to improve the accuracy of every single sub-task, especially the object detection, by using a more complete set of object classes. We also planned to implement a more sophisticated method for the visual-textual entity matching, based on supervised methods, or statistical relational learning methods. We also want to apply the method to a dataset that includes more pictures and text different from captions (e.g., short news with pictures).

References

1. Shen, W., Wang, J., Han, J.: Entity linking with a knowledge base: issues, techniques, and solutions. IEEE Trans. KDE **2**(27), 443–460 (2015)
2. Sukthanker, R., Poria, S., Cambria, E., Thirunavukarasu, R.: Anaphora and Coreference Resolution: A Review. arXiv preprint arXiv:1805.11824 (2018)

3. Venkitasubramanian, A.N., Tuytelaars, T., Moens, M.-F.: Entity linking across vision and language. Multimed. Tools Appl. 1–24 (2017). https://doi.org/10.1007/s11042-017-4732-8
4. Karpathy, A., Fei-Fei, L.: Deep visual-semantic alignments for generating image descriptions. In: Proceedings of the IEEE-CVPR, pp. 3128–3137 (2015)
5. Kong, C., Lin, D., Bansal, M., Urtasun, R., Fidler, S.: What are you talking about? text-to-image coreference. In: Proceedings of the IEEE-CVPR, pp. 3558–3565 (2014)
6. Plummer, B.A., Hockenmaier, J., Lazebnik, S.: Flickr30k entities: collecting region-to-phrase correspondences for richer image-to-sentence models. In: ICCV (2015)
7. Suchanek, F.M., Kasneci, G., Weikum, G.: Yago: a core of semantic knowledge. In: Proceedings of WWW 2007, pp. 697–706, May 2007
8. Corcoglioniti, F., Rospocher, M., Aprosio, A.P.: Frame-based ontology population with PIKES. IEEE Trans. KDE **28**(12), 3261–3275 (2016)
9. Goyal, A., Gupta, V., Kumar, M.: Recent named entity recognition and classification techniques: a systematic review. Comput. Sci. Rev. **29**, 21–43 (2018)
10. Han, J., Zhang, D., Liu, N., Xu, D.: Advanced deep-learning techniques for salient and category-specific object detection: a survey. IEEE SPM **35**, 84–100 (2018)
11. Tilak, N., Gandhi, S., Oates, T.: Visual entity linking. In: 2017 International Joint Conference on Neural Networks (IJCNN), pp. 665–672. IEEE, May 2017
12. Huang, D.A., Fei-Fei, L., Carlos Niebles, J.: Unsupervised visual-linguistic reference resolution in instructional videos. In: IEEE-CVPR, pp. 2183–2192 (2017)
13. Martinez-Rodriguez, J.L., Hogan, A., Lopez-Arevalo, I.: Information extraction meets the semantic web: a survey. Semantic Web (Preprint), pp. 1–81 (2018)
14. Weiland, L., Hulpus, I., Ponzetto, S.P., Dietz, L.: Using object detection, NLP, and knowledge bases to understand the message of images. In: Amsaleg, L., Guðmundsson, G.Þ., Gurrin, C., Jónsson, B.Þ., Satoh, S. (eds.) MMM 2017. LNCS, vol. 10133, pp. 405–418. Springer, Cham (2017). https://doi.org/10.1007/978-3-319-51814-5_34
15. Weiland, L., Hulpu, I., Effelsberg, W., Dietz, L.: Knowledge-rich image gist understanding beyond literal meaning. DKE **117**, 114–132 (2018)
16. Miller, G.A.: WordNet: a lexical database for English. Commun. ACM **38**(11), 39–41 (1995)
17. Ramanathan, V., Joulin, A., Liang, P., Fei-Fei, L.: Linking people in videos with "their" names using coreference resolution. In: Fleet, D., Pajdla, T., Schiele, B., Tuytelaars, T. (eds.) ECCV 2014. LNCS, vol. 8689, pp. 95–110. Springer, Cham (2014). https://doi.org/10.1007/978-3-319-10590-1_7
18. Krishna, R., Zhu, Y., Kravitz, J., Bernstein, M.S.: Visual genome: connecting language and vision using crowdsourced dense image annotations. IJCV **123**, 32–73 (2017)
19. Lu, C., Krishna, R., Bernstein, M., Fei-Fei, L.: Visual relationship detection with language priors. In: Leibe, B., Matas, J., Sebe, N., Welling, M. (eds.) ECCV 2016. LNCS, vol. 9905, pp. 852–869. Springer, Cham (2016). https://doi.org/10.1007/978-3-319-46448-0_51
20. Lin, T.-Y., et al.: Microsoft COCO: common objects in context. In: Fleet, D., Pajdla, T., Schiele, B., Tuytelaars, T. (eds.) ECCV 2014. LNCS, vol. 8693, pp. 740–755. Springer, Cham (2014). https://doi.org/10.1007/978-3-319-10602-1_48
21. Sharma, P., Ding, N., Soricut, R.: Conceptual captions: A cleaned, hypernymed, image alt-text dataset for automatic image captioning. In: ACL, pp. 2556–2565 (2018)

22. Corcoglioniti, F., Rospocher, M., Mostarda, M., Amadori, M.: Processing billions of RDF triples on a single machine using streaming and sorting. In: ACM-SAC (2015)
23. Redmon, J., Divvala, S., Girshick, R., Farhadi, A.: You only look once: unified, real-time object detection. In: IEEE-CVPR, pp. 779–788 (2016)
24. Bracamonte, T., Schreck, T.: Extracting semantic knowledge from web context for multimedia IR: a taxonomy, survey and challenges. In: MTA, pp. 13853–13889 (2018)
25. Dost, S., Serafini, L., Rospocher, M., Ballan, L., Sperduti, A.: VTKEL: a resource for visual-textual-knowledge entity linking. In: Proceedings of ACM Symposium on Applied Computing, pp. 2021–2028 (2020)
26. Antol, S., et al.: VQA: visual question answering. In: IEEE-ICCV, pp. 2425–2433 (2015)
27. Das, A., et al.: Visual dialog. In: Proceedings of the IEEE CVPR, pp. 326–335 (2017)

Human-in-the-Loop Conversation Agent for Customer Service

Pēteris Paikens(✉) , Artūrs Znotiņš, and Guntis Bārzdiņš

University of Latvia Institute of Mathematics and Computer Science, Riga, Latvia
{peteris.paikens,arturs.znotins,guntis.barzdins}@lumii.lv

Abstract. This paper describes a prototype system for partial automation of customer service operations of a mobile telecommunications operator with a human-in-the loop conversational agent. The agent consists of an intent detection system for identifying the types of customer requests that it can handle appropriately, a slot filling information extraction system that integrates with the customer service database for a rule-based treatment of the common scenarios, and a template-based language generation system that builds response candidates that can be approved or amended by customer service operators. The main focus of this paper is on the system architecture and machine learning system structure design, and the observations of a limited pilot study performed to evaluate the proposed system on customer messages in Latvian. We also discuss the business requirements and practical application limitations and their influence on the design of the natural language processing components.

Keywords: Conversational agents · Intent detection · NER

1 Problem Description

The use of chatbots has been growing not only in consumer applications, but is also gaining traction in attempts aim to add conversational agents as another alternative channel for customer service communications, which is a significant expense for many companies and has potential for automation.

However, as chatbots improve towards fluent and varied language, there is an 'uncanny valley' effect where the observed language skills give rise to expectations of true competency in solving the customers' problems which often can not be met by the chatbots at this point, leading to customer dissatisfaction.

In this situation we proposed an approach for integrating conversation agents in the current customer service workflow, reducing operator workload. The customer service agent would be in full control over the customer communication, but the conversation can be automated for many routine cases where the customer service agent would be expected to follow standard guidelines. The notable difference from a full-scope conversational agent is the fact that covering unusual scenarios is not required as long as the agent is capable to identify when the customer is asking something that the automated agent can not understand or answer and human involvement is necessary.

© Springer Nature Switzerland AG 2020
E. Métais et al. (Eds.): NLDB 2020, LNCS 12089, pp. 277–284, 2020.
https://doi.org/10.1007/978-3-030-51310-8_25

2   Related Work

Published research relevant to goal-oriented conversational agents in Latvian is limited. There has been previous work on the chatbot "Anete" [16] for telecommunications provider Lattelecom, however, the technical details have not been published. There are proof of concept systems developed for customer service at an airline and the public library network [15], and there is published work on intent detection models [1] including a review of their applicability for Latvian.

There is substantial relevant related work on such agents for English and other major languages [4,5,12]. A major focus of recent research is work on end-to-end neural systems [13,14,17,19], however, the human-in-the-loop approach requires a natural language understanding system instead of a 'black-box' end-to-end solution. The key natural language processing tasks of such a system are intent detection, entity recognition and information extraction, in particular 'slot-filling'. For intent detection and slot filling tasks state of art results have been achieved with neural network approaches, mostly with recurrent neural networks and attention mechanisms [7,11,18]. Our earlier research [8,21] and other teams [1,2,10] also support the effectiveness of neural network models for specifics of Latvian language in other NLP tasks.

The technical aspects of building human-in-the-loop conversational agent systems have not been well described in existing literature. The core concept of human-in-the loop conversational agents is not novel, we are aware of some research of such systems [6], but most known applications of this approach are proprietary, and the inner workings of these systems are not published.

3   System Architecture

The proposed system architecture, illustrated in Fig. 1, involves an intent detection system for identifying the types of customer requests that it can handle appropriately, a slot filling information extraction system that integrates with the customer service database for a rule-based treatment of the common scenarios, and a template-based language generation system that builds response candidates that can be approved or amended by customer service operators.

The operator actions in correcting the selected intent and the appropriate response continuously provide the system with new, recent training data, and the intent detection modules are periodically retrained on it.

The prototype system was developed using the Tensorflow framework in Python, and deployed as a Docker container.

4   Named Entity Recognition

The named entity recognition system is designed to identify not only common named entities such as people and organization names, but also the specific entities which would be candidates for the slot filling task such as invoice numbers,

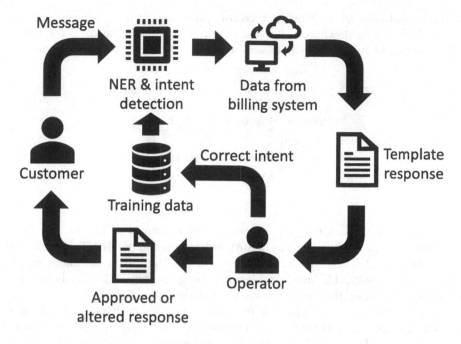

Fig. 1. System architecture

money amounts, dates, relative dates (e.g. 'next month') and date ranges. In total, 16 named entity categories are considered.

The dataset used for initial validation consisted of 1732 customer requests that were prepared in three steps:

1. Replace sensitive text spans with sensitive data markers
2. Manually annotate named entity spans
3. Generate named entities in place of sensitive data markers

For named entity generation, we used list of person names, registry of addresses and regular expression rules to generate invoice, personal legal ID and phone numbers.

The named entity recognition system uses GloVe word embeddings [9] pre-trained on the comment corpus collected from the project Virtual Aggression Barometer[1], character based LSTM representation, two bidirectional LSTM layers and a conditional random field (CRF) loss.

Customer requests usually contain grammatical errors and additional whitespaces for formatting. Sentences are not easily automatically separable, so full request text is used as input to maximally preserve context. Text is split on whitespace and punctuation characters without trying to extract email, date or phone number tokens. Whitespace information is passed as and additional input

---

[1] http://barometrs.korpuss.lv/.

to the neural network in a one-hot vector: no space before the token, newline before the token, whitespace before the token. Word shape feature is used as an additional input to capture emails and named entities with a regular structure.

Table 1. Named entity recognition system results.

System	Precision	Recall	F1
Baseline	76.82	80.20	78.48
GloVe	80.88	78.00	79.41
BERT	81.80	80.45	81.12

Named entity recognition experiment results are shown in Table 1. The baseline system does not include any additional features. The BERT system that uses multilingual BERT model fine-tuned on the Barometer comment corpus achieves best results. The most problematic categories with F1-score below 80% are company names, product names and addresses.

As customer service discussions frequently include sensitive personal information, we implement the data minimization principle required by the General Data Protection Directive by anonymizing the customer messages using the NER results both in the intent detection system processing and in the stored training data. The customer identifying data is passed only to the main operations system, but for intent detection and permanently stored training data we replace it with generic placeholders reflecting the entity type - for example, '[[Phone number]' or '[[Address]]'. This also has a beneficial effect on the intent detection system, reducing data sparsity, overfitting and assigning 'superstitious' significance to irrelevant or potentially discriminatory factors such as particular surnames.

5   Intent Detection

The intent detection system is a LSTM based deep neural network classifier. The classifier was designed to output both a coarse-grained intent topic, suitable for clustering customer requests and assigning some topics to specialized operators, and also fine-grained intent that can be matched to specific actions and answer templates. For initial word embedding layer we used GloVe [9] embeddings pretrained on a large corpus of Latvian [20].

The developed neural network structure and chosen parameter values were the following:

- Tokenization
- Pretrained word embeddings for each token, concatenated with 10-neuron trainable 'miniembeddings'
- Unidirectional LSTM layer with 150 cells
- Dense fully connected layer with 100 neurons, 30% dropout

- Dense fully connected layer with 50 neurons, 30% dropout
- Two separate output layers, for topics and fine-grained intent

We also investigated the application of more complex architectures such as BERT [3] which have achieved state of art results for other tasks, but this did not result in improved accuracy in our testing (see Sect. 5.1) and substantially increased training time, so this avenue was not pursued further.

5.1 Dataset and Experimental Validation

The dataset used for initial validation consisted of 1732 customer requests annotated with fine-grained intent data and named entities relevant to the intent. The data contained 24 topic classes with 115 different specific intents annotated. The intent distribution was representative of incoming customer requests, and thus was not balanced with respect to the topics. The most frequent topic class was billing with 794 requests (46% of total), which also contained the most frequent intents - postponing bills (356 requests) and confirming that an overdue bill has been paid (207 requests), while many specific intents had only a single example request.

Repeated experimentation on various options for neural network structures was performed on this dataset using cross-validation, in order to prepare a single architecture to be evaluated during the pilot study.

Table 2. Intent detection system accuracy

System	Topics	All intents	Postponing	Confirmations
Simple	68%	56%	86%	42%
Proposed	80%	70%	90%	81%
BERT	81%	69%	91%	81%

The key metrics used in evaluation (shown in Table 2) were the system average accuracy scores respectively for all the coarse grained topics, all the fine grained intents, and the F1 scores for the above-mentioned two most frequent intent groups, as they would be the focus of subsequent pilot study. The described systems include a simple multilayer perceptron without precomputed embeddings; the proposed network structure described in the previous section, and a transformer architecture based on fine-tuning BERT [3] for Latvian.

The preliminary results indicated that there was sufficient training data for two most common specific intents, and for the other topics only the coarse-grained topic classes have sufficient accuracy to be practically usable unless significant amounts of additional training data are used.

6   Slot Filling and Pre-filling a Response

If the detected customer intent is one of the prepared scenarios which can be handled by the system, then it is possible to prepare a template answer based on the detected intent and specific conditions. For example, if the intent is to change the payment plan, then it is possible to automatically verify in the core billing system whether the customer is eligible for this plan and prepare an appropriate personalized response template depending on the eligibility.

In addition, a checklist of specific actions for the customer service operator would be generated. For example, if the intent is to assert that a bill has been paid by supplying an attached payment document, then the operator needs to verify the suitability of that document.

For some intents, the system needs to extract specific information from the message in order to fulfil that intent. For example, if the customer is disputing a bill payment, then the date and amount of the payment needs to be identified. If the slot filling system in the proposed architecture would not be able to identify some of the required information, then the generated template answer would include specific sentences explicitly asking for that particular information.

This functionality would require substantial integration work with core billing systems. The proposed architecture is aimed to support this functionality, but development of it was started only after the evaluation of the pilot study and is not complete.

7   Pilot Study

The proposed model was initially validated in a three month pilot study at the mobile telecommunications operator customer service center. The pilot study was aimed to evaluate the feasibility of core technical concepts and proposed architecture in order to justify further integration and development of the full system. While the study involved the actual customer service team, it was primarily a technical feasibility pilot study without a systematic review of the human experience factors.

For the purposes of this study, the intent detection and response generation were limited to two most common types of communication - requests to postpone bill payment, and requests to restore service after payment of overdue bills.

In the scope of this pilot study, the following components of the proposed architecture were prepared and evaluated:

- Integration with message sources
- Named entity recognition
- Data anonymization
- Intent detection
- Integration with customer service systems
- Basic response templates
- Automatic retraining based on customer service agent feedback

Development of the slot filling and decision making component, as well as further work on response generation was not included in the pilot study. The pilot study was implemented only for conversations in Latvian language, but the planned system architecture is trilingual Latvian-Russian-English. Nonetheless we believe that the scope of the pilot study is sufficient to demonstrate applicability of the full proposal.

In the limited pilot study, 14000 customer requests were processed using this system, and continuously used to retrain the intent detection model with additional data. As expected based on the preliminary testing, the detected intent and the automatically chosen answer template (which was selected for the two most frequent topics only) was accurate approximately 90% of the time and required operator intervention for the remaining 10% cases. At the end of the pilot study, the additional data gathered was able to improve the intent detection accuracy by approximately 2% points, so only 8% of the main billing requests needed changes by the operator.

From the perspective of the end users, the pilot study was considered successful, saving time and effort. From the business perspective the study affirmed the feasibility of this concept and supported continuing further development of the proposed system.

8   Conclusions and Future Work

We have described an architecture proposal for a human-in-the-loop system that supports customer service answers to customer enquiries. The initial experiments and a limited pilot study have demonstrated the feasibility of this proposal and support further development of this proposal.

It can be concluded that human-in-the-loop conversational agents are a feasible option for partial customer service business process automation. We argue (but do not conclusively prove in this study) that this approach can save time and effort when handling common customer service enquiries while still maintaining a high quality of service.

Acknowledgements. This research is funded by the Latvian Council of Science, project "Latvian Language Understanding and Generation in Human-Computer Interaction", project No. LZP-2018/2-0216.

References

1. Balodis, K., Deksne, D.: Fasttext-based intent detection for inflected languages. Information **10**(5), 161 (2019)
2. Deksne, D.: Bidirectional LSTM tagger for latvian grammatical error detection. In: Ekštein, K. (ed.) Text, Speech, and Dialogue, pp. 58–68. Springer International Publishing, Cham (2019). https://doi.org/10.1007/978-3-030-27947-9_5
3. Devlin, J., Chang, M.W., Lee, K., Toutanova, K.: BERT: Pre-training of deep bidirectional transformers for language understanding (2018)
4. Følstad, A., Nordheim, C.B., Bjørkli, C.A.: What makes users trust a chatbot for customer service? An exploratory interview study. In: Bodrunova, S.S. (ed.) Internet Science, pp. 194–208. Springer International Publishing, Cham (2018). https://doi.org/10.1007/978-3-030-01437-7_16

5. Jenkins, M.-C., Churchill, R., Cox, S., Smith, D.: Analysis of user interaction with service oriented chatbot systems. In: Jacko, J.A. (ed.) HCI 2007. LNCS, vol. 4552, pp. 76–83. Springer, Heidelberg (2007). https://doi.org/10.1007/978-3-540-73110-8_9

6. Kucherbaev, P., Bozzon, A., Houben, G.J.: Human-aided bots. IEEE Internet Comput. **22**(6), 36–43 (2018)

7. Liu, B., Lane, I.: Attention-based recurrent neural network models for joint intent detection and slot filling (2016)

8. Paikens, P.: Deep neural learning approaches for Latvian morphological tagging. In: Human Language Technologies - The Baltic Perspective. vol. 289. IOS Press (2016). https://doi.org/10.3233/978-1-61499-701-6-160, http://ebooks. iospress.nl/volumearticle/45531

9. Pennington, J., Socher, R., Manning, C.D.: GloVe: global vectors for word representation. In: Proceedings of the 2014 Conference on Empirical Methods in Natural Language Processing (EMNLP), pp. 1532–1543 (2014)

10. Pinnis, M.: Latvian tweet corpus and investigation of sentiment analysis for Latvian. In: Baltic HLT, pp. 112–119 (2018)

11. Qin, L., Che, W., Li, Y., Wen, H., Liu, T.: A stack-propagation framework with token-level intent detection for spoken language understanding (2019)

12. Rizk, Y., et al.: A unified conversational assistant framework for business process automation (2020)

13. Serban, I.V., Sordoni, A., Bengio, Y., Courville, A., Pineau, J.: Building end-to-end dialogue systems using generative hierarchical neural network models. In: Thirtieth AAAI Conference on Artificial Intelligence (2016)

14. Shah, P., Hakkani-Tur, D., Liu, B., Tur, G.: Bootstrapping a neural conversational agent with dialogue self-play, crowdsourcing and on-line reinforcement learning. In: Proceedings of the 2018 Conference of the North American Chapter of the Association for Computational Linguistics: Human Language Technologies, Volume 3 (Industry Papers), pp. 41–51 (2018)

15. Vasiljevs, A., Skadina, I., Deksne, D., Martins Kalis, T., Vira, L.: Application of virtual agents for delivery of information services. In: New Challenges of Economic and Business Development, pp. 702–713 (2017)

16. Vevers, J.: Lattelecom klientu apkalpošanas robotmeitenes anetes projekts: soli pa solim. Dienas Bizness (2017). https://www.db.lv/zinas/lattelecom-klientu-apkalposanas-robotmeitenes-anetes-projekts-soli-pa-solim-468150

17. Vinyals, O., Le, Q.: A neural conversational model. arXiv preprint arXiv:1506.05869 (2015)

18. Wang, Y., Shen, Y., Jin, H.: A bi-model based RNN semantic frame parsing model for intent detection and slot filling (2018)

19. Zhong, P., Wang, D., Miao, C.: An affect-rich neural conversational model with biased attention and weighted cross-entropy loss. In: Proceedings of the AAAI Conference on Artificial Intelligence, vol. 33, pp. 7492–7500 (2019)

20. Znotins, A.: Word embeddings for Latvian natural language processing tools. In: Human Language Technologies - The Baltic Perspective, vol. 289. IOS Press (2016). https://doi.org/10.3233/978-1-61499-701-6-167, http://ebooks.iospress. nl/volumearticle/45532

21. Znotins, A., Cirule, E.: NLP-PIPE: Latvian NLP tool pipeline. In: Human Language Technologies - The Baltic Perspective, vol. 307, pp. 183–189. IOS Press (2018). https://doi.org/10.3233/978-1-61499-912-6-183, http://ebooks.iospress. nl/volumearticle/50320

Author Index

Printed in the United States
By Bookmasters